THE LIVING NOVEL

& LATER APPRECIATIONS

The Living Novel &

RANDOM HOUSE

Later Appreciations

V. S. PRITCHETT

NEW YORK

FIRST PRINTING

Library of Congress Catalog Card Number: 64–14830

Manufactured in the United States of America

The Living Novel was originally published in 1947. In this revised and expanded edition, twenty-seven new essays have been added. The author offers his acknowledgment to the editor of *The New Statesman,* which first published these essays, now amended.

DESIGNED BY JEANETTE YOUNG

TO

My Wife

Contents

THE LIVING NOVEL

& LATER APPRECIATIONS

THE ANCESTOR

When I was young and was reading too many novels the works of Fielding were regarded as one of the pleasant things in store for those about to reach the age of consent. He was the last novelist, as Thackeray said, to be allowed to describe a man, and there were book-soaked critics like Professor Saintsbury to expatiate over their wine upon Fielding's use of the privilege. It is true that Dr. Johnson called Fielding a blockhead and that Richardson—who had reason to spit and squirm—dismissed him as an ostler; but on the whole the warm impression of his genius and character prevailed, the impression which was most frankly but tolerantly conveyed in one of the letters of Lady Mary Wortley Montagu:

> I am sorry for H. Fielding's death, not only as I shall read no more of his writings, but I believe he lost more than others, and no man enjoyed life more than he did, though few had less reason to do so, the highest of his preferment being raking in the lowest sinks of vice and misery. I should think it a nobler and less nauseous employment to be one of the staff-officers than conduct the nocturnal weddings. His happy constitution (even when he had, with great pains, half demolished it) made him forget everything when he was before a venison pastry, or over a flask of champagne, and I am persuaded he has known more happy moments than any prince upon the earth. His natural spirits gave him rapture with his cookmaid, and cheerfulness when he was fluxing in a garret. There was a great similitude between his character and that of Sir Richard Steele. He had the advantage both in learning and, in my opinion, genius; they both agreed in wanting money in spite of all their friends, and would have wanted it, if their hereditary lands had been as extensive as their imaginations; yet each of them was so formed for happiness, it is a pity he was not immortal.

Alas, the vogue of Fielding had passed by the time I grew up. The secret reading of the mid-Victorians, and of late, had lost the spell. The muscular Christians who were privately addicted to his muscular impropriety had given place to a generation with a feminine preoccupation with sex and the fortune-telling science of psychology. If one was going to read the eighteenth-century novelists at all, Richardson was your man and the masculine tradition of Fielding was less congenial. It is typical of our taste that Proust was greatly influenced by Richardson; and that when we look back to the earliest realism, we prefer the ungarnished plate of Defoe to the stylish menu that is handed to us by the author of *Tom Jones* and *Joseph Andrews*. He is said to be altogether too hearty, towny and insensitive. He is said to be that most tiresome of bores, the man's man. He sets up as the shallowest of philosophers: the man of the world, whose world turns out to be a box of tricks. And what does the philosophy amount to beyond a number of small notions: that society is not what it seems, that self-love and self-interest are the beginning and end of human motive, and that the only real and virile view of human nature is the low one? His geniality labored the offense.

One has to admit the force of such a criticism of Fielding, but I am far from thinking it fatal to his rank as a novelist. In the first place the criticism is really aroused by his style rather than by his matter. Fielding is out to cut a figure. When he sets up as a satirist, he believes in the robust satire of the man who lives, not in the more cruel satire of the weak-livered man who abstains and snarls. In their rebellion against the poetic hyperbole of the early romances which had been imitated from the French, the Augustans parodied the heroic style; they were not thereby mocking the noble view of human nature; they were insinuating the sensible one.

Yet, even when we have acquiesced in the brilliant assumptiveness of Fielding's style and have seen beyond his sardonic preoccupation with men of honor and women of discretion, there remains the difficulty that Fielding is the ancestor. In Fielding we are haunted by almost the whole of the English novel. Pages of Dickens, Thackeray, Meredith, even, incongruously, of Kipling, Wodehouse and Amis, become confused in the general panorama: Fielding has the disadvantage of being the "onlie begetter." Not only do we pick out the perennial characters of the main part of English fiction, but he has set many of its idiosyncrasies and limits. Sociable man, social problems, middle-class humor, the didactic habit, the club culture, the horseplay, the gregarious rather than the single eye, the habit of treating country life as an opportunity for the exercise of the body or of the fancy, as though Nature were a mixture of gymnasium and an open-air extension of the Established Church—these are some elements which have continued in the English novel and which date from Fielding. He expressed one kind of Englishness, so that many critics—Sir Hugh Walpole was one—seemed to think that conservative sociability or what is called "the creation of character" contains the whole English tradition; that people who speak of the novel as something inspired by ideas or concerned with a sense of the real situation of society at any given time, were importing tendentious and arid continental ideas. If these critics had considered Fielding's work they could never have made such a wild statement. Fielding was an old Etonian, but he was one of Eton's recalcitrants, sneered at and, in the end, pursued because he let the side down. The fact is that, from the beginning, the English novel set out to protest and to teach. Its philanthropic campaigns in the nineteenth century are paralleled in the eighteenth century by its avowed desire to reform the brutal manners of the age.

The explanation is not necessarily that there has been an extra allowance of public spiritedness in our novelists; it is simply that the crucial problems of his own time provide a novelist with his richest material, whether he deals with it directly or by inference. The reform of manners was as vital in the eighteenth century as the reform of the Poor Law was in the nineteenth. From Elizabethan times, the Dutch, the French and the Spanish visitors had been appalled by the barbarity of English life. When Fielding and Richardson filled their novels with abducted heiresses, Tammany law, bribed judges, faked weddings, duels in Hyde Park, with squalid fights between half-naked women in Gin Alley or on the village commons; with scoundrelly nincompoops, bailiffs and middle-men from the Coffee House and the Court, they were not amusing themselves with the concoctions of artificial comedy. They were attacking the criminal violence and corruption that underlay the elegance of the age. There was a plea for the middle-class virtues at a time when the aristocracy had left the country for the Court and had abandoned its responsibilities in order to milk the Exchequer. Public societies for the Reform of Manners had existed in the early part of the century. Fielding spent his writing life fighting abuses and ended as an excellent Bow Street magistrate, trying to clean up the London streets. "Great characters" there are in all his books, but they are inseparable from his moral purpose.

In an essay on his own work Fielding always said that he drew from life. But like Cervantes, whom he hoped to copy, and whom he so much admired, Fielding had been trained as a writer in the theater. The English novel was not a development from the reporting of Defoe, a way of writing which, of its nature, is prevented from imaginative development. In the end the reporter can do no more than cover more and more ground; his method gives him nothing to till the ground with. Fielding took his slice of life, his chains of picaresque episode which in *Joseph Andrews* had made a promising but inferior version of *Gil Blas,* and let the artifice of the theater break them up and rebuild them. The English novel started in *Tom Jones,* because the stage taught Fielding to break the monotony of flat, continuous narrative. The methods of the theater are abstract and summary; there is an idea before there is a scene; and one of the fascinating things in *Tom Jones* is the use of the summary method to set the scene, explain the types of character, cover the preparatory ground quickly by a few oblique moralizings and antics so that all the realism is reserved for the main action. Is Tom Jones a loyal and honest man? Could he be the opposite if circumstances tempt him? No great paraphernalia of dialogue and literal detail has to be used in order to introduce such questions. Fielding puts them, then illustrates with action, and frames the whole in brief commentary. Scenes do not ramble on and melt into each other. They snap past, sharply divided, wittily contrasted, cunningly balanced. The pace of *Tom Jones* is as fast as farce, and indeed only a theater man's expertness in the dramatic, the surprising, the situation capped and recapped, could cover the packed intrigue of the narrative. The theater taught Fielding economy. It taught him to treat episodes as subjects and not as simple slices of life. Thackeray, who is the only English novelist to have learned from *Tom Jones*—Dickens learned from the inferior middlebrow *Amelia,* which has much more of the drudging realism of the later English novel—developed this method of Fielding's in *Vanity Fair,* going backwards and forwards in time, as well as to and fro in moral commentary. The difference is that Thackeray was born in the time of the sermon, and Fielding in the time of the chorus and the stage aside.

Fielding's own ancestor is Ben Jonson. Coleridge compared the formal excellence of *Tom Jones* with that of *The Alchemist.* The satire in both writers is meaty and brainy, very packed and prolific in ridiculous situations. To every character life is surprising and Fortune perverse. In the love-chase of Sophia Western and Tom Jones, there is the familiar stage situation that when one is willing the other is not available. Tom is a healthy young rake who does not intend to be one, and he reads a severe lecture to Nightingale, the professional Lovelace, who is merely satisfying sexual vanity. In the picaresque novels there is growth or decline in fortune, and rarely is there growth in character; but in *Tom Jones,* Partridge grows once he has got rid of his wife. Sophia, in London, learns to tell a lie to her rival—for which one admires her as much as when she comes headfirst off the horse—and Tom himself passes from the loyal to the careless and, after the shock of being caught out in his infidelities at Upton, into Tom the frantic who will commit any folly. He is a young man in a mess by the time he is mixed up with Lady Bellaston. This intrigue is the one in which first her ladyship and then the lady's maid are hidden behind the curtain in Tom's room, a piece of turn and turnabout which comes straight from the theater; it *does* strike one as artificial, but Fielding brings the whole intrigue to earth by the brilliant short chapter which introduces Mrs. Hunt. Many critics have objected to this chapter as a loose end; but the naïve proposal of marriage from someone to whom Tom has never spoken comes almost affectingly out of the blue. It is a *cri de coeur* among a lot of sharp practice, something beautifully silly in an ill-natured episode.

Joseph Andrews, Jonathan Wild and *Tom Jones* are the three important novels of Fielding, and *Jonathan Wild* is the diamond among them, the most dazzling piece of sustained satirical writing in our language. There remains *Amelia:* a hybrid that lies halfway between the Augustan and the Victorian novel. As a novelist Fielding was subject to two opposite influences which were to leave their mark on the English novel for a hundred years and to ensure that it had little resemblance to the French and Russian novels: he was trained in the rogue's tale which introduced untidiness and irresponsibility into the English novel; and, as I have said, he was trained in the theater, which gave our novel its long obsession with elaborate plot. *Amelia* is a compromise. By the time he came to write this novel, Fielding seems to have lost the heat of the theater's inspiration. The first chapter describing the prison is in the old manner, but presently the narrative digresses and dawdles. The didactic intention comes out frankly and, alas, unadorned. There is white-faced indignation where before there was irony, and indignation is the weaker strain, for it interrupts, where irony undermines. I do not suggest that his old comic gift is dead; far from it. There is Colonel Bath's remarkable duel. And there is the devastating Miss Mathews, the would-be murderess, who is a development from the drawing of that hard old rip, Lady Bellaston, out of *Tom Jones.* Miss Mathews is a superb tart. One is delighted that the Colonel refuses to drop her; delighted, too, though Fielding does not seem to be, that she grows fat. She will so obviously enjoy growing fat. It is she who makes the celebrated remark about the English taste for prudish women: do they attract, inquires the ever-curious Miss Mathews, because they appear to promise to cool the heat of love? In *Amelia,* there is more psychological complexity than there was in *Tom Jones;* it is the book of an older man who has grown tired. If we contrast Tom Jones with Mr. Booth of *Amelia,* we see that Tom commits his sins, repents in a moment and ingenuously forgets them. Mr. Booth is far more complicated. He is a married man to start with; he sins with caution, is transfixed by remorse and then settles down to brood with growing misanthropy. The wages of sin is not death, but worry—middle-class worry. His case never improves, for we see the subtle influence of his affair with Miss Mathews on his relations with other people. Fielding's rising interest in psychology marks a break with his interest in moral types. It is a signal of the coming age. And if *Amelia* indicates a decline from the brilliant fusing of gifts that went to make his earlier books, it points the way the English novel would go when a new genius, the genius of Dickens, seized it.

CLARISSA

The modern reader of Richardson's *Clarissa* emerges from his experience exhausted, exalted and bewildered. The book is, I fancy, the longest novel in the English language; it is the one most crowded with circumstantial detail; it is written in the most dilatory of narrative manners, i.e., in the form of letters. It is a tale perceived through a microscope; it is a monstrosity, a minute and inordinate act of prolonged procrastination. And the author himself is a monster. That a man like Samuel Richardson should write one of the great European novels is one of those humiliating frolics in the incidence of genius. The smug, juicy, pedestrian little printer from Derbyshire, more or less unlettered, sits down at the age of fifty and instructs young girls in the art of managing their virtue to the best advantage. Yet, ridiculous as *Pamela* is, her creator disarms criticism by a totally new ingredient in the novel: he knows how to make the reader weep. And, stung by the taunts of the educated writers of his time, Richardson calmly rises far above *Pamela* when he comes to the story of Clarissa Harlowe; he sets the whole continent weeping. Rousseau and even Goethe bow to him and take out their handkerchiefs; the vogue of sensibility, the first shoots of the Romantic movement, spring from the pool of Richardson's pious tears like the grateful and delicate trees of an oasis. Yet there he is, plump, prosaic, the most middling of middling men, and so domestically fussy that even his gift of weeping hardly guarantees that he will be a major figure. Is there not some other strain in this dull and prodigiously painstaking little man? There is. Samuel Richardson was mad.

I do not mean that Richardson was a lunatic. I do not mean he was mad as Swift was mad. At first sight, an immeasurable smugness, an endlessly pettifogging normality seem to be the outer skin of Richardson's character. We know that from his youth he was an industrious and timid young man who was, for some reason or other, used by young women who wanted their love letters written. Profoundly sentimental, he sat like some pious old cook in her kitchen, giving advice to the kitchen maids, and when he came to write novels he was merely continuing this practical office. He lived vicariously like some sedentary lawyer who has to argue the disasters of other people's lives letter by letter, but who himself never partakes. Genteel, he is, nevertheless, knowing; prim and cozy, he is, nevertheless, the victim of that powerful cult of the will, duty and conscience by which Puritanism turned life and its human relations into an incessant war. There is no love in Puritanism; there is a struggle for power. Who will win the daily battle of scruple and conscience—Pamela or the young squire; Clarissa or Lovelace? And yet what is urging Richardson to this battle of wills? What is it that the Puritan cannot get out of his mind, so that it is a mania and obsession? It is sex. Richardson is mad about sex.

His is the madness of Paul Pry and Peeping Tom. *Clarissa* is a novel written under the microscope; really it is a novel written about the world as one sees it through the keyhole. Prurient and obsessed by sex, the prim Richardson creeps on tiptoe nearer and nearer, inch by inch, to that vantage point; he beckons us on, pausing to make every kind of pious protestation, and then nearer and nearer he creeps again, delaying, arguing with us in whispers, working us up until we catch the obsession too. What are we going to see when we get there? The abduction, the seduction, the lawful deflowering of a virgin in marriage are not enough for him. Nothing short of the rape of Clarissa Harlowe by a man determined on destroying her can satisfy Richardson's phenomenal daydream with its infinite delays.

The principle of procrastinated rape is said to be the ruling one in all the great bestsellers. It was in Richardson's genius that he was able to elevate the inner conflict of the passions and the will to an abstract level, so that the struggle of Clarissa and Lovelace becomes a universal battle-piece; and, in doing this, Richardson was able to paint it with the highly finished realism of the Dutch painters. At the beginning one might simply be reading yet another novel of intrigue, which just goes on and on; and but for the incredible suspense in the narrative I think many readers must have given up *Clarissa* by the end of the first volume. It is not until the third and fourth volumes are reached, when Richardson transposes his intrigue into the sustained and weeping music, the romantic tragedy of Clarissa's rape and long preparation for death, that we get his measure. She dies piously, yet like a Shakespearean conferring greatness upon all around her by the starkness of her defeat. At the beginning we are not prepared for this greatness in Clarissa; even in that last volume we are often uncertain of her real stature. It is not easy for virginity to become Virtue. Would she be anything without Lovelace? And yet, we know, she is the crown upon Lovelace's head. He too becomes tragic under her judgment as she becomes tragic by his act. These two reflect glory upon each other, like saint and devil. But in the first volume there is no difficulty about deciding who is the greater as a character or as an abstract conception. Lovelace has her beaten hands down. A practical and languid correspondence wakes up when he takes pen in hand. Anna Howe, the "pert" friend, makes circles round her. Arabella, with her nose out of joint, is livelier comedy. The scheming brother, the gouty father with his paroxysms, the supplicating and fluttering mother, and the endearing uncles with their unendearing family solidarity, make a greater mark on our minds than the all-too-articulate Clarissa does. Our one hope is that witty Miss Howe is right when she teases Clarissa with maidenly self-deception. "The frost piece," as Lovelace called her, looks exactly like one of those fascinating prudes whose minds are an alphabet that must be read backwards. But no; though she will enchant us when she is rattled, with cries like "Oh, my Nancy, what shall I do with this Lovelace?" her course and her motives are clear to her; and we begin the slow and painful discovery of a virtue which finds no exhilaration except in scruple. We face an inexhaustible determination, and this is exhausting to contemplate, for Clarissa is as interested in the organization of human motives as Richardson himself; and he insinuates himself in her character so thoroughly, niggling away with his "ifs" and his "buts," that he overwhelms her, as Flaubert overwhelmed Madame Bovary.

Still this does not take from the drama of Clarissa's situation, and does, in fact, increase the suspense of it. If we skip—and of course we do, looking up the letters in the obliging synopsis—we do not, as in other novels, find ourselves caught out by an overlooked subplot; we are back in the main situation. Will the family relent? Will Lovelace abduct, marry, rape or reform? There's hardly a subplot worth mentioning in this huge novel. It follows the labyrinth of a single theme. And though we turn to Anna Howe for glimpses of common sense, and for a wit to enliven the glum belligerents of what Lovelace—always a psychologist and nearly a Freudian—called "the Harlowe dunghill" with its wills and deeds of settlement, we see in Clarissa's stand something more than a virtuous daughter bullied by her parents. She is a lawyer in family morals, and in Lovelace's too; but she is the first heroine in English fiction to stand against the family. Richardson called them "the embattled phalanx," and in *Clarissa* he goes to the heart of the middle-class situation; money, accretion of estate, the rise in the world, the desire to found a family, in conflict with the individual soul. She and Lovelace complement each other here. She thinks her family ought not to do evil to her, yet takes their evil upon herself; she is not a rebel but is tricked and driven into becoming an outcast and at last a saint. Like Lovelace, she has asked too much, "for people who allow nothing will be granted nothing; in other words, those who aim at carrying too many points will not be able to carry any." Yes, and those who put up their price by the device of reluctance invite the violence of the robber. By setting such a price upon herself, Clarissa represents that extreme of puritanism which hankers after rape. Like Lovelace's, her sexuality is really violent, insatiable in its wish for destruction.

Lovelace is Richardson's extravagant triumph. How did such a burning and tormented human being come out of that tedious little printer's mind? In the English novel Lovelace is one of the few men of intellect who display an intellect which is their own and not patently an abstract of their author's intellectual interests. He is half-villain, half-god, a male drawn to the full, and he dominates English fiction. He is all the more male for the feminine strains in his character: his hatred of women, his love of intrigue, his personal vanity, his captiousness and lack of real humility. A very masculine novelist like Fielding is too much a moralist, and too confidently a man, to catch a strain like that. And how Lovelace can write! When Clarissa's letters drag, like sighing Sunday hymns, or nag at us in their blameless prose, like the Collect for the day, the letters of Lovelace crackle and blaze with both the fire and the inconsequence of life. His words fly back and forth, throwing out anecdotes and the characters of his friends, with wonderful transitions of mood. In one paragraph he is writing a set apostrophe to Clarissa, full of longing and halfway to repentance. He shakes the mood off like a man who is drunk with grief and throws off this description of his gouty old kinsman:

> And here (pox of his fondness for me; it happens at a very bad time) he makes me sit hours together entertaining him with my rogueries (a pretty amusement for a sick man!) and yet, whenever he has the gout, he prays night and morning with his chaplain. But what must *his* notions of religion be, who, after he has nosed and mumbled over his responses, can give a sigh or groan of satisfaction, as if he thought he had made up with Heaven; and return with a new appetite to my stories?—encouraging them, by shaking his sides with laughing at them, and calling me a sad fellow, in such an accent as shows he takes no small delight in his kinsman.
>
> The old peer has been a sinner in his day, and suffers for it now; a sneaking sinner, *sliding*, rather than *rushing* into vices, for fear of his reputation; or rather, for fear of detection, and positive proof;

> for this sort of fellow, Jack, has no real regard for reputation. Paying for what he never had, and never daring to rise to the joy of an enterprise at first hand, which bring him within view of a tilting or the honor of being considered as the principal man in a court of justice.
>
> To see such a Trojan as this just dropping into the grave which I hoped ere this would have been dug, and filled up with him; crying out with pain and grunting with weakness; yet in the same moment crack his leathern face into a horrible laugh, and call a young sinner charming varlet, encoring him as formerly he used to do the Italian eunuchs; what a preposterous, what an unnatural adherence to old habits.

Or there is the awful description of that old procuress, Mrs. Sinclair, a horror out of Rowlandson, who advances upon Clarissa on the night of the rape, when all Richardson's fascination with carnal horror breaks out. There is a double terror in it, because Lovelace himself is writing as if trying to drive evil out of his mind by a picture of evils still greater:

> The old dragon straddled up to her, with her arms kemboed again, her eyebrows erect like the bristles upon a hog's back, and, scowling over her shortened nose, more than half hid her ferret eyes. Her mouth was distorted. She pouted out her blubber-lips, as if to bellow up wind and sputter into her horse-nostrils, and her chin was curdled, and more than usually prominent with passion.

The temperate, lawyer-like mind of Richardson does not prepare one for passages like this. When there is matter-of-factness in the eighteenth century, one expects it to be as regular as Pope's couplets were. But Richardson is not consistent. In the sheer variety of their styles the letters in this novel are astonishing. The bovine uncles, the teasing parenthetical Miss

Howe, the admonitory Belford, the curt Colonel Morden, heading for his duel, the climbing neurotic brother whose descendants were no doubt in the British Union of Fascists, all have their styles, and they are as distinctive as Lovelace's or Clarissa's. Richardson is the least flat, the most stereoscopic novelist of an age which ran the plain or formal statement to death in the end. Another point: he is a writer of indirect narrative. We are shown scenes at second hand, for the epistolatory method requires it so; and we become used to a sort of memoranda of talk and action which will tire our inward eye because our judgment is called upon at the same time. So there are many reported scenes which are relative failures, for example, the early and rather confusing ones between Clarissa and her mother. One has a muddled impression of two hens flying up in the air at each other and scattering their feathers. Yet even in this kind of scene Richardson can, at times, write talk which is direct and put action wonderfully under our eye. The scene of the rape is tremendous in this respect; and so is the awful picture of the brothel when Mrs. Sinclair breaks her leg and the harridans come out in their night attire; and there is the comic, savage picture of Lovelace defeating the attempt of his family to try him. But where Richardson shook off the slavery of his own method is shown at its best, I think, in Belford's letter describing the prison scene where the two prostitutes offer to bail Clarissa out:

> "We are surprised at your indifference, Miss Harlowe. Will you not write to any of your friends?"
>
> "No."
>
> "Why, you don't think of tarrying *here* always."
>
> "I shall not live always."

Even in those few lines one sees Richardson advancing his inner narrative and, if one continues this conversation, one also sees him patiently and unerringly preserving character. One might almost say that prolix as it was, his method was economical, given his chosen end. The slowness comes from an excess of examination, not an excess of words. No prose has fewer redundancies.

We come to the death scene. The torment of Lovelace pacing his horse past the gate of the house he dare not enter, though Clarissa lies dying within, is not rhetorical. It is defiant as fits a being so saturnine, it is in the mind as becomes a man of intellect, it is the changeable, imploring, raging madness of a clever mind that has met its conqueror. Lovelace is a villain no man hates, because he is a man. He is candid, if he is vain. He can argue like Iago or debate like Hamlet, and in between send a purse of a few guineas to a rogue who has helped him to his present catastrophe. It is strange to think of him—the only Don Juan in English fiction and done to the last Freudian detail. Clarissa dies like a swan amid the formal melody of a prose into which Richardson fell without affectation.

> Her breath being very short, she desired another pillow. Having two before, this made her, in a manner, sit up in her bed; and she spoke then with more distinctness; and seeing us greatly concerned, forgot her own stutterings to comfort us; and a charming lecture she gave us, though a brief one, upon the happiness of a timely preparation, and upon the hazards of a late repentance, when the mind, as she observed, was so much weakened, as well as the body, as to render a poor soul hardly able to contend with its natural infirmities.

It is a strong test of the illusion that Richardson has cast upon us, that we think of Lovelace like a shadow cast upon Clarissa as she dies; and of Clarissa rather than of Lovelace when *he* appears. These lives are known by their absences; they are inextricable, tangled in the thousands of words they have spoken about each other, and are swept away at last into other people's words.

THE SHOCKING SURGEON

The disappearance of illustrations from the English novel, and indeed the decline of the art of illustrating, is a loss to literary criticism. For one of the obligations of the critic is to possess himself of the eyes with which a novelist's contemporaries read him, and this the good illustrator helped him to do. Of course we never achieve this sight, but we can approach it. And how far off the mark we can be is shown by the shock that a good illustrator gives. Cruikshank, for example: he upsets all the weary pieties of realism that lie between us and a comprehension of Dickens; half the silly criticisms of Dickens need never have been written if Cruikshank had been studied as closely as the text. And Rowlandson: pick up an edition of Smollett that has Rowlandson's illustrations and see Smollett come into focus once more, so that his page is almost as fresh to us as it must have appeared to the eighteenth-century reader. It is true that outside this school of illustration the argument weakens; the wooden severity of late-Victorian realism was a lugubrious travesty of the text and one is glad that illustration has been dropped. The fact is that illustration was at its best when the English novel also was in its brash, vital, fantastic youth; when, though wigged in a judicious style, it had only a simple and crude concern with caricature, anecdote and the bad manners of society. Once the novel abandoned travel and developed plot and form, the English novel ceased to need the illustrator, or at any rate ceased to get the right one.

There are two pointers in the engravings which Rowlandson did for *Humphry Clinker*, pointers the reader of Smollett ought to follow. Look at the scrawny figure of that malign virgin, Tabitha Bramble, as she comes accusing into the room where her philanthropical brother has been caught with a lady; look at Humphry in the jail, moaning out his grotesque Methodism to the felons; look at her ladyship, gluttonous, diseased and warty, tearing out her friend's hair. They are not human beings. They are lumps of animal horror or stupidity. To Rowlandson the human race are cattle or swine, a reeking fat-stock done up in ribbons or breeches, which has got into coffee houses, beds and drawing rooms. He was nauseated by the domesticity and the grossness of the eighteenth century's new rich. In fact, every eighteenth-century artist and writer jibbed at the filth of domestic life, at some time or other. These pictures of Rowlandson's (of Hogarth's too) show how urgent was the task of the reform of manners which the writers of the eighteenth century had set themselves, from Addison onwards. (The movement had been revived by William III, who, when he came from Holland, was horrified by the brutality of English life. He encouraged Defoe, especially, to write in the cause of reform.) The second point is that Rowlandson's people are portraits of Swift's Yahoos. In these pictures we see the nightmare lying behind the Augustan manner. The nightmare of the pox, the scurvy, delirium tremens, of obesity and gout, the nightmare of the unsanitary streets, of the stairway which was a dunghill, of the sedate Georgian window which was a place for the emptying of chamber pots; the nightmare of the suppurations that flowed into the waters at Bath, of the stenches that rose from the "elegant" crowds at Assemblies; the nightmare of the lives of children flogged into stupidity—see the boyhood of *Peregrine Pickle*—so that, in Rowlandson and Hogarth, all the virtuous people look like lumps of suet; and, haunting this scene, the nightmare religion of Wesley. Smollett and Rowlandson run so closely together in the drawing of these things that one borrows from the other's brutality. Yet are they brutal? I do not know enough about Rowlandson to say, but I am pretty sure that Smollett, for all his obsession with the bladder and the backside, was not a brutal nor a filthy man. He enjoyed being the shocking surgeon who brings out horrors at the dinner table; but because he was shocked himself. Smollett's sensibility is close to Swift's. There is enough proof of Smollett's intention in the reforms which followed his descriptions of the brutalities of naval life at his time in *Roderick Random.* And though there is a good deal of horseplay, battery and assault in his books, from the comic scene where Hawser Trunnion picks up a turkey from the table to beat an unwelcome visitor, to the one in *Roderick Random* where the hero and a friend tie up the schoolmaster and flog his naked backside with a rope, Smollett has strong views on the stupefying effects of flogging. These are clearly stated in *Peregrine Pickle.* It is true that Perry, after a period of beating, himself becomes the bully of the school, to Hawser Trunnion's great delight, but Trunnion's views are always presented as further fantastic aspects of a fantastic and maimed character. We see more of what Smollett was like in the portrait of Dr. Bramble in *Humphry Clin-*

ker. Generosity and goodness of heart go together with an impetuous temper and a good touch of hypochondria. He has a morbid nose which smells out every stench that Bath, Edinburgh and Harrogate can provide; and Smollett's own nose, in his book of travels in France and Italy, was as fastidious. Smollett may have enjoyed the brutality he described, but his protests and his hypochondria suggest that he felt the pleasure and the agony of the man who has a skin too few. His coarseness, like that of Joyce, is the coarseness of one whose senses were unprotected and whose nerves were exposed. Something is arrested in the growth of his robust mind; as a novelist he remains the portrayer of the outside, rarely able to get away from physical externals or to develop from that starting point into anything but physical caricature.

A course of Smollett is hard for the modern reader to digest. The theater advised and animated Fielding and gave him form and discipline. Smollett might have remained a ship's surgeon—and would probably have been a happier man. (Smollett figures in the elder Disraeli's gallery of literary calamities.) The difficulty of digestion is that he is raw and piquant meat; course follows course without abating, and one has a surfeit. One begins *Peregrine Pickle, Roderick Random, Humphry Clinker* or *Count Fathom*, exclaiming with pleasure at the physical zest and the racing speed of the narrative, but after a hundred and fifty pages one has had enough of the practical jokes, the heiresses and duelists, the cheats and the bawds. Our trouble is that the English novel changed direction after its early lessons with the French and Spanish picaresque writers. The novel of travel gave place to plot and developed character. The kind of thing that Smollett did in *Humphry Clinker*—which all the critics, except the unerring Hazlitt, overpraise—was turned into Young's *Tours* or Cobbett's *Rural Rides*.

One book of Smollett's can be recommended to the modern reader without reservations: the very original *Travels Through France and Italy,* the first ill-tempered, captious, disillusioned and vigorously personal travel book in modern literature. It is a tale of bad inns, illness, cheating customs officials, a thoroughly British book of grousings and manias—the aim of every Frenchman is to seduce your wife, or if not your wife, your sister, and if not your sister, your daughter, as a token of his esteem for you!—but packed with the irritable author and moments of fresh, unperturbed judgment. It annoyed Sterne and was meant to annoy him. Against Sterne's fancies stand Smollett's manias, and how well they stand. Elsewhere, in the novels, one thinks less of whole books than of scenes. *Peregrine Pickle* is not as vigorous in its strokes and movements as *Roderick Random,* but my favorite scenes come from the former book. Hawser Trunnion and his "Garrison" are wonderful fantasies, which tumble upon the reader uproariously as if a party were going on upstairs and the ceiling had given way in the middle of it. Trunnion lying about his naval engagements, fooled by publicans, entrapped by women, and tacking across country to his wedding, is, as they say, "a beauty and no mistake." And his death—that is one of the great scenes of English literature, to be compared with that great death scene at the end of Dostoevsky's *The Possessed.* You can see, as you read, how Fielding's wittier and better-formed imagination would have improved this novel; though Smollett surpasses Fielding, I think, in female portraiture; his leading ladies have more spirit than Fielding's and can amuse themselves quite well without the help of the hero. *Roderick Random* is altogether more sardonic and violent; *Count Fathom* is more polished, an essay after the manner of *Jonathan Wild.* It contains two scenes which stand out—a robber scene, suggested, I suppose, by an early episode in *Gil Blas,* and an appalling chapter describing the Count's mother, who was a camp follower in Marlborough's wars and made a good living by cutting the throats of the wounded and robbing them. This is the kind of scene that reveals the exposed nerve in Smollett.

The physical realism of Smollett and his chamberpot humor are one other link with Joyce and shows how his mind may have had not dissimilar obsessions. Perhaps that is going rather far; but there is some hint of Anna Livia in the Welsh maid's letters in *Humphry Clinker.* Smollett extended the farce of punning and misspelling into new regions for his times:

> Last Sunday in the parish crutch, if my own ars may be trusted, the clerk called the banes of marridge betwist Opaniah Lashmeheygo and Tapitha Bramble, spinster; he mought as well have called her inkle weaver, for she never spun a hank of yarn in her life. Young Squire Dollison and Miss Liddy make the second kipple and there might have been a turd, but times are changed for Mr. Clinker.

Or:

> Who would have thought that mistriss, after all the pains taken for the good of her prusias sole, would go for to throw away her poor body? that she would cast the heys of infection upon such a carrying crow as Lashmyhago, as old as Mathewsullin, as dry as a red herring, and as poor as a starved veezel. . . . He's a profane scuffle, and as Mr. Clinker says, no better than an imp-fiddle, continually playing upon the pyebill and the new burth.

That's going farther than any Malaprop could go. It is more than the rollicking double entendre of Rowlandson's letterpress. It is a Scotsman making a Welsh woman play ducks and drakes with the English language. It is imaginative, festive and, like all Smollett's comedy, broad, bizarre and bold.

THE CRANK

If we are to define the spirit of the eighteenth century by its favorite word, I think the word "man" or "mankind" even more than words like "order" or "reason," is the one we ought to choose. Man dominates the minds and ultimately the hearts of the eighteenth-century writers, where God had dominated the mind of the seventeenth century. After the battles, the factions, the treasons, the private and partisan faiths of the religious wars, the men of the eighteenth century were concerned to impose an order on that chaos, to seek the common denominator, to reassemble the judgment of divided human nature. The warring consciences were to be fused once more into an amenable moral animal with all his greatness and all his folly. The lines of Pope proclaim him:

Know then thyself, presume not God to scan,
The proper study of Mankind is Man.
Plac'd on this isthmus of a middle state,
A Being darkly wise, and rudely great:
With too much knowledge for the Sceptic side,

With too much weakness for the Stoic's pride,
He hangs between; in doubt to act or rest;
In doubt to deem himself a God, or Beast;
In doubt his Mind or Body to prefer;
Born but to die, and reas'ning but to err;
Alike in ignorance, his reason such,
Whether he thinks too little or too much:
Chaos of Thought and Passion, all confus'd;
Still by himself abus'd or disabus'd;
Created half to rise, and half to fall;
Great lord of all things, yet a prey to all;
Sole judge of Truth, in endless Error hurl'd:
The glory, jest, and riddle of the world!

And Man is not yet trapped in our later prefixes and qualifications. He is not yet industrial man, economic man, evolutionary man, civilized man, mass man or man in transition. He is simply himself, a wonder ordained, like a tree watched in a garden. Inconstancy, levity, cruelty may be his habits; but so are generosity, the noble and the useful virtues. Even Swift declares that he loves plain John, Peter and Thomas. The name of Candide is itself a commendation. However ferocious the satire of the eighteenth century, it is always balanced by a pleasure, sometimes trite and complacent, but always ingenuous and warm, in the habits of the new-discovered species; and we ourselves respond to such a fundamentally sanguine and well-found conception of human nature, even as we smile at the neat eighteenth-century labels. The Age of Reason was a revised, replanted and well-tended Eden; the serpent himself did obeisance to the great landscape gardener; and when we look back upon that world we cannot but suspect that half our present miseries date from the dissipation of the common feeling and philosophy that ensured the sanity of the age.

The notion of the sufficiency of man in himself encouraged the growth of peculiar character. The century enjoyed its fantastics. It allowed people to grow as they willed. One delighted in inventing more and more deformities and vices for one's enemies, more and more foibles and scandals for one's friends. The eccentrics of the age grew like cultivated blooms for all to admire; and its cranks could rely on the affection if not on the support of their circle. Misanthropy was especially respected, for among people who live well the melancholy man is slipped in by nature as a kind of sport and to restore the balance; and when the misanthropic man was a crank into the bargain, he was observed with that delighted eagerness which a naturalist feels for the smallest hint of a new mutation.

In this period, there is no more suggestive example than the author of *Sandford and Merton.* Mr. Day is the modest and entrancing crank of the century. He is a crank who is the guide to all cranks, the pattern of the tribe. In their lives few earnest men have been more ridiculous. After his death, the growth of his influence indicated the crank's embarrassing usefulness: if he was ridiculous, we were dreadful; if he was to be laughed at, we were to be wept over. For the case of Mr. Day perfectly illustrates the point that the crank is one of the growing points of society. He shows us not indeed what we shall become, but the direction we are likely to take. The special madness of Mr. Day was the belief that the errors of life were not due to original sin, but to stupidity and the formation of bad habits. If we could be caught young enough, in the age of natural innocence, we could be trained to be wiser and better than our stupid fathers. It was the madness of education. We shall see that when we come to *Sandford and Merton,* but before we do so, a glance at Mr. Day himself, as he is drawn full-length in the *Memoirs* of his friend Richard Edgeworth, is indispensable.

Nature is malicious. She is likely to arrange that

those who have revolutionary ideas about the education of children shall have no children of their own; and here we come upon the first flaw in Mr. Day's private life. He did not succeed in getting any children of his own; he was without the recklessness of the philoprogenitive. An abnormal caution governed the revolutionary life of Mr. Day. He was unable for many years to master the initial difficulty of getting a wife. Women surrounded him, but none came up to his severe requirements. He believed, like any rationalist, in the sufficiency of man; his cross was the insufficiency of woman. The heart of the problem was that Mr. Day was a perfectionist; he not only believed in the perfectibility of man, which is arguable, but he also believed in the perfectibility of women, and women take unkindly to the notion that they can be improved. The susceptible Mr. Day—and he was very susceptible—had either to take what he could get and like what he got, as the common run of men have to do, or—the logic is unanswerable—construct his own wife from blueprints in advance. Admirable mind of the eighteenth century: Mr. Day chose the second course.

What were the requirements of Mr. Day? Like a planner, he wanted to begin from the beginning, to make a fresh start. The whole invention called woman was in error. First of all one had to persuade women of this fundamental error in creation. Then one isolated them, cured them of silliness, frivolity, caprice, love of clothes, love of flirtation, love of chatter, flattery and society, the tendency to disobedience, lying and deception. One cured them of their slavery to fashion. Into the resulting vacuum, one poured modesty, decorum and the higher mental interests; the sex would learn, not indeed to converse themselves, but to follow a man's conversation and to assimilate his opinions. And they would be the most advanced opinions. Mr. Day was sick of the silly women of the eighteenth century, the creatures who were seduced, abducted and swindled, who giggled and fainted, danced and gambled and talked of nothing but clothes. The story is well known. Cautiously he obtained the two famous orphans—two because he realized there might be a failure. Lucretia and Sabrina were immured in the country, and Day waited for them to grow to the point where he could attend to their minds. Alas, the reformer who did not believe in original sin, had not reckoned with invincible dullness! Lucretia turned out to be quarrelsome and trivial. She was married off quickly to a draper. For a time Sabrina seemed more hopeful. But it could not be concealed that she disliked reading. She could not bear science. She could not keep a secret. And she had no control over her emotions. Day established all these points by experiment. For example, to test her self-control he fired pistols close to her ears and her petticoats. She screamed. More serious—she was found secretly to be buying hats and putting lace on her dresses.

The experiment of Mr. Day's is notorious. It caused the greatest astonishment in France where he took the two girls on an educational tour; but incredulous Frenchmen were at last convinced that Mr. Day was genuinely engaged in an educational exercise, and retired from his party in terror. Mr. Day was prepared to fight a duel with anyone who imperiled the curriculum. But the experiment is a mere episode in Mr. Day's search for the right partner. He was only twenty-one when he undertook it.

At this point it is important to reveal the existence of another character who had been experimenting also, and who was the close witness and associate in some of Day's adventures. I refer to Richard Edgeworth. Here comedy fills out. Day is the initiator, but Richard Edgeworth is the foil. One man is the making of the other; and it is through the delightful memoirs of Maria Edgeworth's father that we see Mr. Day drawn full-length with all the century's love of strange human beings and with its special regard for friendship. The two men are examples of the dyspeptic and the eupeptic schools of experiment. They were both rich. They were both country gentlemen.

On the one hand there is the ingenious Mr. Day, the exemplary Mr. Day, the Mr. Day who talked like a book, who neglected his appearance, who refused to dress like a man of fashion, who despised the polite conventions, who began his addresses to women by denouncing the sex. A clumsy man, greasy-haired in the days of wigs, pock-marked and brilliant, Mr. Day scowled cautiously all day over his scruples. At a time when a good masculine leg was admired he was painfully knock-kneed. On the other hand there was Richard Edgeworth, Irish, headstrong, handsome, generous, hot-tempered and gallant, the best dancer in Europe. Like Day, he was a man with theories of education—he was bringing up his son on the lines laid down by Rousseau, to the astonishment of his neighbors and the despair of his lamenting wife. Like Day, he was a man of scruples. But his passions were always growing stronger and his scruples growing less.

And then Day was the theorist and Edgeworth was the man of practice. Day would a thousand times sooner read a book on housing than address a carpenter. His theories about women could be seen as a protective device. Edgeworth's character was the opposite. In the matter of education he got a son and tried his educational theories on him. In the matter of women—Edgeworth married four times, three times very happily. He was an incurable inventor of contraptions—one-wheeled coaches, patent turnip cutters, railway lines, interlocking carriages, telegraphs, patent tips and loading devices, a notable forerunner of the next century's engineers. One can see that a love of mischief was part of his ingenious temperament, and that it must have directed his affection for the prosaic Mr. Day.

There is one remarkable episode in their friendship. It happened when Day had reached the point of desperation in his search for a wife. A delightful young woman called Elizabeth Sneyd who was Edgeworth's sister-in-law (years later she was to become Edgeworth's wife) agreed to consider Mr. Day if he would improve his appearance and polish his manners. Not a simple decision for a man like Day; for him, polish was the Arch Enemy, fashion the Pollution of life. To his drastic and puritan mind, the wearing of a wig meant the renunciation of his republican principles. But he was a desperate man. He agreed. He went off to France with Edgeworth, and, in his own mind, sold himself to the devil. Edgeworth describes how they got to Lyons where he had an enormous social success, while Day went through the pitiless school of a French dancing master. They cropped Day's lank Cromwellian locks. They piled a huge horsehair wig on his head. They dressed his ungainly body in the latest Parisian clothes. They taught him to bow and to dance. It was difficult for him to do this gracefully because of his knees and so soon they had him between boards which were screwed tight so that he could not move. Edgeworth had engineering projects of his own on the Saône, but he took a special and wicked interest in Mr. Day's knee-straightening machine. It was no good. The knees still knocked. "I could not help pitying my philosophic friend," says Richard Edgeworth, "pent up in durance vile for hours together, with his feet in the stocks, a book in his hand and contempt in his heart." Day returned at last to England, but when Elizabeth Sneyd saw the puritan Malvolio come bowing into the room, she collapsed with laughter, and that was the end of that.

Let us leave Mr. Day standing with unbendable rectitude amid the debris of his personal comedy. He did find a wife in the end, exactly the wife he desired, who was delighted to abandon all her personal tastes, including her love of music—an art which distressed him—and to devote her ear to his endless conversation. It was usually about education, and education killed him in the end. Kindness to animals was one of his principles, and Day was killed trying out a new "natural" method of educating an unbroken horse. The Age of Reason conceived wild nature and the noble savage to be tamer than they were.

When we read *Sandford and Merton* we feel that Day had this delusion about children. He had none of his own. Would they have broken him? Or would he have broken them? The father-prig, endlessly eloquent, mellifluously disposed to draw the ever-recurring moral, always pat with the tendentious anecdote, is a strain on his children. They relieve it at last by laughter. Perhaps Day would have become the ridiculous father as *Sandford and Merton* is the father's ridiculous book.

But not basically ridiculous. *Sandford and Merton* is the fruit of the eighteenth century's humane belief in the sufficiency of man and the light of reason. The book is not merely a child's book with a purpose; it is a child's book with a coherent philosophy, and that humane philosophy seems to me to have made *Sandford and Merton* far superior to the religious literature prescribed for children up to and, indeed, after that time. In how many biographies do we read of children who were terrified by *Foxe's Book of Martyrs*? How many were prompted to snivel in misery over *Sandford and Merton's* pious rival of the nineteenth century, *The Fairchild Family*? Some undoubtedly enjoyed the terrors, and I am not sure that it is wise to prevent a child from transposing his inheritance of the guilt and crimes of human nature into the pages of imaginative literature. Throughout the nineteenth century Day's book was disliked because it was said to ignore religion. In fact it did not, for it contains a simple account of Christ's morality; but Day certainly was no friend to the idea of original sin, and he did not set out to take the growing mind from a consideration of its responsibilities to the world outside itself, by nagging it continually with morbid images of the world within. If he was going to talk about hell, it was the hell of poverty, the several hells which men make for their fellows, not the hell invented by sadistic servants. One of the important aims of Day—and also of Edgeworth, who has some claim to be called the father of modern education—was to free the children of the well-to-do from the corrupting influence of nurses, chambermaids and butlers. But Day's philosophy must be judged by the kind of interests it encouraged. No doubt, as Edgeworth at last came to see, we are not certain to choose virtue just because our reason tells us that vice leads to misery and unhappiness; no doubt authority and discipline are required. But what new fields the freedom of philosophy opened to the curious mind! While the fearful and pious child was sobbing over the catastrophes of sin and was enclosed in the dank cloisters of self-pity, the prim little rationalists of *Sandford and Merton* were seeing the world. They were exploring South America, studying elephants and tigers, conducting experiments with the sun and the moon, and learning about the society they lived in.

It is strange that such an uninspiring man as Day, a man so full of crotchets and so devoid of instinct, so poor in response to everything except a generality, should have written a book as limpid and alive as *Sandford and Merton.* He hits one or two tastes of children with nicety: the complacency of children, their priggish and fierce delight in codes of conduct and honor; their love of a crude argument in black and white; their cocky moments of discovery; their passion for being heroes. Day understands the elementary principle that children are human beings who are growing taller and more powerful every day. "We are but little children strong"—not weak. It is true that the tears and the piety of the awful little Harry Sandford mark a stage in the "too noble by half" tradition; but I imagine that the child reader identifies himself with the will of Tommy Merton, and attends to Harry Sandford's remarkable practical capabilities—he knows how to deal with snakes, for example, and can take a thrashing without turning a hair—without being much perturbed by his virtues. Even the sentimentality about the honest poor, with its underhand appeal to childish pity, catches the child's love of showing off and making himself important. Old Mr. Barlow, to do him justice, has an inkling of this.

But the important charm of *Sandford and Merton* is extraneous to these matters. Day succeeds because he has created a kind of traveling zoo, an elegant and orderly zoo whose head keeper maintains a lively and picaresque running commentary. Now he is telling the visitor about the elephant, about elephants he has seen, elephants in the wild, elephants he has tamed, how you ought to handle them, and what happened to a tailor who made the mistake of playing a trick on one. The jungle, the native village, the regal procession are thrown in; and the whole stream of pictures flows smoothly by. They flick away before boredom starts. We have the pleasure of listening to someone talking to himself. This musical and vivid manner comes straight out of Day's own character. He was a man who never stopped talking. The ladies found this suffocating. But a child would listen forever, for Day was so delightfully unreal. "Is not that the country, Sir, where the cruel animal, the crocodile, is found?"

asks Harry Sandford, when Mr. Barlow shows the human weakness of stopping for breath. The invitation is not to be resisted. "It is an animal," says the invincible Mr. Barlow, off again for another couple of pages, "that lives sometimes upon the land, sometimes in the water. It comes originally from an egg. . . ." Little Harry Sandford, so liable to be infected by every germ of virtue blowing casually on the air, catches this manner in his talks with Tom Merton. Harry has just been thrashed by the wicked Squire for refusing to tell him which way the hare went, and Tom is sympathizing:

> H. Oh! it's nothing to what the young Spartans used to suffer.
>
> T. Who were they?
>
> H. Why, you must know they were a brave set of people that lived a great while ago; and as they were but few in numbers and were surrounded by enemies . . .

And so, by yet another happy dislocation of the narrative, the babbling stream of information resumes its cheerful flow.

Sandford and Merton is one of those books which are rich because they have taken a long time to mature and have outgrown their original plan. Day's first notion was to rewrite a number of well-known stories and fables for children; but he gradually saw that the stories could lead to Socratic dialogues and the arguments to still more stories.

> Mr. B. But when a person is not good to him, or endeavors to hurt him, it is natural for an animal to run away from him, is it not?
>
> T. Yes.
>
> Mr. B. And then you say he is wild, do you not?
>
> T. Yes, Sir.
>
> Mr. B. Why, then, it is probable that animals are only wild because they are afraid of being hurt, and that they only run away from the fear of dan-

ger. I believe you would do the same from a lion or a tiger.

T. Indeed I would, Sir.

Mr. B. And yet you do not call yourself a wild animal?

Tommy laughed heartily at this and said No. Therefore, said Mr. Barlow, if you want to tame animals, you must be good to them, and treat them kindly, and then they will no longer fear you, but come to you and love you. Indeed, said Harry, that is very true; for I knew a little boy that took a great fancy to a snake that lived in his father's garden; and, when he had milk for breakfast, he used to sit under a nut tree and whistle, and the snake would come to him, and eat out of his bowl.

T. And did it not bite him?

H. No; he sometimes used to give it a pat with his spoon if it ate too fast; but it never hurt him.

The aim of Day was to give a tendentious education. He loathed all that was meant by a man of fashion. He loathed everything that Lord Chesterfield stood for, almost as much as Lord Chesterfield's son came to do. He loathed idleness, profligacy, the self-indulgence of the rich. He loathed the man of fashion's attitude to children. He was a plain Republican who believed that no one should eat who did not work. He was one of the earliest Abolitionists. All these views are directed at Tommy Merton, whose father is a rich slave owner:

And what right have the people who sold the poor negroes to your father to sell them, or what right has your father to buy them? Here Tommy seemed a good deal puzzled, but at length he said: They are brought from a country that is a great way off, in ships, and so become slaves. Then, said Mr. Barlow, if I take you to another country in a ship I shall have a right to sell you? —T. No, but you won't, sir, because I was born a gentleman. —Mr. B. What do you mean by that, Tommy? —Why (said Tommy, a little confounded), to have a fine house and fine clothes, and a coach, and a great deal of money, as my papa has. —Mr. B. Then if you were no longer to have a fine house, nor fine clothes, nor a great deal of money, somebody that had all these things might make you a slave, and use you ill, and beat you, and insult you, and do whatever he liked with you? —T. No, Sir, that would not be right, neither, that anybody should use me ill. —Mr. B. Then one person should not use another ill? —T. No, Sir. —Mr. B. To make a slave of anybody is to use him ill, is it not? —T. I think so. —Mr. B. Then no one ought to make a slave of you? —T. No, indeed, Sir. —Mr. B. But if no one should use another ill, and making a slave is using him ill, neither ought you to make a slave of anyone else. —T. Indeed, Sir, I think not.

If Day's instruction was tendentious and was written on the revolutionary impulse of the eighteenth century, his methods were also new. Lord Chesterfield's son was intended to be a miniature Lord Chesterfield, an awed and suitably diminished reflection of his father. Day's notion was that a child is a new and independent life. His education in fact and morality was to be gained in the course of living; he was not to inherit a convention. If father's gluttony leads to gout, if father's wealth leads to restlessness, cruelty and guilt, if mother's spoiling leads to ill health, the child's rational faculty must be strengthened until he sees that other courses are better. Education is a guidance in the choice of good habits and the cultivation of a humane disposition.

This was revolutionary. So revolutionary that old Edgeworth was obliged to disinherit his own son who had taken the bit of freedom between his teeth. Reason, alas, could not control him; neither a parent's reason nor his own. Edgeworth hastened to warn parents that he and his friends had been laboring under an appalling error. This was years later; and there is no doubt that Tommy Merton was drawn from Edgeworth's dashing and willful eldest son. And then there was another aspect to the revolution. The coddled manikin of the eighteenth-century portraits was given a healthier life. He was given lighter, freer clothes and was sent to harden himself to sun and cold. The Spartan ideal was established. But, excellent as a revolution and adventure, the Spartan ideal itself became a kind of grim, vested interest, a terrifying convention in the English public schools of the nineteenth century. The cult of nature became the cult of neglect. The gentleman of fashion was succeeded by the gentleman tough.

THE MAJOR'S DAUGHTER

He was greatly mourned at the Curragh where his cattle were well-known; and all who had taken up his bets were particularly inconsolable for his loss to society.

The quotation does not come from *The Irish R.M.*, but from the mother, or should one say the aunt, of the Anglo-Irish novel—Maria Edgeworth. The eighteenth-century note is unmistakable but so, even without the word Curragh, is the Irishness. One will never quite get to the bottom of that sentence out of *Castle Rackrent.* On the surface it is felt and good-natured. "Poor" Sir Kit, after hitting a toothpick out of his adversary's finger in a duel, received a ball in a vital part, and "was brought home in little better than an hour after the affair, speechless on a hand-barrow to my lady." A sad business; but landlords come and go; we know them by their debts; only cattle are eternal. Irish irony has been sharpened to a fine edge; it is more drastic than the corresponding irony of the English writers of the time. Sententious, secure in the collective, educated self-regard of their class, the English ironists regard folly from the strong point of cultivated applause and moral platitude, whereas an Irishwoman, like Maria Edgeworth, has uncertainty under foot. The folly of the death of Sir Kit is only equalled by the absurdity of the mourning; beyond both lies the hopeless disaster of the state of "the unfortunate country."

Behind an ironist like Fielding is assurance, courage and complacency; behind Maria Edgeworth, and Irish irony, lie indignation, despair, the political conscience. The rights and wrongs of Irish politics come into her works by implication. We see the absentees, the rackrenters, the bought politicians, the English, Jewish, Scottish heiresses brought in to save colonial insolvency. We see the buffoon priests and the double-minded retainers. We do not see the rebellion, the boys hiding in the potato fields, but we do catch the tension. The clever, wise daughter of an enlightened father, a woman always ready to moralize about cause and effect in the neat eighteenth-century way, Maria Edgeworth was Irish enough to enjoy without shame the unreasonable climate of human temper and self-will, Irish enough to be generous about the genius for self-destruction. She was a good woman, ardent but—

as Sir Walter Scott said—formidably observant, probably cool, perhaps not strong in sensibility; but she was not sentimental. Her irony—and surely this is Irish from Swift to Shaw—turns a reckless gaiety upon human thick-headedness.

Castle Rackrent is the only novel of Maria Edgeworth's which can be read with sustained pleasure by the reader of today. Its verve and vivacity are as sharp as a fiddle's. It catches on like a jig; if it belongs to the artless time of the English novel, it is not clogged up by old-fashioned usage. I have never read *The Absentee,* which is often praised, but I have tried *Belinda,* a picture of the London smart set, and *Ormonde.* They, too, are vivacious, but there is not much point in finding time for them. They have a minor place in the history of the novel. One can only say that she has an original observation of men and women, an unspoiled eye for types; her moralizings are at any rate free from Victorian sentimentality, but are not in themselves interesting. Is it better for affection to follow esteem, or for esteem to follow affection? How are we to keep the peace between sensitiveness and sensibility, between the natural and the frivolous heart? How do we distinguish the line where generosity becomes self-indulgence? All this is good training, no doubt; but Maria Edgeworth was at her best when she was not being explicit about it. Character for its own sake, as the work of so many women novelists has shown, was the strong subject of this kind, clear-headed, irreverent woman, who never disturbs but also rarely comes to the foregone conclusion.

Belinda is a sharp-eyed tour of the London marriage market. No woman is less deceived by other women than this unsoured spinster who adored her father, wrote handbooks on education with him, managed his estate, "got on" with his four wives and looked after his twenty-one children. The Edgeworths were a nation in themselves. She could draw an old rip like Lady Delacour, a matchmaker like Mrs. Stanhope pushing her debutantes, and a dangerous "metaphysical" woman like Lady Millicent in *Ormonde* with "the sweet persuasive voice and eloquent eyes—hers was a kind of exalted sentimental morality, referring everything to feeling, and to the notion of *sacrifice* . . . but to describe her notions she was very nearly unintelligible." Maria Edgeworth was the Major's daughter; the unintelligible was the unforgivable. It was very plain to her that the Lady Millicents of this world are so exalted that they do not know right from wrong. The men are as firmly drawn as the women. *Ormonde* contains a rich portrait of one of those hospitable, sociable, gallant, warm-hearted Irishmen, the souls of courtesy, whose imagination leads them into difficulties and ends by corrupting them, until the warm heart goes stone cold and they become the familiar Irish politician who will sell himself and anybody. Such a portrait might be done flat in bitterness and satire; Miss Edgeworth works in depth, engages our sympathy for the man, makes him captivate us—as he would in life—and gradually undeceives us without melodrama or ill-nature. None of these is a "great character," but all are faithful observations of character. They are a truthful gallery, as capricious as life, of the figures of a class and an age. Such—we can be certain—was the life she knew.

Her other gift as a novelist is for writing spirited dialogue. The talk of *Belinda* or *Ormonde* is always light, engaging and natural. It is that "modern" talk which goes on from generation to generation—one meets it in Jane Austen; then, after the Regency, it died out, until the modern novel revived it—and which has not been written in, like subheadings, into the story. Maria Edgeworth owed her gift to her indifference to plot, that great torture rack of talk in the

English novel. Plot was forced on her by her father, the brilliant Major, who suffered from a rather delightful excess of confidence in his own powers; but, like Scott at the beginning of his career, Miss Edgeworth was interested only in sketching the people around her, and that is how the true gift for dialogue arises. Yet she owed something even of this to the Major, for it was he who, determined to out-Rousseau Rousseau, made his daughter write down the dialogue of his twenty-one children in order that it could be examined afterwards in his moral and linguistic laboratory.

Of course, she had the Irish ear for Irish expressiveness. In *Ormonde,* King Corny cries out with the gout:

> "Pray now," said he to Harry who stood beside his bed—"now that I've a moment's ease—did you ever hear of the stoics that the bookmen talk of, and can you tell me what good anyone of them got by making it a point to make no noise when they'd be punished and racked with pains of body or mind? Why I tell you all they got—all they got was no pity—who would give them pity, that did not require it? I could bleed to death in a bath, as well as the best of them, if I chose it; or chew a bullet, if I set my teeth to it, with any man in a regiment—but where's the use? Nature knows best, and she says *roar!*"

In a subtler way, she is as good in her plain passages, notably in her scenes between men and women. She hardly can be said to try a love affair, indeed one might say that she has noticed men and women pursue one another but is not sure why they do so. What she likes best is caprice, misunderstanding, the off-days of married life, flirtation: that side of love which, in short, supplies repartee and comedy, sociability or its opposite. Her people are always being interrupted and though this shows some incompetence on the novelist's part, it also allows that crisp animation or restlessness which gives her stories their unaffected drift.

There are no interruptions in *Castle Rackrent.* Thady the steward tells the tale in his plain words and with his devious mind, and he rattles off the decline and fall of the riotous Rackrents over three generations, in a hundred pages. Drink, company, debt and recalcitrant foreign wives ruined these roisterers and Thady's own son, turned lawyer, quietly collected the remnant and indirectly made it his own. At the funeral of one Rackrent, the body was nearly seized for debt:

> But the heir who attended the funeral was against that, for fear of consequences, seeing that those villains who came to serve acted under the disguise of the law; so, to be sure, the law must take its course and little gain had the creditors for their pains. First and foremost, they had the curses of the country and Sir Murtagh Rackrent, the new heir, in the next place, on account of this affront to the body refused to pay a shilling of the debts, in which he was countenanced by all best gentlemen of property and others of his acquaintance, Sir Murtagh alleging in all companies that he all along meant to pay his father's debts of honor, but the moment the law was taken from him, there was the end of the honor to be sure. It was whispered (but none but the enemies of the family believe it) that this was all a sham seizure to get quit of the debts, which he had bound himself to pay in honor. It's a long time ago, there's no saying how it was . . .

That is Defoe, but with whiskey added.

Major Edgeworth did not touch *Castle Rackrent.* He is known to have had a didactic hand in the other works and some have thought he stiffened them. Possibly. Yet his daughter owed her subsequent inspiration to the excitable, inventive, genial mind of the masterful eccentric and amateur. *Castle Rackrent* was the first attempt to present the history of a family over several generations as a subject in itself. It marks a small step in the expansion of the novel. Where the Major's influence is most felt is in the remarkable range of his daughter's work. Ireland is only one of her scenes. English society, Parisian society, are done with the same natural touch. Her work was a triumph for the Major's revolutionary system of free education. Not a patch on Fanny Burney or Jane Austen, no doubt; the minds of father and daughter were too much dispersed by practical and inventive attention to the good, rational life. Scott thought Edgeworthstown a domestic paradise and possibly noted it was an Abbotsford 150 years old without the worry and the expense. Abbotsford meant absurdity, obsession, and imagination; Edgeworthstown meant enlightenment. In the last count, the good life does not produce the great novelists.

A SCOTTISH DOCUMENTARY

While Byron and Hobhouse were at Malta refusing to leave the ship until the Governor ordered the guns of the harbor to salute their arrival, there was another writer in the background. He was getting quiet pleasure out of the fact that the Governor had evidently no intention of wasting his honors on literature. This third person was John Galt, hitherto only a dull Scottish poet and young businessman, but later to become one of the most delightful humorous novelists of the Scottish hearth. Of his work, *The Annals of the Parish* is still entertaining, even for those who, like myself, never take kindly to the Scottish dialect and whose taste for glens, kirks, lochs and kailyards has suffered from an early excess of Scott, George Macdonald and Stevenson. With less pleasure one can also read Galt's *Ayrshire Legatees* and skip through his long novel *The Entail.* There is some well-tipped satire in both these books. Byron said that the Leddy Grippy of *The Entail* was the finest portrait of a woman in English literature since Shakespeare, but he was thinking, I am afraid, not of literature, but of the women who had annoyed him.

Of the three men who waited on board at Malta and who met several times later during Byron's Mediterranean travels, Galt was easily the most versatile, one almost had said the most original. At that time he was traveling with a scheme for capturing the Turkish trade and with an eye for any deal that came by the way. (He just missed buying the Elgin marbles as a speculation and was actually their nominal owner for a week or two while they were on the sea.) Galt showed the same sort of efficiency and enterprise in business which Peacock had, a capacity for large and problematical undertakings; and when one looks at the long list of plays, poems, hack biographies, pamphlets and novels which he wrote, it is a surprise to discover that the main business of his life was buying and selling, pushing plans for colonization, or for damming great rivers like the Clyde and the St. Lawrence, getting canal bills through Parliament and founding towns in Canada. The now thriving town of Guelph, in Ontario, was founded by him; he chose its site and planned its institutions; one other town in the same province bears his name.

Versatility, especially if this includes practical gifts, is a great danger to writers. To Galt, literature was always a side line, a means of making a little extra, which he needed very badly. His work suffers accordingly. But there is always something sympathetic about the businessman novelist, the man who gets a little private amusement out of the Byrons, and himself never quite surrenders to the aberrations of the profession. Into the posing, frantic life of Grub Street, with its suggestion of the intellectual nudist colony, a man like Galt brings the mystery, indeed it amounts to the richness and romance of the conventional; he has the self-possession of one who does not earn his living by exposing his shame. *Tout se paie,* of course; Galt knew that he was a part-timer if not an amateur by temperament. But those writers whose main occupation keeps them on the outside of literary circles preserve a kind of innocence, a modest but all the more determined sense of their merits, and are less tempted to imitate and follow a school. Galt had such an individuality. He was inventive by nature. He made a virtue of his inability to imagine plots and fables by writing documentary works which, in his *Autobiography,* he calls "theoretical histories." And it is interesting to know that *The Annals of the Parish* was written long before *Waverley*—and was for twenty years without a publisher until Scott's work started the interest in Scottish subjects. Galt was indeed an innovator, and innovators do not generally reap fully where they have sown. Not many writers can say that they have founded a town, invented a new kind of book, and have given an important new word to the language: the word Utilitarian was taken by John Stuart Mill from the lips of the Rev. Mr. Balwhidder of *The Annals of the Parish.*

Galt's inspiration for this book came from *The Vicar of Wakefield.* He set out to create a Scottish Dr. Primrose. In fact, the Rev. Mr. Balwhidder, timid, twittering, pious, cautious, decorous, yet possessed of a salty tolerance of nature, is very different. One is never quite certain whether the minister knows how comical he really is. And when I say that *The Annals* is an amusing book I am not addressing myself to the literary critic who can take his amusement spread very, very thin as long as he is sure he is dealing with a standard work. *The Annals* is brisk and diverting, and as succulent, within the bounds of clerical decorum, as local scandal itself. We see the life of the parish of Dailmailing year after year, growing, waning, growing again.

Smuggling seizes Dailmailing's fancy for a time, and along come the illegitimate babies; soldiering seizes it; revolutionary ideas get into its heads; the old laird gives place to a new order; a mill absorbs the free weavers. And on top of these main episodes there is the froth of gossip. Old ladies fly into tantrums, young girls elope, justices roar, and wicked old women conceal smuggled tea in their mattresses and go to bed on them, feigning illness when the Excise officer and his informer come round. If one is in any doubt about the character of this book the first page settles it at once. The Minister of Dailmailing, whose prudence drove him to marry three wives in the course of his lifetime, belongs to the best dry vintage of Scottish humor, with its strange conflicting tangs of primness and animal spirits. He was put in by a patron over the heads of the angry villagers, and over their heads he had to go the Sunday he was "placed" at the church. Pelted with mud and guarded by soldiers, he had to climb in at a window because the church door was locked, only to be greeted inside by one of the zealots with the appropriate Scripture about those who enter "not by the door of the sheepfold but by some other way." And as the dismayed but long-suffering Mr. Balwhidder kneeled at the induction ceremony a loud laugh went up from the congregation when the neighboring minister gave him a tap on the head with a staff, and said, "Timber to timber." Having come in at the window, the minister was obliged to leave by it as well.

The inhabitants of Dailmailing, as can be seen, were people of spirit and with a turn for fantasy, but the quiet Minister was soon their equal. A gamekeeper had seduced the Rev. Mr. Balwhidder's parlormaid, and the Minister obliged the couple to stand in church. This happened after the death of the first Mrs. Balwhidder and was a warning to the prudent Minister that he had better get a second wife. Very different she was from the first, a managing woman with an "over-earnestness to gather gear." She turned the meditative manse into a raucous farm, and worked day and night in the dairy, so that the Minister was left in his study most evenings as lonely as a bachelor. He might have married a factory. But he outlived her, too, and the third one, married in his old age, was nearer his own nature. She was a professor's widow, and the Minister's courtship of her is one of the most remarkable I ever remember in English comic literature. It is like something from Sterne, without the leer. One catches in this scene the frosty sparkle of Galt's comedy at its best:

> On the Thursday the company was invited, came, and nothing extraordinary was seen; but in cutting up and helping a hen, Dr. Dinwiddie put one wing on Mrs. Nugent's plate, and the other wing on my plate, and said there have been greater miracles than these two wings flying together, which was a sharp joke, that caused no little merriment at the expense of Mrs. Nugent and

> me. I, however, to show that I was none daunted, laid a leg also on her plate, and took another on my own, saying, in the words of the reverend doctor, there have been greater miracles than that these two legs should lie in the same nest, which was thought a very clever come off; and at the same time I gave Mrs. Nugent a kindly nip in her sonsy arm, which was breaking the ice in as pleasant a way as could be.

The American war drains the Minister's parish, and then the French revolution divides the village into Government men and Jacobins and the new cults of philosophy, philanthropy and utility grow among the weavers. One angry Tory J.P., on being asked by an arrested weaver whether Christ was not a reformer, replied in a rage: "And what the devil did He make of it? Was He not crucified?" Which, I should say, is a very accurate report of what Christians who are sitting pretty really think of Christ, without realizing it.

The Annals is, besides its comedy, a fascinating social history; and Galt succeeds, where so many artists fail, in showing how his place, his people and their interests grow and change. At the end the Rev. Mr. Balwhidder is far from being the pious clown he was at the beginning. The zest of the narrative springs from its use of everyday speech. Here the dialect words are used sparsely but with vivid effect. Words like "yellyhoo" and "oustrapulous," full of sound and picture, are the hi-jinks of a vastly living vernacular. When we turn to the homely farce of *The Ayrshire Legatees* or the more complicated satire of Glasgow manners in *The Entail,* it is by these phrases and especially by the realism of Galt's dialogue that the eye is taken. A natural, stoical charm, a racy, nutty equanimity, unperturbed and unembittered by the shocks of the world, are in all Galt's books, and in his life too, which was filled with the disappointments that fall to a man who is more inventive than his fellows, as the reader of his *Autobiography* may see. The disappointments of business may indeed prepare a writer to take the dramas of the imagination less extremely and certainly rid him of the artist's temptation to pose. Galt, the part-timer, who reverenced the poet in Byron and wrote his life, was not in the least overawed by him nor deceived. So easily might Galt have sneered or, worse still, have become the prosaic toady; it is the mark of Galt's independence and talent that he kept his moderate Tory head. And in those times it was something to have a level head. When Godwin's works were banned for their Jacobinism in the Ayrshire library, Galt, who detested Godwin's opinions, fought to get the ban removed, and was successful.

SCOTT

"No one reads Scott now": how often one has heard these words! I have no doubt they are true, at any rate true of English readers. At some time in the last fifty years feeling against dialect and especially the Scottish dialect has hardened into a final dislike. It is troublesome to the eye, it is a language which nags and clatters; one would as soon read phonetics. And then dialect suggests the overweening conceit of local virtue, and if anything has died in the last fifty years, it is regionalism. Our society—why pretend—has made war on regionalism and has destroyed it. We may question whether, under any disguise, it can be reborn in the modern world. That is the first difficulty when we look at the long brown row of the Waverley Novels that have stood high out of reach on our shelves, unopened since our childhood. And here the second difficulty arises. We read Scott in our childhood and he is not suitable reading for children; few of the great novelists are. Why should a man, writing in his maturity, scarred by life, marked by the evils of the world, its passions and its experience in his blood, be consigned to the young who know nothing of themselves or the world? The fault is partly Scott's: this great man, the single Shakespearean talent of the English novel, drew far too often the heroes and heroines that used always to appeal to the adolescent and gently reared reader—wooden idealizations, projections of our more refined, sixteen-year-old wishes. At sixteen we are in love with those sexless heroines with their awful school-mistressy speeches. We are in love with those stick-in-the-mud heroes whose disinterestedness and honor pervert the minds of boys with a tedious and delusive idealism. One grows up in the daydream that Scott has generated to discover it is a swindle; and one never forgives him.

Yet, if we except this serious criticism for the moment, and measure Scott in the light of the full noon of life, we see that he belongs to that very small group of our novelists—Fielding and Jane Austen are the chief of them—who face life squarely. They are grown up. They do not cry for the moon. I do not mean that to be grown up is the first requirement of genius. To be "mature" may be fatal to it. But short of the great illuminating madness, there is a power to sustain, assure and enlarge us in those novelists who are not driven back by life, who are not shattered by the discovery that it is a thing bounded by unsought limits, by interests as well as by hopes, and that it ripens under restriction. Such writers accept. They think that acceptance is the duty of a man.

An error of our boyhood reading of Scott is, I fancy, the easy assumption that Scott is primarily an historical novelist. There is more reason to think of him as a comic writer. We would make a similar kind of error about Defoe, Fielding or Richardson if we took them at their word and believed that their only aim was to reform morals. The historical passion of Scott or the moral passion of these other novelists was the engine of their impulse. Where that engine took them is another matter. Hazlitt saw this when, in his too drastic way, he said that Scott was interested in half of life only: in the past of man and not in what he might become; and Hazlitt went to the length of thinking Godwin's *Falkland* fit to be compared with *Waverley*. But Scott's history meant simply his preoccupation with what is settled—and, after all, a great deal *is* settled for better or worse, in human life and character. One might even see in Scott's history the lame man's determination to impose and ennoble normality. The feuds of the clans are done with, the bloody wars of the Border are over, Jacobitism is a mere sentiment notable for its ironical inconsistencies as well as its heroic gestures. A period has ended and, for a novelist, there is no more favorable moment. Now he can survey. Scott gazes upon it all like a citizen who has dressed up. Now, vicariously, he can be physically heroic; but the real product of the historical impulse is not history but an immense collection of small genre pieces, a huge gallery of town and country faces in their inns, their kitchens, their hovels, their farms and their rambling houses. And the painting of them is as circumstantial, as middle-class—in the antiromantic sense—and as nonaristocratic as anything of Hogarth's. Scott does not revive the past or escape into it; he assimilates it for his own time and for his own prejudices. He writes like a citizen. He asserts the normal man, the man who has learned to live with his evil; what Scott's evil might have done with him if he had not learned to live with it can be guessed from the grotesque declamations of *The Black Dwarf*, the creature who cuts himself off from mankind.

The Black Dwarf is not a good novel. There are awkward lumps of unreality in it. The bad thing is the central drama, and this points to Scott's obvious fault as a novelist. He has an immense memory and the necessary gift for improving on memory. He has the power to present the outside of a character and to work from the outside to the inside. But once inside, he discovers only what is generic. That is the fault. He has, I would say, no power to work from the inner to the outer man. There is nothing feminine in him. So the black dwarf is excellent when he is seen as local recollection, a piece of Border hearsay, and no one could surpass Scott in portraying that tortured head, with its deep-sunken, pin-point eyes, the almost legless and hairy little body with its huge feet, and the enormous voice that issues from the abortion. But when we come to the mind of this tortured creature, when he speaks, what we get is not horror but a dreary, savage Calvinist lecture. The black dwarf's misanthropy is a mere exercise, a sermon turned inside out. There is a complete breakdown of the imagination: compare this story with Turgenev's *Lear of the Steppes*. I suspect that as we continue our rediscovery of Scott we shall often find that the chief drama of the novels breaks down in this way, for the great protagonists of fiction begin from the inside of a writer. One is inclined to divide the Scott characters into two classes: the secondary and minor ones who are real and are truly recollected, the children of his wonderful memory; and the major ones who are the awkward, stage figures of an imagination that is cut off from the sap of life. To go back to Hazlitt: Scott lacked a vital sense, the sense of what people may become. His history was not real history. It was the settled, the collectable, the antique.

I turn to *The Chronicles of the Cannongate,* the tales of the second series, to see whether my last sentence is too sweeping. There is *The Highland Widow.* Here is real history—but you notice at once—history without costume. History in the rags of the people. The widow's husband has been a bandit, the Robin Hood of a clan that has almost died out. Her son perceives that times have changed; he enlists in the army which was once his father's enemy. The mother is appalled by the disgrace and plots to restore her son to a life of crime. The tragedy which is enacted springs from the clash of two orders of virtue, and the virtue of one age has become the vice of the age that succeeds it. There is no dialect in this story. It is heroic and not Hogarthian. It is the kind of thing that Mérimée and Pushkin took from Scott. And here, better than in his more elaborate compositions, we see the mark of Scott's genius as a storyteller. I say nothing of the suspense of which he is always a master; I am thinking of his power of suggesting the ominous, the footsteps of fate coming to meet one on the road. Frequently Scott used the supernatural and the hints of second sight to get this effect, and they are all the more effective for being explained as the domestic beliefs of his characters which the author himself hesitates to accept. But in *The Highland Widow* we come upon one of those real omens, one of those chance remarks made by a stranger which have another meaning to the one who hears. It is a device much used by Hardy. In Scott's story the young soldier has been drugged by his fanatical mother so that he shall not return to his regiment. The boy wakes up and rushes out to find what day of the week it is, for he fears more than anything else the degradation of his honor. The first person he meets is a minister, who replies: "Had you been where you should have been yesterday, young man, you would have known that it was God's Sabbath." The two meanings of those words mark the crisis of the tale, and after looking back upon it one realizes how ingenious and masterly has been the construction of a simple story. The end we could foresee; the means we could not, and it is in the means that Scott always shows the power of a master.

It is less the business of the novelist to tell us what happened than to show how it happened. The best things in Scott arise out of the characters. He especially understands, as I said before, the generic differences between people. He understands the difference between the fisherman and the farmer, the shepherd and the drover, and so on. He understands, in other words, what all ordinary, simple, observant men know about one another: the marks of their trade, their town, their family. (His view of women is that of the simple man: he knows them by their habits in the house. In love he does not know them at all.) The tale called *The Two Drovers* is a fine example of Scott's watchfulness of male character. The honor of Robin, the Highland drover, seems to be quaint silliness to Wakefield, the stolid Yorkshireman; the sense and fair play of Wakefield, who cannot believe that enmity will survive a little amateur boxing, are meaningless to the Highlander. Each is reasonable—but in a different way. The clash when it comes is tragic; again two kinds of virtue are irreconcilable. The scene in the inn is wonderfully true to the men there, and the talk slips naturally off their clumsy tongues. Wakefield has challenged Robin to fight with his fists. Robin can't see how this will mend a quarrel.

Harry Wakefield dropped the hand of his friend or rather threw it from him.

"I did not think I had been keeping company for three years with a coward."

"Coward pelongs to none of my name," said Robin, whose eyes began to kindle, but keeping the command of his temper. "It was no coward's legs or hands, Harry Waakfelt, that drew you out of the fords of Frew, when you was drifting ower the plack rock, and every eel in the river expected his share of you."

"And that is true enough, too," said the Englishman, struck by the appeal.

"Adzooks!" exclaimed the bailiff—"sure Harry Wakefield, the nattiest lad at Whitson Tryste, Wooler Fair, Carlisle Sands, or Stagshaw Bank, is not going to show the white feather? Ah, this comes of living so long with kilts and bonnets—men forget the use of their daddles."

"I may teach you, Master Fleecebumpkin, that I have not lost the use of mine," said Wakefield, and then went on. "This will never do, Robin. We must have a turnup or we shall be the talk of the countryside. I'll be d——d if I hurt thee—I'll put on the gloves gin thou like. Come, stand forward like a man!"

"To be peaten like a dog," said Robin, "is there any reason in that? If you think I have done you wrong, I'll go before your shudge, though I neither know his law nor his language."

A general cry of "No, no—no law, no lawyer, a bellyful and be friends" was echoed by the bystanders.

"But," continued Robin, "if I am to fight, I have no skill to fight like a jackanapes, with hands and nails."

And here once more the agent of tragedy is moving slowly down the road toward the two friends—the drover who is carrying Robin's dirk for him, to keep him out of trouble and to circumvent the fate that was foretold at the beginning of the story.

Except in the outbursts of *The Black Dwarf,* Scott appears to see evil as a fatality that ensues from the nature of the times. The civil wars have made men narrow and ruthless, and he writes at the end of an era, surveying the broken scene and pleading for tolerance. The crimes in *The Chronicles of the Cannongate* are "errors of the understanding," not examples of absolute wickedness. When we turn to *The Antiquary* we meet another side of his talent; his humor. I wonder how many of those who, like myself, have not read Scott since their schooldays will recall that Scott is one of the great comic writers? It is not purely Scottish humor, depending on the canniness of the speaker or on a continuous sly, nervous snigger, or on the grotesque and pawky asides of dialect. Scott's humor, like his best prose, is crossbred with the English eighteenth century. Sterne and Fielding have put red blood into it. A character like Jonathan Oldbuck does not make thin jokes down his nose, but stands solidly and aglow beside all the well-found comics of our literature. The secret is that Scott's animal spirits are high, as Fielding's were. I have always enjoyed that strange scene in the early pages of *The Antiquary* in which Oldbuck supervises the rescue of the foolish, snobbish, bankrupt, treasure-hunting Sir Arthur, and his stick of a daughter, from the rising tide. Jonathan Oldbuck who has only an hour before been snubbed by the angry baronet, now watches the men heave the scarcely conscious gentleman up the rock:

> "Right, right, that's right, too—I should like to see the son of Sir Gamelyn de Guardover on dry land myself—I have a notion he would sign the abjuration oath, and the Ragmanroll to boot, and acknowledge Queen Mary to be nothing better than she should be, to get alongside my bottle of

old port that he ran away from, and left scarce begun. But he's safe now, and here a' comes—(for the chair was again lowered, and Sir Arthur made fast in it, without much consciousness on his own part)—— Here a' comes—bowse away, my boys! —canny wi' a tenpenny tow—the whole barony of Knockwinnock depends on three plies of hemp—respice finem, respice funem—look to your end—look to the rope's end."

I can read about half of *The Antiquary* and enjoy the flavors of what I read. After that I skip through the preposterous plot and willingly leave the wooden Lovel and the disdainful Miss Wardour to the pleasure of talking like public statues to each other. In one respect it must be admitted they do surpass modern lovers. Severely regulated by their families and by circumstance, these antique couples are obliged to know their subject. The obstacles to love ensure that the lovers shall concentrate.

The criticism that Scott cannot draw a heroine has to be modified after we have read *The Heart of Midlothian.* To judge by this book Scott could not draw a hero. For neither the pious, pettifogging Butler nor the wicked George Staunton can be called human beings of anything but conventional interest. Effie and Jeanie Deans are quite another matter. They are peasants and Scott condescends to them with the gentlemanliness of his time, but they are alive as his peasants always are. Scott's inability to draw women life-size seems to be due to the fact that he can think of them only as creatures high above him, or safely below him; and the ones below are drawn better than the ones above. The maid is more interesting than the mistress. We owe this romantic and pedestaled conception of women partly to the lame man's feeling of inferiority. He idealized what he could not approach. But these idealizations also arise from that curious split in the puritan middle-class mind which had begun to unsex itself so that it might devote all its will to the adventure of getting on in the world of money or honor, leaving the warmer passions to the lower orders. But unlike the early Victorian novelists, Scott is not a prude. Miss Bellendon's maid, in *Old Mortality*, nudges, winks and uses all her enticements on the soldiery; speech is very free in the farms and the inns; only Miss Bellendon in her castle stands like a statue and talks like an epitaph. Once Scott is free of these inhibitions —and in the main they are fixed by considerations of class—Scott describes women as well as they can be described from the point of view of a man in the house; that is as scolding, fussing, gossiping, pestering, weeping, and mercenary adjuncts of domestic life. They can always answer back. They never forgive a slight, they can always be persuaded to condone a crime. Expressed without satire but with sense and geniality this view has inspired many robust minor portraits of womanhood in Scott. The loveliness and attraction of Di Vernon in *Rob Roy* is due, I fancy, to the fact that she has a good deal of male in her. What is missing from all these portraits is the vitalizing element: the sense a woman has of herself, the sense of what she may become—that sense of our fate which alone gives meaning to our character. And as I have said before, Scott's direct intuitive sense of that fate seems to have been weak; he grasps the importance of it only through the labors of the historian and the documentary artist. His researches, not his instinct, gave us his remarkable portrait of the passionate mother in *The Highland Widow*, and his researches also revealed to him, in the same way, the larger meaning of Jeanie Deans' character in *The Heart of Midlothian*.

A modern novelist who rewrote *The Heart of Midlothian* would certainly stress the unconscious jealousy which Jeanie must have felt toward her younger sister by her father's second marriage. We would say that Jeanie's refusal to tell the lie that would save Effie from the scaffold was not a stern moral act, but an animal retaliation; for psychology alters our interpretation of many ethical dilemmas. Scott ignores the evident jealousy. And though Effie, in a remarkable prison scene, flies out at her sister, we are left with the impression that Jeanie is either too stupid or too conceited in her conscience to be endured. But Scott's strength in the handling of the situation between the two women comes from his knowledge of the effect of history upon them. They are children of history. And the one part of history Scott knew inside out was its effect upon the conscience. Jeanie's refusal to tell a lie had generations of Calvinistic quarreling behind it, the vituperations of the sectaries who had changed the sword of the clan wars and the civil wars for the logic-chopper of theology. Instead of splitting skulls, they had taken to splitting hairs. The comedies, the tragedies, the fantastic eloquence and tedious reiteration of these scruples of conscience are always brilliantly described by Scott, who has them in his blood. And so Jeanie's refusal to lie and her journey to London on foot to seek her sister's pardon are not the result of conceit, heartlessness or even literalness of mind: they are the fruit of history.

And a history which produces not only plump, dumb, resolute figures like hers, but men of roistering violence like the bloody Porteous, tortured believers in predestination like Staunton, fanatics like old Deans, cranks like Saddlebright, lunatic harlots like Madge Wildfire, adventuresses like Effie, wonderful sea-lawyers of the criminal world of old Edinburgh like Ratcliffe, the thief, and wonderful fools like the gaping old laird of Dumbiedikes. There is none of the sentimentality which Dickens spread like a bad fog over the suffocated bastards, baby farmers, harlots and criminals of his novels; none of the melodrama. Scott's realism belongs to the time when gentlemen knew the mob because they were not yet afraid of the mob. There is only one false episode in *The Heart of Midlothian;* and that is the wildly improbable meeting between Jeanie and George Staunton at his father's vicarage in England, and we owe that to the influence of the theater on the English novel. For that matter, none of the English scenes is really good and the final third of the novel is a failure. Here Jeanie is diminished as a character by the condescension of the author. But when she is in Scotland, we feel the force of her country and her fate in her, and these make her into a woman. One sees her even more clearly and fully late in the book when it is she, the rescuer, who has to pay tribute to Effie, the adventuress, who has, after all, got away with it. Scott was too much the man of the world to prevent Effie getting away with a good deal more than Dickens or even Thackeray were later on to allow their giddy-pated or wicked women. Scott recorded willfulness in women with an appreciative eye; and an ear cocked for the back answer.

It has often been said that the decay of our interest in problems of conscience is a major cause of the feebleness of the modern novel; but there have been many poor novels stuffed tight with conscience. Might we not say more justly that the problems of conscience have changed? Our habit is to weigh man against society, civilization against man or nature, individuals against groups. The greatness of *The Heart of Midlothian* arises, first of all, in the scope that the problem of conscience gave to Scott's imagination. He was not arguing in a void. His argument was creating real people and attracting real people to it. He made the story of Effie's murdered baby a national story. And then how wide his range is! The scenes in the Tolbooth are remarkable, and especially those that are built about the figure of Ratcliffe when the governor is working to turn him into an informer. Scott had the eighteenth-century taste for rogues, and their talk is straight from nature.

"Why, I suppose you know you are under sentence of death, Mr. Ratcliffe?" replied Mr. Sharpitlaw.

"Ay, so are a', as that worthy minister said in the Tolbooth Kirk the day Robertson wan off; but naebody kens when it will be executed. Gude faith, he had better reason to say than he dreamed of, before the play was played out that morning!"

"This Robertson," said Sharpitlaw, in a lower and something like a confidential tone, "d'ye ken, Rat—that is, can ye gie us ony onkling where he is to be heard tell o'?"

"Troth, Mr. Sharpitlaw, I'll be frank wi' ye: Robertson is rather a cut abune me—a wild deevil he was, and mony a daft prank he played; but except the Collector's job that Wilson led him into, and some tuilzies about run goods wi' the gaugers and the waiters, he never did ony thing that came near our line o' business."

"Umph! that's singular, considering the company he kept."

"Fact, upon my honour and credit," said Ratcliffe, gravely. "He keepit out o' our little bits of affairs, and that's mair than Wilson did; I hae dune business wi' Wilson afore now. But the lad will come on in time; there's nae fear o' him; naebody will live the life he has led, but what he'll come to sooner or later."

"Who or what is he, Ratcliffe? You know, I suppose?" said Sharpitlaw.

"He's better born, I judge, than he cares to let on; he's been a soldier, and he has been a play-actor, and I watna what he has been or hasna been, for as young as he is, sae that it had daffing and nonsense about it."

"Pretty pranks he has played in his time, I suppose?"

"Ye may say that," said Ratcliffe, with a sardonic smile, "and" (touching his nose) "a deevil amang the lasses."

"Like enough," said Sharpitlaw. "Weel, Ratcliffe, I'll no stand niffering wi' ye; ye ken the way that favour's gotten in my office; ye maun be usefu'."

"Certainly, sir, to the best of my power—naething for naething—I ken the rule of the office," said the ex-depredator.

Then there is Scott's power of describing a crowded scene. I am thinking of the long narrative about the crowd's storming of the Tolbooth and the killing of Porteous. Scott has looked it all up, but his own version is so alive, so effortless, so fast-moving. Every detail tells; the very pedantry of it is pedantry washed down by the rough wine of life. Everything is carried off with the authority of a robust and educated style, the style of a man fit to understand, master and govern, a man endlessly fair and excitingly patient in his taste for human nature. He understands popular clamor. He understands the mysteries of loyalty—all the diverse loyalties of a man's life and trade.

And after that Scott has the storyteller's ability to build a great scene and to make a natural use of it. An instance is the search in the dark on Salisbury Crag when the police have persuaded Ratcliffe to help them catch Robertson, and Ratcliffe has brought Madge Wildfire with him to show them all the way. Madge is semi-lunatic, and Ratcliffe has to use all his guile to keep her to the job. He knows her mind is stuffed full of old wives' tales, and he reminds her of a notorious murder that was done on the Crag years before—a story the reader has already been prepared for: Scott's antiquarian asides ought never to be skipped—but Ratcliffe's cunning is turned against him at the moment of success by the madness of the woman. She accuses him of being as bad as the murderer.

> "I never shed blood," he protested.
>
> "But ye hae sauld it, Ratton—ye hae sauld blood mony a time."

That chance shaft hits Ratcliffe's conscience and wrecks the expedition. In a short chapter Scott has ingeniously extracted every kind of surprise and apprehension; and without any frivolity or artifice. The adventure could have happened; indeed, we say, if we had had eyes at the back of our heads, we would have known that it *must* have happened so, fabulous as it is. Scott's knowledge gives a sense of necessity to his picture of life, and his freedom in mixing the comic with the serious, even at the most dramatic moments, adds to this pleasant sense. He is not overdriven by his imagination, whereas a writer like Dickens was. Scott, like Fielding, has both feet firmly on the ground.

Rob Roy is admired—but for one or two scenes only when we examine the matter, and it is really a poor novel. At first sight the claims of *Old Mortality are* less emphatic upon the reader's attention, and since Scott repeated himself so often one is tempted to neglect this novel. It should not be neglected. Into this book Scott put all his tolerance and civilization, his hatred of fanaticism, and illuminated the subject of the religious wars in Scotland with all his irony, humor, all his wiriness of intellect and all his human sympathy. In Burley he drew the rise and the corruption of the fanatical character, and I do not know any other in Scott whose character grows and changes so convincingly. There is real movement here; elsewhere the sense of movement in his character is more the result of Scott's habit of dissertation than a real enacting of change. The portrait of Claverhouse is debonair, and the battle scene when the insurgents rout him is almost Tolstoyan. How much Scott owes to a sincere pleasure, even a joy, in the accouterment of life. One can see how the Russians, like Tolstoy, Gogol and Pushkin first of all, must have been caught by Scott's wonderful pictures of the eccentric lairds. The miser in *Old Mortality*, or the ridiculous, gaping laird in *The Heart of Midlothian* must have fathered many a landlord in *Dead Souls* and other Russian stories. Where the Russians were to succeed and where Scott failed was in conveying the sense of an abiding destiny going on beyond the characters described. For Scott life is a book that one closes; to the Russians it is a book that one opens. And although one feels his animal zest for life, one feels it as a delightful recollection of hours that are ended, not as the perturbation or languor of the hour which has still to go by on the clock as we read.

One looks up the critics. What did Scott add to the English novel? Is he just another Fielding, but planted in Scottish history? Has he simply added a change of scene and material? It looks like that at first glance: he is a writer from the outside looking in. But I think there is something else. Scott is a complement to Richardson—an analytical and psychological novelist who describes to us the part of our motives formed by public events. He is certainly the first novelist to describe the political influence of religion and the peculiar significance of superstitions and legend in the mind; and he uses them to illustrate the prompting of unconscious guilt and fear. One sees this in the character of Ratcliffe in *The Heart of Midlothian* and in innumerable instances elsewhere; Scott does not use his apparitions and legends merely for the purpose of putting a shiver or a laugh in his story. They are there to convey hidden processes of mind. No English novelist has added to that sense of a general or public mind, and certainly no great novelist—Hardy is the atheistical exception—has used religion as Scott used it.

OUR HALF-HOGARTH

The English humorists! Through a fog compounded of tobacco smoke, the stink of spirits and the breath of bailiffs, we see their melancholy faces. Look at Thomas Hood, his eyes swollen with the cardiac's solemnity, his mouth pouting after tears. There is a terrible account of his last days in Canon Ainger's *Memoir,* where we see the poet famous, forty-six, bankrupt and dying of heart disease, writing farewells to his friends and unable to stop making puns. They beset him like a St. Vitus' dance. They come off his lips in an obsessional patter as if his tongue had become a cuckoo clock and his mind a lunatic asylum of double meanings. And around him his doting family and his friends are weeping, "Poor Tom Hood." This is, alas, one of the too many crying scenes of Victorian biography. It brims with that homemade beverage of laughter and tears which is handed round like a negus from the chiffonier of the lighter Victorian literature. The savage and vital indignation of the eighteenth century, its moral dogmatism, its body full of laughter and its roars of pain, have gone; melodrama replaces morality, a sprite-like pathos, all grace and weeping, and inked by fear of life, steps in where Caliban groaned and blubbered. Charles Lamb called Thomas Hood "our half-Hogarth," and that is the measure of the difference between the two periods.

Hood marks the difference well. Only in Goldsmith do we find a tenderness comparable to his. We look at the eighteenth century and, when all is said, we can hardly deny that it had a coherent and integrated mind, a mind not deeply divided against itself. The proper study of mankind is man, who is very corrupt, but presently Divine Reason will teach him to cast off his chains and he will become a free child of nature. By the end of the century the chains are removed. And what is the result? Hood's early nineteenth century shows us. Man has not become free; he has vanished. Or rather, that humane abstraction called Man has been succeeded by two warring groups. Man has degenerated and has become the middle classes and the poor. No longer, like Swift, do the Victorians feel horror of mankind; on the contrary, looking at the little circle of mankind in which they live, they find the species has very much improved. At Clapham, at Wanstead Flats, even in Russell Square and Fleet Street, he is kindly, charitable and good. Their horror moves from man as a whole to a section of men. They are horrified, they are frightened—philanthropical and well policed though they are—by the poor. For generations now they will not stop talking about the poor. Did they pull down the blinds and turn to conceits and fancies because this fear is outside the window after dark? The feeling is that outside the sitting room is an undefined world of wickedness, hunger, catastrophe and crime. Pickpockets are nabbed, poachers are imprisoned, desperate laborers threaten arson, and children go to the mills and up the chimneys; the press gang and transportation are living memories, and sailors drown—oh, how many sailors drown!—in calamitous storms. These terrible things happen—to the poor. There we have Hood's background. There is his material. But writers are urged and taught to write not by society only but by other writers whose background and intention make them utterly different from their pupils. It is a strange fact that the England of Hood is not delineated by revolutionary realists, but has come down to us in the fantastic dress of German Gothic. The Cruikshank who frightens us; Mr. Punch, with his pot belly, his fairy legs and the arching nose like some cathedral fragment, who squats on Dicky Doyle's cover, are part of the Gothic colony that settle like a migration of gargoyles among the English chimneys and their myth-creating smoke.

Hood, who was a Cockney of Scottish parentage, writes very early in his career of "doing something in the German manner." In his serious verses he is a Romantic, with his eye on Shakespeare, Scott and Keats. But this is the less readable part of Hood. His serious verses, if one excepts pieces of singular purity like "I remember, I remember," hardly amount to more than poetic dilutions for the family album, though contemporaries like Lamb, Southey and Byron had a higher opinion of them. Hood's best work is inflected by the basic early Victorian fear and the fancies to which it led. He is on the side of the poor, of course, and wrote for the early, unsuccessful Radical *Punch:* but the Hood of *The Song of the Shirt*—which trebled the circulation of *Punch*—*The Lay of the Labourer* and *The Bridge of Sighs* is the dying Hood who is touched by the indignation of the hungry Forties. The earlier Hood thinks the poor are quaint and that their crimes can be sardonically disinfected. The result is a vein of fanciful horror which fathered a whole school of ballad writing:

The body-snatchers they have come,
And made a snatch at me;
It's very hard them kind of men
Won't let a body be!

You thought that I was buried deep
Quite decent-like and chary,
But from her grave in Mary-bone
They've come and boned your Mary.

That is from *Mary's Ghost.* I could have quoted from *The Volunteer* or *Death's Ramble.* There is *The Careless Nurse Mayd:*

I saw a Mayd sitte on a Bank
Beguilded by Wooer fayne and fond;
And whiles his flatteryinge Vowes she drank,
Her Nurselynge slipt within a Pond!

All Even Tide they Talkde and Kist
For She was Fayre and He was Kinde;
The Sunne went down before she wist
Another Sonne had sett behinde!

Or from *Sally Simpkin's Lament:*

Oh! What is that comes gliding in
And quite in middling haste?
It is the picture of my Jones,
And painted to the waist.

Oh Sally dear, it is too true—
The half that you remark
Is come to say my other half
Is bit off by a shark.

Gilbert, Lear, Carroll, Thackeray, the authors of *Struwelpeter* and the cautionary tales continue this comic macabre tradition, which today appears to be exhausted. There is Mr. Belloc, who digressed intellectually; and there are the sardonic ballads of Mr. William Plomer. He has added brilliantly the horrors of vulgarity to the horrors of crime and accident.

Hood's special idiosyncrasy is to turn the screw of verbal conceit upon his subject. In *Eugene Aram* alone he cut out these tricks, even forbearing in the last verse when his temptation was always strongest. (How was it Hood failed to ruin what are, surely, the most frightening dramatic lines in English narrative verse?) But if Hood's puns are often disastrous, they do frequently show, as Walter Jerrold (his biographer) has said, a kind of second sight. They are like the cackle out of the grave in *Hamlet.* They add malice to the knife and give the macabre its own morbid whimsicalities. Take that terrible poem, *The Last Man.* The earth has been desolated by plague and only two men are left alive. They meet at a gallows and one, out of jealousy, decides to hang the other. He does so and is left, wracked by conscience, to lament that he cannot now hang himself:

> For there is not another man alive,
> In the world to pull my legs.

The wit in *Death's Ramble* shocks one first of all and then freezes the blood one degree colder. Death sees two duelists:

> He saw two duellists going to fight,
> In fear they could not smother;
> And he shot one through at once—for he knew
> They never would shoot each other.

And the comic funk of *The Volunteer* gets a grotesque double meaning. He fears the alarm:

> My jaws with utter dread, enclos'd
> The morsel I was munching,

And terror lock'd them up too tight,
My very teeth went crunching
All through my bread and tongue at once
Like sandwich made at lunching.

To the poor, Hood draws our attention by shuddering and laughing with them at the same time. His detachment, when he is writing about crime and catastrophe, is dropped when he is putting the case of the poor. Then he writes with something like the garrulous, flat statement of the broadsheets. These odes and poems lumber along. There is the washerwoman's attack on the new steam laundry which has taken her living. There is the chimney boy's lament that the law against street cries forbids him to cry "Sweep" in the streets. Drapers' assistants plead politely with people to shop early. These are pieces of topical journalism which time has blunted, and Hood's pen dipped deeply into that sentimentality which the philanthropical outlook of the period demanded. He was a prolific writer, and knew how to turn out his stuff. Like Dickens he was a sentimental Radical who hoped, as Dickens also hoped, that the problem of the poor could be solved by kindness; but the abiding note is that unpleasant one of Uriah Heep's: "Me and mother is very humble."

Hood prefers to let the poor or oppressed describe their lives uncouthly, rather than to attack the rich. The grotesque poem called *Miss Kilmansegg and her Precious Leg* is an exception. This poem startles because it is the first documented account of the upbringing of the perfect middle-class young lady whose parents are rising in the world. She is brought up to be a proud heiress, and the wonderful picture of arrogant surfeit recalls the awful overfed daughter of the mine owner in Zola's *Germinal.* Money is the only subject of conversation. Then one day Miss Kilmansegg has an accident, her leg is amputated and is replaced by a golden one. A wooden one would not be good enough. Far from spoiling her chances, the golden leg doubles the number of her suitors. Her parents select the most plausible and least trustworthy one who is an alleged aristocrat. He turns out to be a bankrupt gambler who, very soon after the wedding night, gives a knowing look at the leg and

> The Countess heard in language low
> That her Precious leg was precious slow,
> A good 'un to look at, but bad to go
> And kept quite a sum lying idle.

She refuses to sell it. But unhappily she is in the habit of taking it off at night, and the Count sees his chance. Using the leg as a cudgel he bashes her brains out and absconds.

This long poem is like a grotesque novel, something of de la Mare's, perhaps, packed with realistic description, and if its plot groans the lines scamper along as fast as Browning's dramatic narratives and are delighted with their own wit. And here the puns give the poem a kind of jeering muttered undertone. Hood had a great gift for domestic realism and the conversational phrase. In *Miss Kilmansegg* he is not half a Hogarth, but Hogarth whole. Or ought one to say, half a Hogarth and the other half that fanciful melodramatic sermonizer—as Dickens was in the *Christmas Carol*—which the nineteenth century loved? The poem is labored but it is alive.

Hood's wit quietened and compassion melted him in his last years. *The Song of the Shirt* and *The Lay of the Labourer* last very well in their genre, because of their metrical brilliance and because they are taken directly from life. One would want to remove only two or three lines of self-parody from *The Bridge of Sighs*. Hood is as well documented as the realistic novelists were to become. *The Lay of the Labourer* is based on a true incident. An agricultural laborer was convicted for threatening arson because he could not get work or food, and Hood kept the newspaper cutting about the event on his mantelpiece until he wrote the poem. The sentiment is bearable, the rant is bearable, because the facts cry out and are so tellingly reported. One must regret that his feeling for narrative, his instinct for the right tune to put it in and his kind of conscience too, died out of verse with the Victorians. In the higher regions where Hardy lived, as in the lower regions of the music hall, the art of writing dramatic stories in verse seems to have gone for good.

DISRAELI

"The leaders of the People are those whom the People trust," said Sybil rather haughtily.

"And who may betray them," said Egremont.

"Betray them!" said Sybil. "And you can believe that my father . . ."

"No, no, you can feel, Sybil, though I cannot express, how much I honour your father. But he stands alone in the singleness and purity of his heart. Who surround him?"

"Those whom the People have chosen; and from a like confidence in their virtues and abilities. They are a senate supported by the sympathy of millions with only one object in view—the emancipation of

their race. It is a sublime spectacle these delegates of labor advocating the sacred cause in a manner which might shame your haughty factions. What can resist a demonstration so truly national! What can withstand the supremacy of its moral power!"

So writes Disraeli of the rise of the Chartists in *Sybil, or The Two Nations.* His people are speaking the language of opera; yet, after a hundred years, how exactly Disraeli has defined the English political situation. He is our only political novelist; I mean, the only one *saturated* in politics; the only one whose intellect feasts on polity. Strikes, riots, questions of social justice, elections and backstairs politics enliven the other Victorian novelists of the period frequently; but of Mrs. Gaskell, George Eliot, Meredith, Trollope it cannot be said that politics are their blood. These writers do not convert us to this view or that; they are cautious; they do not inflame us; on the whole they leave us with the impression that political action is a disagreeable duty, distracting us from the major interests of human nature. Children of a competitive society, heirs of the Utilitarians, they see politics as the indispensable but tedious regulator. Politics are a method, a humane technique of adjustment; and, in general, it must be said that this has been the English view throughout the nineteenth century and after. To Disraeli, the Jew and alien, such a theory was pragmatic and despicable. It also lacked theatre.

In his early years, at least, and especially in the trilogy of novels of which *Sybil* is the second volume, Disraeli brought to political thought the electric heat of the Jewish imagination and the order of its religious traditions. He demanded the glory of a dogma, the sensation of a rebirth, the emotion of a "new era"—a phrase used for the first time at the accession of Queen Victoria. And when we pick up *Sybil* or *Coningsby,* with their captivating pictures of aristocratic life and their startling, documented pictures of the squalor of the industrial poor, we feel that here at last is a novelist who is impatient of immediate social issues and who has gone back dramatically to the historic core of the English situation. The tedium has gone. We may now be carried away by a faith, snared by a passion. How precise is the diagnosis of the failure of his own party; they are not Conservatives but concessionaries, a party without beliefs. As we read *Sybil* and *Coningsby* we are swept along by a swift exultant mind. It takes us, by a kind of cinematic magic, from the gold plate and languid peers of the Derby dinner to the delectable mansions and heavenly countenances of the exalted, and from them to the sunken faces of the starved and enslaved. We may find ourselves converted to a new medievalism, to those heady "Young England" politics which read like a mixture of Marx, William Morris, Hall Caine and romantic Fascism. Disraeli was wrong; wrong, that is to say, as things turned out. Young England came to nothing, and the English workers followed the solemn prophecies of Sybil and not the aristocratic theory of Egremont; but whether he was right or wrong is not the point. The secret of Disraeli's superiority as a political novelist is that he introduces imagination into politics; he introduces questions of law, faith and vision. He looked upon the English scene with the clear intellect of the alien who, as a Jew, identified himself with both the two English nations; with the race that was to be emancipated and with the aristocracy that ruled them. The romantic, Byronic pride of Disraeli—if we are to take the figure of Sidonia in *Coningsby* as a projection of himself, several times larger than life—is measureless. Under the ancient gaze of the hollow eye of Asia, the Norman family is as crude as a band of tourists standing before the ruin of Ozymandias, king of kings.

Disraeli's gift is for the superb and the operatic. And if there is more than a touch of the de luxe and meretricious in his understanding of the superb, that fits in with the political picture; politics is the world of façade and promises. Disraeli knew God and Mammon. So many political novels have known God, the party line, alone; and without Mammon the people fainteth. He was the romantic poet and yet the *rusé,* satiate, flattering and subtle man of the world. When we are exhausted by visions he can soothe us with scandal. No one, said Queen Victoria with delight when she read his letters—no one had ever told her *everything* before. The novels of Disraeli tell us everything. He not only plants the main spectacle, the house party of history; but he tells us the club gossip and the boudoir gossip—especially that—and speculates with malice on the dubious political career, on the unelevating comedies of political muddle and panic. He knows ambitious human nature. His eye is bright, his wit is continuous. His general surveys, notably those of the shams and disasters which overtook the regime of the Duke of Wellington, are wonderful destructive criticisms. No one describes a ball, or a house party, or a dinner as well as Disraeli, for no one so quickly and neatly gives one the foibles and background of the guests. His family histories are masterpieces of irony; he knows the private cankers of grandeur, the long machinations that have produced a Lord Monmouth or a Lord Marney. (In our own time we can imagine the late Lord Curzon modeling himself on Disraeli's personages.) All his ladies are ravishing; nevertheless, though never losing his sympathy for the female character and never ceasing to flatter, he sets it out with the coolest impartiality. "Although the best of wives and mothers she had some charity for her neighbors"—does that not "get" the good woman precisely? Or take the portraits of Lucretia Colonna and her mother in

Coningsby. They are social generalizations as all his characters are, and yet how definite they are too! I find it difficult to get the hard, grasping, silent and daring daughter out of my mind. Eighteen and a monster of imperiousness already; silent because ill-educated; how she will exploit the old peer who all his life has been exploiting others! Disraeli knows exactly how society has created the character of Lucretia; like Sidonia, he has flattered and observed her. The Lucretia episode in *Coningsby* is rich comedy; for it entangles the egregious Mr. Rigby, Lord Monmouth's awful agent. There is nothing more amusing in this novel than the sight of Mr. Rigby being sent off to subdue the emotions of the mother who has been jilted in favor of her secretive daughter. The vulgar Rigby is a master of tactics:

> He talked wildly of equipages, diamonds, shawls, opera boxes; and while her mind was bewildered with these dazzling objects he, with intrepid gravity, consulted as to the exact amount she would like apportioned independent of her general revenue for the purpose of charity.

Having flown at him like a tigress and poured out epithets—"some of them true"—like a fishwife, the Princess calms down, fanned by his promises, and ends with the faint, pouting complaint that Lord Monmouth "might have broken the news himself." The aristocrat is admired for doing what we would all like to do. Who would not pay a Mr. Rigby to go down and break the brunt of the scenes that are being prepared for one? Still, we cannot call Rigby a great comic character. He is too rapidly generalized in his appearances. He is an essay on a comic character. Libellously drawn from the notorious Croker, he is a portrait, not a person. He is a rich and perennial political type, the yes-man. We add him to our collection of cads and buffoons. The summary of his character is exact:

> The world took him at his word because he was bold, acute and voluble; with no thought but a good deal of desultory information; and though destitute of all imagination and noble sentiment, he was blessed with a vigorous and mendacious fancy, fruitful in small expedients and never happier than when devising great men's scrapes.

Coningsby is a novel of static scenes. There is one that is rightly famous. This is where Coningsby, as a youth, goes to call on Lord Monmouth, his grandfather, for the first time and proceeds from stairway to stairway, apartment to apartment in the great house, until at last he comes into the presence. The emotion is too much for the sensibility of the shy youth, who bursts into tears; and the disgusted old peer, who cannot bear displays of feeling, dismisses him at once. This is one of the human scenes which stands out so movingly against the excess of artificial ones. Where *Coningsby* is still, *Sybil* moves. We pass from the sight of society to the pictures of working-class starvation and slavery. Disraeli investigated the conditions of the poor for himself, and his remarkable eye and ear collected a number of unforgettable notes and dialogues. There is nothing as terrifying in Dickens, for example, as Disraeli's picture of the slum town of locksmiths run by the toughest working men alone, a kind of frontier town without institutions. We see the watchman on his rounds, the starving weaver at his loom, the fever and the gloom of the rain-sodden houses, the new pubs and entertainment halls, the good factories and the bad ones. The conversation of the people is not falsified, but is indeed indigenous and racy. Disraeli drew miners, for example, very well and understood their lives. He could also draw the working-class girl. We have entered into a world already made familiar to us by the prophetic books of Blake. Blake-like cries come out of this darkness: "I wish there was no such thing as coal in the land," says the weaver's dying wife. "And then the engines would not be able to work and we should have our rights again." It is a cry from *The Daughters of Albion.*

Sybil is melodramatic—it would make an excellent opera or film—it lacks the closely finished texture of *Coningsby* but is looser, bolder in argument, wildly romantic in scene. The satire at the expense of the Whig families, who are driving the cottagers off their land and selling out to the railway companies, is scathing: "Sympathy is the solace of the Poor: but for the Rich there is compensation."

The rioting and the attack on Mowbray Castle at the end is tremendous theatrical stuff, though—it must be remembered—Disraeli claimed that all his material about the Chartists was carefully documented. The unreality of certain characters, especially Sybil herself, is, of course, comical; but such characters are not unreal in their context. They are ideals walking and so romantic in their carriage that, in the end, one accepts them and their theatrical lamentations over their stolen heritage.

The *roman à thèse* is not commended as a rule by English critics; we read, as a rule, to be contented, and Disraeli's novels have caused a good deal of polite laughter. Such a world of superlatives invited ridicule. One can never be absolutely sure that Disraeli's imagination would distinguish between a great palace and a great Corner House; just as we can never be quite sure, as Lytton Strachey pointed out, that Disraeli was not himself carried away by the luxurious flatteries he poured into the ears of Queen Victoria.

EDWIN DROOD

When lately I was reading *The Mystery of Edwin Drood* I felt extremely the want of some sort of guidance on the Victorian fascination with violent crime. What explains the exorbitant preoccupation with murder, above all? In earlier periods, when life was cheaper, rape, seduction, incest were the crimes favored by literature. If we look to literature rather than to life, it is certain the Victorian writers took over murder from the popular taste of the eighteenth century, and succeeded—against the outcry of the older critics—in making it respectable. But in the nineteenth century one detects, also, the rise of a feeling (so curiously expressed by a popular writer on the melodrama a few years ago; I have forgotten his name) that "murder is cleaner than sex." There is a clue there, I think. There is a clue, too, in the fact that organized police forces and systems of detection were not established until the Napoleonic wars—we are bound to become fascinated by the thing we punish—and another more sinister clue lies in the relative freedom from war after 1815. A peaceful age was horrified and fascinated, for example, by the ritual murders of the Indian thugs. Where else can we look? To the megalomania that was a natural field for the Romantic movement? To the guilt that is deposited in the mind after a ruthless exertion of the will, such as the Victorians made at the time of the Industrial Revolution? To the social chaos before the fifties, when tens of thousands were uprooted, and if they did not rise with the rising tide were left to sink into the slums or to stand out alone in violent rebellion? The more one reads of the unrest and catastrophes of the nineteenth century, in social or in private life, the more one is appalled by the pressure which is revolution applied to human beings. And when we read again the rant of the melodramas, when we listen to the theatre organ of Bulwer-Lytton in *Eugene Aram*, and read the theatrical pages of Dickens, we feel, after the first shock of distaste, that these people are responding to a pressure which is not exerted upon us in the same degree. The violence of the scene suggests a hidden violence in the mind, and we begin to understand how assuaging it must have been, in novels like *Oliver Twist* or *The Mystery of Edwin Drood*, to see the murderer's conscience displayed in terms of nightmare and hysteria.

Assuaging to the Victorians, but not to us. We are not driven by the same dynamo. *Edwin Drood* stands at the parting of the ways between the early Victorian and the modern attitude to murder in literature, and also, I suspect, at the beginnings of a change in Dickens himself. The earlier murders of Dickens belong to the more turbulent decades of the nineteenth century. By the late fifties a calm had been reached; the lid had been levered back on to the pot of society and its seething had become a prosperous simmer. When Wilkie Collins wrote *The Moonstone* and Dickens, not to be outdone, followed it with *Edwin Drood*, we begin the long career of murder for murder's sake, murder which illustrates nothing and is there only to stimulate our skill in detection and to distract us with mystery. The sense of guilt is so transformed that we do not seek to expiate it vicariously on the stage; we turn upon the murderer and hunt him down. Presently, in our time, the hunt degenerates into the conundrums of the detective novel which, by a supreme irony, distracts us from our part in the mass murders of two wars. One or two critics have suggested that the struggle with the unfamiliar technique of the hunt was too much for Dickens and that it killed him and his novel. We cannot know whether this is so; but both those who dismiss the book as the last leaden effort of a worn-out man, and those who observe that it is the most careful and private of Dickens's novels, are agreed that it is pitched in a key he has never struck before.

What is that key? Before I add my answer to the dozens that have been made, it seems important to define one's own attitude to Dickens. I am totally out of sympathy with the hostile criticism of Dickens which has been made during the last twenty years, which has ignored his huge vitality and imaginative range and has done no more than to say he lacked taste and that he sacrificed a profound view of human nature to the sentimentalities and falsities of self-dramatization. To me it is a perversion of criticism to suggest that you can have the virtues of a writer without his vices, and the discovery of Dickens's failures does not make his achievement less. I swallow Dickens whole and put up with the indigestion. I confess I am not greatly interested in the literary criticism which tells me where he is good and where he is bad. I am glad to be instructed; but for us, at the present time, I think there is far more value in trying to appreciate the nature of his creative vitality and the experience that fed it —a vitality notably lacking in our own fiction. Now when we turn to *Edwin Drood* we do find some of the old Dickens. There is Mr. Sapsea, for example, with his own account of his courtship, that beautiful shot plumb in the middle of romantic love and Victorian marriage:

"Miss Brobity's Being, young man, was deeply imbued with homage to Mind. She revered Mind, when launched or, as I say, precipitated, on an extensive knowledge of the world. When I made my proposal, she did me the honor of being so overshadowed with a species of Awe, as to be able to articulate only the two words 'Oh Thou!' meaning myself. Her limpid blue eyes were fixed upon me, her semi-transparent hands were clasped together, pallor overspread her aquiline features, and, though encouraged to proceed, she never did proceed a word further. . . . She never did and never could find a phrase satisfactory to her perhaps—too—favorable estimate of my intellect. To the very last (feeble action of the liver) she addressed me in the same unfinished terms."

That is the old Dickens, but a shadow is upon Mr. Sapsea. The tomb of Mrs. Sapsea is, we are told, to be used by Jasper, the murderer, for his own purpose. Durdles, the drunken verger, tapping the walls of the Cathedral for evidence of the "old uns," is to be roped in. The muscular Christian, Mr. Crisparkle, sparring before his mirror in the morning, is marked down by the plot; and that terrifying small boy, the Imp or Deputy, who is employed by Durdles to stone him homewards when he is drunk, will evidently be frog-marched into the witness box. Dickens is submitting to discipline, and how fantastically severe it was may be seen in Edmund Wilson's *The Wound and the Bow.* The background loses some of its fantasy, but the best things in *Edwin Drood* are the descriptions of the cathedral, the town and countryside of Rochester which are recorded with the attentive love one feels for things that are gracious and real. Chesterton thought that something of the mad, original Dickens was lost in this realism; other critics explain it as the influence of mid-Victorian settling down. Mr. Edmund Wilson seems to suggest that in *Edwin Drood* one finds the mellowness and the bitterness of the man who sets out with some confidence equipped to master his devil and to dominate his wound. I do not find a loss in this picture of Cloisterham:

> Cloisterham is so bright and sunny in these summer days, that the cathedral and the monastery-ruin show as if their strong walls were transparent. A soft glow seems to shine from within them, rather than upon them from without, such is their mellowness as they look forth on the hot cornfields and the smoking roads that distantly wind among them. The Cloisterham gardens blush with ripening fruit. Time was when travel-stained pilgrims rode in clattering parties through the city's welcome shades; time is when wayfarers, leading a gypsy life between haymaking time and harvest, and looking as if they were just made of the dust of the earth, so very dusty are they, lounge about on cool doorsteps, trying to mend their unmendable shoes, or giving them to the city kennels as a hopeless job, and seeking others in the bundles that they carry, along with their yet unused sickles swathed in bands of straw. At all the more public pumps there is much cooling of the bare feet, together with much bubbling and gurgling of drinking with hand to spout on the part of these Bedouins; the Cloisterham police meanwhile looking askant from their beats with suspicion, and manifest impatience that the intruders should depart from within the civic bounds, and once more fry themselves on the simmering high roads.

The shocks in *Edwin Drood* come not from the sudden leveling of his fantasy and the appearance of realism. They occur when Dickens acts his realism—see the showdown between Jasper and Rosa—and we realize that it is really alien to Dickens's gift that his people should be made to talk to each other. When he attempts this he merely succeeds in making them talk *at* each other, like actors. His natural genius is for human soliloquy not human intercourse.

In criticism of the English novel and in appeals to what is called "the English tradition," there has been a misunderstanding, I think, about this intrinsic quality of Dickens. One hears the word Dickensian on all sides. One hears of Dickens's influence on the English novel on the one hand, and of the failure of the English novel to produce a comparable genius. While the word Dickensian lasts, the English novel will be suffocated. For the convivial and gregarious extravagance and the picaresque disorder which are supposedly Dickensian are not Dickens's especial contribution to the English novel. They are his inheritance from Sterne, Smollett and, on the sentimental side, from Richardson, an inheritance which may be traced back to the comedy of Jonson. What Dickens really contributed may be seen by a glance at the only novelists who have seriously developed his contribution—in Dostoevsky above all and, to a lesser degree, in Gogol. (There is more of Dickens, to my mind, in James Joyce's *Ulysses* than in books like *Kipps* or *Tono Bungay.*) For the distinguishing quality of Dickens's people is that they are solitaries. They are people caught living in a world of their own. They soliloquize in it. They do not talk to one another; they talk to themselves. The pressure of society has created fits of twitching in mind and speech, and fantasies in the soul. It has been said that Dickens creates merely external caricatures, but Mr. Sapsea's musings on his "somewhat extensive knowledge" and Mr. Crisparkle's sparrings in front of his mirror are fragments of inner life. In how many of that famous congress of "characters"—Micawber, Barkis, Moddles, Jingle, Mrs. Gamp or Miss Twitteron: take them at random—and in how many of the straight personages, like Jasper and Neville Landless in *Ed-*

win Drood, are we chiefly made aware of the individual's obliviousness of any existence but his own? The whole of Dickens's emotional radicalism, his hatred of the Utilitarians and philanthropists and all his attacks on institutions, are based on his strongest and fiercest sense: isolation. In every kind of way Dickens was isolated. Isolation was the foundation not only of his fantasy and his hysteria, but also—I am sure Mr. Edmund Wilson is correct here—of the twin strains of rebel and criminal in his nature. The solitariness of people is paralleled by the solitariness of things. Fog operates as a separate presence, houses quietly rot or boisterously prosper on their own. The veneer of the Veneerings becomes almost tangible, whipped up by the repetitions. Cloisterham believes itself more important than the world at large, the Law sports like some stale and dilapidated circus across human lives. Philanthropy attacks people like a humor or an observable germ. The people and the things of Dickens are all out of touch and out of hearing of each other, each conducting its own inner monologue, grandiloquent or dismaying. By this dissociation Dickens brings to us something of the fright of childhood, and the kind of realism employed in *Edwin Drood* reads like an attempt to reconstruct and co-ordinate his world, like a preparation for a final confession of guilt.

THE BRUTAL CHIVALRY

Robert Surtees is a sport, in both senses of the term, who flashes in and out of the English novel, excites hope and reduces the critical factions to silence. He has all the dash, all the partiality and all the prospect of an amateur. There is a rush of air, a shower of rain drops from the branches, a burst of thundering mud, a crashing of hazel, the sight of a pink coat and, as far as the English novel is concerned, he has gone. In that brief appearance he has made the genial suggestion that all the other English novelists have been mistaken; they have missed the basic fact in English life—that we are religious, that our religion is violent sport. The unwritten life of a large proportion of the characters in English fiction is passed in playing or watching games in the open air; nature is being worshipped with the senses and the muscles. We are either bemused by fresh air or are daydreaming of some lazy, cunning and exhausting animal life in the open. In that condition, our hourly and sedentary habit of worry as a substitute for thought vanishes and we become people in love. It takes an amateur, like Surtees, to see an obvious thing like this and to exaggerate so that the part becomes the whole of English life. He was a north country squire, an excellent sporting journalist, but handsomely innocent of the future of hunting in England. He really thought that the Industrial Revolution would make the sport democratic! His assumption is that English violence can be appeased only by the horse. He is the final authority on our horse civilization, and Jorrocks is a sort of Don Quixote of the last phase of a brutal chivalry. *Après moi* (he might have said) *le garage.*

It is natural that hunting people should admire Surtees. It is not surprising that serious literary critics should admire him also. He creates a complete world. It is the world which Fielding's and Thackeray's people knew in their off-stage lives. It has no relation with the feeble subculture of horse lovers, pony worshippers, or with the gentility of the jodphur that spread over England as the coach gave way to the railway, provoking the cult of the New Forest pony. The natural democrats of England live in the north and, though Surtees was a Tory squire, he sincerely believed that the horse was an insurance against the new, snobbish exclusiveness of the shot-up Victorian middle class. He imagined, as so many have done before, that class revolutions will not become snobbish and exclusive. Happy pastoral delusion! Surtees did not foresee either the hardness or the sentimentality of the coming urban England. Or, perhaps, he half guessed it. For the point about Jorrocks is that he is (1) not a horse lover but a fox lover, (2) that he rides, buys and sells horses, (3) that he has not an aitch to his name. He is, boldly, incontrovertibly, aggressively, in mid-nineteenth-century—a grocer. His fame is that he is not merely a sportsman, but a Cockney sportsman. He has all the trading sharpness and romanticism of a man who sells tea. Surtees is content (purposefully content) with this reality. Jorrocks is as vulgar as Keats; and, as a northerner and a gentleman, Surtees refuses to accept the improved accents of the new rich in the south. He exploits the rewards our class system offers to our literature. We are continually supplying a number of vulgar geniuses who stand out against the new snobberies which the Puritan streak in us is liable to create; and, in the case of Surtees, there is the anomaly that a Tory squire provides the vulgar protest. The heir of Jorrocks is Mr. Polly. Both are native protests against the mean and successful revolutions that deny the instincts of genial, sincere and natural men.

Surtees owes a lot to the low side of Thackeray and does seamy society a good deal better. His dialogue is as quick and true as the master's. He extends a robust and native tradition: the masculine strain of English comic writing. This comedy is broad and extraverted. It grins at the pleasures and pains of the human animal—if it is male—and has little time for the female. Occasionally Surtees sees a tolerable female, but very rarely. We need not suppose that he agreed with Jorrocks that a man ought to kick his wife out of bed three times a month, but we suspect this was only because he regarded the act wistfully as an ideal unfortunately unattainable. The fact is that our comic extraverts are like Mr. Sponge and bring a horse-dealer's eye to the consideration of women—"fifteen two and a half is plenty of height" for them. In its male world, the comic tradition likes the misfortunes of the body, the bruises, the black eyes, the drinking sessions, the gorging at table; prefers the low to the refined, the masterful and unreasonable to the sensitive and considerate. There is a strong regard for the impossible element in human character, for the eccentric and the obsessed. The brutes have their engaging moments. (They give the right kind of girls half a dozen smacking kisses.) But their transcendent emotions emerge in another direction. Jorrocks will quarrel with his huntsman, Pigg, but be reconciled, to the point of embracing him, at the kill. These people are dedicated. They will suffer anything, from drowning upwards, for their sport. They will experience an ecstasy which goes beyond the animal into the poetic. And, in the meantime, they will rollick. Thoroughly non-Puritan, they understand that the life of animal pleasure is the life of animal dismay and they accept it. What these writers in the masculine comic tradition dwell on is the variety of human character. They know that action brings this out and, with a kind of mercy, they will forgive anything so long as action, not introspection, has revealed it.

Mr. Aubrey Noakes has written a good brief appreciation of Surtees in *Horses, Hounds and Humans.* It does not add to earlier studies, but it does bring out the importance of his experience with the law and his adventures in politics. Mr. Noakes also goes into the interesting reluctance of the Victorians to take to him until Leech illustrated his novels. On the one hand, Surtees was a man of the eighteenth century—hence Thackeray's understanding of him; on the other, he was an amateur who dealt almost entirely with background figures, the great Jorrocks excepted. He was deeply knowing about English sporting life, the squirearchy and the law, but he did not construct the melodramas and elaborate plots of the other Victorian novelists, nor did he issue their moralizings. He often excelled them in the recording of ordinary speech and day-to-day incident. He is fresher than the masters, but he is artless. A good deal of his humor is the humor of shrewd sayings which, later on, we find in Kipling. His original contribution is in the field of invective. Surtees has a truly Elizabethan power of denunciation. Here is Jorrocks loosing off to his servant:

> "Come hup, you snivellin', drivellin' son of a lucifer-match maker," he roars out to Ben who is coming lagging along in his master's wake. "Come on," roars he, waving his arm frantically, as, on reaching Ravenswing Scar, he sees the hounds swinging down, like a bundle of clock pendulums

> into the valley below. "Come hup, I say, ye miserable, road-ridin', dish-lickin' cub! And give me that quad, for you're a disgrace to a saddle, and only fit to toast muffins for a young ladies' boarding school. Come hup, you preter-pluperfect tense of 'umbugs. . . . Come on, ye miserable, useless son of a lily-livered besom-maker. Rot ye, I'll bind ye 'prentice to a salmon-pickler."

This is all the more splendid because Jorrocks keeps to the " 'ard road" as much as possible, and can't bear taking a fence. He is eloquent, perhaps because he is as cowardly as Falstaff and yet as sincere in his passion. He knows what he wants to be. His is the eloquence of romance. And this is where we come to the Dickensian aspect of Surtees, too. Dickens has several degrees of comic observation. There is the rudimentary Dickens of caricature, of the single trait or phrase turned into the whole man. And there is the Dickens where this is elaborated into soliloquy, in which the character is represented by his fantasy life. Like the rudimentary Dickens, Surtees has the feeling for caricature. *Handley Cross, Facey Romford's Hounds* and *Mr. Sponge's Tours* are packed with minor eccentrics of the field, the fancy and the law; but in Jorrocks, Surtees enters upon the more complex study of people who live out the comic orgy. "By 'eavens, it's sublime," says Jorrocks, watching the hounds stream over a hundred acres of pasture below him. " 'Ow they go, screechin' and towlin' along just like a pocketful o' marbles . . . 'Ow I wish I was a heagle." A "heagle" he is, in that moment; sublimity is his condition. He has shrewdly built up his pack, he has given his uproarious lectures, he has had his vulgar adventures in country houses; he has got the better of his betters and has outdone the new rich in vulgarity—making among other things that immortal remark about mince: "I like to chew my own meat"—he has disgraced Mrs.

Jorrocks, but he has pursued an obsession utterly so that it has no more to teach him, beyond the fact that it has damaged his credit among the unimaginative in the City. Fortunately, Surtees has given him power of speech. Jorrocks is never at a loss for repartee or for metaphor. He is remarkable in his duels with Pigg, and the only pity is that Pigg's dialect is nearly incomprehensible. But Pigg and his master are well matched. They battle like theologians about the true business of life: the pursuit of foxes.

Surtees is a specialist. But he is, to an important extent, outside his speciality. He had strong views about sport. He hated the drunkenness of sporting society and the old squirearchy. He hoped the new age would bring in something better. He was hostile to the literary conventions. His parodies of *Nimrod* show him as an opponent of literary snobbery. He disliked the obsequious regime of servants and the rogueries of the stable, the auctions and the law. It is odd that one so saturated in his world should have seen it all with so fresh an eye. Perhaps he had that morbidity of eye which is given to some men at the end of a period, when they can see things with the detachment which considerable art demands. He was too much the gentleman and amateur to construct a great novel; but he was independent enough and sufficiently instructed by obsession to create in Jorrocks a huge character who could go off and live an episodic life of his own. The Victorians were shy of Surtees's honesty. They were moving away from the notion that there was a level on which all Englishmen could be united. They were building the split culture of our time. Surtees was trying to save England on the acres of Handley Cross.

GEORGE ELIOT

She looked unusually charming today from the very fact that she was not vividly conscious of anything but of having a mind near her that asked her to be something better than she actually was.

It is easy to guess which of the mid-Victorian novelists wrote these lines. The use of the word "mind" for young man, the yearning for self-improvement in the heroine, and, lastly, the painful, reiterating English, all betray George Eliot. This description of Esther Lyon in *Felix Holt* might have been chipped out in stone for George Eliot's epitaph and, as we take down a novel of hers from the shelf, we feel we are about to lever off the heavy lid of some solid family tomb. Yet the epitaph is not hers alone. The unremitting ethic of self-improvement has been the sepulcher of all mid-Victorian fiction except *Wuthering Heights.* Today that ethic no longer claims the Esther Lyons of the English novel. The whole influence of psychology has turned our interest to what George Eliot would have called the downward path, to the failures of the will, the fulfillment of the heart, the vacillations of the sensibility, the perception of self-interest. We do not wish to be better than we are, but more fully what we are; and the wish is crossed by the vivid conflicts set up in our lives by the revolution that is going on in our society. The bottom has fallen out of our world, and our Esthers are looking for a basis, not for a ceiling, to their lives.

But this does not mean that Esther Lyon is falsely drawn or that she is not a human being. Using our own jargon, all we have a right to say is, that the objects of the superego have changed; and, in saying this, we should recall a minor point of importance. It is this. Not only English tradition from Fielding onwards, but no less a person than the author of *Les Liaisons Dangereuses* delight in the delectable evasions of the prig and the reserve of the prude; and it would indeed be absurd to cut the aspirations to virtue out of characters and to leave only the virtue that is attained or is already there. The critic needs only to be clear about the kind of aspiration that is presented to him; and here we perceive that what separates us from Esther Lyon and her creator is a matter of history. She is impelled by the competitive reforming ethic of an expanding society. One might generalize without great danger and say that in all the mid-Victorian novels the characters are either going up in the world, in which case they are good; or they are going down in the world, in which case they are bad. Whereas Goldsmith and Fielding reveled in the misadventures of the virtuous and in the vagaries of Fortune—that tutelary goddess of a society dominated by merchant-speculators—a novelist like George Eliot writes at a time when Fortune has been torn down, when the earned increment of industry (and not the accidental coup of the gambler) has taken Fortune's place; and when character is tested not by hazard but, like the funds, by a measurable tendency to rise and fall.

Once her ethic is seen as the driving force of George Eliot we cease to be intimidated by it, and she emerges, for all her lectures, as the most formidable of the Victorian novelists. We dismiss the late Victorian reaction to her work; our fathers were bored by her because they were importuned by her mind; she was an idol with feet of clay and, what was worse, appeared to write with them. But it is precisely because she was a mind and because she was a good deal of the schoolmistress that she interests us now. Where the other Victorian novelists seem shapeless, confused and without direction, because of their melodramatic plots and subplots and the careless and rich diversity of their characters, George Eliot marks out an ordered world, and enunciates a constructed judgment. If we read a novel in order to clarify our minds about human character, in order to pass judgment on the effect of character on the world outside itself, and to estimate the ideas people have lived by, then George Eliot is one of the first to give such an intellectual direction to the English novel. She is the first of the rulers, one of the first to cut moral paths through the picturesque maze of human motive. It is the intimidating role of the schoolmistress. And yet when we read a few pages of any of her books now, we notice less the oppression of her lectures and more the spaciousness of her method, the undeterred illumination which her habit of mind brings to human nature. We pass from the romantic shadows into an explicit, a prosaic but a relieving light.

Two of George Eliot's novels have a permanent place in English literature. As time goes by *Adam Bede* looks like our supreme novel of pastoral life; and I cannot see any novel of the nineteenth century that surpasses *Middlemarch* in range or construction. With *Adam Bede,* it is true, the modern reader experiences certain unconquerable irritations. We are faced by a sexual theme, and the Victorians were constitutionally unable to write about sexual love. No English writer since the eighteenth century has been happy in this theme, for since that time we have lost our regard for the natural man and the equanimity required for writing about him. In *Adam Bede* we are shocked by two things: the treatment of Hetty Sorel and the marriage of Dinah and Adam at the end. It is clear that George Eliot's attitude to Hetty is a false one. The drawing of Hetty is neither observation from life nor a true recasting of experience by the imagination; it is a personal fantasy of George Eliot's. George Eliot was punishing herself and Hetty has to suffer for the "sins" George Eliot had committed, and for which, to her perhaps unconscious dismay, she herself was never punished. We rebel against the black and white view of life and when we compare *Adam Bede* with Scott's *Heart of Midlothian,* to which the former confessedly owes something of its plot, we are depressed by the decline of humanity that has set in since the eighteenth century. Humanity has become humanitarianism, uplift and, in the end, downright cruelty. The second quarrel we have with this book arises, as I have said, from the marriage of Adam and Dinah. There is no reason why a man who has suffered at the hands of a bad woman should not be rewarded and win the consolations of a good woman. If Adam likes sermons better than infidelity, we say let him have them; we all choose our own form of suffering. But George Eliot told lies about this marriage; or rather, she omitted a vital element from it. She left out the element of sexual jealousy or, if she did not leave it out, she did not recognize it, because she could not admit natural passions in a virtuous character. In that scene where Hetty pushes Dinah away from her in her bedroom, where Hetty is dressing up and dreaming her Bovary-like dreams, the reader sees something that George Eliot appears not to see. He is supposed to see that Hetty is self-willed; and this may be true, but he sees as well that Hetty's instincts have warned her of her ultimate rival. The failure to record jealousy and the attempt to transmute it so that it becomes the ambiguous if lofty repugnance to sin, springs from the deeper failure to face the nature of sexual passion.

This failure not only mars George Eliot's moral judgment but also represses her power as a storyteller. When Adam comes to Arthur Donnithorne's room at the Hermitage, Arthur stuffs Hetty's neckerchief into the wastepaper basket out of Adam's sight. The piece of silk is a powerful symbol. The reader's eye does not leave it. He waits for it to be found. But no, it simply lies there; its function is, as it were, to preach the risks of sin to the reader. Whereas in fact it ought to be made to disclose the inflammatory fact that the physical seduction took place in this very room. George Eliot refuses to make such a blatant disclosure not for aesthetic reasons, but out of her own regard for Victorian convention; and the result is that we have no real reason for believing Hetty *has* been seduced. Her baby appears inexplicably. The account of Hetty's flight is remarkable—it is far, far better than the corresponding episode in *The Heart of Midlothian*—but the whole business of the seduction and crime, from Adam's fight with Arthur Donnithorne in the woods to Hetty's journey to the scaffold, seems scarcely more than moralizing hearsay to the reader. And the reprieve of Hetty at the gallows adds a final unreality to the plot. It must also be said—a final cruelty.

Yet, such is George Eliot's quality as a novelist, none of these criticisms has any great importance. Like the tragedies of Hardy, *Adam Bede* is animated by the majestic sense of destiny which is fitting to novels of work and the soil. Majestic is perhaps the wrong word. George Eliot's sense of destiny was prosaic, not majestic; prosaic in the sense of unpoetical. One must judge a novel on its own terms; and from the beginning, in the lovely account of Dinah's preaching on the village green, George Eliot sets out the pieties which will enclose the drama that is to follow. Her handling of the Methodists and their faith is one of the memorable religious performances of English literature, for she neither adjures us nor satirizes them, but leaves a faithful and limpid picture of commonplace religion as a part of life. When she wrote of the peasants, the craftsmen, the yeomen, the clergy and squires of Warwickshire, George Eliot was writing out of childhood, from that part of her life which never betrayed her or any of the Victorians. The untutored sermons of Dinah have the same pastoral quality as the poutings of Hetty at the butter churn, the harangues of Mrs. Poyser at her cooking, or the remonstrances of Adam Bede at his carpenter's bench. In the mid-Victorian England of the railway and the drift to the towns, George Eliot was harking back to the last of the yeomen, among whom she was born and who brought out the warmth, the humor, the strength of her nature. We seem to be looking at one of Morland's pictures, at any of those domestic or rustic paintings of the Dutch school, where every leaf on the elm trees or the limes is painted, every gnarl of the bark inscribed, every rut followed with fidelity. We follow the people out of the hedgerows and the lanes into the kitchen. We see the endless meals, the eternal cup of tea; and the dog rests his head on our boot or flies barking to the yard, while young children toddle in and out of the drama at the least convenient moments. Some critics have gibed at the dialect, and dialect is an obstacle; but when the great moments come, when Mrs. Poyser has her "say out" to the Squire who is going to evict her; or, better still, when Mrs. Bede laments the drowning of her drunken husband, these people speak out of life:

> "Let a-be, let a-be. There's no comfort for 'e no more," she went on, the tears coming when she began to speak, "now they poor feyther's gone, as I'n washed for and mended, an' got's victual for him for thirty 'ear, an' him allays so pleased wi' ivery-

thing I done for him, an' used to be so handy an' do the jobs for me when I war ill an' cambered wi' th' babby, an' made me the posset an' brought it upstairs as proud as could be, an' carried the lad as war as heavy as two children for five mile an' ne'er grumbled, all the way to Warson Wake, 'cause I wanted to go an' see my sister, as war dead an' gone the very next Christmas as e'er come. An' him to be drowned in the brook as we passed o'er the day we war married an' come home together, an' he'd made them lots o' shelves for me to put my plates an' things on, an' showed 'em me as proud as could be, 'case he know'd I should be pleased. An' he war to die an' me not to know, but to be a-sleepin' i' my bed, as if I caredna nought about it. Eh! an' me to live to see that! An' us as war young folks once, an' thought we should do rarely when we war married. Let a-be, lad, let a-be! I wonna ha' no tay; I carena if I ne'er ate nor drink no more. When one end o' th' bridge tumbles down, where's th' use o' th' other stannin'? I may's well die, an' foller my old man. There's no knowin' but he'll want me."

Among these people Dinah's religion and their quarrels with her about it are perfectly at home; and George Eliot's rendering is faultless. English piety places a stress on conduct and the guidance of conscience; and George Eliot, with her peasant sense of the laws and repetitions of nature, easily converted this working theology into a universal statement about the life of man. Where others see the consequences of sin visited upon the soul, she, the Protestant, saw them appear in the events of a man's or woman's life and the lives of others. Sin is primarily a weakness of character leading to the act. To Arthur Donnithorne she would say, "Your sin is that your will is weak. You are unstable. You depend on what others say. You are swayed by the latest opinion. You are greedy for approbation.

Not lust, but a weak character is your malady. You even think that once you have confessed, your evil will turn out good. But it cannot, unless your character changes." And to Hetty she says, "Your real sin was vanity." It is a bleak and unanswerable doctrine, if one is certain that some kinds of character are desirable and others undesirable; psychologically useful to the novelist because it cuts one kind of path deeply into human nature, and George Eliot knows each moral character like a map. If her moral judgment is narrow, it enlarges character by showing us not merely the idiosyncrasy of people but propounds their type. Hetty is all pretty kittenish girls; Arthur is all careless young men. And here George Eliot makes a large advance on the novelists who preceded her. People do not appear haphazard in her books. They are not eccentrics. They are all planned and placed. She is orderly in her ethic; she is orderly in her social observation. She knows the country hierarchy and how a squire is this kind of man, a yeoman another, a teacher, a publican, a doctor, a clergyman another. They are more than themselves; they are their group as well. In this they recall the characters of Balzac. You fit Dinah among the Methodists, you fit Methodism into the scheme of things, you fit Adam among the peasants. Behind the Poysers are all the yeomen. George Eliot's sense of law is a sense of kind. It's a sense of life which has been learned from the English village where every man and woman has his definition and role.

I doubt if any Victorian novelist has as much to teach the modern novelists as George Eliot; for although the English novel was established and became a constructed judgment on situations and people after she had written, it did not emulate her peasant sense of law. Hardy alone is her nearest parallel, but he differed from her in conceiving a fate outside the will of man and indifferent to him. And her picture of country life is really closer to the country we know than Hardy's is, because he leaves us little notion of what the components of country society are. The English peasant lived and still lives in a milder, flatter world than Hardy's; a world where conscience and self-interest keep down the passions, like a pair of gamekeepers. It is true that George Eliot is cut off from the Rabelaisian malice and merriment of the country; she hears the men talk as they talk in their homes, not as they talk in the public houses and the barns. But behind the salty paganism of country life stands the daily haggle of what people "ought" and "didn't ought" to do; the ancient nagging of church and chapel. All this is a minor matter beside her main lesson. What the great schoolmistress teaches is the interest of massive writing, of placing people, of showing how even the minds of characters must be placed among other minds.

When we turn from *Adam Bede* to *Middlemarch* we find a novel in which her virtues as a novelist are established and assured; and where there is no sexual question to bedevil her judgment. No Victorian novel approaches *Middlemarch* in its width of reference, its intellectual power, or the imperturbable spaciousness of its narrative. It is sometimes argued by critics of contemporary literature that a return to Christianity is indispensable if we are to produce novels of the Victorian scale and authority, or indeed novels of any quality at all; but there are the novels of unbelievers like George Eliot and Hardy to discountenance them. The fact is that a wide and single purpose in the mind is the chief requirement outside of talent; a strong belief, a strong unbelief, even a strong egoism will produce works of the first order. If she had any religious leanings, George Eliot moved toward Judaism because of its stress on law; and if we think this preference purely intellectual and regard worry, that profoundly English habit of mind, as her philosophy, the point is that it was congenital, comprehensive worry. A forerunner of the psychologists, she promises no heaven and threatens no hell; the best and the worst we shall get is Warwickshire. Her world is the world of will, the smithy of character, a place of knowledge and judgments. So, in the sense of worldly wisdom, is Miss Austen's. But what a difference there is. To repeat our earlier definition, if Miss Austen is the novelist of the ego and its platitudes, George Eliot is the novelist of the idolatries of the superego. We find in a book like *Middlemarch,* not character modified by circumstance only, but character first impelled and then modified by the beliefs, the ambitions, the spiritual objects which it assimilates. Lydgate's schemes for medical reform and his place in medical science are as much part of his character as is his way with the ladies. And George Eliot studied her medical history in order to get his position exactly right. Dorothea's yearning for a higher life of greater usefulness to mankind will stay with her all her days and will make her a remarkable but exasperating woman; a fool for all her cleverness. George Eliot gives equal weight to these important qualifications. Many Victorian novelists have lectured us on the careers and aspirations of their people; none, before George Eliot, showed us the unity of intellect, aspiration and nature in action. Her judgment on Lydgate as a doctor is a judgment on his fate as a man:

> He carried to his studies in London, Edinburgh and Paris the conviction that the medical profession as it might be was the finest in the world; presenting the most perfect interchange between science and art; offering the most direct alliance between intellectual conquest and the social good. Lydgate's nature demanded this combination: he was an emotional creature, with a flesh and blood sense of fellowship, which withstood all the abstractions of special study. He cared not only for

"Cases," but for John and Elizabeth, especially Elizabeth.

The Elizabeth, who was not indeed to wreck Lydgate's life, but (with far more probability) to corrupt his ideals and turn him into the smart practitioner, was Rosamond, his wife. Yet, in its own way, Rosamond's superego had the most distinguished ideals. A provincial manufacturer's daughter, she too longed idealistically to rise; the desire was not vulgar until she supposed that freedom from crude middle-class notions of taste and bearing could only be obtained by marriage to the cousin of a baronet; and was not immoral until she made her husband's conscience pay for her ambitions. The fountain, George Eliot is always telling us, cannot rise higher than its source.

Such analyses of character have become commonplace to us. When one compares the respectable Rosamond Lydgate with, say, Becky Sharp, one sees that Rosamond is not unique. Where *Middlemarch* is unique in its time is in George Eliot's power of generalization. The last thing one accuses her of is *unthinking* acceptance of convention. She seeks, in her morality, the positive foundation of natural law, a kind of Fate whose measures are as fundamental as the changes of the seasons in nature. Her intellect is sculptural. The clumsiness of style does not denote muddle, but an attempt to carve decisively. We feel the clarifying force of a powerful mind. Perhaps it is not naturally powerful. The power may have been acquired. There are two George Eliots: the mature, experienced, quiet-humored Midlander who wrote the childhood pages of *The Mill on the Floss;* and the naïve, earnest and masterly intellectual with her half-dozen languages and her scholarship. But unlike the irony of our time, hers is at the expense not of belief, but of people. Behind them, awful but inescapable to the eye of conscience, loom the statues of what they ought to have been. Hers is a mind that has grown by making judgments—as Mr. Gladstone's head was said to have grown by making speeches.

Middlemarch resumes the observation and experience of a lifetime. Until this book George Eliot often strains after things beyond her capacity, as Dorothea Casaubon strained after a spiritual power beyond her nature. But now in *Middlemarch* the novelist is reconciled to her experience. In Dr. Casaubon George Eliot sees that tragedy may paralyze the very intellect which was to be Dorothea's emancipation. Much of herself (George Eliot said, when she was accused of portraying Mark Pattison) went into Casaubon, and I can think of no other English novel before or since which has so truthfully, so sympathetically and so intimately described the befogged and grandiose humiliations of the scholar, as he turns at bay before the vengeance of life. Casaubon's jealousy is unforgettable, because, poisonous though it is, it is not the screech of an elderly cuckold, but the voice of strangled nature calling for justice. And notice, here, something very characteristic; George Eliot's pity flows from her moral sense, from the very seat of justice, and not from a sentimental heart.

Middlemarch is the first of many novels about groups of people in provincial towns. They are differentiated from each other not by class or fortune only, but by their moral history, and this moral differentiation is not casual, it is planned and has its own inner hierarchy. Look at the groups. Dorothea, Casaubon and Ladislaw seek to enter the highest spiritual fields—not perhaps the highest for us, because, as we have seen, the world of George Eliot's imagination was prosaic and not poetic—still, they desire, in their several ways, to influence the standards of mankind. There is Lydgate, who is devoted to science and expects to be rewarded by a career. He and his wife are practical people, who seek power. The pharisaical Bulstrode, the banker, expects to rise both spiritually and financially at once, until he sits on the right hand of God, the Father; a businessman with a bad conscience, he is the father of the Buchmanites and of all success-religions. The Garths, being country people and outside of this urban world, believe simply in the virtue of work as a natural law and they are brought up against Fred Vincy, Rosamond's brother. He, as a horsey young man educated beyond his means, has a cheerful belief in irresponsible Style and in himself as a thing of pure male beauty with a riding crop. We may not accept George Eliot's standards, but we can see that they are not conventional, and that they do not make her one-sided. She is most intimately sympathetic to human beings and is never sloppy about them. When Vincy quarrels with Bulstrode about Fred's debts, when Casaubon's jealousy of Ladislaw secretes its first venom, when Lydgate tries vainly to talk about money to his wife or Fred goes to his mad old uncle for a loan, vital human issues are raised. The great scenes of *Middlemarch* are exquisite, living transpositions of real moral dilemmas. Questions of principle are questions of battle; they point the weapons of the human comedy, and battle is not dull. In consequence, George Eliot's beliefs are rarely boring, because they are energies. They correspond to psychological and social realities, though more especially (on the large scale) to the functions of the will; they are boring only when, in the Victorian habit, she harangues the reader and pads out the book with brainy essays.

I see I have been writing about *Middlemarch* as though it was a piece of engineering. What about the life, the humor, the pleasure? There are failures: Dorothea and Ladislaw do not escape the fate of so many Victorian heroes and heroines who are frozen by their creator's high-mindedness. Has George Eliot forgotten how much these two difficult, sensitive and proud people will annoy each other by the stupidity which so frequently afflicts the intellectual? Such scruples, such play-acting! But Lydgate and Rosamond quarreling about money; Rosamond quietly thwarting her husband's decisions, passing without conscience to love affairs with his friends and ending as a case-hardened widow who efficiently finds a second father for her family—these things are perfect. Mary Garth defying the old miser is admirable. But the most moving thing in the book—and this is the real test of a novelist—is given to the least likeable people. Bulstrode's moral ruin and his inability to confess to his dull wife are portrayed in a picture of dumb human despondency which recalls a painting by Sickert. One hears the clock tick in the silence that attends the wearing down of two lives that can cling together but dare not speak.

The humor of George Eliot gains rather than loses by its mingling with her intellect. Here we feel the sound influence of her girlish reading of the eighteenth-century novelists who were above all men of education. This humor is seen at its best in scenes like the one where the relations of the miser come to his house, waiting to hear news of his will; and again in the sardonic description of the spreading of the scandal about Bulstrode and Lydgate. George Eliot followed causes down to their most scurrilous effects. She is good in scandal and public rumor. Her slow tempo is an advantage, and it becomes exciting to know that she will make her point in the minor scenes as surely as she will make it in the great ones. Mrs. Dollop of The Tankard has her short paragraph of immortality:

> (She had) "often to resist the shallow pragmatism of customers disposed to think their reports from the outer world were of equal force with what had 'come up' in her mind."

Mr. Trumbull, the auctioneer, is another portrait, a longer one, smelling of the bar and the saleroom. Dickens would have caricatured this gift from heaven. George Eliot observes and savors. Characteristically she catches his intellectual pretensions and his offensive superiority. We see him scent the coming sale and walk over to Mary Garth's desk to read her copy of Scott's *Anne of Geierstein,* just to show that he knows a book when he sees one:

> "The course of four centuries," he reads out unexpectedly, "has well enough elapsed since the series of events which are related in the following chapters took place on the continent."

That moment is one of the funniest in the English novel, one of those mad touches like the insertion of a dog stealing a bone, which Hogarth put into his pictures.

There is no real sickness in George Eliot. Both heavy feet are on the ground. Outside of *Wuthering Heights* there is no madness in Victorian fiction. The Victorians were a histrionic people who measured themselves by the Elizabethans; and George Eliot, like Browning and Tennyson, was compared to Shakespeare by her contemporaries. The comparison failed, if only because madness is lacking. Hysteria, the effect of the exorbitant straining of their wills, the Victorians did, alas, too often achieve. George Eliot somehow escapes it. She is too level-headed. One pictures her, in life, moralizing instead of making a scene. There is no hysteria in *Middlemarch;* perhaps there is no abyss because there is so much determination. But there is a humane breadth and resolution in this novel which offers neither hope nor despair to mankind but simply the necessity of shaping the moral life. George Eliot's last words on her deathbed might be placed on the title-page of her collected works: "Tell them," she is reported to have said, "the pain is on the left side." Informative to the last and knowing better than the doctor, the self-made Positivist dies.

MEREDITH'S BRAINSTUFF

Does anyone know what to think of Meredith's novels now? I think not. The lack of sympathy is complete. Difficult to read in his own time, he is almost impenetrable to ourselves. "Full of good brainstuff," Gissing said of *Diana of the Crossways,* and added joyfully that the true flavor of this book came out only after three readings! It was Meredith's brain that annoyed his early critics; today we suspect his heart. Insincerity and freakishness are held against him. Yet, we ought to feel *some* contact for he is the first modern highbrow novelist in the sense of being the first to write for the minority and to be affected, even if unconsciously, by the split in our culture. George Eliot, his rival intellectual, was not so affected.

Those who visited the chalet at Box Hill in the period of Meredith's old age and fame were astonished by the mass of French novels there. He set out, as the French do, to facet life so that it became as hard as a diamond, to shape it by Idea. (At the time of the death of his second wife, he wrote: "I see all round me how much Idea governs," and Idea was "the parent of life as opposed to that of perishable blood.") The notion sometimes gave an intellectual dignity to his creations, but just as often dignity was merely stance. For Meredith's imagination housed the most ill-assorted ideas: there was dandyism, there was the oracular Romance of his claim to be a Celt, there was the taste for German fantasy, the feeling for supermen and women and the heroic role of the fittest. If we follow his own habit of metaphorical association, we find ourselves saying that the descendant of two generations of naval and military tailors in Portsmouth was born to the art of dressing up. In fact, his grandfather, and his father before him, had been as fantastic in their lives as he was in his novels; the son was able to survive his own self-deceptions by the aid of wit. The difficulty of Meredith does not lie in his thought, but in its conceits, in the flowered waistcoats of his intellectual wardrobe. Gosse used to object to this passage from the description of a scene at the gaming table:

> He compared the creatures dabbling over the board to summer flies on butcher's meat, periodically scared by a cloth. More in the abstract, they were snatching at a snapdragon bowl. It struck him that the gamblers had thronged on an invitation to drink the round of seed-time and harvest in a gulp. Again they were desperate gleaners, hopping, skipping, bleeding, amid a whizz of scythe blades, for small wisps of booty. Nor was it long before the presidency of an ancient hoary Goat-Satan might be perceived with skew-eyes and pucker-mouth, nursing a hoof on a tree. Our medieval Enemy sat symbolical in his deformities, as in old Italian and Dutch thick-line engravings of him. He rolled a ball for souls, excited like kittens, to catch it tumbling into the dozens of vacant pits.

Brainstuff, indeed. For our welfare (Meredith warned us) Life was always trying to pull us away from consciousness and brainstuff. On the other hand, "Matter that is not nourishing to brains can help to constitute nothing but the bodies that are pitched on rubbish heaps." Human felicity is always trying (he said in a letter) to kill consciousness. There is often an extraordinary violence in Meredith's neo-Pagan metaphors.

Meredith, like Browning, had too many ideas. And, as in his novels, so in his life, the brilliant egoist appeared to be an artificial construction. An American biographer, Professor Lionel Stevenson, notes, in *The Ordeal of George Meredith,* that by the time he was fifty, Meredith "had completely molded himself in a dramatic personality." He had become the Comic Spirit in person and if there was overstrain, it was for clear personal reason: "The components had been collected with a kind of genius. Impenetrably screened behind it lurked the Portsmouth tailor shop, the bankrupt father, and the dreadful decade of his first marriage." The price was that he did not inspire intimacy:

> It was not that he seemed either aloof or insincere; but he created the effect of a perpetual and consummate theatrical performance and the pilgrims to Box Hill were not so much consorting with a friend as they were appreciating a unique work of art.

It would be misleading to continue to press a comparison between Meredith's life and his work as a novelist. Professor Stevenson is concerned with the writing life and very little with literary criticism. He comments on the novels, as they come along, but does not examine them in much detail. He notes (what Henry James deplored) Meredith's evasion of the *scène à faire;* for example, it is the point of all Meredith's novels, as Professor Stevenson admirably says, that the chief characters shall be tried by ordeal. They are burned in the fire of their own tragic or comic illusions and emerge from self-deception into self-knowledge. Yet, in *Diana of the Crossways*, the scene where Diana commits the folly of letting a political secret out of the bag is skipped. Is she an hysterical egoist? Is she as immoral as she appears? Has she merely lost her head? Only a direct account of the scene at the newspaper office, where she hands over the secret, can tell us. Meredith was no storyteller—a fatal defect, above all in the days of the three-volume novel. He is a novelist who gesticulates about a story that is implicitly already told. The cage of character is his interest. The rest of Professor Stevenson's criticism is appreciative but not considerable. I find only one point of disagreement. He says that Meredith was the first to introduce something close to natural dialogue in the English novel. Certainly Meredith breaks the convention in which dialogue had been written up to his time; the result is not natural speech. Meredith simply applied his own allusiveness to dialogue, and allusiveness happens to be a characteristic of ordinary speech anyway; he was too full of himself to see the characters or speech of other people, except in so far as they could be elaborated as "idea" and in stylized form. Meredith's dialogue is simply Meredith cutting a figure in his own society.

As a biography Professor Stevenson's *Life* tells a well-known story competently. A writer has not much time for living and Meredith's life is one more variant on the theme of the calamities of authorship. There is the aloof, handsome, snobbish youth making that first break with his environment by sheer pride of obsession. There is the unhappy marriage to Peacock's daughter and the hardening of the heart—yet Meredith's heart must have hardened in childhood. And then the literary grind follows. *The Ordeal of Richard Feverel* is a failure, so is *Evan Harrington. Harry Richmond* gets a few admirers. His integrity was untouched by neglect; he worked without a public until he was fifty, and by that time, his health went to pieces. The tall, eagle-faced man, the nonstop wit, talker and laugher, with his bouts of "manly" boisterousness and back-slapping, had always been a dyspeptic. Now he suddenly became deaf. He presently had the symptoms of locomotor ataxia. To keep his family he had ground away for years as a publisher's reader and wrote three articles a week for a provincial newspaper. For years also he made a small annual sum by reading to an old lady once a week. His letters are full of the groans of laborious authorship. At fifty he had had enough, but he was fated to live into his eighties, unable to hear speech or music; unable to walk, which had been his chief pleasure in life. He was drawn about in a donkey chair. He was sixty before he became famous; the relative comfort of his old age was only in part due to his success—he inherited a little money from an aunt. In his personal life, he had seen the death of his two wives and the son whom he had once adored, but who had become estranged from him after his second marriage. A psychologist might say that Meredith's life is an ironical illustration of the theory that we get what we are conditioned to desire. The death of his mother in very early childhood, and the pride and fecklessness of his father, had formed Meredith for self-sufficiency and loneliness: the brain rapidly filled in the hollows left by affections which had been denied. His own affections certainly became intellectual; his love letters are clearly of the kind that exhaust the feeling in an excessive flow of lyrical expression. He grieved over the death of his wife, but he *had* compared her to a mud fort! Friends found an annoying disconnection between brain and heart. There was one reward. It seems frequently to come to the egoistic temperament: the exciting, if heartless, power of living in the present. He tore up old letters and, in old age, is said to have scorned the common consolation of that time: living in the past. The torrential talker, the magician, was in short a picturesque monster, relishing his scars. One whimsical young American admirer—mentioned by Professor Stevenson—made the shrewd, even Meredithean remark, that he would probably have been happier and better organized if he had been a woman.

To return to the "unreadableness" of Meredith. He is not unreadable; he exists a page at a time; he is quotable, to be skipped through. The large characters like Sir Willoughby Patterne or Richmond Roy, are myths. Meredith is tedious only in his detail; when he intends to be preposterous he is wonderful, as he is in that scene in *Harry Richmond,* where Richmond Roy poses publicly as an equestrian statue. Meredithean irony is excessive, as all the brainstuff is, but it is excellent when the character or the scene is fantastic enough for him. He is impossible until one submits to his conception of Romance; after that he is only hard work. He is a rhapsodist who writes about people who are really souls moving impatiently out of their present into their future, toward destruction or self-knowledge. They are pagan souls in the poetic sense, not characters in the moralistic sense; giants of the Celtic tradition, grotesques in the German; all their geese are swans. Their lives are portrayed as heightened exercises in their integrity and their sense of honor. Professor Stevenson remarks that Meredith was attacked with ridicule until he was fifty, not only because he was a pagan who could not tell a story and at odds with popular realism, but because Romance was out. His fame began when Romance came in. Stevenson and Conrad contain strange echoes. Chesterton's suburban romance owes a lot to him. D. H. Lawrence was the last to be influenced by him. Another element in making his fame was the rise of feminism. It is very hard for ourselves to imagine another revival in Romance. What a future generation of novelists may find stimulating in him is that preoccupation of his with what he called "the idea." He enlarged the novel with a brilliant power of generalization. It was spoiled, as so much English fiction has been, by the obsession with romantic class consciousness, but in *Beauchamp's Career*, or even in a clumsy novel like *One of Our Conquerors*, he has an ability to generalize about society as living history. And his presentation of character—Diana Merion, for example, in *Diana of the Crossways*—as idea and person at once, is a fertile addition to the old English tradition of character types, removed from our moralizing habit. The pile of French novels at the chalet, the attempt to turn Molière into English, had their point.

Harry Richmond is a novel with fewer difficulties of style than most of Meredith's work, chiefly because it is written in the first person. He was a poetic or rhapsodic novelist, and *Harry Richmond* is a romance about the serious deceits and comedies of romance. Several of the characters are more than life-size, or speak and live in the heightened language of an imagination which is sometimes fine, at other times wooden or uncertain of its level; but there is no doubt that Meredith creates a complete world. Critics have often said that Meredith's taste for the chivalrous and high-sounding takes him clean out of the nineteenth century and sends his novels floating away in clouds of nonexistent history. They have said that we can never pin him down to time and place, and that he is intellectually Ruritanian. This is only superficially true. We must take into consideration a novelist's temperament before we judge like that. Because Meredith's mind was macroscopic, because his subject again and again is people's imaginative, ideal, future-consuming view of themselves and of their environment, this does not mean that they have no known place in a recognizable world. Nothing could be more thoroughly Victorian in imagination than *Harry Richmond;* if the neo-medieval coloring is precisely that, this novel reads as if it were an attempt to glamorize Victorian life out of recognition. This is a well-known habit among the poets of the nineteenth century. The cult of the picturesque history can be described as an escape from the grim squalor of the Industrial Revolution; but we can also think of it as a confident and imperial enterprise of colonization. The Victorians were high feeders on what is felt to be foreign in time or place. *Harry Richmond* is cast in the imperial frame of mind, and if Meredith can be justly accused of being merely Ruritanian, he did not fall into the ludicrous which so often imperils (shall we say?) Tennyson's historical or legendary poems. The very pretense of Harry Richmond's fantastic father to the throne of England and to royal blood expresses a rising, exuberant aspect of the situation in England at that time when people were very liable to be plethoric about the greatness of their history. The plot and many details of narration are also true to the period. It was a time of violent changes of fortune in private life, of tremendous claims to estates and titles. Meredith is known to have got the idea for Richmond Roy's wild claim from the fact that William the Fourth had many children by an Irish actress, and also from the marriage of George IV to Mrs. Fitzherbert. Meredith's remoteness has been exaggerated by critics brought up on realism.

The spell of *Harry Richmond*—for to read it is to pass into trance—exists because of the brilliant handling of an impossible subject. If Meredith had confronted Richmond Roy's claim squarely and realistically he would have been lost. His art lies in building up the character of the father as the romantic and charming figure seen by his child, and then in gradually disclosing that he is first an adventurer, living in state one minute and in a debtor's prison the next; at last, by evasive insinuation, comes the royal claim. Richmond Roy grows larger and larger, richer in resource and effrontery, more and more triumphant for every setback, but skating on thinner and thinner ice the farther he goes. Meredith learned from French novelists the method of working up to the key phrase. The moment the farmers on whom Harry Richmond is boarded when he is a child start deferring to him, and are heard at last to whisper superstitiously "Blood rile," the thrill is aesthetic. It has exactly the effect of the words, "You are an egoist," when they are spoken to Sir Willoughby Patterne in *The Egoist,* and when they transform the tension and tighten the focus of that book. Richmond Roy has been compared too obviously with Micawber; he is far more complex than that; his follies and dreams have genius. He is not a windbag; he is a fine actor. He is nearer to Falstaff. Richmond Roy alarms. He alarms when he brazenly orders scarlet liveries, permitted only to the Royal Family, for his postillions. He alarms by his knowledge of our weaknesses. He can bounce his way into buying a chateau or a yacht. He can spellbind a foreign court and rout the hostess of Bath. Notoriety he thrives on. His impudence when he poses as an equestrian statue at the German court is splendid. These fantastic episodes set off the scurvy ones: the father's nasty relationships with the Press, his unscrupulous robbery of his adoring son, his caddish exploitation of the young man's love for the German princess, his cold-hearted swindling of his sister-in-law. He pretends that the money came from personages who are anxious to keep him quiet. He is a mountebank, and if we are glad in the end that Squire Beltham exposes him in good Squire Western style, it is not really because we like to see vice punished, but because the rogue has got too maddening and has reached an hysterical and pathetic stage where he will become a figure too farcical to bear his real weight as a symbol; hence his tragedy. Meredith works up to that proper conclusion but, like a great artist, explores all the other possibilities first. He has the piling-on instinct of the storyteller. We are delighted toward the end when Richmond Roy is confronted with another false claimant, a so-called Dauphin who claims to have marks on his body which prove his heredity. Meredith is clever enough to give this episode twice; in two different kinds of gossip, one showing Richmond Roy the master of an insulting situation, the other through Square Beltham's hilarious British scorn. Meredith's mastery of comedy does not exclude the low and, indeed, in the low he is not tempted to his vice of over-polishing. When the ladies retire from the dinner table—a nice touch that—the Squire lets go:

> They got the two together, William. Who are you? I'm a Dauphin; who are you? I'm Ik Dine, bar sinister. Oh, says the other; then I take precedence of you! Devil a bit, says the other; I've got more spots than you. Proof, says one. You first, t'other. Count, one cries. T'other sings out. Measles. Better than a dying Dauphin, roars t'other; and swore both of 'em 'twas nothing but port wine stains and pimples. Ha! Ha! And, William, will you believe it?—the couple went round begging the company to count spots to prove their big birth. Oh Lord, I'd ha' paid a penny to be there! A Jack of Bedlam Ik Dine damned idiot!—makes the name o' Richmond stink.

It has been said that Meredith is not a storyteller—but a story need not depend very much on plot; it can and does in Meredith depend on pattern and the disclosure of character through events. The weakness is that the fantastic father engrosses the great part of the interesting incident; when he is offstage our interest flags. Meredith's narrative is not a straight line; it is a meandering back and forth in time, a blending of events and commentary and this Meredith must have gone for instinctively because he is wooden in straightforward narration. We follow an imagination that cannot bear precision. He depends on funking scenes, on an increasing uncertainty about how exactly events did occur. There is a refusal to credit reality with importance until it has been parceled out between two or three minds and his own reflections on it. Even in the duel scene in Germany, the excellence is due to the ironical telescoping of the event; we are hearing Meredith on the duel, telling us what to look at and what not to bother about. The effect is of jumping from one standstill scene to another. Life is not life, for him, until it is over; until it is history. (One sees this method in the novels of William Faulkner). The movement is not from event to event, but from situation to situation, and in each situation there is a kernel of surprising incident. In realism he is tedious. One can almost hear him laboring at what he does not believe in and depending on purely descriptive skill.

The love scenes in *Harry Richmond* present a double difficulty to ourselves. The mixture of realism and high romance is awkward; we are made to feel the sensuality of lovers in a way remarkable to mid-Victorian novels; their words appear to be a highfalutin' means of taking the reader's mind off it and, in this respect, Meredith's pagan idealism is no more satisfactory than the conventional Christian idealism of other novelists. Like Scott, Meredith is always better at the minor lovers than the major ones. His common sense, touched by a half-sympathetic scorn, is truer than his lyricism which is too radiantly egocentric. In Meredith's personal life, his strongest and spontaneous feelings of love were those of a son and a father, and this is, of course, the theme of *Harry Richmond.* That is why, more than any of his other works, this one appears to be rooted in a truth about the human heart. In erotic love, Meredith never outgrew his early youth and the fact over-exhilarates and vulgarizes him by turns.

Harry Richmond is thought to be less encumbered than Meredith's other novels because it is written in the first person. Unfortunately, as Mr. Percy Lubbock pointed out some years ago in *The Craft of Fiction,* the first person has to be both narrator and actor in his own story, and in consequence stands in his own light. I do not believe that this is a serious fault in *Harry Richmond* as a story, for what carries us forward is Meredith's remarkable feeling for the generosity, impulsiveness and courage of youth and its splendid blindness to the meaning of its troubles. Harry is blinded by romantic love for his father and the German princess; he is weak in not facing up to the defects of the former and in not being "great" enough for the latter; but both these sets of behavior are honorable and have our sympathy. With his father he shares a propensity for illusion and romance and is cured of them. Since he is the narrator we have only his word for it, and one is far from convinced that Harry Richmond has been cured or even examined. Put the story in Henry James's hands and one sees at once that the whole question of illusion or romance would have been gone into far more deeply. It is the old Meredithean trouble: he is an egoistical writer, fitted out with the egoistical accomplishments, and one who can never be sufficiently unselfed to go far into the natures of others. His portraits start from him, not from them, and the result is that he is only picturesque, a master of ear and eye, a witty judge of the world, a man a good deal cutting a figure in his own society; we are given brilliant views of the human heart, but we do not penetrate it. He has no sense of the calamitous, no sense of the broken or naked soul, and—fatally—no sense of evil. More than any other novelist of his age, he has the Victorian confidence in a manner so dazzling and profuse that it is natural he was called Shakespearean. In the effusive Victorian sense, he was; but Shakespearean merely linguistically, by inheritance, at second hand, without any notion of human life as passion or of suffering as more than disappointment. He is a very literary novelist indeed.

AN IRISH GHOST

The leaves fly down, the rain spits and the clouds flow like a dirty thaw before the wind, which whines and mews in the window cracks and swings the wireless aerial with a dull tap against the sill; the House of Usher is falling, and between now and Hogmanay, as the drafts lift the carpets, as slates shift on the roof and mice patter behind the wainscot, the ghosts, the wronged suitors of our lives, gather in the anterooms of the mind. It is their moment. It is also the moment to read those ghosts of all ghosts, the minor novelists who write about the supernatural. Pushed into limbo by the great novelists with their grandiose and blatant passion for normality, these minor talents flicker about plaintively on the edges of fame, often excelling the masters in a phrase or a character, but never large enough to take the center of the stage. Such a writer is J. Sheridan Le Fanu. In mid-Victorian literature Le Fanu is crowded out by Dickens and Thackeray, talked off the floor by Lever, that supreme raconteur, surpassed or (should one say?) by-passed on his own ground by Wilkie Collins: yet he has, within his limits, an individual accent and a flawless virtuosity. At least one of his books, a collection of tales republished sixteen years ago with Ardizzone's illustrations and entitled *In a Glass Darkly* is worth reading; it contains the well-known *Green Tea.* His other books show that, like so many talented Irishmen, he had gifts, but too many voices that raise too many echoes.

Le Fanu brought a limpid tributary to the Teutonic stream which had fed mysterious literature for so long. I do not mean that he married the Celtic banshee to the Teutonic poltergeist or the monster, in some Irish graveyard; what he did was to bring an Irish lucidity and imagination to the turgid German flow. Le Fanu's ghosts are the most disquieting of all: the ghosts that can be justified, blobs of the unconscious that have floated up to the surface of the mind, and which are not irresponsible and perambulatory figments of family history, mooning and clanking about in fancy dress. The evil of the justified ghosts is not sportive, willful, involuntary or extravagant. In Le Fanu the fright is that effect follows cause. Guilt patters two-legged behind its victims in the street, retribution sits adding up its account night after night, the secret doubt scratches away with malignant patience in the guarded mind. We laugh at the headless coachman or the legendary heiress grizzling her way through the centuries in her nightgown; but we pause when we recognize that those other hands on the wardrobe, those other eyes at the window, those other steps on the landing and those small shadows that slip into the room as we open the door, are our own. It is we who are the ghosts. Those are *our* own steps which follow us, it is *our* "heavy body" which we hear falling in the attic above. We haunt ourselves. Let illness or strain weaken the catch which we keep fixed so tightly upon the unconscious, and out spring all the hags and animals of moral or Freudian symbolism, just as the "Elemental" burns sharp as a diamond before our eyes when we lie relaxed and on the point of sleep.

Some such idea is behind most of Le Fanu's tales. They are presented as the cases of a psychiatrist called Dr. Helvetius, whose precise theory appears to be that these fatal visitations come when the psyche is worn to rags and the interior spirit world can then make contact with the external through the holes. A touch of science, even bogus science, gives an edge to the superstitious tale. The coarse hanging judge is tracked down by the man whom he has unjustly hanged and is hanged in turn. The eupeptic sea captain on the point of marrying an Irish fortune is quietly terrorized into the grave by the sailor whom, years before, he had had flogged to death in Malta. The fashionable and handsome clergyman is driven to suicide by the persecutions of a phantom monkey who jumps into his Bible as he preaches, and waits for him at street corners, in carriages, in his very room. A very Freudian animal this. Dark and hairy with original sin and symbolism, he skips straight out of the unchaste jungle of a pious bachelor's unconscious. The vampire girl who preys on the daughter of an Austrian count appears to be displaying the now languid, now insatiate, sterility of Lesbos. I am not, however, advancing La Fanu as an instance of the lucky moralist who finds a sermon in every spook, but as an artist in the dramatic use of the evil, the secret, and the fatal, an artist, indeed, in the domestic insinuation of the supernatural. With him it does not break the law, but extends the mysterious jurisdiction of nature.

Le Fanu might be described as the Simenon of the peculiar. There is the same limpid narrative. He is expert in screwing up tension little by little without strain, and an artist in surprise. The literature of the uncanny scores crudely by outraging our senses and our experience; but the masters stick to the simple, the *almost* natural, and let fall their more unnerving revelations as if they were all in the day's work. And they are. The clergyman in *Green Tea* is describing the course of his persecution, how it abates only to be renewed with a closer menace.

> "I traveled in a chaise. I was in good spirits. I was more—I was happy and grateful. I was returning, as I thought, delivered from a dreadful hallucination, to the scene of duties which I longed to enter upon. It was a beautiful sunny evening, everything looked serene and cheerful and I was delighted. I remember looking out of the window to see the spire of my Church at Kenlis among the trees, at the point where one has the earliest view of it. It is exactly where the little stream that bounds the parish passes under the road by a culvert; and where it emerges at the roadside a stone with an old inscription is placed. As we passed this point I drew my head in and sat down, and in the corner of the chaise was the monkey."

Again:

> "It used to spring on a table, on the back of a chair, on the chimney piece, and slowly to swing

itself from side to side, looking at me all the time. There is in its motion an indefinable power to dissipate thought, and to contract one's attention to that monotony till the ideas shrink, as it were, to a point, and at last to nothing—and unless I had started up, and shook off the catalepsy, I have felt as if my mind were on the point of losing itself. There are other ways," he sighed heavily, "thus, for instance, while I pray with my eyes closed, it comes closer and closer, and I see it. I know it is not to be accounted for physically but I do actually see it, though my lids are closed, and so it rocks my mind, as it were, and overpowers me, and I am obliged to rise from my knees. If you had ever yourself known this, you would be acquainted with desperation."

And then, after this crisis, the tortured clergyman confides once more to his doctor and makes his most startling revelation in the mere course of conversation. The doctor has suggested that candles shall be brought. The clergyman wearily replies:

"All lights are the same to me. Except when I read or write, I care not if night were perpetual. I am going to tell you what happened about a year ago. The thing began to speak to me."

There is Henry James's *second* turn of the screw.

We progress indeed not into vagueness and atmosphere, but into greater and greater particularity; with every line the net grows tighter. Another sign of the master is Le Fanu's equable eye for the normal. There is a sociability about his stories, a love of pleasure, a delight in human happiness, a tolerance of folly and a neat psychological perception. Only in terms of the vampire legend would the Victorians have permitted a portrayal of Lesbian love, but how lightly, skillfully and justly it is told. Vigilance is a word Le Fanu often uses. We feel a vigilance of observation in all his character drawing, we are aware of a fluid and quick sensibility which responds only to the essential things in people and in the story. He is as detached as a *dompteur;* he caresses, he bribes, he laughs, he cracks the whip. It is a sinister but gracious performance.

One doesn't want to claim too much for Le Fanu. For most of his life he was a Dublin journalist and versatility got the better of him. He is known for two of his many novels: *Uncle Silas* and *The House by the Churchyard. Uncle Silas* has ingenious elements. Le Fanu saw the possibility of the mysterious in the beliefs and practices of the Swedenborgians, but the book goes downhill halfway through and becomes a crime puzzle. A good man dies and puts his daughter in his brother's care, knowing his brother is reputed to be a murderer. By this reckless act the good man hopes to clear his brother's name. On the contrary, it puts an idea into his head. This brother, Uncle Silas, had married beneath him, and the picture of his illiterate family has a painful rawness which is real enough; but such a sinister theme requires quiet treatment, and Le Fanu is too obviously sweating along in the footsteps of Dickens or Wilkie Collins. Lever is another echo. It is his voice, the voice of the stage Irishman which romps rather too nuttily about *The House by the Churchyard,* into which Le Fanu seems to have thrown every possible side of his talent without discrimination. There are ghosts you shrink from, ghosts you laugh at, cold murder is set beside comic duels, wicked characters become ridiculous, ridiculous ones become solemn and we are supposed to respect them. It is all a very strange mixture, and Sterne and Thackeray, as well as Lever, seem to be adding their hand. A good deal is farcical satire of the military society in eighteenth-century Dublin, and Le Fanu is dashing and gaudy with a broad brush:

> Of late Mrs. Macnamara had lost all her pluck and half her colour, and some even of her fat. She was like one of those portly dowagers in Nubernip's select society of metamorphosed turnips, who suddenly exhibited sympathetic symptoms of failure, grew yellow, flabby and wrinkled, as the parent bulb withered and went out of season.

His comic subalterns, scheming land agents and quarreling doctors, his snoring generals and shrill army wives, are drawn close up, so close up that it is rather bewildering until you are used to the jumpy and awkward angles of his camera. One gets a confused, life-size impression, something like the impression made by a crowded picture of Rowlandson's, where so much is obviously happening that one can't be sure exactly what it is and where to begin. Le Fanu was spreading himself as Lever had done, but was too soaked in the journalist's restless habits to know how to define his narrative. He became garrulous where Lever was the raconteur. He rambles on like some rumbustious reporter who will drop into a graceful sketch of trout fishing on the Liffey or into fragments of rustic idyll and legend, and then return to his duels, his hell-fire oaths and his claret. I can see that this book has a flavor, but I could never get through it. The truth is that Le Fanu, the journalist, could not be trusted to *accumulate* a novel. You can see in *Uncle Silas* how the process bored him, and how that book is really a good short story that has unhappily started breeding. His was a talent for brevity, the poetic sharpness and discipline of the short tale, for the subtleties and symbolism of the uncanny. In this form Le Fanu is a good deal more than a ghost among the ghosts.

TROLLOPE WAS RIGHT

The comfort we get from Trollope's novels is the sedative of gossip. It is not cynical gossip for Trollope himself is the honest check on the self-deceptions of his characters, on their malicious lies or interested half-truths about each other. It is he, a workaday surrogate of God, sincere, sturdy, shrewd and unhopeful, who has the key. Trollope does not go with us into the dangerous region that lies just outside our affairs and from which we draw our will to live; rather, he settles lazily into that part of our lives which is a substitute, the part which avoids loneliness by living vicariously in other people. If it is a true generalization—as some say—that the English, being unimaginative, are able to live without hope but not without the pleasure of thinking they are better than their neighbors, Trollope's are the most English of our novels. But the generalization is not true. Trollope himself—as Mr. Cockshut says in a very intelligent study—is saved by eccentricity. There is something fervent, even extreme, in his admiration of endurance. He was a man whose temper could flare up. His preoccupation with what is normal is the intense one of a man who has had to gain acquaintance with normality from an abnormal situation outside it. His special eccentricities are his mania for work and his passion for spending energy. From his point of view, novel writing was obsessional. It convinced him that he, the outsider in a society of powerful groups of people, was justified in being alive. Even his most contented novels leave an aftertaste of flatness and sadness. He has succeeded in his assertions, to the point of conveying a personal satiety.

The plots of Trollope and Henry James have much in common. But if we compare a novel like *The Eustace Diamonds,* one of the most ingenious of Trollope's conundrums, with, say, Henry James's *The Spoils of Poynton,* we see the difference between a pragmatic gossip and an artist of richer sensibility. Sense, not sensibility, governs Trollope; it is fine good sense and, though he lumbers along, most notable for the subtlety of its timing. He is an excellent administrator and politician of private life. But whereas James saw how the magnificent spoils of the Poynton family could corrupt by their very beauty, Trollope did not envisage anything morally ambiguous in the imbroglio of the Eustace diamonds. The *Spoils* were treasure; the *Diamonds* are property. The former are made for the moral law; the latter for the courts. It is true, as Mr. Cockshut says, that the brilliantly delayed climax where Dove, the lawyer, points out the stones are worthless, has its overtones. But to Trollope's imagination the diamonds are ultimately meaningless; one might defend the wicked Lady Eustace and say that she alone gave them a symbolical meaning. They at least stand for her will. But Trollope in fact dislikes her childish will as much as her propensity for lying; her poetic side is shown to be false. One wonders if he could have portrayed it if it had been genuine. She is a perjurer, a bitch and a coquette and, quite rightly, ends up as a bore; but in a novel filled with irritable and spiritless people, she is the one figure of spirit. Trollope merely knows that she is wrong.

With all his mastery, Trollope is only interested in what people are like, not in what they are for. The limitation comes out most clearly in his political novels when we see how politics work and never for what purpose, beyond those of personal career. Some critics have put down this fundamental virtue of Trollope to his good-natured and sensible acceptance of mid-Victorian society, and would say that he accepted his world just as Jane Austen accepted hers. Others—and I think Mr. Cockshut would be among them—point to his constitutional melancholy. It has the effect of devitalizing his characters. I do not mean that old harridans like Lady Linlithgow, the delightful self-willed Lady Glencora, or Lord George in *The Eustace Diamonds* lack personal vitality; the deficiency is in artistic vitality. If we compare the portrait of Lady Eustace with Thackeray's Becky Sharp it is interesting to see how much passivity there is in Lady Eustace and how much greater is the adventuress than the stubborn fool. Lady Eustace drifts. Her wickednesses are many, but they are small. She is little more than a tedious *intrigante* who relies on chance. She, of course, succeeds with us because of her obstinacy, her wit, her courage, her seductiveness and her beauty and because her wickedness is that of a child. Indeed Lord George, the "corsair," pats her on the head and treats her as such. Becky is a more positive and interesting figure of badness because she is grown up.

In *The Eustace Diamonds,* there are only two moments when Trollope breaks through his melancholy to write out of strong feeling. The first is an unpleasant outbreak: the anti-Semitism of his portrait of Mr. Emilius, "the greasy Jew." Trollope, honest observer that he is, notes that Lady Eustace is far from being physically repelled by the preacher who is said to be repulsive. The female masochist—as Mr. Cockshut says—has recognized a master, the coquette her master-hypocrite. The second outbreak occurs in describing the brutal, forced engagement of Lucinda Roanoke to Sir Griffin, and the violence with which the Amazon repels him when he tries to take her on his knee. Here the revulsion is physical. These are two disconcerting glimpses into the Trollopian alcove and both are blatant. Trollope with his blood up is better seen on the hunting field; he will be kinder there to the women who are to be humiliated.

Mr. Cockshut has read the whole of Trollope and I have not. His book provides an able analysis of the novels and a fresh approach to Trollope himself. The critic might have said, with advantage, more about Trollope's curious life; Mr. Cockshut is more detailed than other critics have been about Trollope's response to mid-Victorianism; he is fascinated by the moral issues which Trollope propounded, but he is apt to digress. As a critic he depends on paraphrase which is always suggestive and enjoyable though it also runs into the danger of crediting a novelist with ideas he may only dimly have discerned. Is it true, for example, that masochism is Lady Eustace's central characteristic? Surely it is a lack of interest in truth. Mr. Cockshut's main point is that there are three phases in Trollope's prodigious output; the daydream stage; the genial middle period when he accepts the world; and the final one, beginning with *He Knew He Was Right,* when he is bitterly disillusioned about the society which he has affirmed his right to. Mr. Cockshut cannot think of any special reason for the change. Perhaps Trollope's leaving the Post Office and failing to get into Parliament had something to do with it. Leisure depressed, indeed terrified him and, perhaps, what Mr. Cockshut calls his "belated understanding of the changes that were coming over Victorian England" became unpleasantly observable with leisure. We need not think that hard work exhausted him, but men who are hard on themselves become harder on other people as time goes by. "He knew he was right" could have been his device, the rightness not lying especially in his opinion, but in his choice of what might be called "practical hallucination" as a way of living. He was perhaps reverting in late middle age to the misanthropy of his early, unhappy youth. The cycle is common enough. Dickens, too, became harsh and, to contemporary taste, the harsh or obsessional phase of novelists happens to have become attractive.

He Knew He Was Right and *The Eustace Diamonds* are not genial books. There is something savage in them. The values of society are rotten, the people are fools, brutes or lunatics. Lady Eustace may be bad; but what are we to say of the virtuous Mrs. Hittaway, the social climber, who does not scruple in the name of virtue to employ Lady Eustace's servants to spy upon her and who is so morally exalted by her own slanders that she does not even want to consider the evidence for them? They are a nasty, money-grubbing lot, no better than they should be. Their story is redeemed and "placed" by Trollope's smiling remark that the scandal managed to keep the old Duke of Omnium alive for three months and gave everybody in London something to talk about at dinner. Trollope may be pessimistic but he was too alert a comedian to be misled into rancor. His good nature was truthful if it grew less and less hopeful. Himself morbidly subject to loneliness and boredom and capable of portraying characters who were destroyed by these evils, he never fell into exaggeration—nor indeed rose to it.

The Eustace Diamonds is a triumph of ingenious construction and of storytelling. Trollope is a master of that dramatic art which the English novel seems to have inherited from its early roots in the theatre; the art of putting the right in the wrong and the wrong in the right. He also understands Society and the difference between the weary meaninglessness of the conventional and the vicious aimlessness of the unconventional. The fast set and the Grundys, like Mrs. Hittaway, are opposite sides of the same coin. Yet if, as Mr. Cockshut's analysis patiently shows, the gossip is morally organized, it is not schematic. The characters are various in themselves. A dull man like Lord Fawn becomes fascinating. We see the figure of Frank Greystock in all the colors of a merely moderate honesty. Each character is brought to its own dramatic head. Will Greystock jilt the governess and marry Lady Eustace? Trollope is not content to stop at answering that question, but goes one better and shows Greystock falling asleep in the train, bored stiff by a flirt who had captivated him. Trollope's observation can make even a Commissioner of Police interesting. Nor does the comedy remain on one level. The love affair of Lucinda and Sir Griffin approaches the grotesque and the horrible and the sharp financial deals and recriminations of Lady Eustace and Mrs. Carbuncle are as savage as anything in *Jonathan Wild.* Trollope is a remorseless exploiter of fine points. If he had been a mere plot-maker he would have been satisfied to expose the perjuries of Lady Eustace in the court scene, but he squeezes more than that out of it. He sees to it that a sadistic counsel, powerless to be other than cruel, makes the liar tell the truth a dozen times over, unnecessarily. And when the bogus preacher proposes, Lady Eustace doubts if he is bogus enough.

The critic must admire these skills. He must admire Trollope's knowledge of the groups in the social hierarchy. He must notice how fertilizing was Trollope's own dilemma: that he was a man of liberal mind crossed by strong conservative feeling. There remain the serious limitations that his manner is slovenly, repetitive and pedestrian, that his scene has no vividness, that—as Mr. Cockshut says—the upper steps of his moral stairway are missing, that he lacks fantasy. There will be sin but no sanctity. It is after all Lady

Eustace's crime that she was not the average woman and it is supposed to be Mrs. Hittaway's justification that she is. And so, when we emerge from Trollope's world, we, at first, define him as one of the masters who enables us to recognize average life for what it is. On second thoughts, we change the phrase: we recognize that he has drawn life as people say it is when they are not speaking about themselves.

The latest addition to the attractive Oxford Crown edition of Trollope is one of the chronicler's "failures" —*The Prime Minister.* It was the penultimate volume of what Trollope considered his best work: the series which begins with *Can You Forgive Her?* and runs on to the Phineas novels. As Mr. Amery says in his introduction, it raises the question of politics in the novel. The failure of *The Prime Minister* is, of course, relative; no novel containing Lady Glencora could be called dull. But this one has no personable young hero like the frank and susceptible Phineas Finn and Emily Wharton is a bit of a stick as the meek but obstinate young bride in love. On the other hand, Lopez, the speculator and fortune hunter, is a genuine figure of the age; drama is created by his shifty fingers, he is bold and credible. The only bother with Lopez is that he is made the vehicle of Trollope's peculiar dislike of "outsiders" and foreigners—he loathed Disraeli really because he was a Jew—and a hostile lecturing tone comes into Trollope's voice when he writes of him, which is absent from the portrait of that other rapscallion—Burgo Fitzgerald. Yet Trollope tries very hard to be fair to Lopez, who is presented with objective care and is never all of a piece. He has courage, for example, and one notices that he does not lie until he is kicked when he is down. Only his suicide, at the end, is out of character, for obviously a man like Lopez will always start again from the bottom. He perfectly illustrates what a novelist like Galsworthy would have made a lot of moral fuss about: that in a rich oligarchic society, the Lopezes will always be sacrificed when their heads are turned or when it is a question of class solidarity and self-defense. Trollope is very accurate as a psychologist of the uncomprehending rogue; a little cynical as he shows how mad it is to think of succeeding in England if you use your imagination and disobey the rules. It is a tremendous moment when Lopez attempts to blackmail the Duke of Omnium and the best kind of surprise: the brilliant Lopez has lost his head. We had forgotten how stupid cleverness can be. Finally, in the major conflict between the lofty-minded Prime Minister and his wife, Lady Glencora, whose whole idea is to exploit her husband's political eminence socially, there is wit, and drama too.

Where is the specific failure, then? I do not mean the general criticism of Trollope that he is commonplace, that reading him is like walking down endless corridors of carpet, restful to walk on, but in the end enervating. What is the failure within Trollope's own honest terms? The reader is bound to agree with the experienced opinion of the politician who introduces the book: as Mr. Amery says, it was possible for Trollope to write about the Church without engaging in religious controversy, because this is only fitful in religion and, anyway, is only one aspect of it. But controversy is the living breath of politics, and Trollope leaves it out altogether. He purposely makes the Duke of Omnium Prime Minister of a Coalition, in which controversy is momentarily quiet. The fact is that Trollope the civil servant despised politicians; the Duke of Omnium is no more than a Treasury official, with an immense sense of rank and a vast income. And so, though we hear in detail of the machinery of Parliament, the intrigues for safe seats, the machinations of the drawing rooms and have an excellent picture of political comedy and humbug, we have no notion of politics as anything more than a career disputed between the "ins" and the "outs."

It infuriated Trollope to see that Disraeli's political novels were more highly thought of than his own. He wrote of them:

> Through it all there is a feeling of stage properties, a smell of hair oil, an aspect of buhl, a remembrance of tailors, and that pricking of the conscience which must be the general accompaniment of paste diamonds.

Even so, Disraeli's *Sybil* and *Coningsby* are far more convincing as political novels. They burn with the passions of the day and if there is falsity in the lighting, that is an essential political quality. Disraeli presents politics as prophetic dogma; he understands that politics grow out of beliefs, interests and conditions, though they degenerate into expedients. The working class are not excluded as Trollope excludes them; and though Trollope lived in a quieter political period, it can hardly be said that the workers were without voice. Disraeli's vision of politics in his novels was exotic and perhaps no purely English novelist is capable of this, any more than he has been capable of the dialectical fantasies of Shaw; to write well about politics one has got to believe in them in the abstract and to regard them as a possible imaginative world. Trollope hated the idea of such a thing, and in consequence, though he gets the surface brilliantly, he misses the reason for its existence.

Character is the whole interest of Trollope and if his portrait of the Prime Minister, the Duke of Omnium, is meant to be a picture of the perfect gentleman and statesman, it is not idealized nor schematic. The Duke's skin is too thin, he has scruples, he is moody, morose and capable of ducal temper. Though he is in conflict with his wife who gives a fantastic house party—forty guests a night for six weeks, and none to stay more than forty-eight hours; think, says the housekeeper at Gatherum Castle, as if she had Arnold Bennett at her elbow, of the towels and the sheets!—the Duke clearly understands that if she is a woman with no scruples, she is kept straight by her feelings and convictions. And Trollope is expert in crossing the intentions of his people with the accidents of life. The climber Lopez might have got his safe seat, if only the bumptious Major Pountney—"a middle-aged young man"—had not annoyed the Duke on another matter. But we get, I think, a better idea of the political entanglement in the earlier book, *Phineas Finn.* Phineas is not an outsider, and therefore Trollope is in a better temper. He is the ingenious, penniless, handsome young fellow, going into politics against the author's affectionate advice and we are led with him step by step into his career. There are even glances at the Irish Question. We see Phineas funking his first opportunity to speak and making a mess of it when he does get up, full of indignation, on another occasion.

There are shrewd portraits of the Whips—but there is nothing to equal Disraeli's wonderful libelous sketch of Croker—and Trollope knows how to grade his politicians according to the condition of their careers. There is a hostile portrait of John Bright. He is Turnbull who is contrasted with Monk, an imaginary Radical "ever doubting of himself, and never doubting himself so much as when he had been most violent and also most effective, in debate." But Turnbull-Bright has no doubts:

> I think that when once he had learned the art of arranging his words as he stood on his legs, and had so mastered his voice as to have obtained the ear of the House, the work of his life was not difficult. Having nothing to construct he could always

> deal with generalities. Being free from responsibility, he was not called upon either to study details or to master even great facts. It was his business to inveigh against existing evils, and perhaps there is no easier business. . . . It was his work to cut down forest trees, and he had nothing to do with the subsequent cultivation of the land. Mr. Monk had once told Phineas Finn how great were the charms of that inaccuracy which was permitted to the opposition.

That is all very well, but the very irony at the expense of politicians shows the failure to rise to the imaginative opportunity. As Mr. Amery says, Disraeli would have plunged for the excitements of foreign policy. He would have risked.

Indeed, although *Phineas Finn* is an amusing guide to Parliamentary life as it then was, it interests us really for things like the famous portraits of the violent red-eyed Lord Chiltern—this plunging, dangerous man would be the hero of a contemporary novel, not a minor character—the superb Mr. Kennedy, so gloomy, so evangelical, who adroitly lengthens family prayers when he is jealous of his wife's lover:

> [He] was a man who had very little temptation to do anything wrong. He was possessed of over a million and a half of money, which he was mistaken enough to suppose he had made himself. . . . He never spoke much to anyone, although he was constantly in society. He rarely did anything, though he had the means of doing everything. He had seldom been on his legs in the House of Commons, though he had been there ten years. He was seen about everywhere, sometimes with one acquaintance, sometimes with another—but it may be doubted whether he had any friend . . . though he would not lend money, he gave a great deal—and he would give it for almost every object. "Mr. Rbt. Kennedy, M.P., £105" appeared

> on almost every charitable list that was advertised. No one ever spoke to him as to this expenditure, nor did he ever speak to anyone. Circulars came to him and the cheques were returned. The duty was an easy one to him and he performed it willingly. Had any moment of inquiry been necessary it is possible the labour would have been too much for him.

That is a close study of something not often observed: the neutrality, the nonentity of rich men. And then there are the women of the book who all talk so well and who are very well distinguished from each other. The stress on sex in the modern novel has meant that women have lost their distinctiveness as persons. Trollope excels in making the distinctions clear.

Trollope is a detailed, rather cynical observer of a satisfied world. Honest, assertive, sensible, shrewd, good-humored, he is content. As Henry James said, he gives us the pleasure of recognition. But content is, so to speak, a summit that he has attained, not a torpor into which he has fallen. He grew worldliness like a second skin over the raw wounds of his youth, and the reason why he describes what is normally observable about people so well, is that he longed merely for the normal. He had been too insecure to want anything more than that security, and it was by a triumph of personal character that he attained it. Trollope might excusably have become a neurotic—and without talent. It is maddening to see the themes of Henry James taken back to the platitude of their starting point and left there; strange to have to recognize that what are called "things as they are" can be soothing. It is dangerous to marry for money, but it is also dangerous to marry for love; it is dangerous to commit adultery for society will drop you, yet society is greedy and hypocritical. It is bad to borrow; it is mean not to lend. One is listening to human nature muddling along on its old rules of thumb. The only pattern we can discern is that made by the struggle of the individual within his group: politics, the law, the Church. It is not a passionate struggle. It is mainly a question of faintly enlightened self-interest. We feel about his people what we feel about our relatives: the curiosity that distracts us from a fundamental apathy. The sense of danger and extremity which alert us in the warlike compositions of Jane Austen, is dulled. His novels are social history, without the movements of history; life as we see it without having to think about it. It has no significance beyond itself; it is as pleasant, dull and restful as an afternoon in an armchair. The footpads in the London parks, the frightened family of the crooked bankrupt, the suicide on the suburban line, are there, not to frighten us unduly, but to give further assurance to normal people that normality is stronger than ever. Can we wonder, in these times, at the Trollope revival?

A VICTORIAN SON

The Way of All Flesh is one of the time bombs of literature. One thinks of it lying in Butler's desk at Clifford's Inn for thirty years, waiting to blow up the Victorian family and with it the whole great pillared and balustraded edifice of the Victorian novel. The book Thackeray failed to write in *Pendennis* had at last been written. After Butler we look back upon a scene of devastation. A spiritual slum has been cleared, yet one is not entirely heartened. Was that the drawing room where mamma daydreamed about marrying off her daughters to the school friends of her sons? Was that the fireplace where papa warmed the seat of his trousers and worked up the power politics of godly inertia? Did guilty sons go up those stairs? Did catty sisters hiss from those landings and aunts conduct their warfare of headaches and slammed drawers in those upper rooms? Yes, says Samuel Butler, this was Heartbreak House. Yet not all of his very few admirers agreed with him. Butler writes to Miss Savage in 1883 when the book was circulating in manuscript:

> "Mr. Heatherley said I had taken all the tenderest feelings of our nature and, having spread them carefully on the floor, stamped upon them till I had reduced them to an indistinguishable mass of filth, and then handed them round for inspection."

I think it must be agreed that at least Butler spread them on the floor. Now that the floor has collapsed twice in a generation we begin to wonder whether it is still the best place for them; whether Norman Douglas was not right when he said, in *South Wind,* that Butler lacked the male attributes of humility, reverence and sense of proportion?

As Irish life runs to secret societies, so English life seems to run naturally to parricide movements. We are a nation of father haters. *The Way of All Flesh* assuaged a thirst which, one supposes, began with the law of primogeniture and the disinheritance of younger sons. In the working class which gets little material start in life from its parents and which has to support them and house them in their old age, the obsession is noticeably rare. The normal human desire seems to be to bite the hand that feeds us, and not the hand we feed. But one has only to compare the quarrels of fathers and sons in, say, the eighteenth-century theatre, with Butler's development of the theme, to see a private struggle turning into a national disease. The thunder of the eighteenth-century father as he is helped out of the coach toward the trembling figure of a young scapegrace who has rejected one heiress in order to abduct another and prettier one, comes from a Jupiter engorged (by the generosity of nature) with biological authority and the gout. The eighteenth-century father is a pagan bursting a blood vessel in the ripeness of time; the nineteenth-century father is a Jehovah dictating an inexhaustible Deuteronomy. Money, as Butler saw, makes the difference; and money, in the nineteenth century, is very different from money in the eighteenth century. Fortune, the speculator's goddess—not money—pours out its plenty from the South Sea bubbles and the slave trade in the eighteenth century. Sacks of gold descend from heaven by fantastic parachute, and are stored in the gloating caves, and trade is still spacious and piratical. How different is the nineteenth century, when Economics appears as a regulated science. With the rise of industrialism, Fortune has given place to cash, cash has become Consols and debentures. Investment does not float down from on high. It seeps in, it is secreted, it accumulates. Its accumulation gives birth to new laws of property and these become moral laws and obtain divine sanction. Investment is a token of energy and a huge will to power, and the fathers who exerted this will expected their families to run like the machines that were making their money.

The Way of All Flesh struck this system at its most vulnerable points: its sentiment, its priesthood and their myth. Butler ignored questions of justice and went for the enfeeblement of religious life and the paralysis which crept upon the emotions. The Musical Banks of *Erewhon* pour out a useless coinage, and when Ernest Pontifex kneels in prayer he fails to save either the souls of the poor, who have no time for him, or his own investments. He is useless to God and Mammon, and to offend Mammon is as serious, for Butler, as to offend God, for Mammon is so much richer in vitality and meaning than the stuffed Anglican God. But what Butler really opposed to Victorianism was not the sort of responsibility we would oppose to it; Butler opposed a system and its myth not with another system but with the claims of human personality. Against Victorianism he placed himself; himself with both feet on the ground, telescope to blind eye and in perverse self-possession, against people whose dreary will to power—and whose hold on spiritual and material property as well—had dried the sap of sense and life.

We cannot think of Butler without the Butleriana. We always come back to Butler as a man. We come back to the undigested slice of rebel egotism. Full of theories himself, he is constantly leaving the ranks of the specialists and joining the amateur ranks of the human beings. George Eliot may be all very fine, but he has bought a dictionary in order to read *Daniel Deronda* in the original! Now this is not nineteenth century at all. To start with, there is no ambition in it; and the more one thinks of him and his failure to fit in, the more one feels he is not a prophet, or at any rate not the prophet of Mr. Shaw's invention. On the contrary, he is a sport or throwback. He looks more and more like a throwback to the eighteenth century. His science—with its affection for Buffon—smacks of it. That science, one suspects, is a rather literary science. His literary antecedents suggest the eighteenth century, too. *The Way of All Flesh* by its egocentricity, its very flatness and discursiveness, calls to mind the autobiographies of the eighteenth century, things like the *Autobiography* of Gibbon.

The genius of that age was to display a man to the full and yet to contain him within some intellectual assumption. The worldliness, the curiosity, the plainness, the tolerance, the irony, the comeliness of the eighteenth century are qualities which *The Way of All Flesh* revives. Not wholly so, for he was kicking irritably against the pricks; but he leapfrogs over the backs of the Victorians to alight beside the author of *Jonathan Wild* and *Amelia*—those novels in which Fielding was especially concerned with the moral and financial illusions of the virtuous. Butler would be at home in the cudgeling matches of Johnson or in Swift's dry and incinerating indignations. *Erewhon* is a straight descendant of *Gulliver*—a poorer book because it lacks savagery and the sublime, plain figure of Gulliver himself—it is no fellow to a mild book like *News from Nowhere*. Where, but in Swift or Fielding, shall we find the suave parallel to this passage from *The Way of All Flesh:*

> "It seems to me," he continued, "that the family is a survival of the principle which is more logically embodied in the compound animal—and the compound animal is a form of life which has been found incompatible with high development. I would do with the family among mankind what nature has done with the compound animal, and confine it to the lower and less progressive races. Certainly there is no inherent love for the family system on the part of nature herself. Poll the forms of life and you will find it in a ridiculously small minority. The fishes know it not and they get along quite nicely. The ants and the bees, who far outnumber man, sting their fathers to death as a matter of course, and are given to the atro-

cious mutilation of nine-tenths of the offspring committed to their care, yet where shall we find communities more universally respected? Take the cuckoo again—is there any bird which we like better?"

Shooting out his hatred and his contradictions, taking back his hatred with laughter, begging us, like Montaigne, to get our dying done as we go along, Butler is certainly an attempt at a rotund man, even though we know that the common-sense view of life is so often a refuge of the injured and the timid, and is neighbor to the conventional.

One's criticism is that the priggishness of Butler, rather than the roundness, gets into the characters of *The Way of All Flesh.* We must except Butler's working-class characters, those collector's pieces, like Mrs. Jupp, the landladies, charladies and servants. A novelist picks those up as he goes along. It is the great weakness of *The Way of All Flesh* that the characters are dwarfed and burned dry by Butler's argument. They are often very tedious. He chose them for their mediocrity and then cursed them for it. They can't stand up to his tweakings. Here Miss Savage was a sound critic when she pointed out the dangers of his special pleading; and although one can feel the years ripening the book, one ends with the feeling that Ernest Pontifex does not amount to much. Why should he come into his fortune? Merely that the unrighteous should have their reward? One does not feel that Ernest has very deeply developed because of suffering or fortune. He has escaped only. And he seems rather lost without his enemy. The weakness is that Butler is doing all the talking. There is no contradictory principle. Ultimately the defense of orthodoxy, even an orthodoxy as dim as Theobald's, is the knowledge of human passions. The strange thing is that Ernest does not give us the impression of a man who enjoys himself; he sounds like a man whose hedonism is a prig's hygiene. He looks like becoming the average bachelor of the room marked Residents Only.

One would give anything to have met Butler. For Ernest, Butler's shadow, one cares very little. Unlike Butler he does not act; because of the necessities of the book he is acted upon. His indiscretions are passive. He has no sins; he has merely follies. Still, Butler made more of a hand of self-portraiture in this reminiscence than Thackeray made of Arthur Pendennis and Butler seems to have learned from Thackeray's disquisitional method. These two misfit novelists, born a hundred years too late, have many things in common. Christina is another Amelia from the latter pages of *Vanity Fair*, but filled out with richer comic truth. Her ruthless daydreams are wonderful, her play-acting diplomacy is observed with wicked affection. She is one of those mothers whose right breast never lets on what the left breast is feeling. We are given the great Jekyll and Hyde masquerade of the female bosom:

> As regards Ernest, the suspicions which had already crossed her mind were deepened, but she thought it better to leave the matter where it was. At present she was in a very strong position. Ernest's official purity was firmly established, but at the same time he had shown himself so susceptible that she was able to fuse two contradictory impressions concerning him into a single idea and consider him as a kind of Joseph and Don Juan in one. This was what she had wanted all along, but her vanity being gratified by the possession of such a son, there was an end of it; the son himself was naught.

"The matter" she was "leaving," as the reader will remember, was a maternal plot to make him betray his friends. The paragraph goes on just as penetratingly into the male version of this kind of humbug:

"No doubt if John had not interfered Ernest would have had to expiate his offense with ache, penury and imprisonment. As it was the boy was 'to consider himself' as undergoing these punishments. . . ."

One is made to feel the pathos of human jealousies, hatreds and humbug. One is tricked into forgetting that they are inevitable. Butler believed that living, like money, should be in the foreground of human life and not an anxiety in its background. He hated the efficient mechanic doctrine, the mechanistic science and (as one sees in *Erewhon*) the machine with its stereotyped response. He pitied the conscious Ernest who toes the line and tried to inflame in Ernest the healthy sabotage of the unconscious. What, strangely enough, Butler failed to find, in this early introduction of the unconscious into English fiction, was the passion. It was odd going to the unconscious and finding there —what? That chronic perversity: common sense.

A PLYMOUTH BROTHER

The reaction from puritanism has been so strong and general in the last forty years or more that we too easily assume the extreme forms of it are dying. I do not believe they are. One kind of puritanism goes, after a long battle, and a new one takes its place. In an irreligious age, puritanism simply becomes scientific or political. Or it becomes a severe, exclusive addiction to psychological method. We may suppose that the Plymouth Brethren are a declining sect; but their place is taken by new international sects like the Jehovah's Witnesses, and this group is manifestly on the increase. It is not difficult to see why. The attack on science, the attack on social and political effort, does not affect the educated alone; it is eagerly followed by the ignorant and powerless. And then there are more intimate attractions. Extreme puritanism gives purpose, drama and intensity to private life. One of the greatest mistakes which the genial critics of puritanism make is to suppose that puritanism seen from the outside is the same as puritanism seen from the inside. Outwardly the extreme puritan appears narrow, crabbed, fanatical, gloomy and dull; but from the inside—what a series of dramatic climaxes his life is, what a fascinating casuistry beguiles him, how he is bemused by the comedies of duplicity, sharpened by the ingenious puzzles of the conscience, and carried away by the eloquence of hypocrisy. He lives like a soldier, now in the flash of battle, now in the wangling of camp and billet. However much he may bore others, he never suffers from boredom himself.

That distress eats into the lives of the children of the puritans. Puritanism burns up the air and leaves a vacuum for its descendants. When we read Edmund Gosse's *Father and Son* which describes the remarkable life of a family of Plymouth Brethren, we see that an insufferable ennui drove the son from his father's faith. Extreme peculiarity in a religious sect is exciting, even stimulating and enlarging to a child; it isolates him, and in doing so gives him a heady importance, an enormous lead (in some respects) over his more orthodox fellows. But the experience is too fierce. It creates that "chaffiness"—so quickly burned out—which the early Quakers were always talking about. The real reason for the boredom to come lies in that war against the imagination which all puritan sects—the political and scientific it should be observed, as well as the religious—have undertaken. Sir Edmund Gosse's parents would not allow their child to read or hear stories. Fact, yes; but stories were not true, therefore they were lies. The young Gosse, whose father was a scientist, was familiar with birds, insects, the creatures of the sea, and with books of scientific travel; but he had never heard of Jack the Giant Killer or Little Red Riding Hood.

> So far as my "dedication" was concerned [he writes] I can but think that my parents were in error thus to exclude the imaginary from my outlook upon facts. They desired to make me truthful; the tendency was to make me positive and sceptical. Had they wrapped me in the soft folds of supernatural fancy my mind might have been longer content to follow their traditions in an unquestioning spirit.

Yet it would be hard to call the elder Gosse a totally unimaginative man. As a scientist he was unimaginative, and so nipped the promise of his own intellect and career; but as a religious man he was riotously imaginative. He lived in the Eastern imagery of the Bible; he believed in it literally; he apprehended the instant end of the world and prepared himself for a literal flight upwards into the air toward the arms of the angels. His was simply an intense and narrow imagination. And there is a comment by the son here which is very suggestive. We might assume that Gosse senior was a typical middle-class Victorian scientist and Nonconformist, presumably conditioned by his class and his age and bent on the general purpose of practical self-improvement; but, as the son points out, the father's religious life really sprang from a far earlier period. Gosse senior was not a nineteenth-century man; his Calvinism had survived, intact, from the seventeenth century. Conduct, which meant everything to the nineteenth-century man, meant little to the elder Gosse; vision, the condition of grace, was everything. Later on, when the boy grew up and went to live in London, the father was worried very little by what the boy did; but was in agony about what he might think or feel. Was he still a dedicated soul, had he fallen from grace? To such questions the elder Gosse might bring the exhausting and pettifogging inquiry of a lawyer, rather than the imaginative anxiety of the religious mystic; but the attitude, as the son says, is nearer Bunyan's or Jeremy Taylor's than it is to the nineteenth century.

In our talk about environment we too easily assume that people living in the same time, in the same place, under the same conditions, are alike in their responses. We forget the time lags, the overlaps, the sports and faults of history. It is surprising to find that American travelers to London in Victorian times saw an eighteenth-century city. We detect such lags and fixations in nations which are far enough away, in the Germans, the Spaniards, the Irish. We do not so easily detect them in private life. What was it that prolonged the seventeenth-century stamp upon the elder Gosse? A possible explanation is that, on both sides, the family was a genteel one of steadily declining fortune, and no family is more tenacious of the past, more prone to fixation than the declining family. We have only to compare Gosse's quarrel with Butler's to see the difference between two contemporaries. Gosse was fortunate; for Butler's nineteenth-century father had become a kind of practical Jehovah who thrashed prayer and Latin into his son indifferently. Gosse never hated his father. There was a break, a tragic and passionate break, not a clash of wills so much as a division of principles; and, since the breach was tragic, its agony was without resentment. Butler and his father, in their common hatred, were vituperative to the end; the Gosses gazed helplessly, emotionally across the gulf of history between them. Centuries separated them. The violence of the revolutionary nineteenth century did not possess them; and so it was the scorn, the satire and hatred of Butler and not the scrupulous, unavailing sympathy and impartial regret of Gosse that were to whip up the violent reaction against the Victorian family, and especially the Victorian father.

Gosse's attitude to his father is acquiescent and almost Gibbonian. If Gosse's imagination had been fed in childhood he might have used his father as a starting point for one of those imaginative libels, like Dickens's portrait of Micawber, which are fatherhood's vicarious and unwilling gift to literature. But from Gosse, the ex-puritan and melodious prig, we get instead a positive, literal, skeptical document. What an incredible story the mere facts make. Nothing fixes the fantastic note like the episode of the moth. The naturalist, his wife and his child were at prayer one morning in 1855:

> . . . when through the open window a brown moth came sailing. My mother immediately interrupted the reading of the Bible by saying to my father, "Oh, Henry, do you think that can be *Boletobia?*" My father rose up from the sacred book, examined the insect, which had now perched, and replied "No! It is only the common *Vapourer Orgyia antiqua!*" resuming his seat and the exposition of the Word, without any apology or embarrassment.

I said earlier that Gosse senior could not be called unimaginative, but as the son points out, he was certainly deficient in sympathetic imagination. In one sense his fanatical religion was scientific, an exhaustive classification and checking up. There was, for example, the question of Prophecy. The father said that no small element in his wedded happiness had been the fact that he and his wife were of one mind in the interpretation of Sacred prophecy. They took to it as profane families take to cards or the piano. They played with the Book of Revelation as if it were Happy Families or Snap:

> When they read of seals broken and of vials poured forth, of the star which was called Wormwood that fell from Heaven, and of men whose hair was as the hair of women, and their teeth as the teeth of lions, they did not admit for a moment that these vivid mental pictures were of a poetic character, but they regarded them as positive statements, in guarded language, describing events which were to happen, and could be recognized when they did happen. It was the explanation, the perfectly prosaic and positive explanation, of all these wonders which drew them to study the Habershons and the Newtons whose books they so much enjoyed. They were helped by these guides to recognize in wild Oriental visions direct statements regarding Napoleon III and Pope Pius IX, and the King of Piedmont, historic figures which they conceived as foreshadowed, in language which admitted of plain interpretation, under the names of denizens of Babylon and companions of the Wild Beast.

The conviction that the last days of the queenly arrogance of Rome had come so affected Gosse's mother that her husband wrote in his diary that it "had irradiated her dying hours with an assurance that was like the light of the Morning Star." As the years went slowly by—and how slowly they passed for the bored and ailing child who was expected to live at this pitch—it began to dawn on him that there was something incredibly trivial about such convictions. The elder Gosse could swallow one Eliot's stuff about prophecy and yet reject Darwin. He was an educated man, yet he could say that Shakespeare, Marlowe and Ben Jonson endangered the soul and that Dickens was preferable to Scott "because Dickens showed love in a ridiculous light." The child of such a man was obliged to develop two selves. One assented, got itself publicly baptized and dedicated at the age of ten, and confounded the wise with his theology and unction; the other quietly built up a very different mind—and as the sons of puritans will—an inveterate irony. This came out at the time when his father was thinking of marrying again. The father (the child sharply detected) was put, for once, in the position of the penitent. One was required, the child remembered, "to testify in season and out of season." Was the lady (he therefore asked) "one of the Lord's children"? Had she, he pressed, "taken up her cross in baptism"? The father had to admit that the lady had been brought up in the "so-called Church of England." "Papa," said the little prig, wagging his finger, "don't tell me that she's a pedobaptist?"

Gosse was encouraged to draw this portrait by the revolt of the times. He was faced by the difficulty that at the moments when narrow or peculiar religion is behaving most ludicrously, it is also providing its adherents with emotions or intentions that one must respect. Nothing could have been more intellectually disgraceful and spiritually disastrous than the boy's public dedication; nothing more dingily farcical; or more humiliating when one considers that Gosse's father was, after all, an educated man. Yet one must respect the emotions that the participant felt. There is, as Gosse said, something comic and tragic, really tragic, in the theme. On a similar subject Mark Twain became savage; he was driven to a kind of insulting nihilism. Gosse, in the end, was rather more bored than outraged by his father, for he understood the defect of character that had caused the malady. He saw that the sin was the denial of the imagination and the pestering of the judgment. He saw that, at the time of the Darwin crisis, his father had really sold his intellect and perhaps his soul. That flight to Devonshire was a flight from the society of his equals, who would challenge his faith every day, into a society of rustics who could be guaranteed to swallow everything he said. We smile with amusement and irony at the two figures; the father examining his insects under the naturalist's microscope, the son applying the lens of the biographer and producing one of the most brilliant specimens of his century.

GRUB STREET

"Gissing: the English Gorky with a butterfly collar," says Mr. G. W. Stonier in his introduction to *New Grub Street.* Moscow, transmuted, becomes Camberwell and is lamed. It is as well to remember the Russian quality of our very suburban novelist for, like Meredith and Disraeli, Gissing brings an alien's or exile's unconventional insight into English society. They are all self-created foreigners: Disraeli, the Jew;

Meredith with his German education and his Welsh illusions; Gissing living abroad in dreams of Renaissance man and the Greek classics while he listens to the Museum cough in the Reading Room of Great Russell Street. (A scholar, Gissing must be one of our few novelists who is also a linguist; he spoke French perfectly, read German and Italian easily, beside the classical tongues. He knew some Spanish and attempted Russian.) One sees what moods and material the English novel has lost in being written by Englishmen; that is to say, by those Englishmen who, in Mr. Stonier's good phrase, could "only dramatize their own self-satisfactions." And we recall that the great Russian novels of the nineteenth century arose from the failure of a class, whereas the English sprang out of its success.

Gissing's failure and his exile are the cause of his fame. We are driven back, as always with imperfect artists, to the entanglement of the person and his work. As Mr. Walter Allen has pointedly said in *The English Novel* the fiction of Gissing is "too personal, the powerful expression of a grudge." No other English novelist until then had had a chip the size of Gissing's; self-pitying, spiritless, resentful, humorless, his lucid bleat drags down his characters and his words. There is a disturbing complacency in him as he stands at the sink and tells us that life is wretched and defeating, and many an indignant reader must have felt that Gissing was myopic. Like the young Jasper Milvain in *New Grub Street* he seems to raise his chin and talk to the upper air when talking about himself. And then, like many men whose life is shut in by unbelievable domestic wretchedness, Gissing was self-centered and did not recognize that, if one is going in for this sort of thing, one had better open one's eyes and recognize that life is not merely dreary and miserable; it is savagely cruel and utterly appalling. Gissing wrote less of the horror he knew than of the apathy which it engendered. He writes as if he were a mere effect. To return to Mr. Stonier:

> One need only lose oneself in London or in the similar streets of any large town, to experience the monotony of anguish uppermost in Gissing. He respects the low affront, not hurrying, in imagination, to overpaint it with bright colors; the life behind windows does not grow comic or enormous; distance lends no enchantment, and no music steals up the gutters to transform what is into what is not. He lacks the fairy or imp of entertainment; but as the bias of fiction writing goes, that is not such a disadvantage. He cannot help seeing plain, being faithful, taking the bad tooth into account.

Gissing is very Russian in his overpowering sense of the stale and unoccupied hours we have to lug around with us and this is his peculiar importation into the English novel.

Today, Mr. Walter Allen's suggestion of the grudge is more interesting. In some ways the grudge of several of our young novelists resembles Gissing's, as if Gissing were their perverse prophet and progenitor. There are hints of it in all his work and it is particularly strong in *New Grub Street.* The grudge is concerned with education and opportunity. It has two aspects. Why pass an Education Act, giving clever Board School boys the chance to become cultivated men when they will only find themselves in stultifying and unseemly surroundings and without the means to live in some accord with their minds; and why educate ordinary boys so that they can become the customers for everything that is vulgar and trivial in popular, commercial culture? When Gissing wrote *New Grub Street* the new journalism with its obsession with things like "What the Queen Eats" was showing its first signs.

Now, it is easy to show that either the competitive instinct or the reforming spirit of social conscience—both of which Gissing lacked—were required of the clever Board School boy in return for his privilege. Gissing resented that only the rich could join the Past. For the unclever, Gissing had somehow got the idea (as Mr. Walter Allen says) that the aim of education was merely to teach people to read books. He was the scornful scholarship winner. (He appears to make one exception in his dislike of the new journalism; in its higher forms of popularization it educates women. One recognizes here the man who suffered from the tongues of ignorant viragoes.)

The grudge of Gissing is the grudge of the outsider. He shows this psychological characteristic in his attitude to the prostitute and the servant girl he married. The violence in these vicious women is really matched, not by the passivity of his temperament, but by what one suspects to be the isolation and ruthlessness of his own mind. Morley Roberts, in his disguised biography of Gissing, now happily issued with a key, believed that Gissing simply desired the whole sex and, in his self-imposed loneliness and incapable of love, thought anyone would do. One has the horrible suspicion that he felt punishment justified him and so set him free. But—to get on more certain ground—Gissing was an outsider in rejecting modern society altogether because it did not provide a place for the recalcitrant scholar and the pure artist who was poor. The theme of *New Grub Street* is the tragedy of the intellectual worker. The book is a full conspectus of the literary situation done with Gissing's gray exactitude and clarity. The vulgar comic view of writers as a collection of eccentrics is dropped; he catches their fundamental dignity, anxiety and egotism. It is bad enough to be an artist, with its appalling gift of self-knowledge, without being obliged to kill the love of your wife, slave till you are blind, and end ill, half-starved and counting the pennies, behind the tightly drawn curtains of lower-middle-class respectability. The portrait of the wretched, gifted and only moderately salable Reardon in this book is masterly, for Gissing is unremitting in observation. Without money a James or a Shaw would just as certainly go down to the smell of last night's dinner in the seedy backroom. Gissing's simple description of the writer's day as he sits at his desk is exact, touching and terrifying; one feels half-elated, half-sickened at the end of it. For, allowing for one deficiency in Reardon's character, the morbid lack of will, the portrait would serve for any novelist.

Those who have the grudge nowadays have, of course, no interest in Gissing's concept of the artist or in his belief in the culture he belongs to. All the same, the conditions of literary society have not changed much since Gissing's times. Journalism, with its short-term shots of success, its weekly injection, still offers its therapy to the writer who can stand the ulcers and suicidal depressions of creative writing no more. Inflation and high taxation have wiped out the rewards of the successful and have reduced the less successful to the role of commentators frantic for a new slant. Our society will reward highly any writer who agrees to compound on his gifts and abandon them. A creative writer must have time. In Gissing's day he had time but little money and, after the first successful start, the lack of money ate into the time. Still, the little money Gissing had was his and he lived in a low-cost society. In our high-cost society we have money, but a large portion of it goes back to the State and we may not invest in our talent. In consequence, we have no time.

Morley Roberts, who was an intimate of Gissing, thought that he shared with most English novelists the ability to create situation and the inability to develop it owing to the national *mauvaise honte* and dread of feeling. But Gissing excelled, as many have, in irony. Each character is solid in *New Grub Street* and if the dialogue is still and the action is slow, there is nothing wooden in the people. Their temperature is, indeed, low. In their varying ways, they are all afflicted, of course, with Gissing's chronic passivity; but in two instances, in the characters of Reardon's wife Amy, and the young, climbing, versatile journalist Jasper Milvain, he introduces us to two new and disturbing developments of the passive character. Milvain is not passive in his profession; he climbs boldly, cleverly, even engagingly; it is his conscience that is passive. He practices an ingenious technique of self-deception, *i.e.*, he believes that if he is frank about his motives, if he tells the truth, this will clear him of moral obligations. He has the insincerity of the detached. Amy's passivity is feminine, and realistic. She has no will but she drifts with skill. Gissing is unusual among English male novelists in discerning the mental life of his women. Living in an ideal world himself he understood their ideal world. It did not shock him that Amy should resent her husband's failure; and that her love would not stand up to it. It was natural to wish to marry a great man, but it was also natural that, under his influence, she would develop into a creature alien to him and with an intellect of her own. She marries the conscienceless Milvain with her eyes open and with a delicate lack of scruple. Easy enough to make fun of her as a female climber; Gissing sees the comedy but he is detached enough to see she has a right to drift with her self-esteem. She will become genteel. Poverty is over.

When we wince at Gissing's uncritical acceptance of the lower-middle-class dream of gentility and respectability, and at its emblem, the butterfly collar; when we shudder at the tepid, timid ideal world he obtained from classical scholarship, we ought also to point out that he saw people in two troubled phases: as they are and as they would wish to become. To him the individual dream was or could become a serious extension of their emotional range as characters. Indeed, it is out of the soured homes, where dreams have gone bad, or have become ludicrous or catastrophic, that the vitality of this class has sprung. To most English novelists, invigorated but narrowed by class consciousness, one class has always seemed comical to another; that is where Gissing is so un-English, a foreigner or an exile. He sees nothing comic in class. He writes as if it exists chiefly as a pathos or a frustration, a limitation of the human keyboard.

THE SCIENTIFIC ROMANCES

A cloud of dust travels down the flinty road and chokes the glossy Kentish greenery. From the middle of the moving cloud come the ejaculations of an unhandy driver; the clopper of horses' hoofs, the rumble of a wagonette or trap. One catches the flash of a top hat or a boater. One smells horse manure and beer. And one hears that peculiar English spoken by the lower middle class, a language in which the syllable "-ing" either becomes "-ink" or loses its final "g," and which is enlivened by cries of "Crikey" and

"Golly." The accent is despairing, narrow-voweled yet truculent, with something of the cheap-jack and Sunday League in it, and it is broken by a voice, not quite so common, which says things like, "We're not the finished thing. We're jest one of Nature's experiments, see. We're jest the beginning." And then there is a crash. Over goes the wagonette, the party inside hit out with their fists, noses bleed, eyes are blackened. Most surprising, a nearby house catches fire. Do not be alarmed. The time is the late 'nineties and you have simply been watching the outing of a group of early H. G. Wells characters who have become suddenly aware that science is radically changing the human environment. No Frenchified or Russianized fiction this, but plain, cheerful, vulgar, stoic, stupid and hopelessly romantic English. It is as English as the hoardings.

There are always fist fights and fires in the early Wells. Above all, there are fires. They occur, as far as I remember, in all the scientific romances except *The Island of Dr. Moreau*—a very pessimistic book—and are an ingredient of the Wellsian optimism, an optimism whose other name is ruthlessness. There was a time, one realizes, when science was fun. For the food of the gods is more entertaining than the prosaic efficacy of vitamins; the tripods of the Martians are more engaging than tanks. And then, here you have Wells at his best, eagerly displaying the inventive imagination, first with the news and at play, with an artist's innocence. Here you see his intoxicated response—a response that was lacking in his contemporaries—to the front-page situation of his time, and here you meet his mastery of the art of storytelling, the bounce and resource of it. Above all, in these early books, you catch Wells in the act, his very characteristic act, of breaking down mean barriers and setting you free. He has burst out himself and he wants everyone else to do the same. "Why," cries the engineer in *The Food of the Gods*—the poorest of these books—"Why don't we do what we want to do?"

For that matter, I have never read any book by H. G. Wells, early or late, which did not start off by giving me an exhilarating sense of personal freedom. Every inhibition I ever had faded from me as I read. Of course, after such a high, hard bounce one comes down again. The answer to the engineer's question is that we do not do what we want to do because we want to do opposite things at the same time. Yet that infectious Wellsian sense of freedom was not all anarchy, romantic ebullience or Utopian uplift. That freedom was a new fact in our environment; one pays for everything—that is all. I do not know what date is given to the second scientific revolution, but one had to go back to the great centuries of geographical discovery for a comparable enlargement of our world; and it is a suggestive fact that we had to go back to Swift, the Swift of Lilliput and Laputa, before we found another English novelist going to science for his data and material as Wells has done. (The influence of science, in the one hundred fifty years that lie between those two writers, is philosophical, not factual.) Wells's eager recognition of the new environment is one of the sources of the sense of freedom we got from him. I make no comparison of the merits of Wells and Swift—though the Beast-Men of *The Island of Dr. Moreau* are derivatives of the Yahoos and are observed with Swift's care for biological detail—but in his best narratives Wells does go back to the literary traditions of the early eighteenth century, the highest traditions of our narrative literature. The ascendancy of Swift is a question of imaginative range and style; above all it is due to a humanity which is denied to Wells because he arrived at the beginning, the crude beginning, of a new enlargement, whereas Swift arrived toward the end of one. None of Wells's narrators, whether they are South Kensington scientists or people, like the awful Bert, who appear to be suffering from an emotional and linguistic toothache, is capable of the philosophical simplicity and sanity of Gulliver; for Wells has only just spotted this new world of agitating chemicals, peculiar glands, and obliterating machines. The sense of wonder has not grown far beyond a sense of copy. He is topical and unstable, swept by eagerness yet visited by nauseas sudden and horrifying. Suppose we evolve into futility or revert to the beast from which we have arisen? Such speculations are alien to the orthodox eyes which were set in Swift's mad head; he had no eye to the future; the eighteenth century believed in a static world. The things Swift sees *have happened.* To Wells—and how typical of an expanding age—the things he sees have *not* happened. They are possibilities. In these scientific romances one catches occasionally the humane and settled note: in *The Time Machine,* in *The Island of Dr. Moreau* and in *The War of the Worlds,* which are the most imaginative stories of the group and are free of the comic Edwardian horseplay. The practical experiment has been detached from the practical joke; the idea is untainted by the wheeze. The opening sentence of *The War of the Worlds* suggests a settled view of humanity, besides being an excellent example of Wells's mastery of the art of bouncing us into belief in anything he likes to tell us:

> No one would have believed in the last years of the nineteenth century that human affairs were being watched keenly and closely by intelligences greater than man's and yet as mortal as his own.

It is not surprising that the passages of low comedy, which elsewhere are Wells's excellence, should be a failure in the scientific romances. Naturally they break the spell of the illusion with their clumsy realism. And if love is born, Wells is Walt Disney at his worst. The love scenes between the giants in *The Food of the Gods* are the most embarrassing in English fiction, and one wonders that the picture of the awful Princess, goggling in enormous close-up and fanning herself with half a chestnut tree, did not destroy the feminist movement. But except for faint squirms of idyllic petting in *The Time Machine,* none of these aberrations misdirects the narratives of the three books I have mentioned. I cannot include *The War in the Air* among the best; it *is* an astonishing piece of short-term prophecy and judgment. One remembers the bombing of battleships and the note on the untroubled mind of those who bomb one another's cities; but the book is below Wells's highest level. So, too, is *The Invisible Man,* which is a good thriller, but it develops jerkily and is held up by horseplay and low comedy. Without question *The Time Machine* is the best piece of writing. It will take its place among the great stories of our language. Like all excellent works it has meanings within its meaning and no one who has read the story will forget the dramatic effect of the change of scene in the middle of the book, when the story alters its key, and the Time Traveler reveals the foundation of slime and horror on which the pretty life of his Arcadians is precariously and fearfully resting. It is fair to accuse the later Wells of escaping into a dream world of plans, of using science as a magic staircase out of essential social problems. The best Wells is the destructive, ruthless, black-eye-dealing and house-burning Wells who foresaw the violence and not the order of our time. However this may be, the early Wells of *The Time Machine* did not escape. The Arcadians had become as pretty as flowers in their pursuit of personal happiness. They had dwindled and would be devoured because of that. Their happiness itself was haunted. Here Wells's images of horror are curious. The slimy, the viscous, the fetal reappear; one sees the sticky, shapeless messes of pond life, preposterous in instinct and frighteningly without mind. One would like to hear a psychologist on these shapes which recall certain surrealist paintings; but perhaps the biologist fishing among the algae, and not the unconscious, is responsible for them. In *The Time Machine*—and also in the other two books—Wells is aware of pain. None of his investigators returns without wounds and bruises to the mind as well as the body, and Dr. Moreau is, of course, a sadist. *The Island* is hard on the nerves and displays a horror more definite and calculated than anything in Wells's other books. Where *The Time Machine* relieves us by its poetic social allegory, *The Island of Dr. Moreau* takes us into an abyss of human nature. We are left naked at the end of the shocking report, looking with apprehension at the bodies of our friends, imagining the tell-tale short legs, the eyes that shine green in the dark, the reversion to the wolf, the hyena, the monkey and the dog. This book is a superb piece of storytelling from our first sight of the unpleasant ship and its stinking, mangy menagerie, to the last malign episode where the narrator is left alone on the island with the Beast-Men. Neither Dr. Moreau nor his drunken assistant is a lay figure and, in that last episode, the Beast-Men become creatures of Swiftian malignance:

> The Monkey Man bored me, however. He assumed, on the strength of his five digits, that he was my equal, and was forever jabbering at me, jabbering the most arrant nonsense. One thing about him entertained me a little: he had a fantastic trick of coining new words. He had an idea, I believe, that to gabble about names that meant nothing was the proper use of speech. He called it "big thinks," to distinguish it from "little thinks"

> —the sane everyday interests of life. If ever I made a remark he did not understand, he would praise it very much, ask me to say it again, learn it by heart, and go off repeating it, with a word wrong here and there, to all the wilder of the Beast People. He thought nothing of what was plain and comprehensible. I invented some very curious "big thinks" for his especial use.

The description of the gradual break in the morale of the Beast-Men is a wonderful piece of documented guesswork. It is easy enough to be sensational. It is quite another matter to domesticate the sensational. One notices, too, how Wells's idea comes full circle in his best thrillers. There is the optimistic outward journey, there is the chastened return.

It would be interesting to know more about the origins of *The Island of Dr. Moreau,* for they must instruct us on the pessimism and the anarchy which lie at the heart of Wells's ebullient nature. This is the book of a wounded man who has had a sight of sadism and death. The novelist who believed in the cheerful necessity of evolution is halted by the thought of its disasters and losses. Perhaps man is unteachable. It is exciting and emancipating to believe we are one of nature's latest experiments, but what if the experiment is unsuccessful? What if it is unsurmountably unpleasant? Suppose the monkey drives the machine, the gullible, mischievous, riotous and irresponsible monkey? It is an interesting fact that none of Wells's optimistic contemporaries considered such a possibility. Shaw certainly did not. Evil, in Shaw, is curable. He believes in the Protestant effort. He believes that men *argue* their way along the path of evolution, and that the life force is always on the side of the cleverest mind and the liveliest conscience. When he reflects on the original monkey, Shaw cannot resist the thought that the monkey was a shrewd animal going up in the world, and Shaw feels a patronizing pride in him which the self-made man may feel about the humble ancestor who gave him his start in life. There is certainly no suggestion that he will ever lose his capital, which is civilization, and revert. There is no thought, in this quintessential Irish Protestant, that the original monkey may be original sin. Nor could there be: the doctrine of original sin is a device of the emotions, and about our emotions Shaw knows absolutely nothing at all. But to the emotional Wells, the possibility of original sin in the form of the original monkey is always present. The price of progress may be perversion and horror, and Wells is honest enough to accept that. Shaw appears to think we can evade all painful issues by a joke, just as Chesterton, the Catholic optimist of his generation, resolved serious questions by a series of puns.

Wells can be wounded. It is one of his virtues. One is reminded of Kipling, another wounded writer—was Wells satirizing Kipling in that chapter of *The Island of Dr. Moreau* where the Beast-Men are seen mumbling their pathetic Law?—and Kipling and Wells are obviously divergent branches of the same tree. Wells the Utopian, Kipling the patriot—they represent the daydream of the lower middle class which will either turn to socialism or fascism. Opposed in tendency, Wells and Kipling both have the vision of artists; they foresee the conditions of our time. They both foretell the violence with a certain appetite. Crudity appeals to them. They are indifferent or badhearted, in human relations. They understand only personal independence which, from time to time, in their work is swallowed up in mass relationships. In the final count, Kipling—like Wells's man in the sewer in *The War of the Worlds*—falls back on animal cunning. It is the knowing, tricky, crafty animal that survives by lying low and saying nothing. Kipling, for all his admiration of power, believes in the neurotic, the morbid and defeated mind. This strain is in Wells also, but he has more private stoicism than Kipling has, a stoicism which blossoms from time to time into a belief in miracles and huge strokes of luck. Impatient of detail, mysteriously reticent about the immediate practical steps we must take to ensure any of his policies, Wells believes—like Kipling—in magic: a magic induced by impudence or rebellion. Wells and Kipling—these two are light and shadow to each other.

Wells's achievement was that he installed the paraphernalia of our new environment in our imagination; and life does not become visible or tolerable to us until artists have assimilated it. We do not need to read beyond these early scientific works of his to realize what he left out. The last war, whose conditions he so spryly foresaw, has made that deficiency clear. When we read those prophetic accounts of mechanized warfare and especially of air bombardment, we must be struck by one stupendous misreading of the future. It occurs where we should expect it to occur: in the field of *morale*. Wells imagined cities destroyed and the inhabitants flying in terror. He imagined the soldiers called out to keep order and the conditions of martial law and total anarchy. He imagined mass terror and riot. He did not reckon with the nature, the moral resources, the habits of civilized man. Irresponsible himself, he did not attribute anything but an obstructive value to human responsibility. That is a serious deficiency, for it indicates an ignorance of the rooted, inner life of men and women, a jejune belief that we live by events and programs; but how, in the heyday of a great enlargement of the human environment, could he believe otherwise? We turn back to our Swift and there we see a mad world also; but it is a mad world dominated by the sober figure of the great Gulliver, that plain, humane figure. Not a man of exquisite nor adventurous spirituality; not a great soul; not a man straining all his higher faculties to produce some new mutation; not a man trying to blow himself out like the frog of the fable to the importunate dimensions of his program; but, quite simply, a man. Endowed with curiosity, indeed, but empowered by reserve. Anarchists like Wells, Kipling, Shaw and the pseudo-orthodox Chesterton, had no conception of such a creature. They were too fascinated by their own bombs.

THE FIVE TOWNS

It is a long time now since the earth seemed solid under the feet to our novelists, since caprice, prophecy, brains and vividness meant less than the solid substance of time and place. And Arnold Bennett, in books like *The Old Wives' Tale* and *The Clayhanger Family*, seems to be the last of the novel's four-square gospelers. I return to him often and always, once I get into him, with satisfaction. A book like *The Clayhanger Family* has the sobriety as well as the tedium of a detailed engraving; and there is, oddly, enough of the connoisseur in Bennett to induce our taste. He is not a dilettante in the ego's peculiarities and he is without interest in elegance; he is the connoisseur of normality, of the ordinary, the awkward, an heir—one might say—of the makers of the Staffordshire figures who thought Moody and Sankey as good a subject as equestrian princes of the blood. We speak of the disciplines of belief, of art, of the spirit; Bennett speaks of the discipline of life itself, reveres its frustrations, does not rebel against them; kneels like some pious behavior to the drab sight of reflexes in process of being conditioned. He catches the intolerable passing of time in our lives, a passing which blurs our distinctiveness and quietly establishes our anonymity; until our final impression of him is as a kind of estate agent's valuer walking with perfunctory step through the rooms of our lives, ticking his inventory and treating us as if we were long deceased. He cannot begin—and I think this is his inheritance from the French Naturalists—until we are dead, until we and our furniture have become indistinguishable evidence. I find this very restful. Frustration—*pace* H. G. Wells—is one of the normal conditions of life, and calming is the novelist who does not kick against the pricks.

Fidelity and sincerity are the words one puts first to Arnold Bennett's work. Some years ago there appeared an anthology called *The English in Love*, containing love passages from the English novelists, and I was much struck by the superiority of Bennett's contribution to the work of specialists like Meredith and D. H. Lawrence. Bennett was not describing passion; but against his quiet exactitude and sincerity, the lyricists looked forced and trite. The very matter-of-factness of Bennett made him one of the best portrayers of women we have had. The vices of romanticism or of misogynist satire passed him by in his best work completely. What other words come to mind when we think of him? They are his own words: "detracting" is one, "chicane"—a great favorite—is another; but there is a sentence in the early pages of *The Clayhanger Family* which contains a volume of criticism on him. He is writing of young Edwin Clayhanger coming home from his last day at school in the Five Towns: "It seemed rather a shame," Bennett says of Edwin, "it seemed even tragic, that this naïve, simple creature, immaculate of worldly experience, must soon be transformed into a man wary, incredulous and detracting." The essence of Bennett's mind is packed into that awkward sentence with its crick in the neck at the feeble beginning and the giveaway of its three final words. Bennett had borrowed the manner and methods of the French Naturalists without being seriously formed by the scientific, political and philosophical ideas which made them Naturalists and gave them their driving force. Timidity rather than conviction is behind the brevity of his address. The result is that the apostle of will, efficiency and success appears to us hesitant and uncertain; he is between two stools; he cannot make up his mind whether life is "rather a shame" or "tragic." And when you compare *The Clayhanger Family* with the contemporary French *Les Thibaults* —which, like *Clayhanger,* contains a prolonged study in fatal illness and is also concerned with the relation of father and son—you feel at once, though you recognize the conscious artist, Bennett's lack of imaginative stamina and resilience. What Bennett observes will be truthfully, almost litigiously, observed. Hazard will set the points wrongly in the lives of humdrum people and push them off the rails. Time will get its teeth into them more deeply year by year. We shall feel, as Edwin felt, that we must "brace ourselves to the exquisite burden of life." We shall feel we are interpenetrated "by the disastrous yet beautiful infelicity of things." What we shall miss is the sense that life is conceived of as anything in particular, whether it be the force that makes the Five Towns or forms the bleak impetuosity of Hilda Lessways. We shall not feel that life is much more than a random collection of *things*.

Admitting the absence of a frame, allowing for some lagging of narrative which the modern novelist would speed up, everything else in *Clayhanger* is good. Bennett, as I have said, was the connoisseur of the normal, the ordinary and the banal. Where other novelists add, he—as he said—detracted. For example, how easy for the novelist to identify himself with the sixteen-year-old Edwin and to exaggerate that sense of being alone with the universe which the boy had when he sat in his room alone at night. Bennett collects that emotion, astutely yet compassionately—but he collects it, labels it—it becomes part of the collection of human samples which make up Edwin Clayhanger's life. Bennett's pursuit of the normal is even better illustrated by his treatment of the character of the hard, impulsive, passionate figure of Hilda Lessways. Here he uses a characteristic device: he makes two full-length portraits of her from two different points of view, a method which gives a remarkable suspense to the story. The first portrait of Hilda is romantic and mysterious outline. In the second, with enormous dramatic effect, he fills in the plain reality of her life. That second appearance of hers, as she cleans the house and quarrels with her mother about money, is a remarkable portrayal of the relationship of two women. As spectators of Hilda's character we might easily exaggerate, romanticize and misread her disaster; but Bennett's gift as a novelist is to abolish the role of spectator. He almost painfully domesticates the reader, puts him in the slow muddle, murmur and diurnal perturbation of a character's life, so that the reader knows no more than Hilda knows, where she is going or why she is going there. Where most novelists live by a sort of instinct for imaginative scandal, Bennett—by some defect of imagination which he is able to turn to advantage—clings like a cautious puritan to sober likelihood. He doesn't bet: "It's a mug's game." The result, in the portrait of Hilda, is a staggering probability. There is a passage when she discovers her husband is a bigamist and a crook, that the child she is expecting is illegitimate, and that she will be left penniless in their boarding house at the mercy of bailiffs. She is faced by ruin. How do people face ruin? Variously, unexpectedly; they traipse, protected by conviction, through their melodramas. Bennett seems to reply:

> Hilda in a curious way grew proud of him. With an extraordinary inconsequence she dwelt upon the fact that was grand—even as a caterer, he had caused to be printed at the foot of the menu forms which he had instituted the words: "A second helping of all or any of the dishes will willingly be served if so desired." And in the general havoc of the shock she began to be proud also of herself because it was the mysterious power of her individuality that had originated her disaster.

The determination to avoid the dramatic has led to something far more dramatic: revelation, a new light on character, the unexpected vistas in ordinary life.

Bennett's characters have three dimensions; the slow but adroit changing of the light that is thrown upon them makes them stereoscopic and gives them movement. And this movement is not the swift agitation of the passions but the dilatory adjustment to circumstance.

One of the reasons why bad novels are bad is not that the characters do not live, but they do not live with one another. They read one another's minds through the author. In *Clayhanger*, we feel at once that the characters are living together because, quite without prompting and entirely in the course of nature, they misunderstand one another. Edwin never understands his father because he does not know his father's past.

The father cannot understand the son because the father's whole attitude to life is that his rise from barbarous poverty is a primitive miracle. He is primitive, the son is rational. Each one bumps awkwardly along in the wonder of his own nature. When the father is stricken by fatal illness the son becomes the tyrant. Their emotions about each other are strong; but the two men do not feel these emotions for each other at the same time. The fierceness of the father's battle for life in the long, gray death scene startles the son—and yet he feels how strange it is that a dying man should be strong enough to return again and again to the struggle, whereas he, the son and slave, should be at the point of collapse. A writer with little poetic feeling, Bennett thinks of our awkwardness with each other, of the unbridgeable gaps of time, experience and faculty which separate us, and not of our ultimate isolation. That is why he is a pathetic and not a tragic writer; one who feels uncertainly that "it is rather a shame," that we have to bear time's burden of "beautiful infelicity."

Bennett's collector's passion for ordinariness is a kind of poor relation of Meredith's passion for the fantastic. It is amusing to make an irreverent comparison between Meredith's chapter *On an Aged and Great Wine* with Bennett's fervent hymn to building materials and plumbing in *Clayhanger.* This tedious literalness of Bennett's culminated in that nightmare of deified gadgets, *Imperial Palace.* But the virtues of Bennett lie in his patient and humane consideration of the normal factors of our lives: money, marriage, illness as we have to deal with them. Life, he seems to say, is an occupation which is forced upon us, not a journey we have chosen, nor a plunge we have taken. Such a view may at times depress us, but it may toughen us. Bennett really wrote out of the congenital tiredness of the lower middle class, as Wells wrote out of its gambling spirit and gift for fantasy; and in the end, I think,

Bennett's picture, with its blank acceptance of the Sunday School pageants, the Jubilees, the Band of Hope, the fear of the workers, the half-baked attempts at culture, is the more lasting one. It is history. History presented—when we glance back at Bennett's French masters—with the dilettante's and collector's indifference to any theory of what history may be about.

KIPLING'S SHORT STORIES

After Dickens, Kipling is the only very considerable English writer of fiction to have been popular in the most popular sense and to excite the claim to genius. He might dabble in popular myth-making and put on the swank that goes with journalistic writing, but impurity had to be reckoned as in the nature of his bristling and generous gift. By 1910, the critical esteem had begun to go; for anyone who grew up in the twenties it had gone; when one looked at a page or two of Kipling in the thirties, he looked like a progenitor of The Thing we all hated. It was easy to tie his politics round his neck and sink him. Long after that, it was a shock (when we opened one of his books) to discover that his politics might not have been as important as we had made out; that his real themes were anterior and that he had an independent gaiety and authority in his sentences suggesting a much darker experience than the political. One was faced by a variable but continuous exhibition of musketry over an enormous terrain, which alerted the mind so long as he never allowed his own feelings or those of his characters to come out into the open, but left them to be guessed. He was, in any case, better at what was choked and strangled and, puritanically, he admired pain. But, of course, he did not always leave us guessing; blatancy, emphasis, the breezy sentences beginning with a relative came back and, being sensitive, we put the book down and resumed our ignorance, preferring those writers who had grown up and who were not ashamed of the heart.

It is in this mixed state of prejudice, ignorance and unwillingness to go back to old topicality that I approach a subtle and partial critical study of Kipling, *The Art of Rudyard Kipling*, by Miss J. M. S. Tompkins. She invites one to enter a labyrinth and to trace the course of a genius she believes to be undeniable and which went on painfully growing until, in his later, complex and allusive work, it was purified and at its fullest. It is a little embarrassing, when one looks from her book into Kipling's tales, to find she is more sensitive than her subject was. The study does not claim to be comprehensive; startlingly but firmly, she leaves his politics out altogether. ("I was a child of the British Empire, as I am a subject of the British Commonwealth, and I have never found either position embarrassing. I regret that I shall not live long enough to see our humanly imperfect but undeniably great achievement of Empire fairly assessed in the long view of history.") This decision is not as damaging as it might sound, for she is not a biographer, nor a critic who runs the writer and the man together at every point. She is concerned only with the writer and, even there, most of all with the short stories. It is by these, she conveys, that what he did must be judged. To say that Kipling is the greatest English writer of short stories is to astonish oneself. He is—because no others before him made it expressly their métier.

Kipling's choice and aptitude are un-English; they are a little French; they are very American. If one were to raise political questions, one would say that Englishness was thrashed into him, that it was imposed. He invented myths for the sahibs, full of moral words, tribal signs and masonic grips, but the matter of his stories has often more in common with that of American predecessors like Twain, and successors like Hemingway and Faulkner, than it has with anything English writers have done. *Mary Postgate* is a foreigner's searching portrait of an English spinster. We cover that sort of thing up. The fantasy of *The Man Who Would Be King* is a frontier story, a natural for Mark Twain—see the King and Duke episode in *Huckleberry Finn*—and the preoccupation with toughness, cunning and shrewdness, and above all with the testing of personality, is not restrained by our sociability, dignified by our severity of satire or confined by a sense of character seen in security. In fact, the common opinion is that Kipling failed precisely in character-drawing where traditional English novelists have succeeded. I do not think he felt much need to draw character; from his Anglo-Indian point of view he thought the islanders too set, smug and narrow. This would have to be the starting point of any discussion of his politics; he became an English patriot in a most un-English way—except for the sentimentality—not by rebellion from within but from a sense of grandeur from without, and from that sense of colonial superiority which always made Anglo-Indians an annoyance and a joke. But the theory of a crypto-American Kipling is mine; it is not Miss Tompkins's. Indeed, far from it. For her he is an Elizabethan:

> . . . a traditional writer with a traditional and recurrent cast of English temperament . . . he delighted in the Elizabethan dramatists. Man in a state of strong excitement stretched beyond his normal stature on the rack of anguish, passion, or his own will, was as much his theme as theirs though in him the will is stretched to service rather than to self-assertion. In Kipling, as in his elder brothers, the moral and sensational go hand in hand. Strain, the oppression and horror of melancholy throw up for him, as for them, eccentricities of behavior which he observes with curiosity, and open up tracks of mental experience, of which he seeks to convey the strangeness. . . . Like the Elizabethans he had an original and unembarrassed love of eloquence . . . his danger, like theirs, was excess, the premature outbreak of the imagination into extravagant emphasis and unsupported hyperbole.

Kipling loved pattern, craftsmanship and the science of all trades. Yet the novel he could not master. Perhaps he had learned brevity too young; perhaps it was due to his facility as a poet; perhaps he burned up himself and his material too quickly or—as Mr. Edmund Wilson suggested in *The Wound and the Bow* —failed to confront himself. Miss Tompkins thinks Kipling mastered the novel by relinquishing its form and became our unique short story writer, and one of the greatest in all literatures, by straining into the short form the intense, highly charged essences of the longer one. He sought complexity as he sought discipline. The greater the material—*Mrs. Bathurst,* for example, which covers the affections of a lifetime, trails across a continent and ends in passion and horror—the more the essentials are reduced to a line or two, the quicker and more cunning the dodging among events and time. He proceeds, as a novelist does, less by narrative than by changing structure. We have seen

Hardy reduce a novel to a dozen lines of verse. Kipling's dramatic cutting is more like Browning's, and the art of both writers lies in making us supply the missing scenes and often the most important one. Time is no difficulty for him. The setting he always gives us vehemently—after that, it is all fencing as if he were outmatching us, driving us into a corner, until we give in, and it is we who tell him, not he who tells us, what happened.

Kipling is not one of those short story writers who settle on a mere aspect of a subject, a mood, an emotion or a life. He takes the whole subject and reduces it, in form, to the dramatic skeleton. Important issues are left obscure as if the author himself did not know what had happened or was trying to trade on mystery, and we often have to read back to see where we went wrong; yet the effect is of extent, panorama and crowded life. One explanation lies in Kipling's genius for conveying place and physical presence; the more important one is his triumph over what, as a novelist, would have been his failing: his incapacity to write of character in detail. What he tells us about people, what by a paradox makes them vivid, is that they belong to the common run; they are ordinary engineers, seamen, soldiers, housemaids, reliable villagers, conventional youths, Indians anonymous within their sects, occupations or races. They have no character; they have, simply, a fate; and it is this that evokes the presence of hundreds like them. Kipling is able to suggest that he has no life of his own but has lived by knowing all about such lives. He may be—he often is—too much of a know-all, swaggering shrewdly in and out with the low, the mean or the extravagant view, but this basic losing of himself and knowing is a powerful gift.

Miss Tompkins is aware that Kipling presents difficult problems of taste. The exaggeration, the sentimentality, the horseplay, are dealt with as best she can. I doubt whether his sentimentality can be discussed as a question of fashion: sentimentality—as distinct from sentiment—arises when we impose an idea upon a feeling in order to obscure it. Kipling is sentimental about duty, when he wishes to conceal his ambiguous feelings about suffering and cruelty. *Mary Postgate* is an unsentimental story because it does not evade the terrible fact that old Miss Postgate looked beautiful, attractive and satisfied when she had experienced a sadistic revenge. The most displeasing sentimentalities in Kipling relate to his guesswork magic and mysticism and they lead to mistakes in craftsmanship—the letter box which sticks out like a gadget in the superb story of *The Wish House*. But in sketching out the map of Kipling's pilgrim's progress, from the period of brashness and hurt into the arenas of revenge, anger, healing, pity and the terror of illness, breakdown and the abyss, she shows us a Kipling who is far less a trickster and far more a man deeply caught by injury, pain, hatred and the craving for purgation, and who uses every ounce of his experience. He had been born in the Methodist tradition and knew the burden is on the individual soul. It is also one of the splendid characteristics of Kipling as an artist that he can consider this burden disrespectfully, in jeering and fantastic terms, as well as in terms of mercy, pity, horror and resignation.

To make her point about the density of Kipling's art, Miss Tompkins makes a long and ingenious analysis of the baffling *Dayspring Mishandled.* Like many of the late stories it requires minute attention from the reader, but although it has all the marks of a master of building and technique, and although the theme of the emptiness and irrelevance that waits on a lifelong scheme of revenge is a good one, the story seems to me an example of Kipling's vice of attitudinizing in order to avoid the explicit. Miss Tompkins suggests it may be a story about the dangers of his own imaginative obsession with revenge and, in this sense, the tale has the interest of a piece of ingenious self-criticism. As a tale it is dim and esoteric; who and what poisoned whom with what? we ask. The late Kipling was a conjuror, not a mystifier like the later Henry James.

Mr. Edmund Wilson has said that Kipling lacked faith in the artist's vocation and put the doers, makers and rulers of the day before the artist in esteem. This is true when we consider Kipling as a propagandist, and Miss Tompkins has purposely avoided that aspect of his work. At his best—*On Greenhow Hill, The Wish House, Love-o'-Women, The Gardener, The Man Who Would Be King* or *The Bull That Thought*—the criticism misses. In this last tale, indeed, the artist is the explicit conqueror, and *The Man Who Would Be King* can be read as farcical and deadly satire on the British in India. Kipling had the gaiety of the word in his veins and he saw himself as an artist through and through. What Mr. Wilson may be getting at is Kipling's often showy and evasive pose of common sense, in which the average comes out on top; or that hard, no-nonsense grin on his face which flatters average human insensibility by calling it experience. Pain is over and over again his subject; so much so that he cannot evoke simple feeling without encasing it in bandages or see the fullness of love except in the perspective of its dire consequences.

He is indeed afraid of deep feeling in the foreground and the fear—perhaps because of his enormous gifts—leads him into stretches of middling vulgarity. But, in fact, Kipling grew out of clever journalism to have the strongest feeling for the means of art and all the artist's deference to difficulty. He can even be said to have had this feeling exorbitantly; but, given the man he was and his populous mind, it is what made him our most prolific and unique writer of short stories. The art thrives on personal limitations.

SONS AND LOVERS

What of the writers who emerged from the First World War? D. H. Lawrence, for example—can he tell us anything; how does he seem now? A great influence, like Wells was, on ordinary conduct; a whole generation dropped the puritan tradition and made love after the fashion of Lawrence's new puritanism. The cult of sex was also a protest against the ignoble atmosphere of city life. Wells supplied the blueprint for free love; Lawrence replied with the content. It was a new content for marriage. Free love awakens Lawrence's irony; he admires the restlessness of it but sees that it is governed by the law of diminishing returns. Like Wells, too, Lawrence is one of the journalist-novelists. He writes a novel a year about his travels and the mistakes of his friends—a religious journalist where Wells is political. Has Lawrence had any influence on contemporary writers? Yes, he is responsible for the fact that no living writer has any idea of how to write about sexual love. Lawrence's phallic cult was a disaster to descriptive writing. The ecstasies of sexual sensation are no more to be described than the ecstasies of music which they resemble. The realism of the Chinese *Golden Lotus,* for example, makes Lawrence look silly. But above all, it was fatal for imitators of Lawrence to pick up his contagious manner and leave the beliefs that did so much to create the manner; on the other hand, no one could possibly believe what Lawrence believed, and Lawrence hated people if they tried, because he believed in the inviolable, personal contradictions. One day when Lawrence and Frieda were out riding in Mexico, Frieda cried out, "Oh, it's wonderful, wonderful to feel his great thighs moving, to feel his powerful legs!" "Rubbish, Frieda," Lawrence shouted back. "Don't talk like that. You have been reading my books. You don't feel anything of the sort." Quite rightly and consistently Lawrence allowed no one to believe what he believed. All the same, Frieda persisted; she did feel like that! Certainly she *wanted* to feel like that. Lawrence's teachings are interesting because they are a compendium of what a whole generation wanted to feel, until Hitler arose, just after Lawrence's death, and they saw where the dark unconsciousness was leading them. Seen in this light, Lawrence represented the last phase of the Romantic movement: random, irresponsible egotism, power for power's sake, the blood cult of Rosenberg. And Lawrence was representative, because tens of thousands of people in England and Europe were uprooted people, like himself.

Still, that was only one of the dubious lights in which he could be read. The man of genius is a melting pot and everything that came to the surface in the English soul between 1910 and 1940 can be found in Lawrence. We are interested now not in what he taught—if it *was* teaching—but in his disposition: and that is vivid the moment we pick up any of his writings. First of all, *the whole of England,* before and after World

War I, acted upon Lawrence's imagination. His angry paganism of demigods released a repressed religious imagination in English literature. He reintroduced the direct apprehension of experience. He wrote from within—from inside the man, the woman, the tree, the fox, the mine. His people and his scene, whether it is a German road, a Nottingham kitchen or a Mexican village, are no longer fingered with one hand in the manner of naturalistic writers; they are grasped with both hands, with mind and senses. The impersonal novelist, the god with the fountain pen, has gone; the people, the trees, the mines, the fields, the kitchens come physically upon the page. And although Lawrence is the most personal of novelists, and quite as personal as Thackeray or Meredith were, he does not continually obtrude. At his best, he puts the reader instantly in the scene; instead of drawing it up neatly to be considered with all the feeling left out.

> "He saw the whitish muddy tracks and deep scores in the road where part of the regiment had retired. Now all was still. Sounds that came, came from the outside. The place where he stood was still, silent, chill, serene; the white church among the trees beyond seemed like a thought only."

To you, who are not a writer, the white church *would* have been exactly that: a thought, a mark on the skin of your mind. Or:

> "He, in his semi-conscious sleep was vaguely aware of the clatter of the iron on the iron stand, of the faint thud, thud on the ironing board. Once roused, he opened his eyes to see his mother standing on the hearth rug with the hot iron near her cheeks, listening, as it were, to the heat. Her still face with the mouth closed tight from suffering and disillusion and self-denial, and her nose the smallest bit on one side and her blue eyes so young, quick and warm, made his heart contract

> with love. When she was quiet so, she looked brave and rich with life, but as if she had been done out of her rights."

"Listening to the heat"; "Done out of her rights"—those are instantaneous, intimate, non-literary observations. They are natural, personal and not considered. Personal to Lawrence, they become personal to us. The greater part of our observation of the world has no conscious purpose; from the point of view of the good life, society, our work and so on, it is refractory. It feeds the unorganizable soul. And the soul cannot be ordered about and cannot compromise: see the miner in *Jimmy and the Desperate Woman:*

> "I'm nothing but made use of," he said now talking hard and final to himself, and staring into space. "Down the pit I'm made use of, and they give me a wage, such as it is. At the house I'm made use of, and my wife sets the dinner on the table as if I was a customer in a shop."
>
> "But what do you *expect?*" cried Jimmy, writhing in his chair.
>
> "Me? What do I expect? I expect nothing. But I tell you what . . ." he turned and looked straight and hard into Jimmy's eyes.—"I'm not going to put up with anything either. . . . If I give in to the coalface and go down the mine every day to eight hours' slavery more or less, somebody's got to give in to me."

He is an impossibilist: one of the stock comic characters or simply the obstinate brute; but he is a piece of nature and it is useless to argue with him. Lawrence writes of that part of our nature with which it is useless to argue. He shows us things carelessly, as they cannot help being:

> "A flat, shallow, utterly desolate valley, wide as a bowl under the sky, with rock slopes and grey stone slides and precipices all around, and

the zig-zag of snow stripes and ice-roots descending, and thin rivers, streams and rivers rushing from many points downwards, down in waterfalls and cascades and threads, down into the wide, shallow bed of the valley, strewn with rocks and stones innumerable, and not a tree, not a visible bush."

It is interesting to contrast a very consciously made novel like Bennett's *Old Wives' Tale* with Lawrence's *Sons and Lovers.* Both novels cover a lifetime of family life and truthfully recreate English sentiment. Bennett feels from the outside. He puts down what he has known. He sympathizes, pities and invents. And he condescends. In the mind's eye the characters of any novel can be measured for height, and Bennett's characters always seem to me small people, miniatures seen from a height as Bennett looks down upon them on the writing table. The characters of *Sons and Lovers* are less complete in their detail, there is a blur in many of them so that we are not always sure of the focus; but they are life-size. They are as big as Lawrence is. He has got inside them until they have grown to normal size. We *follow* Constance in *The Old Wives' Tales;* we walk *with* Mrs. Morel in *Sons and Lovers.* We are as uncertain as she is, from day to day. The very muddle of the narrative in this book with its puzzling time sequences, its sudden jumps backward and forward, gives us a sensation that is familiar and real; the sensation that life sprawls, spreads sideways, is made up of reminders and recapitulations, and sags loosely between one point of definition and the next. The Russian novelists had this interest in the loose texture of life whose crises begin so far away from their overt moment, and sometimes clean off the track of the expected drama. Not only that, they and Lawrence see that what we call a crisis in human relationships is a collection of crises, a rumbling and grumbling, a gabble and to-ing and fro-ing of human intercourse. Rarely does a crisis come to its final decisive outburst; nothing is final; we do not boil over, we leak away. Lawrence's sense of the life-size of people is his gift; it is also his weakness; but if we are to look for the virtues of a novelist we shall find them in those places where he is wriggling his way round his weaknesses. Lawrence is a muddling narrator, totally unskilled in construction; all right, he seems to say, let the living people drag on as best they can. They will move and compel because they live, because he will make us share their life in the collier's cottage, in the factory where Paul Morel works, on the farm where he spends his holidays. Instantaneously we shall breathe with them. And it is this power to make the reader's chest rise and fall, as it were, with the breathing of the characters in all the off moments, the lost hours, the indecipherable days of their life, that gives *Sons and Lovers* its overwhelming intimacy. There is no novel in English literature which comes so closely to the skin of life of working-class people, for it records their feelings in their own terms. The description of the older son's death, the many scenes describing the father's halting resentment or remorse, little moments of daily life when the children hang round the father's chair, are beautifully done. Common English life wears the habit of things gone wrong, of awkwardness and frustration, and Lawrence touches this quality with faithful hands. To the fidelity and the submissive spirit of the early part of *Sons and Lovers,* he returned in only a handful of short stories of which the *Odor of Chrysanthemums* seems to me the most impressive. He wrote unanswerably well—and this is true of so many English novelists—only of the environment of his childhood.

Sons and Lovers goes wrong when Lawrence begins telling lies, that is to say when he starts arguing, as in the Miriam episode which is often boring and obscure.

English novelists are afraid and ashamed of adolescence because, later in life, to be serious about oneself is considered priggish and conceited. The young prig is taken at his own valuation in French literature—see Stendhal and Flaubert's *Sentimental Education*—and is generally admired because the French respect the gradual formation of the mature nature. They are also interested in the structure of artists. But Lawrence grew up in a community and indeed in a country where the biography of an imagination embarrasses and is despised. I have always liked the Clara Dawes episode in *Sons and Lovers,* partly because it begins well, and partly for the grotesque scene where Clara's mother sits up belligerently determined to prevent the lovers from going to bed together. There is a guilty hang-dog humor and great truth of observation in this episode, although the character of Clara Dawes is overglorified, by her sexual excitement of the author. Certainly *Sons and Lovers* is patchy—it was much rewritten—and English novelists who write autobiographical novels seem to plunge in and have no idea where to bring their life story to an end. Lawrence cheats about the story of his adolescence; the spirit of rebellion brought with it a shame not only of his shames but of his happiness. The suppressed secret is that the pressure of Paul's environment made him a snob. He half admits it, but only in discussion. It is never enacted. Imagine Stendhal, the supreme portrayer of very young men in European literature, missing that!

To the English novel as a form Lawrence made one or two important contributions. He brought in new subject matter. He put the reader more or less in the position of writing the novel for himself, by giving him instantaneous observation and by slackening the strings that move the puppets. Like the Russians, he made the days of his characters' lives more important than the plot. From Meredith he developed the notion that people are not individual characters, but psychic types, flames lit by the imagination. They do not (after *Sons and Lovers*) develop, but leap higher and higher until they strike their certain fate. This conception of character was used in another sense by Marxist satirical writers who followed him. Lawrence gave novels a subject instead of a plot. Especially in his short stories, Lawrence used a summary, standstill description of character, so that the whole story (see *The Prussian Officer*) is a series of dramatic assertions and reiterations about two men, culminating in the tragedy. This tense and even frenzied method, was made tolerable by the colloquial sound of his own voice, *i.e.*, the reader believes he is instantly saying it all himself. This manner arises because Lawrence is often clumsy and commonplace in straight narrative and because he is too egotistical and lacking in humility to know what people are really like; it accounts for much that is boring incantation. But to the short story, which can support the tour de force, these dramatic summaries are an excellent addition, though we must allow, as in Meredith, for a certain air of theatre. Like Meredith (and Hall Caine) Lawrence writes at the top of his voice and is railing against his subject. Only his extraordinary sense of physical life and his lapses into accidental nature, save these rhetorical stories. In the end, the mining stories, things like *The Fox* and the rich irony of pieces like *The Rocking-Horse Winner* survive whole. For the rest, we must dip for his descriptions. Once he was uprooted from the Midlands and his class, he ceased to be a novelist; he was a traveler, a remarkable letter writer, brilliant in discoveries which he buried under pulpit-loads of nonsense about people and a life he could not tolerate.

CONRAD

Conrad exists in English literature but he is a harsh exotic who can never quite be assimilated to our modes. No English novelist has his peculiar accent in psychological and moral curiosity; it is, like the knowing accent of Kipling, a foreigner's acquired slang, but expressing a far more elevated sensibility than Kipling had; only Henry James, another alien, with his pursuit of fine consciousness, approaches Conrad's fencing with extremes. Yet here, all Conrad's critics have been dissatisfied. They have felt, as Forster did, that he was following extremes into a fog of argument or rhetoric; or they have been obliged to agree with the comment of Dr. Leavis—the most substantial of Conrad's critics—on the inequalities of *Heart of Darkness* and that

> he is intent on making a virtue out of not knowing what he means. The vague and unrealizable, he asserts with a strained impressiveness, is the profoundly and tremendously significant.

Even in *Nostromo,* where Conrad's powers of concretion were married to a great subject, we shall not exactly know where we stand. We are always liable in his work to lapse from the certainties of art into the restless brilliance of opinion, to find the matter in hand being explored with the cleverness of the café writer and the moral dilettante. We shall be haunted by the special and tragic brilliance of the exile who, as he exhibits himself and acts his role, is never unconscious of the fact. So, as Mr. Douglas Hewitt says in a short recent assessment of Conrad's novels, they are not tragedies—but they *resemble* tragedies. They are, generally speaking, one must add, inhibited from tragic fullness by his famous, defensive and histrionic irony. He is, at bottom, a rather sadistic and sardonic writer. His irony is ultimately perverse—or, as earlier critics used to say, morbid—because it is a personal irony and does not always lie in the nature of the events he describes. Is *Nostromo* a great classical novel or a brilliant commentary? That is to say, superb as it is, does it not strike one as being a commentary on the kind of novel or dramatic work that could, at some time, be written on the subject?

Nostromo is the most strikingly modern of Conrad's novels. It might have been written in the last decade and not, as it was, in 1904. All the issues of the economic exploitation of a backward country are here; the politics of Costaguana over two or three generations are telescoped in depth without losing the focus on the present. We see both the ideal and fraud in colonial exploitation, in the fight for liberalism, progress, reform, the bent for revolution and the advent of a foreign power. Even the rise of two of the now dominant forces in his kind of situation is clearly noted: the desire of America to take over everything in the world and, against or with that, the rise of the masses. Conrad did not set these things down in a political or historical essay, nor in a novel of propaganda, but in the impure and, above all, inflected detail of a large sceptical and imaginative work. Every moment is physically realized not by a right-minded and insensitive political reporter with a mind hardened or softened by his program, but by an artist dealing, as art must, in the wasted, the elusive, the incalculable. It is one of the prophetic felicities of this work that it is pervaded by a profound, even morbid sense of insecurity which is the very spirit of our age, and that sense is (as it must always be) personal. Before anyone else—though we may pause to give Mr. E. M. Forster his due—Conrad the exile had the luck to foresee that in half a century, we should all in a sense become exiles.

One or two reflections follow from our astonishment with *Nostromo*. The first is a general reflection on the social soil in which the modern English novel is planted. The great English subject—one is inclined to say—and at any rate the great subject which includes a picture of society, lies outside England, simply because English life itself has for long been parasitic on life abroad and does not wish to recognize the fact. "Abroad" is where English institutions have been put to the test and not in South Wales, Tyneside, Birmingham or Surrey. As I say, apart from Conrad, only E. M. Forster seems to have known this; possibly Lawrence, too, in a book like *Kangaroo*. The second reflection is one that throws a light on some of Conrad's defects as a novelist. He suffers from being before his proper time. It is a freak of time that he is a Romantic. Even in small yet not unimportant matters like the use of dialogue, Conrad was unlucky. If he could be writing *The Secret Agent* or the bandit pages of *Victory* now, he would certainly not write the wooden Cockney or the ludicrous melodrama of his gangster's dialogue; the intellectual energies of the refugee would not have been spent on acquiring literary English, but the English of speech.

Conrad is a man in what we may call the post-1940 situation, but who is obliged to conceal the fact under a dramatic fog of rhetoric. He, of course, loved rhetoric and became—as Mr. Hewitt says—more prone to it when his talent went to pieces from *Chance* onwards;

vaguely emotive words like "unspeakable," "nameless," "inscrutable," "horror," "pure evil," "mystery," "Woman" are the well-known pedals of the Romantic organ. Behind them lay things which, a generation or so after, he could have named, and as an incipient nihilist he would have been bound to name them. He would have been obliged to live or set down in precise physical detail, the nihilism which he feared so much in his nature. It would have been drawn out by a nihilist age. The case of Kurtz in *Heart of Darkness,* the case of Heyst in *Victory,* or Decoud in *Nostromo* is contemporary, but now the full glare of the interrogator's lamp is on their faces. Conrad would have been drawn out of the grandiloquent shadows that exasperate us and which seem to exasperate him; he would have found less to opine upon and more, cruelly, to state. The morbidity of which early critics complained—quite rightly; before 1914 certain values seemed impregnable—would not strike one in our imaginary Conrad who had been drawn out by times that would fit his temperament like a glove. Betrayal, guilt, isolation, the double self, corruption, the undisguised sadism that has appeared in our life, the anarchy, are not matters of speculation and pious lament. They are contemporary facts.

Mr. Hewitt is of the opinion that the decline of Conrad's work which began with *Chance,* comes from a failure to see any secure or positive values which could counter the force of his negative criticism. The alternative was to plump for popular Romance and an unreal, black and white world of wholly good or wholly evil people. These later books are simply the early rhetoric expanded. Mr. Hewitt's book is a short one which sticks to the text of a few of the novels and is concerned with the specific moral health of Conrad's genius at different times; it is far from comprehensive and though its main points are excellent, one misses a sensibility to detail. Gould and his wife, for example, are hardly realized characters in *Nostromo:* they are states of mind, like the Dukes who hold the Court in a Shakespearean drama. Why in comparison does Mr. Hewitt find Heyst in *Victory* so fatally unrealized? Are Heyst's conversations with the girl on the island less acceptable than Mrs. Gould's conversations with Decoud in *Nostromo?* The dialogue is wooden in both instances; the matter is suggestive and subtle. Is not the difference between Gould and Heyst simply that one is a practical and obsessed solitary scheming for his mine, whereas Heyst is a passive solitary? Mr. Hewitt warns us of the danger of paraphrasing Conrad, but Conrad paraphrases himself in characters like Gould, Heyst and Decoud. They are attitudes, not people, though they are attitudes lit up here and there by the novelist's power to give them flashes of individual life. The fact is that Conrad was a writer of restless and changeable conceptions, but he was poor in invention. His imaginative eye did not easily move; it was fixed upon brilliant detail so that the sound of a thing like the clank of railway trucks, with its suggestion of prisoner's fetters, becomes so powerful as an image, that it is more real to us than the people who have to be explained or talked-on in brilliant but ultimately elusive colloquies. He is a jumpy, attitudinizing, artificial writer, bedeviled by his eye. The selection of the isolated subject is, in part, the expression of his maddened desire for a subject that can be made to stand still so that it can be forcibly elaborated. The pattern of *Nostromo* is wonderful. It is like some grim brocade; yet was it necessary to be so elaborate in order to get the utmost out of the subject? And did Conrad get the utmost? On the level of a great tragic conception, I think, it must at last be thought he did not. We are overburdened by detail, by a too constant intensity.

We are hypnotized. We "come to," but there has been no purgation.

The Secret Sharer, in Mr. Hewitt's opinion, marks the deciding crisis in Conrad's life as a novelist. In this excellent tale he thinks Conrad exorcised his personal devil and thereafter turned away from the central conflict which had fertilized his art. Leggatt, the man who takes refuge in the young Captain's cabin, has killed a man in some squabble, and he plays the part of the Dostoevskian "double" as Gentleman Brown had done to Lord Jim. Leggatt is the hidden transgressor in the unconscious, an embodiment of the fear "that there are parts of himself which he has not yet brought into the light of day" and which may interfere "with the ideal conception of one's own personality every man sets up for himself secretly." The Captain is put to a strain leading almost to madness by his secret partnership and actually risks his ship; but having pushed the pact to the limit, he conquers and sails off, free at last, where Kurtz, Gentleman Brown of *Nostromo* and Lord Jim represent failures in this struggle with the unconscious. *Chance* with its optimism of black and white Romance, the reliance on the sailor's simple code—Mr. Hewitt says—follows at once. This is a shrewd point. Conrad's pessimism, his lack of a positive scheme of spiritual values, clearly left him, as a Romantic artist, in an intolerable situation.

Exile—the fact of being uncommitted—is at the bottom of Conrad's triumphs and his failures. He is a writer of great vanity. One has the impression of a mind more suited to the theatre than to the novel. The wonderful faceting of *Nostromo* is essentially theatrical in effect; self-consciousness, artifice, the sense of his role which every Conrad character feels, including Marlowe himself, strengthen our impression. Of course, he was no more a dramatist than Henry James was, but there is this straining towards the drama. It is indeed the self-dramatizing, evasive, speculative quality in his own comments on his work which make him an unusually unreliable guide to his achievement.

M. Jean-Aubry's work on Conrad is well known; his biographical study, *The Sea Dreamer,* has been available in French for some years. It is informed but incurious and can hardly now be up to date. Conrad was very much an autobiographical writer and was very explicit in his memories; this has made him too easily the coeval of his biographer who simply runs beside him.

Two things strike us about Conrad. The first is that despite his life of action, his true heritage was political and literary. He took to the sea, as a writer might, if he had a good stomach, out of a romantic passion for travel and geography. He was not a born seaman who eventually takes to writing as another form of extraversion. Conrad's father was a well-known if minor literary figure in Poland, a dilettante of reckless political nerve, and the son's decision to go to sea was a violent break with the formative influences of his upbringing. It was a protest, an adventure, could almost be thought an aberration, and was likely to recoil. Secondly, we must note the immense importance of politics and especially of political defeat in his life. He saw defeat lived out in tragedy, in the death of his father and mother after their exile in Russia. He was with them there; he nearly died there. He learned exile as a child. The "gloom" of Conrad was not the broad, passive gloom of the Russians which seems to arise from the dull excess of space; he disliked being called a Slav. He was a Westerner who despised the Dostoevskian Russia. Conrad's "gloom"—as his biographer says—began with his early schooling in sorrow. It grew, later on, into something hard and sardonic. It is the bitter irony of the active man of strong imagination who sees, with personal indignation, the relativeness of experience. The exile has the illusion of moral freedom and becomes a connoisseur of the ironies of his situation. One is haunted throughout Conrad's writing by inhibition.

There is some parallel in the lives of Conrad and his father. The dangerous political gestures of the father were patriotic, noble, passionate and romantic, but they were carried on in the futile void created by an all-powerful tyranny. There was a total lack of prospect. It was oceanic. In the life of the son the conception of tyranny that wastes life has changed into the embittering notion of Destiny. There is something odd about Conrad's idea of Destiny; so often it is merely exasperating, when it should surely be dreadful; perverse when it should be impassive. The men of the generation of Conrad's father knew evil by direct experience. The police rapped on the door. The arrest was made. The lies were told. The trial took place and the protests. The sentence to Siberia, which was really a sentence to fatal illness and the loss of everything valued in life, was a fact—to Conrad's father. To the son, when he grew up, evil was a bad dream, a sinister memory, a dark rhetorical suggestion. Again and again in his work, the evil thing becomes diffused and generalized into an indefinable reek of corruption. It is indeed Conrad's special contribution to the English novel, to have insinuated into it the sense of an atmosphere of evil which is notoriously lacking. On the other hand, we have to note that Conrad is better at the evil fact—the cannibal helmsman lying dead in the wheelhouse in *Heart of Darkness;* the crew disappointed that they cannot eat the body—than he is at evil in the general sense. There are times when the belief in original sin sounds either histrionic or professional; and in *Heart of Darkness* far too much play is made with words like "inscrutable," "unfathomable," "impalpable," "mysterious," "inconceivable" in a manner that suggests an attempt to create a system or dogma of evil by sheer oratory. Conrad's description of the Congo is unforgettable, but his moral reflections look like stage drawings or temporary constructions. I think the exile's temperament gave Conrad his obsession with the allusive. He could never resist a symbol; and his images tend to submerge his people at their crisis, as if they were evasions. Even so, such a concern for texture does not really explain why "Mistah Kurtz," the whole focus of *Heart of Darkness,* is a ghost or figment. His extreme lusts—what are they? What unnamable things did he do? Was he a cannibal? He murdered, we suppose. It is curious that when Marlowe actually sees the heads on the poles outside the hut, he sees them not by the defenseless naked eye but by the magnifying intervention of binoculars. At the very crisis of the story we do not directly face the fact; we are given the distorting illusion.

Kurtz is, of course, made into an ubiquitous, diffused, romantic symbol in this manner and is the symbol of two kinds of corruption: the primordial, and the disgusting aspect of colonial exploitation in its first greedy rush. The Whites have gone mad with greed. Kurtz has simply been logical. He has gone over the borderline into "complete freedom." He has accepted the union of "desire and hate"; he has split into the prim hypocrite citizen and the savage lunatic. In love (we are led to conclude) he found "horror." All this is psychologically absorbing, for Conrad means it to apply as a potential to all of us; but it is mere hearsay in the novel. The novelist does not show us an instance of it in action.

Conrad was concerned with fear, guilt, remorse and the tincture of corruption in good things. He is preoccupied by betrayal. It is the rootless who betray. His greatness lies in the handling of a large range of moral types who suffer these evils each in a different way, so that we feel he understands a universal condition. The preoccupation stirred up certain Polish critics years ago. What crime or betrayal had Conrad on his conscience? Why did he write *Lord Jim*? What about *The Secret Agent*? His work is close to personal experience —did he commit some fault at sea? It seems certain that he did not. He may have felt a morbid anxiety, M. Jean-Aubry says, as a foreigner, that he might not come up to the codes of the nation he had made his own. The Poles suggested that Conrad felt the guilt of the emigré, a guilt all the sharper because he was the son of a man who had been a national martyr. Conrad did not evade the criticism and answered it very sensibly. He was especially unlucky, because he reached forward prophetically to a time when exile has become, to our sense, a general experience.

THE IRISH R.M.

"Did you ever eat my grandmother's curry?" said Flurry, to me, later, as we watched Bernard Shute trying to back his motor into the coach house.

I said I had not.

"Well, you'd take a splint off a horse with it," said Mrs. Knox's grandson.

The Aussolas woods were full of birds that day.

Birds bursting out of holly bushes like corks out of soda-water bottles. . . .

Yes, there is no doubt about it: the *Experiences of an Irish R.M.* are your grandmother's curry. They are a light literature which takes the skin off your tongue, the breath out of your lungs and—to quote a favorite phrase of the authors—"puts your eyes on sticks." And then, even those sentences I have quoted have a horse in them. There are horses on nearly every page of this book, malicious and heroic creatures of deep character which seem to be out on a perpetual hunt. It is indeed hard to know which are the people and which are the horses. Perhaps they are all horses. Flurry Knox would willingly have become one. So would his grandmother. Most of the Somerville and Ross women, with their rain-fiercened complexions, their long heads and box-like bodies, their sprained ankles and strained shoulders and their frightful high spirits, are unimaginable without their chestnuts and their grays. Their pace is spanking, their talk flies out like froth. It was not a freak of satire that in the beginning of Anglo-Irish literature, Swift drew the Houyhnhnms as the master race; he was simply recording the national religion.

With a malice and madness that match the Somerville and Ross characters, the Irish climate acts as a mirror to their antics. The frost is crisp on the fallen leaves in the bare woods, the woodcock rise out of the trees or the snipe zip away over the frozen bogs into a sky of Neapolitan enamel; but within an hour rain is spouting off the hat brims of the sportsmen, and days of mugginess or downpour jail the mind and drive it to thoughts of the whisky bottle, the long meditated intrigues of tribal life, the treacheries and despondencies of the lonely colonial wits. A world that was on the verge of becoming Turgenev's turns into a jumble of Surtees, Tom Moore and *The Fall of the House of Usher;* and half the farce lies not in the horseplay, but in the ingredients themselves. We begin to laugh before we start reading and that is apt to mean that we stop laughing before the end, and wonder why the authors dare not be quiet for a moment. What would happen if they were quiet? What did the Major do when he was not trying to keep pace with Flurry Knox's mare or (far more complex) follow Flurry's mind? There were mornings, we are told, when he spent the time in the gentlemanly task of writing letters. What was he writing? Or what was old Mrs. Knox thinking as she sat with her stockinged feet in the fireplace, oblivious of the good feed for poultry which always lay under the Louis Quinze chairs on her drawing-room floor at Aussolas, and lulled by the pompous cooing of the doves which flew into the room and perched on the picture frames of the smoke-kippered portraits of her ancestors? Unless there is an answer to these questions there is force in the criticism of Somerville and Ross that used to be made in the sour, wan yellow dawn of the Irish revival, when it was a crime for anyone to laugh in Ireland, unless they laughed for the right party: the criticism that these ladies were simply purveying the stage Irishman to English magazines and winding up the old parish hurdy-gurdy of Irish farce.

And, of course, they were. The tradition of Irish farce is permanent. The stage Irishman is permanent. He is as permanent as the Irish narrative gift and the use of words as an intoxicant. The puritanism of Maynooth and Merrion Square cannot put its gooseflesh on the warm native fancy. But there is more than one Somerville and Ross. An early novel, written before the *R.M.* made them popular, does attempt to say what the Anglo-Irish were like between one View

Hallo or one Petty Session and the next. That book is *The Real Charlotte.* I don't want to be a spoil-sport, especially now the *R.M.* has been canonized by *Everyman,* and I write as a foreigner, but *The Real Charlotte* did something which had not, up to the nineties, been done in Irish literature. It portrayed the Anglo-Irish with the awful, protracted mercy of the artist. It "placed" them as no novelist had thought of "placing" them before; as surely, for example, as Mrs. Gaskell knew how to place her world in *Wives and Daughters.* I do not mean that *The Real Charlotte* is as sound or as accomplished a novel as Mrs. Gaskell's. It was a first novel, awkwardly built, and, like so many Anglo-Irish writers, the authors never got rid of an amateur, almost a juvenile streak; but *The Real Charlotte* was a beginning of great promise. One went to Ireland looking for the characters of the Irish R.M.; one found oneself, thirty years after it was written, surrounded by the disquieting people of this one serious novel.

The scene is Galway and the long loch beyond it. There is the big estate on the lake. There is the agent's modest place nearby. There are one or two absurd houses. And then, back in Dublin or the worst end of Bray, there is the genteel squalor of Francie Fitzpatrick's life. In England Francie would be a lower-middle-class beauty on the make; in the Ireland of the nineties she is a beautiful hoyden, a tomboy and a flirt, coarse grained yet childlishly unaffected. If she ceases to be prim she will be a mess, a noise without innocence. She goes to Galway to hook a husband, preferably a mindless young officer who will mend her family fortunes. Too ingenuous to be called an adventuress, too beguiling to be thought entirely vulgar in her man-hunt or her manners, Francie will never find her place.

In England, the class system would provide repose for Francie's soul; in Ireland the tribe system, with its withering snobberies, punishes her at every point of her social climb. She is doomed to be second-rate, to attract second-rate behavior. And though *The Real Charlotte* is a novel about jealousy and the never-ceasing intrigue and treachery of Irish life, its main stuff is this snobbery. Not a plain, excluding snobbery that tells us where we may go and where we may not, but a snobbery that is in the blood. Not a snobbery versed in distinguished ancestors only, but a snobbery bedeviling the character with the pretensions of second cousins and the mildewed memories of better times. It is a snobbery that has become the meaning of life. It permeates everything: good sense, idealism, hatred, tenderness, religion—even pity. We must allow something for the fact that this book is written in the nineties; and when the Dysarts wince because Francie keeps her gloves on at tea, we are charmed by the comedy of the manners of a period. Anglo-Irish snobbery was pretty genial about such quaintness. But underneath this are the inturned passions of a small, defensive and decaying colonial society: Francie is a social casualty in the everlasting skirmish with the other Ireland. Only by exaggerating their exclusiveness and remarking low comedy around them can the Ascendants keep their ascendancy.

Of course, we may read in the Dysarts a devotion to manners, sensibility and excellence; but the devotion is so defensive that it becomes negative. It has become a mania like Lady Dysart's acrostics. And the mania spreads downwards. So Lambert, the land agent, wishes to impress as much as the Dysarts do, and his desire turns to self-destructive hatred of them. He ends by trying to cheat them. Francie's cousin Charlotte, who is half peasant and whose clumsy mind can yet devise labyrinthine schemes, bids too high on Francie's behalf, hopes to capture a Dysart for her, and is betrayed by the girl. In a curious passage, the young Christopher Dysart feels a mingled envy and pity for Francie's vital but ill-judged insouciance; and Francie to whom he is incomprehensible because he is too far above her, rubs her low breeding into him in order to cause him pain and, by causing pain, to bring him nearer to her understanding. Again, Lambert enjoys making a fool of Charlotte by arousing her feelings in order to exploit her purse and cut a figure. Snobbery creates victims to pity, and all these characters discover the strange pleasure of forgiving the people they have injured. If they all only knew it, the logical end of their mania was the sensitive, tedious ineffectuality of Christopher Dysart. In him there is a masterly portrait of the lifeless, hopelessly neutral, decent young aristocrat of the period.

Cousin Charlotte has been compared to Cousine Bette and, allowing for the change to the raw Irish scene, there is something in the comparison. The money motives, the class structure, are there. To these elements one must add a peculiar psychological quickness to catch the perversity of human feeling and the cross-ruffing of Fate: for example, in her jealous plottings Charlotte cannot bear not to give herself away. Feeling presents itself as intrigue. Francie is not the only flirt; they are all flirting with every dream and issue. They cross one another and double-cross themselves. Pity becomes hatred, hatred turns into tenderness, tenderness into cruelty. We watch with fascination while the dull, irritable land agent with his debts, his horses and his ailing wife, ingeniously plots his own downfall.

All this must be visualized against an animated scene which is broken by some of the *R.M.* comedy that was to come. The absurd pleasure launch on the lake, tooting away at the least convenient moment, and its inane comment on the people is a delightful invention. The awful English officer and Don Juan is an excellent cad. The middle-class carpet dance is a fearful romp. A hundred small touches keep this small world in a continual ripple and change of color. On the other hand, the chorus from peasant life is boring. Fifty years of politics lie between us and these skirling *commères,* with their high-pitched domestic life and the loquacity of displaced Elizabethans. But the narrative writing has the Irish visual gift, so bold in its metaphors, so athletic in its speed, as if tongue and eye were racing against each other. There is the native animism:

> Tall brick houses, browbeating each other in gloomy respectability across the street.

The shrewd is punched home by the baroque:

> She was losing hold of herself; her gestures were of the sort that she usually reserved for her inferiors, and the corners of her mouth bubbled like a snail.

And then, though there is hardly a breath of Irish politics in the story, they are there by implication. For the characters are exclusively the Irish Protestants and their isolation gives a strength to the strokes in which they are drawn.

The faults of *The Real Charlotte* are obvious. The national malady of not "letting on" what you are up to enables the novelist to catch the changeableness of human character; but toward the end the elusive becomes the frantic. It is unforgivable that Francie is killed out riding; especially as her death, one is pretty sure, is due to the profound snobbery of the authors. There is no way of making a lady of her, so she has to be killed. But after one has removed the old-fashioned trappings, the irony, the insight and portraiture of this novel show that Anglo-Irish society might have got its Mrs. Gaskell, if the amateur tastes of the discursive colonial had not breezily ridden the chance off the page.

AN EAST END NOVELIST

"And the effect is as of stables." My eye has been often baffled by lack of the word which would define the poor streets of the East End, as they used to be before the last war; and here in Arthur Morrison's *Tales of Mean Streets* which were written in 1894, I find it. Those acres of two-story houses which lay below the level of the railway arches of Bethnal Green and which stood like an alien stretch of unfeatured plowing beyond the Commercial Road, are particularized at last. The mind has won a foothold in a foreign city.

For, east of Aldgate, another city begins. London flattens and sinks into its clay. Over those lower dwellings the London sky, always like a dirty window, is larger; the eyes and hands of people are quicker, the skins yellower, the voices are as sharp as scissors. Every part of London has its smell, and this region smells of rabid little shops, bloated factories, sublet workrooms and warehouse floors; there is also the smell of slums, a smell of poverty, racy but oftener sour; and mingling with these working odors, there arises an exhalation of the dirty river which, somewhere behind these streets and warehouses and dock walls, is oozing toward the flats of the Thames estuary like a worm. The senses and the imagination of the stranger are so pricked by this neighborhood that he quickly gets a fevered impression of it; it will seem dingier or more exotic than it really is. And when we turn to literature for guidance, we are even less sure of what we see. For the literature of the East End is very largely a stranger's literature. It lies under the melodramatic murk and the smear of sentimental pathos, which, in the nineteenth century, were generated by the guilty conscience of the middle classes. They were terrified of the poor who seethed in a trough just beyond their back door. The awful Gothic spectacle of hunger, squalor and crime was tolerable only as nightmare and fantasy—such as Dickens provided—and the visiting foreigner alone could observe the English slums with the curiosity of the traveler or the countenance of the anthropologist. And there was another difficulty. Philanthropy, for all its humbug, did slowly have its effect on the public conscience in every generation, so that it was genuinely possible to say "things have changed." The Ratcliffe Highway went. Limehouse had been purged, and there arose a romantic literature of the East End, based on a riotous evocation of the bad old times. The stranger's literature was the literature of a time which first strengthened morale by giving the reader a fright, and then went on to make the fright pious, sentimental and picturesque.

But what of the literature written from within the East End, the really saturated literature which has been lived before it has been written? For many years now, in accounts of the realism which came into fashion at the time of Gissing, I had noticed a recurring title: *Tales of Mean Streets,* by Arthur Morrison, and lately I have been put on to *The Hole in the Wall* and *Child of the Jago* by the same author. They are written from the inside and they have extraordinary merit; *The Hole in the Wall* strikes me as being one of the minor masterpieces of the last sixty years. It has the kind of fidelity to scene that the modern documentary writers have sought, yet is never flattened, as their work is, by concern for conditions; let us not allow "conditions" to deflate the imagination or argue away the novelist's chief delight and greatest difficulty: the art of constructing and telling a story complete in itself. For unless he learns this art, a novelist neutralizes his power of observation, his power to observe more than one thing at a time, his power of writing on different planes and varying perspectives, and discriminating among the accumulated incrustations of fact that clog an impressionable mind. Arthur Morrison had this power. "Conditions" were in his bones; his books stand apart from the worthy and static pathos of Gissing, from the character albums of the writers of low comedy, from the picturesque and the nightmare schools. Mr. Morrison's early novels and sketches are often modest in their art, like the work of someone learning to write, but they have an anthropological drama of their own, and, at any rate, are not more awkward than Bennett's *Tales of the Five Towns*. What is missing from these novels is the modern novelist's sardonic exposure of the economic rackets which make the poor man poor; the brutality of poverty is subject enough for Mr. Morrison. A book like *Child of the Jago,* the story of a young thief in Bethnal Green, shows a sharp-eyed and intimate knowledge of how East End society used to behave as a society, of how it used to deploy its cunning and uphold its customs. Injustice is done and the President of the Immortals has already abandoned the hopeless scene to the human instinct of self-preservation when Mr. Morrison comes in to record it. Out comes the cosh, the street wars begin, the half-naked harpies run at each other with broken bottles, the pimps and fences step over the bodies of the drunks who lie, pockets turned inside out, in the gutters. It's a world of sullen days in backrooms with the baby lying half dead on the bed and the hungry women gaping listlessly at the empty cupboards, while the men go out in search of loot and drink and come back with their eyes blackened and their belts ready to flay the undeserving family. I have picked out the seamier side of *Child of the Jago* not to gloat over the horrors but to indicate the material. Such incidents are not raked into the book without discrimination; these novels are not pools of self-pity in the Gissing manner; nor are they worked up with that sadistic touch of angry ecstasy which Dickens brought to his pictures of poverty. In Mr. Morrison's book slum life is the accepted life, a dirty but not a turgid stream. In their position, you say—as one ought to say of all human beings—these people have lived, they've kept their heads above water for a spell. Man is the animal who adapts himself.

Child of the Jago describes the brutal, drunken, murderous London of the late nineteenth century which used to shatter the visiting foreigner and send him home marveling at English violence and English hypocrisy. Its picture of the street wars is unique. *The Hole in the Wall* raises this material to a far higher plane of narrative. Here is a thriller set in Dockland, where the filthy river, its fogs and its crimes, stain the mind as they did in *Our Mutual Friend.* Every gas-lit alley leads abruptly to some dubious business. The average thriller takes us step by step away from probability. It strains away from likelihood. *The Hole in the Wall* belongs to the higher and more satisfying kind, which conducts us from one unsuspected probability to the next. Mr. Morrison has employed what is, I suppose, the classical method of writing this kind of book; he shows us the story mainly through the eye of a young boy. The child goes to live with his grandfather who keeps a pub at Wapping and there he gradually discovers that his heroic grandfather is really a receiver of stolen goods. The old man comes by a wallet containing £800 which has been robbed from a defaulting shipowner—who has been murdered—and the plot is made out of the attempts of various criminal characters to get this money back. The merit of the book lies in its simple but careful reconstruction of the scene—the pubs and gin shops of the Old Ratcliffe Highway, the locks and swing bridges, the alleys and gateways of Dockland with their police notices, the riverside jetties and their lighters, the way over the marshes to the lime kilns. I take it to be a mark of the highest skill in this kind of novel that nothing is mentioned which will not have, eventually, an importance to the tale; and that the motives for action arise in the characters and are not imposed on them by the need of working up a mystery and creating suspense. We do not know what their next step will be, because these people are still ruminating upon it themselves. Marr, the absconding shipowner, disguises himself as a sailor, but forgets that he will blab if he gets drunk; Dan Ogle who merely intends to take his watch, gradually sees that murder will be necessary if the £800 is to be taken; the blind fiddler who does not mind very much being double-crossed, thinks otherwise when he is assaulted and ridiculed as well as cheated. And Mr. Morrison succeeds with them because he shows them to us, first of all as ordinary shady characters muddling along the path of shifty illegality, and then suddenly faced by a new, a more terrible temptation and jumping at it.

The Hole in the Wall moves calmly from one major scene to the next; there is no sagging of the narrative. We see Marr, stunned and tottering, led like a broken marionette between his murderers. They are bawling at the tops of their voices so that, in the night, passers-by will think they are drunken sailors helping a pal, instead of murderers, dragging an almost lifeless body to the river. We see the body fished out—and what a remarkable piece of description that is. It "tells"—as Henry James used to say—because of the very homeliness of the boy's narrative. (There is a lesson to the modern tough writers here. They lose their effect because they are tough all the time. They do not allow us to have the homely, frightened, law-abiding emotions. They do not allow us the manly fear, and they lose the interest of moral conflict.) And then there is the tremendous scene where the blind fiddler takes his revenge on Ogle, the murderer. He is hiding in a lime quarry. At night the fiddler gropes across the marshes to the shed where Ogle is sleeping:

> He had been gone no more than a few seconds, when the snore stopped. It stopped with a thump and a gasp, and a sudden buffeting of legs and arms; and in the midst arose a cry; a cry of so hideous an agony that Grimes the wharf-keeper, snug in his first sleep fifty yards away, sprang erect and staring in bed, and so sat motionless for half a minute ere he remembered his legs and thrust them out to carry him to the window. And the dog on the wharf leaped the length of its chain, answering the cry with a torrent of wild barks.
>
> Floundering and tumbling against the frail boards of the shed the two men came out at the door in a struggling knot; Ogle wrestling and striking at random, while the other, cunning with a life's blindness, kept his own head safe and hung as a dog hangs to a bull. His hands gripped his victim by ear and hair, while the thumbs drove at the eyes the mess of smoking lime that clung and dripped about Ogle's head. It trickled burning through his hair and it blistered lips and tongue, as he yelled and yelled again in the extremity of his anguish.

The blind man had blinded his persecutor.

One puts the book down looking back on the ground

it has covered, seeing how economically it implanted that sinister Dockland of the eighties on the mind, with a simple warmth and precision; how it mocked the little criminals, and then, suddenly, struck out into the squalor behind the drink in the snug bar and the bawling songs in the upper room; and how finally it pierced one with human fear and horror, without once cutting adrift from probability and an identifiable daily life. It is a masterly course, sustained, calm and never exaggerated. The style is a little old-fashioned, but it never scuttles away for safety into period dress. There was a London like this—we are convinced—mean, clumsy and hungry, murderous and sentimental. Those shrieks were heard. There were those even more disturbing silences in the night. Dockland, where the police used to go in threes, has its commemoration.

AN AMATEUR

The businessman who is a novelist in his spare time, an occasional and amateur novelist, is a character who must always be envied by professionals. For here is a man who has avoided the treadmill of talent and the catastrophes which lie in the path of genius. The businessman who is a novelist is able to drop in on literature and feel no suicidal loss of esteem if the lady is not at home, and he can spend his life preparing without fuss for the awful interview. There need be no last-minute slapdash à la Dostoevski; no years of painful groping among the hallucinations of the intellect, such as Flaubert suffered; no spiritual crises which will split a masterpiece in two; no flagging hack-work to patch the interval between one work and another. The amateur can afford to be thorough, and he usually is thorough precisely in those places where the professional slurs, skimps, and hopes for the best. But there is yet another advantage to be envied. I am not thinking of the solid income of the businessman whose leisure really *is* leisure and not a haunted escape from contracts and creditors; I am thinking of the businessman's solid character. To have that and yet also to have the gift, to know that the gift can never play the devil with his life—those seem to be outrageous advantages.

The novels of J. Meade Falkner, an almost forgotten writer of the late nineties, brings such reflections to the mind. Falkner was not a businessman novelist of the Italo Svevo size; but he has his small place. *The Nebuly Coat* and *The Lost Stradivarius* are mystery stories tinctured by scholarship and are now, I think, too slow and unmysterious for our taste—the last war hurried the pace of these things—but in *Moonfleet* he wrote a story of adventure that will have a permanent place among the minor *genre* pieces of our literature. A word about Falkner, first of all. He was a most remarkable man. By taste and education a scholar whose researches in archeology, folklore, paleography, architecture, church music and medieval history earned him a papal medal and many honors at the Universities, Falkner spent all his life in Armstrong Whitworth's, whose chairman he was during and after the last war. He was a brilliant diplomatist and negotiator with foreign governments. He traveled all over the world for his firm. He said that he owed his versatility to his medieval mind, and in her preface to the abridged Penguin edition of *The Nebuly Coat,* Lady Longford says that he applied the same minute care to his reports for Armstrong Whitworth and his researches in the Vatican library. In the Civil Service the various mind has been common; in the bustle of industry it is rare. And during his packed career, Falkner wrote works of learning and these three novels.

The Nebuly Coat and *The Lost Stradivarius* recall the books of Sheridan Le Fanu, but they are not on the level of the Irish master. Falkner lacked Le Fanu's psychological curiosity and the uneasiness of his imagination. Where Le Fanu was skilled in disturbing the mind, Falkner, with the habits of research, spoiled things by setting our minds at rest. It is true that the character of Westray, the young architect in *The Nebuly Coat,* is peculiar, and that he is distressed about the morality of shielding an impostor who is possibly a murderer; but the episode is so obscure that I cannot help suspecting Westray's real motive was snobbery. He thought it blasphemy to expose a lord or to throw doubt upon the records of Somerset House and the College of Heralds. Again, in *The Lost Stradivarius,* there is a suggestion of wicked practices in the occult. Le Fanu would never have descended to anything so gentlemanly and so scholarly as the suggestion that the habits of Medmenham Abbey had had a secret revival. When Le Fanu's characters are haunted by guilt, the guilt is guilt, not a connoisseur's lucky historical find. If either of these two novels of Falkner's are attractive light reading, it is because of their antiquarianism and because of the precision of their setting. We are at the beginning of that passion for antiques which started in the nineteen-hundreds, I suppose, and which so oddly foreshadowed the genteel auctioning off of heirlooms which swept Britain and Europe after the last war. *The Nebuly Coat* is an antique in itself. With wonderful verisimilitude, Falkner invented a cathedral town and worked out a carefully documented and imaginary catalogue of its family stains and historical dilapidations, and he hinged his plot on no less a matter than the technical delicacies of architectural restoration. There is also some heraldry in this book and, in *The Lost Stradivarius,* a good deal of musical scholarship. This material and his use of it to create an atmosphere interest us a little now, for he wrote with clarity; but Falkner showed up to this point small sense of character or narrative. This is a mark, so often observed, of the diligent amateur. No professional would document his work so well; but no professional would throw it all away on uninteresting people.

Moonfleet is another matter altogether. Here is a novel which has the sustained excitement, if not the richness of character, of the best work of Stevenson. It is a brilliant pastiche of eighteenth-century adventure, limpid, tender and running over the complicated score of its great detail without ever striking a wrong note or a superfluous one. How true the note always is. Pedantry has vanished. Now when Falkner is describing the history of the wicked Mohunes and the legends of their wickedness and burial in the church beside the sea; when he describes how the tides flood the crypt and the evils that come from it; and later on, when he troubles us with an account of the disused marble quarries of Dorset and the habits of the quarrymen, he pours these things into a story which flows more swiftly on, because of them, to fresh eddies of excitement. The elements of detection and mystery are multiplied. We want to know about those quarries as badly as we want to know about the escaping smugglers who have gone to earth in them. A whole coast with its cliffs, its marshes and its shingle roaring in the storms, has become urgent to us, such is the life which Falkner can impart to topography. These descriptions cannot be skipped, for Falkner achieved here, with an apparent ease, the art of gradual revelation. It was the eighteenth century's great lesson to narrators who had not yet been disorganized by the cult of nature, and who therefore did not throw in a ton of scenery for emotion's sake. Nature was used and useful, and the gradual disclosure of its usefulness was an invaluable accompaniment to the voice of narrative. This is apparent in writers as widely different as the circumstantial Defoe and the melodious Abbé Prévost. There is something of the latter's tone in Falkner's writing, a modest candor, which sets the young hero a little apart from the too stalwart ranks of boy heroes, and gives a tenderness to the circumspect descriptions. Here is Falkner's picture of the country into which the boy and the smuggler escaped after their climb up the cliff face. They are on the edge of the abandoned quarries:

> We had left the stony tillage fields, and the face of the country was covered once more with the closest sward, which was just putting on the brighter green of the spring. This turf was not smooth, but hummocky, for under it lay heaps of worthless stone and marble drawn out of the quarries ages ago, which the green vestment had covered for the most part, though it left sometimes a little patch of broken rubble peering out at the top of a mound. There were many tumbledown walls and low gables left of the cottages of the old quarrymen; grass-covered ridges worked out of the little garden-folds, and here and there still stood a forlorn gooseberry bush or a stunted plum or apple tree with its branches all swept eastward by the up-channel gales. As for the quarry shafts themselves, they too were covered round the tips with the green turf, and down them led a narrow flight of steep-cut steps, with a slide of soapstone at the side, on which the marble

> blocks were once hauled up by wooden winches. Down these steps no feet ever walked now, for not only were suffocating gases said to beset the bottom of the shaft, but men would have it that in the narrow passages below lurked evil spirits and demons. . . . We waited a few minutes and then he took me in his arms and began to descend the steps, back first, as one goes down a hatchway.

That is a fairly static description, a breathing space in the action of the story. Yet how it moves, how it flows and coils like the water receding along the snaky course of one of those southern estuaries that Falkner liked to write about. And the same, simple, inevitable movement is in the passages of action. This is the scene at the end where Elzevir loses his life in trying to rescue the boy on the terrible Chesil Beach.

> I saw the string of men lashed together and, reaching down as far as man might, to save any that came through the surf, and heard them shout to cheer us, and marked a coil of rope flung out. Elzevir was by my side and saw it too, and we both kept our feet and plunged forward through the quivering slack water; but then there came an awful thunder behind, the crash of the sea over the wreck, and we knew that another mountain wave was on our heels. It came in with a swishing roar, a rush and rise of furious water that swept us like corks up the beach, till we were within touch of the rope's end, and the men shouted again to hearten us as they flung it out. Elzevir seized it with his left hand and reached out his right to me. Our fingers touched, and in that very moment the wave fell instantly, with an awful suck, and I was swept down the beach again. Yet the undertow took me not back to sea, for amid the floating wreckage floated the shattered maintop and in the track of that great spar I caught, and so was left with it upon the beach

thirty paces from the men and Elzevir. Then he left his own assured salvation, namely the rope, and strode down again into the very jaws of death to catch me by the hand and set me on my feet.

But the secret of the success of *Moonfleet* does not lie first of all in its ingenious and masterly unveiling of an adventure; nor even in the naturalness of it all. The secret, I think, is that Falkner makes us feel for the church and village of Moonfleet something of that touching emotion which we have had for a place we have lived in and unaccountably loved in its smallest particular. He has hit upon our love for place and on the feeling that, in such a place, great happenings may start as innocently, but as irreparably, as spring water bubbles up from the earth to start a river. And once he had struck this note he sustained it. Not once does it falter. It grows clearer and stronger like a rising wind, like the high note of *Treasure Island,* which never loses its eagerness, or the grave and ominous accent of *The Fall of the House of Usher*.

I do not rank *Moonfleet* with these tales, for it has not their scope. Falkner was no great maker of characters. The boy-narrator and Elzevir the smuggler, who slowly adopts him in place of his dead son, are simple beings; not wooden, not lay figures indeed, but simple. They grow a little, experience makes them, and the dumb growth of their affection into an austere and self-sacrificing love is a moving undertone to the story. Theirs is not the conventional relationship of partners in adventure. One sees the passage of time reversing, or at least modifying, their attitude to each other. But outside of these two there is nobody. In this book, Falkner does not attempt what he could not do excellently; and like one of those small academic paintings in which we detect the flash of a minor master, *Moonfleet* arrests the mind because it has satisfied the eye. We have seen something that is small, perhaps, but exquisitely, affectingly well done.

THE PERFORMING LYNX

"I'm living so far beyond my income," says one of the characters in Saki's *The Unbearable Bassington,* "that we may almost be said to be living apart." That is a pointer to Saki's case: it is the fate of wits to live beyond the means of their feeling. They live by dislocation and extravagance. They talk and tire in the hard light of brilliance and are left frightened and alone among the empty wine glasses and tumbled napkins of the wrecked dinner table. Saki was more than a wit. There was silence in him as well. In that silence one sees a freak of the traveling show of storytellers, perhaps a gifted performing animal, and it is wild. God knows what terrors and cajoleries have gone on behind the scenes to produce this gifted lynx so contemptuously consenting to be half-human. But one sees the hankering after one last ferocious act in the cause of a nature abused. The peculiar character called Keriway who crops up unexplained in the middle of the Bassington novel tells the story of a "tame, crippled crane." "It was lame," Keriway says, "that is why it was tame."

What lamed and what tamed Saki? The hate, passion, loneliness that closed the hearts of the children of the Empire-builders? Like Thackeray, Kipling and Orwell, Saki was one of the children sent "home" from India and Burma to what seemed to them loveless care. Saki did not suffer as Kipling suffered, but we hear of an aunt whom his sister described as a woman of "ungovernable temper, of fierce likes and dislikes, imperious, a moral coward, possessing no brains worth speaking of and a primitive disposition." A Baroness Turgenev, in short. She is thought to be the detested woman in *Sredni Vashtar,* one of Saki's handful of masterpieces, the tale of the boy who plotted and prayed that she should be killed by a ferret. Boy and ferret were satisfied. But something less pat and fashionably morbid than a cruel aunt at Barnstable must lie behind Saki's peculiarity, though she may go some way to explain his understanding of children. We are made by forces much older than ourselves. Saki was a Highland Scot and of a race that was wild and gay in its tribal angers. Laughter sharpens the steel. He belonged—and this is more important—to an order more spirited, melancholy, debonair and wanton than the puddingy Anglo-Saxon world south of the Border, with its middle-class wealth, its worry and its conventions. He could not resist joining it, but he joined to annoy. *The Unbearable Bassington* is a neat piece of taxidermy, a cheerful exposure of the glass case and contents of Edwardian society, a footnote to *The Spoils of Poynton.* In a way, Saki has been tamed by this society, too. Clovis likes the cork-pop of an easy epigram, the schoolboy hilarity of the practical joke and the fizz of instant success—"The art of public life consists to a great extent of knowing exactly where to stop and going a bit further" and so on—he is the slave of the teacup and dates with every new word. He is the pathos of the bubble. But Saki has strong resources:

he is moved by the inescapable nature of the weariness and emptiness of the socialite life, though unable to catch, like Firbank, the minor poetry of fashion. Francesca is too shallow to know tragedy, but she will know the misery of not being able to forget what she did to her son, all her life. She is going to be quietly more humiliated every year. And then, Saki's other resource is to let the animals in with impudent cruelty. The leopard eats the goat in the Bishop's bathroom, the cat rips a houseparty to pieces, the hounds find not a fox but a hyena and it comfortably eats a child; the two trapped enemies in the Carpathian forest make up their feud and prepare to astonish their rescuers with the pious news, but the rescuers are wolves. Irony and polish are meant to lull us into amused, false comfort. Saki writes like an enemy. Society has bored him to the point of murder. Our laughter is only a note or two short of a scream of fear.

Saki belongs to the early period of the sadistic revival in English comic and satirical writing—the movement suggested by Stevenson, Wilde, Beerbohm, Firbank and Evelyn Waugh—the early period when the chief target was the cult of convention. Among these he is the teaser of hostesses, the shocker of dowagers, the mocker of female crises, the man in the incredible waistcoat who throws a spanner into the teacup; but irreverence and impudence ought not to be cultivated. They should occur. Otherwise writers are on the slippery slope of the light article. Saki is on it too often. There is the puzzling, half-redeeming touch of the amateur about him, that recalls Maurice Baring's remark that he made the mistake of thinking life more important than art. But the awkwardness, the jumpiness in some of these sketches, the disproportion between discursion and incident or clever idea has something to do with the journalism of the period—Mr. Evelyn Waugh's suggestion—and, I would add, some connection with the decadence of club culture. The great period of that culture was in the mid-nineteenth century: by the early 1900's it had run into the taste for the thin, the urbane and the facetious; and to sententious clichés: Lady Bastable is "wont to retire in state to the morning room"; Clovis makes a "belated appearance at the breakfast table"; people "fare no better" and are "singularly" this or that. The cinema, if nothing else, has burned this educated shrubbery out of our comic prose. But Saki's club prose changes when he is writing descriptions of nature (at which he is a minor master) when he describes animals and children or draws his sharp new portraits. His people are chiefly the stupid from the county, the natterers of the drawing room and the classical English bores, and though they are done in cyanide, the deed is touched by a child's sympathy for the vulnerable areas of the large mammals. He collected especially the petty foibles and practical vanities of women (unperturbed by sexual disturbance on his part), and so presented them as persons, just as he presented cats as cats and dogs as dogs.

> Eleanor hated boys and she would have liked to have whipped this one long and often. It was perhaps the yearning of a woman who had no children of her own.

Or there is the scene between the pleasant Elaine who, having just become engaged to be married, decides to increase her pleasure by scoring off her aunt, and her country cousin who has also just got engaged. Saki is clear that Elaine is a thoroughly nice girl:

> "There is as much difference between a horseman and a horsy man as there is between a well-dressed man and a dressy one," said Elaine judicially, "and you may have noticed how seldom a dressy woman really knows how to dress. An old

> lady of my acquaintance observed the other day, some people are born with a sense of how to clothe themselves, others acquire it, others look as if their clothes had been thrust upon them."

A stale joke? Beware of Saki's claws; he goes on in the next sentence:

> She gave Lady Caroline her due quotation marks, but the sudden tactfulness with which she looked away from her cousin's frock was entirely her own idea.

Saki's male bores and male gossips are remarkable in our comic literature, for he does not take the usual English escape of presenting them as eccentrics. Bores are bores, classifiable, enjoyable like anacondas or the lungfish. There is Henry Creech with "the prominent, penetrating eyes of a man who can do no listening in the ordinary way and whose eyes have to perform the function of listening for him." And bores have lives. When Stringham made a witty remark for the first time in his life in the House of Commons one evening, remarking indeed that, "the people of Crete unfortunately make more history than they can consume locally," his wife grasped that some clever woman had got hold of him, and took poison.

E. V. Knox's edition of the tales is a pleasant one, but it inexplicably omits all the stories from *Beasts and Superbeasts* in which Saki was at his best. I do not much care for Saki's supernatural stories, though I like the supernatural touch: the dog, for example, in *The Unbearable Bassington,* at the ghastly last dinner party. His best things are always ingenious: the drama of incurring another's fate in *The Hounds of Fate,* the shattering absurdity of *Louis,* the artificial dog; and the hilarious tale of the tattooed Dutch commercial traveler who is confined to Italy because he is officially an unexportable work of art. The joke, for Saki, is in the kill. On the whole, it is the heart that is aimed at. He is always richly informed in the vanities of political life and does it in a manner that recalls Disraeli. Except for novels by Belloc, there has been none of this political writing since. Artificial writers of his kind depend, of course, on the dangerous trick logic of contrivance. Success here is a gamble. For morality he substitutes the child's logic of instinct and idea.

The Unbearable Bassington is one of the lasting trifles. Its very surprising quality is the delicate apprehension of pleasure and misery. Saki was short of pity. He was an egotist and had no soothing word for pain. He knew that certain kinds of pain cannot be forgotten. Self-dramatization, self-pity, none of the usual drugs, can take that stone from the heart. He is thoughtful but will offer nothing. In this frivolous novel Saki begins to mature. His next novel, *The Coming of William,* written in 1912 and warning lazy and corrupt Society of the German menace, was good propaganda. He imagined an England annexed to Germany and it makes uncomfortable reading; for silly Society turns instantly to collaboration. There is a more serious discomfort here; a disagreeable anti-Semitism shows more plainly in this book and one detects, in this soldierly sado-masochist, a desire for the "discipline" of authoritarian punishment. He is festive and enjoyable as the wild scourge; but the danger obviously was that this performing lynx, in the demi-monde between journalism and a minor art, might have turned serious and started lecturing and reforming his trainer. In earlier and more spontaneous days, he would have eaten him.

TWO WRITERS AND MODERN WAR

"And so good-bye to the war. I know not how it may have been or may be to others—to me the main interest I found (and still in recollection find) in the rank and file of the armies, both sides, and in those specimens amid the hospitals and even the dead on the field."

This passage comes from *Specimen Days,* from those pages where Whitman described his work in the hospitals during the American Civil War. The interest of Whitman's pages about this war lies in the fact that he is the first to reveal a modern attitude. He stands at the breaking point with the past.

The American Civil War was the first modern war. It is true that the Crimean War, some eight years earlier, has resemblances with the American conflict. There is the awakening of public concern for the care of casualties, a concern which had grown with medical knowledge. But the Crimean War was fought in a small area. It was fought by professional soldiers—the British commander-in-chief directed operations from his private yacht to which he returned to dine and sleep every night—and the casualties, though heavy, were less than half of those suffered in America, where a million men died in the field, the hospitals and the prison camps. The Civil War involved everyone, the armies became conscript armies almost at once. The professional soldiers were put to the task of training the man in the street. Similar conditions, it will be said, existed in the Napoleonic wars—for Napoleon was the first to use conscription on a great scale. But the Napoleonic army was the Grande Armée. The conscript was transformed by the professional and national notions of Glory and the impulse of the Revolution. He was, in a sense, a party man and not a citizen in military dress. And then, when we read the memoirs of those wars, in English or in French, we notice that they are the work of men bent on the military career. They have the professional officer's outlook. Gleig—a subaltern of Wellington's—who wrote an account of his adventures in the Peninsula, is typical of them. One can imagine Gleig reborn in the sixties and exclaiming at the moral deterioration of his profession, once it is overweighted by every Tom, Dick and Harry. There is a loss of style and manner, both in action and in the narratives written afterwards. The precise horrors of war are sometimes mentioned in the classical records but, generally, rhetorical clichés are preferred: carnage, slaughter and so on.

If Gleig were to return and read Whitman's notes, he would first be struck by the importance given to the casualties and the hospitals; and then by the unprotected nakedness of human feeling. The classical manner was not inhumane; but it put military dignity and professional virtue first. It was the manner of leaders. War, the most lawless of activities, was given a frame of decorum; you might not always fight by the code of honor, but a code of honor existed and, above all, you spoke and wrote in accord with it. The British troops sacked San Sebastian and fired at the officers who tried to stop them; but Gleig in *The Subaltern* speaks in the voice of a gentleman when he describes and deplores the event. There is no suggestion that war is a human tragedy. This suggestion is not made until the civilian fights. He cannot shrug his shoulders and say, "C'est la guerre." He is stunned by his own fears, stupefied by his own atrocities, amazed at his happiness, incredulous at the point of death. When all people are at war, no code, no manner, can contain the experience. The nearest writers to Whitman are Tolstoy and Erckmann-Chatrian—it is interesting to note that they were all writing about war at the same time—but Tolstoy's ironical pacifism and Erckmann-Chatrian's mildness and peaceableness are a branch of the main stream of popular feeling. They are not, like Whitman, the stream itself. The *Histoire d'un Conscrit de 1813* was written in 1864. It has been called *l'Iliade de la peur* and it portrays the pathos of the conscript's situation. The tragedy of the conscript is a passive one: that a quiet, peaceable man like himself should be *killed!* But in Whitman—as in Wilfred Owen—the tragedy is not passive; it lies not only in what is done to a man but in what he himself does and in what happens to him inside. When we compare these things with the sentiment of Erckmann-Chatrian we see that these authors are propagandists concerned with society. The freshness of their document is deceptive. They describe the Napoleonic wars with wonderful verisimilitude; but the wars are not taken direct from life. These writers have digested the moving simplicities of old men's hearsay. They are propagandists with an uncommonly delicate ear. They write to warn opinion in the fond domestic parlor behind the little shop.

Compared with them, Whitman does not know his mind. He is all over the place. He is the public. It is typical of *Specimen Days* that its first picture of the war is of the news spreading in the streets at night.

The emotion of the street catches him. He is not intoxicated with patriotism but he does not deny the message of the pennants and the flags in the street. He is the man in the parlor who goes out into the street and loses his head. He feels the herd instinct. Two great wars have made us guarded, and when we read *Specimen Days* and especially the poems called *Drum Taps,* we resist this old-fashioned war. The sun has faded the defiant and theatrical photograph, and paled the headlines to a weak-tea brown. The uniforms are shabby. We suspect Whitman's idea that out of this a nation is born; it sounds like the cracked bugle and slack drum of propaganda. And yesterday's propaganda puts no one in a flurry. Yet, in all this, the loquacious Whitman is right. It is the bewildering thing in all his work, that this dressed-up egotist with all the air of a ham actor, is always half-right when he is most dubious. He is the newspaper man who reflects the ambiguous quality of public feeling. His virtue is that he begins on the pavement and that, like the streets, he has no shame and no style. Excitement and incantation take the place of it. The soldiers straggle into Washington after the defeat at Bull Run:

> The men appear, at first sparsely and shame-faced enough, then thicker, in the streets of Washington—appear in Pennsylvania Avenue, and on the steps and basement entrances. They come along, in disorderly mobs, some in squads, stragglers, companies. Occasionally, a rare regiment, in perfect order, with its officers (some gaps, dead, the true braves), marching in silence, with lowering faces, stern, weary to sinking, all black and dirty, but every man with his musket, and stepping alive; but these are the exceptions. Side-walks of Pennsylvania Avenue, Fourteenth Street, etc., crowded, jamm'd with citizens, darkies, clerks, everybody, lookers-on; women in the

windows, curious expressions from faces, as those swarms of dirt-cover'd return'd soldiers there (will they never end?) move by; but nothing said, no comments. . . . Amid the deep excitement, crowds and motion, and desperate eagerness, it seems strange to see many, very many, of the soldiers sleeping—in the midst of all, sleeping sound. They drop down anywhere, on the steps of houses, up close by the basements or fences, on the sidewalks, aside on some vacant lot, and deeply sleep. A poor seventeen- or eighteen-year-old boy lies there, on the stoop of a grand house; he sleeps so calmly, so profoundly. Some clutch their muskets firmly even in sleep. Some in squads; comrades, brothers, close together—and on them, as they lay, sulkily, drips the rain.

All that effort to produce one last remarkable phrase—there you have Whitman.

After this the reality begins. And the reality, as the first modern war drags on, is the casualty list. In the classical narratives men are merely shot. Sometimes they are blown up. The aftermath was not minutely described. "Bloodshed," "carnage," generalize it. Whitman, too, uses those words but with all his voice. And he went round the hospitals and saw the gangrene, the amputations, the unspeakable wounds. He smelt the ether. Saw the tiptoe walking. The screens put round. He saw the stretcher cases lying out in the rain and glad to be cooled by it. He knew men crawled under bushes to die by inches. He took down the last words and wrote letters for men too weak to write. The men were not sorry for themselves. They talked very little. They had become detached and incredulous. Thousands, he knew, died and were never identified. It struck him, when he saw the burial trenches, that the typical soldier of this first modern war was "unknown."

That discovery marks the beginning of the modern

attitude to war. We write as followers, not leaders. And though Whitman likes the heroic act, the message in the leader's eye, enjoys seeing the President ride past with his escort of cavalry and feels the public emotion of the "great convulsive drums," he writes more surely when he goes back to the rank and file, when he recovers his sense of anonymity. (Odd that this huge and often so flaccid egotist should be able to puff himself large enough until he is identified with all the people and lost in them: it is his paradox.) It is his paradox, too, that doggerel and the real thing traipse along together like the blind leading the blind, unable to see, unable to stop. In avoiding literary jargon, he easily wallowed in the tear-jerking stuff of small town In Memoriam notices—to emerge from the bathos with perhaps one line or two worth writing:

"Grieve not so, dear mother" (the just-grown daughter speaks through her sobs,
The little sisters huddle around speechless and dismay'd)
"See, dearest mother, the letter says Pete will soon be better."

Alas, poor boy, he will never be better (nor may-be needs to be better that brave and simple soul),
While they stand at home at the door he is dead already,
The only son is dead.

But the mother needs to be better,
She with thin form presently drest in black,
By day her meals untouch'd, then at night fitfully sleeping, often waking,

In the midnight waking, weeping, longing with
one deep longing,
O that she might withdraw unnoticed, silent from
life escape and withdraw,
To follow, to seek, to be with her dear dead son.

Blake could be simple, but he was never maudlin. And there are the curious parallels with the poetry of the last war, the same mixing of the romantic note with the realism. We turn from Wilfred Owen's

I am the enemy you killed, my friend,
I knew you in this death.

to Whitman's

Word over all, beautiful as the sky,
Beautiful that war and all its deeds of carnage
must in time be utterly lost,
That the hands of the sisters Death and Night in-
cessantly softly wash again, and ever again,
this soil'd world:
For my enemy is dead, a man divine as myself is
dead,
I look where he lies white-faced and still in the
coffin—I draw near,
Bend down and touch lightly with my lips the
white face in the coffin.

Well, there it is. The set piece has gone, the full-bottomed formal patriotism of the eighteenth century, the episodic poetry of the early nineteenth. The sense of occasion has gone. There are no more "incidents from the French camp," there is no loss of the *Revenge*, no *Charge of the Light Brigade*, no *Burial of Sir John Moore*. The serving soldier has been outnumbered and swamped by the civilian soldier. The profession has been drowned in the classes. Nor can we attribute the change to a decay of the love of country—as some critics tried to do at the beginning of the last war—for Whitman was a bombinating patriot, yet he wrote no pieces of occasion of that kind. *Drum Taps* describe the general scene, what the unknown and anonymous man did and saw and how filthily he died. Patriotism has not decayed; but the human being has emerged. He emerged first of all, it is interesting to observe, in a civil war, a war of ideas; and in the country which, to so many people, had seemed the Promised Land, where no formal tradition of war existed. Whitman himself observed, in his confused groping way, that a new way of warfare was necessary to America. A new way of writing about war certainly emerged; perhaps that is what he was trying to say.

It is worth while turning at this point to an American novelist who is the child of the Tolstoy-Whitman movement, the child of the Crimea and Bull Run. I am thinking of Stephen Crane and his book *The Red Badge of Courage* which was published in the nineties. The achievement of Crane was individual and high, but in placing it we must now confess that it came in on the Tolstoy wave; and that but for Tolstoy, it would never have been written. There is an important difference of experience between Tolstoy and Crane. In writing respectively about the Napoleonic and the American Civil Wars, both writers were reconstructing wars they had not seen; but Tolstoy *had* seen the Crimea, he had been a soldier, whereas Crane had read Tolstoy but had never seen war at all when he wrote his famous book, just as Defoe's *Journal of the Plague Year* was done by a writer who had never seen the plague: Crane became a war-correspondent after his book was written. It is in fact a romance or fable, subjective in impulse, in the tradition of Poe, Hawthorne, Melville, and James. An American critic has suggested that it was the fruit of a conflict of religious conscience and, indeed, the battle is compared with a mad religion and, at times, with a war of sectaries. The writer has been committed to "fight the good fight," is frightened at the open clash and then has to reassemble his self-respect out of fear, doubt and lies and learn to live with his experience. This may or may not be true of the origins of the book; what matters is that, Tolstoy and War Memoirs aiding, Crane has completely transposed himself into an imaginary eye-witness. One curious common emotion nevertheless unites the master and the disciple. They reject the formal, the professional and rhetorical attitude to war; they reject the illusions of the profession and the traditional litanies of patriotism; but they cannot quite conceal a certain sadness at the passing of these things. In Tolstoy one so often suspects the secret longing of the repentant, the too-repentant soldier.

The Red Badge of Courage is a tour de force. Crane starts a bugle call and sustains it without a falter to the end of the book. The scene is a single battlefield in the American Civil War, and the purpose of the novel is to show the phases by which a green young recruit loses his romantic illusions and his innocence in battle, and acquires a new identity, a hardened virtue. War has ceased to be a bewraying and befogging dream in his mind; it has become his world and he derives virtue from his unity with it. There is a second element in the story. To Crane a battlefield is like a wounded animal. The convulsions of its body, its shudders, its cries and its occasional repose, are the spasmodic movements and dumb respites of the groups of soldiers. There is not only the individual mind in the battlefield, but there is the mass mind also. Crane watches the merging of the individual with the herd. There is no plot in this book; it is a collection of episodes. We do not know which battle is being described or what are its objects. The rights and wrongs of the war itself are not discussed. No civilian and hardly a sight of the work of man, like a house or a cultivated field, comes into the picture. Few of the characters are named; the central figure is known simply as "the young man." The enemy are just the enemy, something fabulous and generally invisible in the blue smoke line of the engagement, terrifying and dragon-like at the worst, and at the best a singularity to be mistrusted. Who wins or loses is obscure. The whole thing is almost as anonymous as a poem or a piece of music and has the same kind of tension and suspense. For we are not specially interested in the mortal fate of the boy. We do not specially fear that he will be killed, nor do we privately hope he will cover himself with glory. Our eyes are fixed on something different in him; on each adjustment in his character as it comes along. At the end of this book, we say to ourselves, we too shall know how we shall behave when we discard our illusions about war and meet the reality. Romantically we fear or hope for battle as a way of singling ourselves out and dying; but underneath this daydream is the awe of knowing that battle is a way of living before it is a way of dying, and one in which we cannot calculate our behavior in advance. It was one of the discoveries of the unrhetorical attitude to war in literature, that even the men on the right side and in the just cause are afraid; and to Crane—an adventurous man who died young from the effects of going to see trouble all over the earth—the deep fear of fear was a personal subject.

This comes out in the first chapter of *The Red Badge of Courage,* where the young man is seen in the camp listening to the rumors and torturing himself with questions. He feels courageous but will courage stand? Will he stay or will he run in panic? These are overmastering questions. The first dead do not scare him, nor does the early uproar. He can stand the first attack and face the fear hidden in the wall of forest where the enemy lie, and after the frenzy of the first onslaught he lies for a few moments in the trench overcome by a sense of fellowship with his companions and experiencing with astonishment "the joy of a man who at last finds leisure." But, fixed on their intense personal problem, his heart and mind have not yet understood that while the imagination expects decisive and single answers, reality does not deal in such simplicities. The attack, to everyone's despair, is renewed. The second phase has begun. It is too much. The youth throws down his rifle and runs. Here Crane shows his power as a novelist, for in this part of the story he writes those dramatic scenes and draws those portraits which have given the book its place in the literature of war. This is where the dying soldier, walking white and erect like a rejected prince among his broken court, goes stiffly toward his grave. Crane was a dreamer of the ways of dying, but this death is one of the most terrible, for it is a *progress* to death:

> The spectral soldier was at his side like a stalking reproach. The man's eyes were still fixed in a stare into the unknown. His gray, appalling face had attracted attention in the crowd, and men, slowing to his dreary pace, were walking with him. They were discussing his plight, questioning and giving him advice. In a dogged way he repelled them, signing to them to go on and leave him alone. The shadows of his face were deepening and his tight lips seemed holding in check the moan of great despair. There could be seen a certain stiffness in the movement of his body, as if he were taking infinite care not to arouse the passion of his wounds. As he went on he seemed always looking for a place like one who goes to choose a grave. Something in the gesture of the man as he waved the bloody and pitying soldiers away made the youth start as if bitten. He yelled in horror. Tottering forward he laid a quivering hand upon

the man's arm. As the latter slowly turned his wax-like features toward him the youth screamed:

"Gawd! Jim Conklin!"

The tall soldier made a little commonplace smile.

"Hello, Henry," he said.

If the boy's horror and quivering seem conventionally overemphatic in that passage, the rest is not. Writers are always faced by two sets of words before they write; those which will draw a literary curtain over reality, and those which will raise the veil in our minds and lead us to see for the first time. Crane's gift for raising the veil is clear. The presence of "spectre" and "commonplace smile" in that portrait is imaginative observation at its best.

The book is filled with observation of this kind. Some is placed there by poetic intuition:

> The sun spread disclosing rays, and, one by one, regiments burst into view like armed men just born of the earth. The youth perceived that the time had come. He was about to be measured. For a moment he felt in the face of his great trial like a babe, and the flesh over his heart seemed but thin. He seized time to look about him calculatingly.
>
> But he instantly saw that it would be impossible for him to escape from the regiment. It enclosed him. There were iron laws of tradition and law on four sides. He was in a moving box.

This inner sensation of the experience is matched by wonderful, small phrases of verisimilitude: "His *forgotten feet* were constantly knocking against stones or getting entangled in briars." Or there is this picture—how common it has become in modern realism, which Crane anticipates by thirty or forty years:

> Once the line encountered the body of a dead soldier. He lay upon his back staring at the sky.

> He was dressed in an awkward suit of yellowish brown. The youth could see that the soles of his shoes had been worn to the thinness of writing paper, and from a great rent in one the dead foot projected piteously. And it was as if fate had betrayed the soldier. In death it exposed to his enemies that poverty which in life he had perhaps concealed from his friends.

The only word a modern reporter would not have written in that passage is the word "piteously."

Toughness, that is to say fear of facing the whole subject, as Crane faced it, has intervened to make the modern writer's picture purely visual and inhumane—one remembers the turned-out pockets of the dead in Hemingway and his bravado about writing a natural history of the dead. The pathetic fallacy abounds in Crane's prose and we hear of "the remonstrance" and "arguments" of the guns; but for all the Whistlerian artiness—noted by H. G. Wells—there is pity, there is human feeling. There is a background of value and not a backdrop gaudy with attitudes. There is a quest for virtue—what else is the meaning of the young boy's innocent odyssey among his fears, his rages and his shames?—and not, as one sees in Kipling, the search for a gesture or some dramatic personal stand which avoids the issue and saves the face. Crane ignores the actor in human beings, the creature with the name on the personal playbill; he goes—at any rate in *The Red Badge of Courage*—for the anonymous voice in the heart.

THE TRIPPERS

One of the nice things about foreigners is their faithful regard for English light humor. When we disclaim it, when we snobbishly indicate that this fanciful persiflage goes out of date very quickly, they reproach us. If we explain that the speciality had become sententious at the turn of the century and was in decline after 1914, when wit, impatience, cruelty and vivid scorn returned to our comic writing, the foreign reader persists that our gracious light humor was civilization itself. Victorian civilization, we may reply; but millions have read a book like Jerome K. Jerome's *Three Men in a Boat,* and in all the languages of Europe and Asia. One would hardly have thought that this modest little tale of the misadventures of three can-opening suburban clerks on the Thames would stand up to American connoisseurs of Mark Twain's Mississippi, but it did. Pirated at once, the book conquered America as it amused the students of Bombay, Peking and Valparaiso.

The gag-book, of course, follows the flag. It is now American. The American response to Jerome arose possibly because he had the episodic digressing, garrulous quality of their vernacular writers. He is close to the Twain of *The Jumping Frog.* But Jerome, like the authors of *The Diary of a Nobody,* and like W. W. Jacobs, belongs to a secure, small Arcadia where the comic disasters of life are the neater for being low. Jerome's humor is a response of the emerging lower middle class to the inconvenience of their situation. Their dreams have left a legacy of small comic defeat. Overworked, they regard idleness as a joke. They have to do everything in penn'orths and ha'porths. Genteel, they have to repress their hilarious envy-disapproval of any burst of bad language on the part of the undeserving poor. The humor of life's little troubles was called the "too real," the joke lying in deadly and misleading accounts of humiliating trivia. One might take Jerome as the signal that, in 1889, holidays for this overworked and masochistic class became possible. It is "too real" that the tin-opener (new emancipating gadget of democracy) has been forgotten. It is "too real" that George and Harris have to share the same bed; that the bed is two foot six wide and that they have to tie themselves together with the sheets in order to keep themselves from falling out. It is "too real," *i.e.*, only too likely, that the dog will bring a rat to drop into the terrible stew they are making. It is "too real" that a worn-out child will drop a half-eaten bun in the maze at Hampton Court. The packing, the rain, the clubbing together to hire a cab, the mockery of small boys, the troubles with towropes, laundry, butter, the belief that the banjo is a lovely instrument and that *Two Lovely Black Eyes* is a beautiful song are the vulgarities of life. There is nothing surreal about the "too real"; it is the chronic. We know little about the inner lives of Jerome's characters. It is true that Harris has a comic nightmare, but this is merely the traditional joke about strong drink. The odd thing is that the "too real" could be appreciated in Bombay. Is the tale of Uncle Podger a universal domestic myth? Would Arabs laugh at it? The appeal of Jerome lies in his gentleness and irony, in his habit of digression, his gift of capping his comic moments with a final extravagant act that outbids life altogether. Above all, his book is an idyll. Jerome himself, astonished by the book's success, guilefully argues that it could not be due to its vulgarity alone. The absence of women gives us a clue—there is one, but she is a mere body that floats by, drowned; *Three Men in a Boat* has the absurdity of a male pipe dream. *Huckleberry Finn* is basically this also; but the tobacco is stronger and indeed, generally, chewed.

The idyll is of the stream on which the loud, bickering, banjo-playing boatload floats lightly along. Not lightly, of course; sculling blisters and half kills them. The joke lies in the modesty of the incident; bumping the bank, getting someone else's shirt wet, eating the horrible camping food, annoying fishermen and motor launches, singing with self-confidence and out of tune, drifting unawares toward the weir, getting the tent up for the night. A lot of it is stock comedy. We know the tent will fall down; the question that awakens the ingenuity of the masters is, how will it fall down? At Cookham these suburbans will imagine themselves in the "wild heart of nature." They are not mugs; they have to match their bounce against the primeval cunning of landladies and the pensive malice of innkeepers, anglers and boatmen. Skillfully Jerome plays everything down. He relies on misleading moral commentary and on that understatement which runs like a rheumatism through English humor. Certain jokes date. Bad language is no longer a joke since swearing came in after the first World War. Idleness is no longer a joke—we have moved into an age that says it believes in leisure. And we find nothing piquant in the silliness of girls. The silly girl in light humor was soon replaced by Wodehouse's pretty power stations. (The light humorists of Jerome's period were obliged to avoid sex; they became experts in femininity.) But the dating of a joke does not matter; the laughter in

Jerome is caused less by any fact than by the false conclusions drawn from it. He will mildly note that bargees are sometimes "rude" to one another and use language "which, no doubt, in their calmer moments, they regret." Again the work joke has the intricacy of a conceit in Jerome's skillful hands.

> It always seems to me that I am doing much more work than I should do. . . . But though I crave for work I still like to be fair. I do not ask for more than my fair share. But I get it without asking for it—so at least it seems to me and this worries me. George says that he does not think that I need trouble myself on the subject. He thinks it is only my over-scrupulous nature that makes me fear I am having more than my due; and that, as a matter of fact, I don't have as much as I ought. But I expect he says this only to comfort me.

The son of a preacher, Jerome saw that one of the funniest things in a human being is his conscience.

The light humorists get too much pleasure out of educated periphrasis and self-congratulatory club wit. These lead inevitably to heavy prose. Jerome, like W. W. Jacobs, escaped the danger. His prose is clear and simple. It muses on like some quiet, ironical tune played on a malicious whistle. He is free from the journalistic vice of exhibitionism and frantic juggling with bright ideas. He sits by himself on the river bank and drifts on from tune to tune, happily and regardless. He is a very economical writer. In anecdote, he is a master of leading the reader on quietly and then of rushing in a line that suddenly makes the joke take to the air and go mad. The tale of Uncle Podger hanging the picture is a notable piece of technical virtuosity. The packing of the trunk begins as a joke but ends in the complexity of French farce or Restoration comedy. The good light humorist is not a careless fellow with one or two brainwaves and surprises only; he is a deedy lover of the detail that delays the action until the pressure has reached the proper bursting point. There are some conventional phrases in Jerome's famous account of opening the can of pineapple, but it is a model. They had tried the penknife, a pair of scissors and a hitcher: the tin merely rolled over, broke a tea cup and fell into the river. George and Harris were no more than a little cut about the face:

> Then we all got mad. We took that tin out on the bank and Harris went up into a field and got a big sharp stone and I went back into the boat and brought out the mast, and George held the tin and Harris held the sharp end of his stone against the top of it and I took the mast and poised it high in the air and gathered all my strength and brought it down.
>
> It was George's straw hat that saved his life that day . . . Harris got off with a flesh wound.
>
> After that I took the tin off myself and hammered at it with the mast till I was worn out and sick at heart whereupon Harris took it in hand.
>
> We beat it out flat; we beat it back square; we battered it into every form known to geometry. Then George went at it and knocked it into a shape so strange, so weird, so unearthly in its wild hideousness that he got frightened and threw away the mast. Then we all three sat down on the grass and looked at it.
>
> There was one great dent across the top that had the appearance of a mocking grin and it drove us furious, so that Harris rushed at the thing and caught it up and flung it into the middle of the river, and as it sank we hurled our curses at it and we got into the boat and rowed away from the spot and never paused until we reached Maidenhead.

This is pure music hall, of course; much of Jerome is quiet comic patter. He was, in fact, something of an actor. But the idyll frames it all. And peacefully transforms it. A collection of light sketches becomes a complete mirage. A world is never created on any level without the secret structure of conflict. Jerome's case was like that of Dickens in the *Pickwick Papers*. He was commissioned to write an historical guide to the Thames and bits of that survive in the book. He was also a meditative man with a religious background. One or two little sermons are embedded in the text. To us they are incongruous, but late-Victorian farce was not hostile to sentiment. These pieties give an engaging wash of pure sentimental purple to Jerome's water color. He was always saved by his lightness of touch. He succeeds less with history. Jokes about Queen Elizabeth and Magna Carta are heavy going. It takes a schoolmaster or a Mark Twain to get the best out of them. Nonconformists like Jerome are apt to be too fervently conventional about history. As for the landscape, it is agreeably kept in its place. The glitter of the main stream, the rankness of the shadows, the gushing of the locks and the streaming of the weirs at night are done with a pleasant subdued versifying. These sights do not overwhelm his true business—that row of elderly anglers (for example) sitting on their chairs in a punt, who are suddenly knocked off, fall into the bottom of the boat and are left—in sublime phrase—"picking fish off each other."

Mr. D. C. Browning who writes an introduction to the Everyman Edition of the book which contains also *Three Men on the Bummel* tries to persuade us that the latter is as good. What the German tour does is to point to the reason for the superiority of the book about the Thames. It is an idyll of youth. In the German book the heroes are older. They are married. They have lost the happy, impartial rudeness of unattached young men. This time they have to be informative. They still sparkle but the lark has turned into a tour. Jerome was very shrewd about the Germans and these, sedulously trying to penetrate the mystery of English fancy, used *Three Men on the Bummel* as a textbook in German schools.

MR. FORSTER'S BIRTHDAY

"May I never resemble M. de Lesseps," E. M. Forster wrote when he considered the famous statue by the Suez Canal on one of his journeys to India. "May no achievement upon an imposing scale be mine." He has indeed been a haunting absence in the English novel, but on the occasion of his eightieth birthday, we can allow ourselves to dress up our prose in the boater and blazer of 1905 and think of his silence, since *Passage to India,* as "a rotten business," without a moral—like Harold's dropping of the oars and dying, in *The Point of It*—and of Forster's survival in our literature as a "cert." How does one survive if one does not impose? Forster has survived so far by interposing. Where his elders, Shaw, Wells, Kipling, imposed by sheer efficiency and manpower, Forster has interposed and influenced by a misleading slackness, by the refusal to speak in a public voice. This has given the personal a startling strength. He has had, one guesses, more influence on the educated middle classes than any other

English writer in the last thirty or forty years; for it is he who has taught them to disengage themselves from their inherited official, not to say imperial, personality. The Empire Kipling celebrated, Forster destroyed, and by a handful of out-of-date novels—for it was his fate to have a great deal of his material pulled from under his feet by the 1914 war. In saying his say against imperialism, he exhausted in advance what he could have said, as a novelist, against totalitarianism. He was kind enough to write articles.

One can rely on English life to produce these personal voices: a Samuel Butler, a Mary Kingsley, a Forster; in our own generation, a George Orwell. Their voices are direct, natural, distinct and disengaged, malignly flat. The machine stops when they start talking. We are so used to various sorts of "side" in English life, that we are startled and pleased by the note of authority from nature. Outside of our poetry we find that voice hard to hit on. Forster's gift has been just that: the private voice, carrying without effort, in the public place. The refusal to be great; the attack on the will and the bad heart; the two cheers instead of the usual three for democracy, the third being reserved for "love the Beloved Republic, which feeds upon Freedom and lives"; the belief in personal relationships—"the heart signs no document"—and an aristocracy of "the sensitives, the considerate and the plucky"; the debating-point plea for a "period of apathy, inertia and uninventiveness"—these are not withdrawals. Some are principled assertions of the supreme value of individual life; some are there to redress a balance. None is a brilliant paradox put down by a consuming brain. The apologist for softness is intellectually hard; the liberal who has been forced out of economic *laisser faire* and who believes that, nevertheless, *laisser faire* is the only doctrine that "pays"—a favorite ironic word—in the world of the spirit, is not proposing to let us do what we like. No one is let off in Forster's novels; like Jane Austen, he is a moral realist. Leonard Bast, the prototype of the angry young man, will get a rap on the knuckles for being a crushed soul. Having a chip—a maiden aunt seems to say—is no excuse for hysteria and making messes. Mr. Wilcox catches it for being a soul-crusher. No tears, I seem to remember, are shed in Forster's novels. The sins of the heart, the failure to "connect," don't pay: they end in emptiness and panic. Those are better words than the jargon we have learned to use since the nervous breakdown, if only because they imply the moral imperative which is necessarily lacking in scientific studies of the mind.

There is the voice of the decided moralist in Forster; fortunately for the English novel, it has been transposed into the accents of the brusque and off-hand sanity which is in the central tradition of our comedy. Like Shaw's—though in the private interest, being more concerned with intimate feeling than with justice—Forster's is a comedy of ideas, and the danger there was that it would be expressed in a comedy of types or that he would have chosen people possessed of too great a skill in debate. He escaped this danger by his brilliant use of people who had been thoroughly unfitted to deal with their situations; like so many of Henry James's characters they are null or dull. Looking again at the early short stories which try out the themes to be taken up by *Where Angels Fear to Tread* or *Howards End* one is, at first, shaken by their pedestrian characters. How faded the people are now; they were born faded. Everyone outside Cambridge, one suspects, had to bear that accusation. Pompous, shabby, fussy suburbans they are, a collection of dim widows, daughters genteel or bossy, sons emasculated or emotionally congested. There are the mild, mechanical soldiers and all are liable to the blood pressure, the willfulness or the frostbite of a class consciousness that has passed out of our knowledge. Formidable to deal with, these injured families are in danger of suffering (as Gissing's characters do) from an initial social pathos which is unforgivable in works of art. (Class theories play the part of the famous pathetic fallacy.) But, at second glance, the pathos goes. For these unlikely dullards are suddenly shaken by issues that had never occurred to them as existing; they are tripped up by melodrama, and their dullness makes their situation more arresting. They are made to skip and look lively. Mr. Forster's beliefs are gentle, but he has no sentimental indulgence for weakness, and we remember that behind the fineness of his spiritual scrutiny lie the scrupulous traditions of the Clapham Sect; working in him is a spirited agnosticism and he does not see why the moral stakes for these muddled gamblers should not be put very high or why the upper middle classes should not have to risk all. In a way, he treats the English as if they were foreigners—a good idea considering how anti-foreign we have always been. His people swing between two states of mind—the disinterested and the benighted; and they fall into four foreign groups: the Teutonic—heading toward suicide in a sea of general ideas; his Latins—vulgar, avaricious but redeemable because they have not been castrated by good taste, are in the sink-or-swim of the instinctive life, and are liable to racial memories of Mediterranean paganism; the Oriental—passive, touchy and affronted; and the inhabitants of Tonbridge. Where have we seen the Forster situations before? In the novel-poems of the poet Clough, but whereas Clough is torn in half and is half-guilty, half-aggressive about his passivity and his escape into abstract thought, Forster presents the picture of a united personality who knows his mind. He knows what he is committed to.

It is not like the committal of Shaw or Butler—with

whom he has, however, some affinity—nor any of the other committals of those who attacked the official late Victorian or Edwardian personality. His comedy is not freakish; it is not accommodating; there is no comfort in his skepticism. He is not scabrous and not at all the satirist, even if he caricatures; he is without the orgiastic sense of the full comic writers who revel in meaninglessness. He is not very sociable. His comedy is positive and spiritual; it has one most alarming trait: assurance. It is lonely. It has courage. He has always got his deadliest effect from a pretense of sloppiness, from a casual, slangy disregard of the spirit of composure, or from a piece of parenthetical bathos. That opening argument about the cow in *The Longest Journey* is an example. If he is casually disrespectful, he is also casually abrupt about matters of life and death: the echo in the cave, Gino's outbreak of physical cruelty at the crux of sorrow in his child's death, young Wilcox getting three years for hitting someone with an old sword, Leonard dying perfunctorily because a bookcase falls on him, the baby falling out of the carriage, and those brief, dismissed sudden deaths in boats, playing fields and at the level-crossing. The intellectual must face casualty; but he had better remember casualty and the inexplicable. None of these famous incidents will "do" in a realistic novel; the shock is too great and one might attack them as pointers to a suspicion that Mr. Forster has exaggerated the device of not belonging to the world, and even that he grew up so quickly because he refused to join it. But these incidents, of course, succeed in romance where the writer has the license to load his dice as he wishes. He has, also, a hankering after the pagan acceptance of mercilessness and the absence of tears.

Since his time, anyone in the nature of a personage has vanished from the English and American novel. The official has gone. The conversational, the vernacular voice has come in, but only in the interests of naturalism. It is common now to read novels in which physical life is rendered so clearly that we have the impression of seeing it before our eyes like the pebbles of a clear-running stream. That impression can be had from Mr. Forster's novels also—but with an important difference. It is the moral life that has the pebble-like clarity in *his* writing; he has made it tangible and visible. He has, so to say, speeded up the process of contemplation by making clear what, in his view, needed to be contemplated. The plain conversational style is truly conversational in the sense that we feel several people are talking and trying to find out; in spite of James's influence, there is no sense of monologue. Forster's talk, like all good talk, has the quality of surprise.

It is easy enough to demonstrate that Forster represents the end of something. He has almost said so himself, though not quite: civilizations are a string of intermissions in the anger of time. He speaks at the end of liberal culture and, since there is no other, there is no implicit accusation. He agrees that this firm attachment owes something to privilege and we all know the dogma that, in its penultimate phase, a culture sees spiritual order in art alone; in its ultimate post-Forsterian phase it crumbles into a sort of Byzantine pedantry.

Forster's contribution to our present collective society is the reminder that it will be an arid and destroying desert if we remove the oases of private life. But he is a dangerous master. All very well for him to refuse to be great: he had to fight the portentous. Educated and inured by the powerful, he was free to develop apathy and softness as an unexpectedly useful muscle. He had something pretty unscrupulous to disbelieve in. Does he feel, now, that burden peculiar to famous old age, that an age has caught up with him? Does he feel, that in England at any rate, a younger generation is carrying the cult of privacy and personal relationships to the lengths of whimsicality and eccentricity? It often strikes one that far too large a portion of educated energy is going into running England as a kind of private joke, an ingenious personal crossword. We are more gentle with one another, but we spend an inordinate amount of time being gentle; we are bathed to the point of sleep in tolerance and understanding. Forsterian teaching has been taken on without our recognizing that it had the virility of a reaction. It is very pleasant to relax, as he taught us, and to believe (for example) in his notion that the bucket drops down into the unconscious and brings up the substance of the work of art. It is true. But isn't it Mr. Forster's old enemy, the will, that has turned the handle and let the bucket down? It is a mistake to take this infertile and original writer literally. Thus his "apathy" really means "integrity." One other writer of his generation, Boris Pasternak, has it, and has demonstrated its phenomenal spiritual strength. Like him, Forster hands back the ticket, bored by the verbosity of the strong-willed, knowing that there is a creative force in the secrets of life. He is fresh because he is unable to conceive of a life without free choice; perhaps we would think him more than courageous, and actually great, if his novels had conveyed the other half of the argument: that we have to choose for others and that choice is made by others for us. But this is to ask for an inrush of ungoverned emotion beyond the scope of comedy.

FORDIE

"I once told Fordie that if he were placed naked and alone in a room without furniture, I would come back in an hour and find total confusion." Ezra Pound's joke about Ford Madox Ford hits the mark. Confusion was the mainspring of his art as a novelist. He confused to make clear. As an editor, as a source of literary reminiscence, he attracts because he is always sketching his way from inaccuracy to inaccuracy in order to arrive at some personal, translucent truth. His unreliability may have annoyed, but it is inspired.

As a novelist—and he wrote some thirty novels, nearly all forgotten—he is one of those whose main obstacle is his own talent. A Conrad cannot invent; a Lawrence cannot narrate: such deficiencies are fortunate. They force a novelist to compensate, with all his resources, so that we shall hardly be aware of what is lacking and shall, in any case, think it unimportant. Ford is obstructed less by his defects than by the effusiveness of total ability. He has been called brilliant, garrulous and trivial, but what really happened was that, with the exception of *The Good Soldier,* parts of the Tietjens trilogy and most of *The Fifth Queen,* he never sank into the determined stupor out of which greater novelists work. It is comforting to think that the unduly brilliant may eventually have their stroke of luck: *The Good Soldier* is a small masterpiece.

Interest in Ford's work is now reviving in England and in the United States, where technicians are studied with a useful if exhausting piety. Mr. Richard Cassell has got in early with a handy, basic investigation. He is alert to the peculiar effects of the Pre-Raphaelites on Ford, the French influence on the English novel of the period, and so on, but does not discuss the curious romanticizing of the idea of "the gentleman" which has made Ford seem tiresome and false to the modern reader. The dilemma of "the gentleman" preoccupied Shaw, James, Conrad, Galsworthy, and has even been revived in the latest novels of Evelyn Waugh. It was once a burning topic—one that Forster, with his marvelous aversion to burning topics, ignored. But there are overtones in Ford's writing on the subject which recall his own criticism of what the Pre-Raphaelites felt about love—they swooned. Swooning about love was a way of not knowing the facts. Ford swooned about the country gentry, and nothing dates so much as fashions in love.

Still, *The Good Soldier* survives the swooning over the character of Colonel Ashburnham and does so because, for once, Ford had his excessive gifts under control. For once he remembered that if he was to be an Impressionist writer, he had better not confuse writing with painting. The confusion of memory need not be colored; indeed, in writing, if the parts are too prismatically brilliant, the whole will become gray instead of luminous. As this novel shows, Ford was equipped by intelligence and by grief to be a moralist once he could be freed from the paint box and, above all, from High Art. Conrad must have been a very bad influence on a man who had already too much vagueness in him; Henry James can have only been harmful to one with already so much consciousness. To them Art did nothing but good; the idea is excellent in itself; but it is dangerous to a man of talent who only very seldom in a laborious literary life hits upon a subject that draws out all his experience.

The Good Soldier and *The Fifth Queen* succeed. The former has the compact and singeing quality of a French novel; it is a ruthless and yet compassionate study in the wretchedness of conventional assumptions and society's war upon the heart. The latter is a historical romance and tells the story of Henry VIII and Katharine Howard; it suffers a little from Ford's chronic allusiveness, but a great issue is at stake and the ambiguities in it awaken all his interest in intrigue. His mind was one that hated conclusions, not because it was a skeptical mind but because it wanted to be put to one more test. From this spring his ingenuity as a storyteller—a gift so rare that it is often scorned—and his constant concern with technique. Critics have usually praised this technical capacity, but have said that this was all he had; yet it is—and one ought not to have to say so—a capacity of enormous importance. (Imagine that Jane Austen had left *Sense and Sensibility* in its epistolatory draft!) One can see that to a mind as given to confusion and to posture as Ford's was, technical capacity was his one reality. He asks nothing better than to be seen making difficulties work for him. The famous device of the "time-shift," which was a mania with him, enabled him to begin his scene in the middle and yet arrive with a whole tale of suspense that was thick with suggestion and memories caught on the way ashore.

In *The Good Soldier* the time-shift enabled him to effect those dramatic revaluations of people which give his novels their point. We had supposed, for example, that Leonora was vulgarly jealous when she slapped Mrs. Maiden's face; but in a page or two we dart back in time to discover that there was another and stronger motive, one that exposes a hidden part of Leonora's nature: her shocked frigidity, her greed for money. When that is threatened, her passion for appearances collapses. In choosing for the narrator a dull and unemotional man who fumbles his way through a tale of passion which leads to death and madness, Ford has found someone who will perfectly put together the case of the heart versus conventional society, for he is a mild American Quaker perpetually astonished by Catholic puritanism. Meanwhile his own do-gooding wife is, unknown to him, a destroyer and nymphomaniac. Ford is often accused, by the hospital nurses of criticism, of triviality, but in this book the trivia are sharp and enhance the awful dull force of the tragedy.

Rewrite *The Good Soldier* in straightforward narrative and Ford's vision of life as a minutely operating process of corrosion vanishes, and with that, of course, his particular Catholic outlook. Corrosion, as it is presented in this novel, means that we have more parts to our lives than one and that they work fatally upon each other. One has a quite extraordinary sense in the book of the minds of people perpetually thinking away their heartbeats.

Ford's preoccupation with technique—point of view, time-shift, *progression d'effet,* rendering and so on—was both a godsend and a curse, for he was constitutionally distracted, impatient and shy of coming to terms. By concentrating on the *means* of creating an impression he seems to have hoped in some of his novels to find that the means would suggest an End darker, more inscrutable and mysterious, than anything in the author's mind at the outset. Life was an intrigue that was never resolved, a meaningless experiment. This approach might lead, as it does in the works of Conrad, to fogginess; in Ford it could lead only to an excessive highlighting of detail and to staginess. The secret Romantic Ford leans too much on the ominous and sardonic outsider, the shadow figure breathing heavily down the neck of the reader, Art pretending to be Destiny. But when Ford is at one with his subject, as he is in *The Fifth Queen*, he stages well. His delight in playing fast and loose with time, in beginning a scene in the middle of a broken sentence, dropping it and picking it up again until the crisis is built up, his whole patterning and puzzling, are vividly justified.

He succeeds, more often than not, in his ingenious system of getting at the inside of things by looking intensely at the surface alone. This, of course, he inherited from the painters. He may see more than we can in the way people's hands lie in their laps, or how their legs look when they are kneeling, or how much of Henry VIII appeared as he went upstairs; but in the larger pictorial actions—Tom Culpepper rushing up drunk from Greenwich to Smithfield eager to see some martyrs at the stake because he'd never seen a burning before—the sense of daily life dancing by in a man's mind is wonderfully conveyed. Ford was a master of episode. If he is stagey, he does not ham. We notice, for example, that Tom Culpepper doesn't in fact see the actual burning because he gets into an absurd brawl. As a storyteller Ford recognized life when he saw complication and chance. His brutal scenes are benevolently comic; his women are originals; wherever there's human naïveté and deviousness he is as happy as Kipling was, but with compassion. And throughout there is no detail that fails to bear on the religious quarrel which is his central subject. He responded very much in all his work to the margin men and women leave in their minds, to their longheadedness; and one can see that he found a parallel between the corruption of the Reformation and that of the Edwardian world which had killed the heart, he would have said, by reducing virtue and honor to the condition of masks.

No doubt *The Fifth Queen* is too close to the eye in a cinematic way to have the spacious historical sense of a great historical novel like *Old Mortality;* it hasn't the coolness of Mérimée's short novel on the Massacre of St. Bartholomew; but it makes most of our historical fiction up to 1914 look like the work of interior decorators. Literature for Ford was a passion; its rituals were sacred. But there is no doubt about his moral seriousness or the cumulative effect of the main story. How, by what stages, will Katharine bring the King to the point of making his submission to Rome? How will the King procrastinate? What lies will trap the Queen? Will the King, for once, be able to escape from his changeable and fatally political nature? What belongs to Caesar, what to God—and what to Good Learning? There is nothing allusive in the handling of this massive central conflict and it is brought to its climax without melodrama. One thing Impressionism could do was to catch the day as it passed through the minds of the actors in it. It could record confusion by a scrupulous and ingenious use of the means of art. Allowing for Ford's pleasant vanity in the imposture, this bravura piece—as Graham Greene calls it in his introduction to these volumes—is rather fine.

Half-English, half-German and, by fancy, French, Ford Madox Ford was nature's expatriate. His only country, he said, was literature. To be precise, it was "the Novel." He simply lived for it. Consider him as an incurable and dedicated work of fiction, one of the most diverting yet serious and instructive of "living lies," and he becomes comprehensible. As a brilliant human being he was self-dispersing, moving from one hallucination to another, dumping his luggage in the hotel room of two or three cultures; he reassembled himself, for a while, in words and stories and in them he believed with an industrious and short-lived intensity. He succeeded in only three remarkable stories—

The Good Soldier, the *Fifth Queen* trilogy and *Parade's End.* They vindicate his happy yet tortured incapacity to go straight from a starting point, for he had none. They put his lack of self-confidence, his shortness of spiritual breath, his indolence, to use. They brought out and exploited with full resource the price he had to pay for his extraordinary cleverness: the emotion of anguish. One is tempted to say "passion" also—but one has to hesitate here. The writers who convey passion also convey the terrible calm of its purgation and aftermath and Ford is too full of his own skill and ironical humor to allow that. But he does leave us with an indignant sense of unforgettable pain. One always finds that at the bottom of the baggage Ford left about the world.

Some pain is self-sought—the pain, for example, of our choice of impossible incarnations. It is hard, here, to separate the factitious from the inevitable. When he became incarnate as Tietjens in *Parade's End,* Ford could not obliterate Ford. One does not want him to do so, for Tietjens is Ford's anguished hallucination. No novelist can completely become another character; in Tietjens Ford constructed an English gentleman as only something like German romanticism or idealism could see him. Ford was no gentleman; he was a fine artist. He seems minutely to have observed the type, and at the same time to have loaded him with history and an inhuman willingness to suffer everything for the sake of suffering. So often one has seen expatriates find their home in a past that has not existed: Ford's plain feudal Yorkshire squire, with his love of the pre-industrial way of life, his scorn of the vulgar modern world, his dislike of ambition, his irritable abstention, his martyred sense of decency, looks today like a romancing not about a man but a code.

When Ford created Tietjens the dilemma of the gentleman was very much the fashion, as I have said. These talented agrarians existed. The coarse businessmen, speculators and careerists were breaking in on them, the Press had turned yellow, the conventions were shocking when they worked and even more shocking when they did not. If Tietjens and his scruples about sex and society seem odd now, they did not fifty years ago. Rock-like before the unanswered slanders of his bankers, his military friends, his father, his cold, promiscuous wife who tricked him over the paternity of his child, Tietjens was exactly the figure to expose by his silence and his suffering the rottenness of Edwardian society. Further, he was not a Roman Catholic but his wife was, and the curse on the Tietjens family is thought to go back to the Reformation and the thieving of Roman Catholic lands. This adds to Tietjens's martyrdom, a touch of Destiny which is pretty gamey stuff. That old row has been hung too long to be digestible. One is rather exasperated by Tietjens's stubborn determination to collect all the slings and arrows going; after all, where does the family get its millions from? From the sacred soil of a great estate? Hardly. Toward the end of the novel there is a hint that the family controls a lot of industry in Middlesborough. Tietjens is just as much a child of the industrial revolution as anybody else. He may not like the men of the new order who were coming in just before 1914: not being gentlemen they were certain to cheat. But isn't he simply an idealizer of convention? One has a sneaking sympathy for his wife who at one moment complains that her husband is trying to be Jesus Christ as well as the misunderstood son of a great landowner. Her cruelties are an attempt to turn a martyr into a man.

In creating Tietjens, Ford chose a character utterly unlike himself and did the detail admirably. He caught the obtuse pride of the social masochist. He caught the spleen of the gentleman because this accorded well with the ironic spleen that Ford himself felt as an artist, even when it was a pose. The gregarious, voluble, intelligent nature of Ford could not be prevented from mingling with the Yorkshire squire; what one does not accept in Tietjens is the romantic German aura. Any German can do a better job of being an English gentleman and Tietjens is just a Germanized squire. He is even a classical scholar.

Two more able American critics, John Meixner and Paul Wiley, have written studies that will stimulate the Ford addict, and both agree that *Some Do Not* is the best of the Tietjens novels. It is a complete "Affair"; the famous time-shifts are well patterned. And both understand that Ford, being an indolent man with little self-confidence and an observer before everything else, was best at beginnings. Any paragraph is better than a page. All the good things, large or small, are beginnings. The boredom we experience in Ford comes, indeed, from the strain of reading innumerable beginnings on every page. So these critics find that Tietjens does not grow. His wife turns melodramatically wicked as the book goes on. I don't entirely agree with the first part of the verdict: Tietjens may be better done in the earliest volume but he becomes more representative and important as a human being in the account of the war in France, and especially because his puzzling private life is in abeyance.

Ford's response to the war brought out his highest quality: his historical sense and his exactitude. He surveyed with sardonic relish the chaos of the staff officer's labors: the numbering and allotting, the terrible paperwork in a war no one understood. The Canadians are going up the line, but where are they? They have been held up somewhere by a train smash. What is to happen to the men they are supposed to relieve? Ah, now the Canadians have been found! And now we've got them, the orders have been countermanded. The intrigue and the rot at the Base produce a natural defensive reaction: the chaos is intended by the politicians, the *embusqués* at home. And who are they? The new men, of course, the climbers and careerists. (This certainly was the legend of the period.)

The general picture of a whole society floundering is done with a wonderful precision and not in the form of easy diatribe. Tietjens is just the right kind of numbed Homeric figure to record the sudden killing of a man in the staff dugout, a man to whom he had refused leave; or the explosion of a mine and the rescuing of the buried. As a character Tietjens escapes from the cliché of almost all the war novels of that time in which the hero conveys that the whole war has been declared against him personally. Tietjens knows that a civilization, or at any rate a class, is sinking. Responsible and capable, Ford-Tietjens has an unselfed and almost classical sub-Olympian view of the experience. Although he was self-consciously an impressionist, Ford has some inner sense of a moral order. Or, if not that, a moral indignation at the lack of it. Or if not that, a taste for the moral consolations of defeat. He brings not only an eye but a judgment to what he sees.

There is something odd but also—from a novelist's point of view—tolerant about this judgment. A craftsman, through and through, in everything, Ford is interested in the way things are done. Even corruption has its curious status. What are gunners like, what are their interests, their follies, what is the *virtu* of the trade? He is deeply interested in the idle detail of human nature and his own lazy aloofness enabled him to catch the detail perfectly. A variety of scenes come to mind: the death of O Nine Morgan or the astonishing scene where a gunner chases a solitary German with shells.

> His antics had afforded these gunners infinite amusement. It afforded them almost more when all the German artillery on that front, imagining that God knew what was the matter, had awakened and plastered heaven and earth and everything between them for a quarter of an hour with every imaginable kind of missile. And had then abruptly shut up.

And it had all happened merely because Tietjens had lightly told a gunner that any Italian peasant with a steam plough could pulverize a field at a cost of thirty shillings, which was cheaper than the cost of high explosives. As a craftsman the gunner was put on his mettle.

That incident is anecdotal, but Ford could create the people who lived the anecdotes. His art—particularly the theory of the time-shift—was in part based on an analysis of talk, the way it plunges and works back and forth. The method was perfected in *The Good Soldier;* in the later Tietjens novel, it does not succeed so well. It often becomes a device for refusing to face a major scene. One has only a confused notion of what went on in the hotel bedroom when the drunken General broke in on Tietjens and his wife at a crucial point in their sado-masochistic relationship, when it is important that we should know all. Ford's view seems to have been that no one ever quite knows what goes on at the crucial moments of life. His craftsmanship becomes obscurely crafty at such moments, as though, with tiresome cleverness, he had decided that it was the business of art to impose chaos on order. At his worst, he turns never saying Yes and never saying No into an aesthetic neurosis.

Where do we place Ford in relation to the contemporaries he admired—James and Conrad? For Mr. Meixner Ford was "locked in the prison of his own theories" and lacked "the personal audacity, the conquering boldness," required by a masterpiece. He was a penetrating historian, a man of fundamental insights, but he did little with them; his ingenuity made him intellectually thin. *The Good Soldier* succeeds because it is done in the first person, which allows him to rid himself of the stiff aloofness and impersonality he thought he was copying from the French—by a paradox this is his unmistakably French novel. He has not the range of a James or a Conrad, nor the mass of good work; but Conrad's characters are "static and inert," despite the subtlety and penetration of his analysis; and Ford (for Mr. Meixner) surpasses Conrad in *The Good Soldier* and *Some Do Not* because Ford's people have greater inner life, are more various, more real, more fluid and more pleasing and more moving. I would have thought Conrad's skeptical moral sense, as a *déplacé,* was richer than Ford's. Compared with James, Ford goes deeper (for Mr. Meixner) into the range of spiritual terror and anguish. If after a lot of wrangling, one came to agree with this last point, one would have to qualify it by saying that the very nature of Ford's methods made these depths brief and rare; and that they came as a result of calculated shock. We feel the shock felt by Tietjens when O Nine Morgan is killed before his eyes; we are startled by the picture of Tietjens trying to recover his memory when his brain has been affected by bombardment—but these episodes remain superb fragments.

Mr. Wiley is good at showing the consistency of Ford's career as a novelist and as theorist of the novel and pays a lot of attention to the forgotten works. Although the discussion of Ford's methods in his last novel, *Vive le roy,* is interesting, it does not succeed in making this maddening work more readable. Like a first-class teacher Ford gives his ideas the force of his personal life. But, except in his two best books, he had so many ideas that he was exhausted by the time he got to the page. He had not the breath. He creates the spell of someone always on the move; the pen itself was expatriate. His theories, in the end, become devices for postponing the novelist's task: which is to settle and confront. Impressionism—and with it a desire to impress—becomes an unconscious journalism. One sees him, and his characters also, wearing themselves out by continually changing trains.

KNIGHTSBRIDGE KENNELS

Why do the novels of Ada Leverson survive? How is it that these water ices of the Edwardian drawing room have kept their crispness and have not melted away? One can put it down to the Wilde revival; one can regard it as a side-effect of the present turdish taste for chichi; or as a passing nostalgia for the tritenesses of small, safe, set, satiny world of teacups and little dinners, where the gravest dangers are things like being seen riding in a hansom with a wan Bohemian girl from the wrong side of the Park. Ada Leverson's urban males are vulnerable to pity for ill-provided females through whose designs any well-appointed woman can see. We are offered a life lived according to "the rules," which smoothly prevent the emotions from becoming more than inconvenient.

To cover the inevitable boredom there are always the bitchings and counter-bitchings of the Knightsbridge kennels. Thus, a rather too jolly Mr. Mitchell will be "almost any age between sixty and sixty-five"; a Sir Charles is "distinguished to the very verge of absurdity." All this is pleasant enough, but—I agree with Colin MacInnes who writes an ardent preface to Ada Leverson's best-known trilogy *The Little Ottleys*—it has little to do with her merits. The only unconvincing touches that occur in her last novel are those that are closest to the modern world: they record one or two glimpses of the outbreak of the 1914 war. It is natural that they should be unconvincing, for that war killed the comedy of manners. She survives because she is an original and considerable artist.

A writer can be a considerable artist without being more than a minor novelist. If they are to last, the minor novelists depend on sparkle, a freshness of view and a perfection of means; if they are comedians, on the gift of living in a perennial present. Economy and distinction of style and—in Miss Leverson's case—skill in construction are indispensable. They must delight in their limits if we are to delight in them: they must always refuse—and how few middling novelists do make this refusal!—to borrow the courage of other people's convictions. Miss Leverson understood this. It is possible that the pleasure she gives owes a lot to a clever adaptation of the methods of the theatre: the two-dimensional tale passes as quickly as an expert charade. A scene never lasts too long; it is as sharp as repartee. She is careful, even when moralizing, to keep to the surface of life and it is often when she appears to be most trivial that she is life-enhancing and most serious.

To the somewhat extravagant praise given by Mr. MacInnes, I would add the warning that she has not the range of, say, an Edith Wharton; and although it is true that, in a general way, she writes in the tradition of Congreve, she dilutes with the very different comedy of *The Diary of a Nobody,* the Ottleys being the Pooters, but younger and smarter and moved from Finchley to Knightsbridge. They are little Somebodies. This is the comedy of "life's little ironies" which came in during her lifetime. When the clownish Bruce Ottley and his wife chase from one Hamilton Place to another in London looking for where they are supposed to be dining and find they have got the week wrong; above all, in Bruce Ottley's querulous time as an amateur actor, we have pure Grossmith:

> "I told Mitchell what I thought of him in very plain terms. I went so far as to threaten to throw up my part, and he said, 'Well, all right, if you don't like it you can give it up any time.' I said 'Who else could you get at the last minute to play a footman's part?' and he said 'Our footman.' "

The other strain in her comedy is her concern for integrity. She rejoices in the banality of her characters; but in her heroine, Edith Ottley, she has created a young wife who clings to the conservative conventions of her world yet is disturbed to find that she may in her marriage be sacrificing herself to them when she supposes she is doing something sensitive and fine. In other words, Miss Leverson introduces the question of personal truth into her comedy. There is a point at which Edith, despite her coquettishness, is in danger of becoming as tiresome as Thackeray's Amelia; it is no great credit to Edith's probity that she is rescued from having to solve her dilemma by her husband's inane flight with the chief comic character of the book and, ultimately, by the breakdown of the standards of Knightsbridge in the war. I find Edith a shade calculating. Her asinine husband is at his shamefaced worst when the marriage collapses and, in a wonderful scene, comes out with the one honest remark of his life, a ridiculous, fierce *cri de coeur* that punctures the basic assumption of her ethic and her comedy:

> "No, Edith. I can't endure married life any longer. It doesn't suit me."

This cry from a prime domestic fusspot who is always carrying on about being master in his own house is marvelously funny, but it has a wildness about it suggesting that the Ottleys, like the rest of this Edwardian world, had somehow begotten two children without having done more than meet socially.

It is sometimes said that artificial comedy in English suffers from a lack of brain. It really celebrates the English genius for hardening off, refusing to face issues and creating an ennui which will be the great guarantor of social, moral and emotional eventlessness. The most boring and self-centered of men, Bruce Ottley, thrives on boredom and develops, in consequence, a character so eccentric that it never ceases to fascinate his friends. Our comedy, like our way of life, depends on the evasion of ideas or knowledge and on the creation of character. Edith is about to marry a fine fellow at the end of the novel, but as far as comedy is concerned he is a dead loss: he bores us with his £5,000 a year and his undoubted enlightenment. And it is an odd conjunction of life and art that, after she wrote this novel in 1916, Miss Leverson wrote no more.

But she had by then created a comic character far more original than the lunatic Bruce—Madame Frabelle. This portrait is satisfying because it is not caricature. It is the truth about Madame Frabelle that is so funny; and the fact that she is a likable monster makes her funnier. She is the Life Force gone dowdy, shady and kind, but never dormant. Indeed, advancing years make her phoniness redoubtable. It is she who runs off with Bruce in the end—one can imagine her picking him up like a puppy in her teeth and wobbling off with him—and anyone who is interested in skill in writing must admire the cleverness with which Miss Leverson insinuates the stages that lead to this dénouement. The splendid thing about Madame Frabelle is that she is absurd, false, but sympathetic—this comes from Miss Leverson's truthfulness:

> Madame Frabelle (of course) was dressed in black, *décolletée* and with a good deal of jet. A black aigrette, like a lightning conductor, stood up defiantly in her hair. Though it did not harmonize well with the somewhat square and *bourgeoise* shape of her head and face, and appeared to have dropped on her by accident, yet as a symbol of smartness it gave her a kind of distinction. It appeared to have fallen from the skies; it was put on in the wrong place, and it did not nestle, as it should do, and appear to grow out of her hair, since that glory of womanhood, in her case of a dull brown going slightly grey, was smooth, scarce and plainly parted. Madame Frabelle really would have looked her best in a cap of the fashion of the Sixties. But she could carry off anything; and some people said that she did.

Madame Frabelle's great gift is that of being wrong about everything. She is a monument to the failures of feminine intuition. She is an exciting store of inaccurate facts and false conjectures. She is the queen of nonsensical law-giving, masterfully inhabiting a very heaven of self-deception, as dotty as a horoscope. But people are charmed—again Miss Leverson's truthfulness—because Madame Frabelle is helplessly charmed by them. When she carries off Bruce, no one really minds. Two absurdities will have fulfilled themselves. Edith's excellences bored Bruce: he needed the dramatic companionship of a fellow self-deceiver.

Miss Leverson's admired males are too psychologically decorative: they are "connoisseurs of human nature," "urbane observers," "collectors of experience." They call Edith "*impayable*" when, frankly, she is really a moral coquette. But Miss Leverson's wit and perceptions are original. There are Lady Cannon's florid and massive clothes which, like her furniture, "express a violent, almost ominous conventionality, without the slightest touch of austerity to tone it down." Edith Ottley's appearance has "the rather insidious charm of somehow recalling the past while suggesting something undiscovered in the future." The random dialogue of parties turns, with hardly a pause, from the disturbing perception—"something in his suave manner of taking everything for granted seemed to make them know each other almost too quickly, and gave her an odd sort of self-consciousness"—to the hilariously vapid:

> Captain Willis lowered his voice to a confidential tone and said:
>
> "D'you know what I always say is—live and let live and let it go at that: what?"
>
> "That's a dark saying."
>
> "Have a burnt almond," said Captain Willis inconsequently as though it would help her to understand.

Writers of comedy have to bear as best they can the charge of triviality, in spite of the fact that their eye for detail and their instinct of selection give them an exceptional power to render the surface of life. How rarely do realists catch that surface. The other charge that they are evasive or, of all things, not "serious" is even more stupid, for they above all convey by their laughter the sense of danger that is inseparable from delight in the moment. In artificial comedy and the comedy of manners this sense of danger is intense.

Miss Leverson lives by this. But the quality that has helped most to keep so much of her work in the perennial present is, quite simply, her feminine appetite for news:

> All women love news of whatever kind; even bad news gives them merely a feeling of pleasurable excitement . . .

Heavier novelists die off in a decade or two from a surfeit of information.

NEW YORK, 1900

A novel by Mrs. Wharton in her best period is a correcting experience, a pain when the correction seems to be directed at ourselves, a pleasure when it is being handed out to other people. She is—so many of the important women novelists have been this—a mother-figure, determined, pragmatic, critical and alarming. How inevitable not to come up to her moral, intellectual, above all her social standards. Once we get out of the room where we have been sitting alone with the formidable lady, we foresee that we shall break out or go downhill once more. We know she is no fool; she can startle us by her range of observation; but we shall suspect that what she calls discipline is really first cousin to puritanism and fear, and that what she calls the Eumenides are really projections of the aunts who run the conventions and man the barricades of the taboos. The acerbity of a novelist, like Mrs. Wharton is *mondain* before it is intellectual; it denotes a positive pleasure in the fact that worldly error has to be heavily paid for spiritually. Her sense of tragedy is linked to a terrifying sense of propriety. It is steely and has the hard efficiency of the property market into which she was born. When, in *The House of Mirth,* Lily Bart is told that she will have to choose between the values of the smart set in New York and the "republic of the spirit," we are not absolutely convinced that this republic is not a new kind of puritan snobbery. The men who belong to this republic signally fail to rush the women off their feet into this excellent world, and Mrs. Wharton is drily aware of their failure. In its first decades the rise of American Big Business created an upper class whose sensitive men cut themselves off from a crude society that shocked them and which was dominated by women. She noted this in her autobiography and it is plain in all her books. Her own interesting situation is that there is an emotional force held back in her, which resents the things her mind approves of and it is this dilemma that gives her mind its cutting edge—at any rate in the books she wrote before she found personal happiness. That happiness, it now seems, dulled her talent.

There is, of course, more than all this to Mrs. Wharton, both as person and novelist. She elaborated the balance sheet of renunciation and became the accountant-historian of a rich society, and nothing passed her merciless eye. She wrote best when the pressure had been hardest to bear, even though that pressure may have frozen the imaginative and enhanced the critical character of her talent. Her prose has a presentable cold pomp: "The cushioned chairs, disposed expectantly under the wide awning, showed no signs of recent occupancy." Under great bitterness and frustration we have learned to expect outbursts of sentimentality—as a far greater writer, like Mauriac, has shown us—and when she drags the Eumenides into three or four melodramatic pages of her best novel, *The House of Mirth*, we are embarrassed. But it is exceptional for her control to go. Her study of rich New York in the early 1900's in that book will pass for smart sets anywhere and at any time, for even in our day, when most conventions have gone, when people no longer behave like "deaf mutes in an asylum," the cheerless figure of the socialite remains. The smart set is the quintessential dust bowl. In a later comment on this novel Mrs. Wharton wrote "that a frivolous society can acquire dramatic significance only through what its frivolity destroys. Its tragic implication lies in its power of debasing people and ideals." The idea is Jamesian and if the execution of it lacks the poetry, the heightened recitative of Henry James, we do get from Mrs. Wharton the hard, unpitying moralist who will forgive but not forget, and the derisive critic of social architecture.

Indignation about the sins of another social class is, of course, easy money, and does not, of itself, get a novelist very far. One strongly suspects that Mrs. Wharton did not like new people getting rich. But she did examine her subject with scientific efficiency, and in Lily Bart she created the most rewarding kind of socialite: one who was morally a cut above the rest of her circle, but who had been fatally conditioned from the first. Lily Bart is a beautiful and very intelligent girl, delightful company and really too clever for any of the men her society was likely to offer. On the lowest level, she is hopeless about money, about pushing her way in first, about intrigue, about using people, about the main chance. Her own view is that she behaves as she does because she has no money. It is Becky Sharp's cry: virtue on five thousand a year. But this is only half her case. She is a superb artist in the business of being in the swim, a brilliant contriver of success; she has a wonderful sense of timing—when to be in the spotlight and when not. Her startling weakness is that she sows but she does not reap. At the last moment she is wrecked by the sudden boredom and carelessness of the very clever. On the day of victory she oversleeps. Her self-confidence is such that she does not bother to play her ace; and she imagines her gift for dispensing with success at the last minute will make her impervious to her enemies. It does not. Selden, who wants to marry her, imagines that her last-minute failures are signs of grace, impulses from the unconscious. They make her very likable, but they must be considered as opportunities for further displays of courage and sangfroid rather than happy, nonsocial backslidings into "the republic of the spirit." Her courage is half vanity. So low are the standards of her set that she is encouraged thereby to mistake thrilled nerve for an access of intelligence:

> She . . . listened to Ned Silverton reading Theocritus by moonlight, as the yacht rounded the Sicilian promontories, with a thrill of the nerves that confirmed her belief in her intellectual superiority.

Theocritus is, in fact, the right poet, at the right moment, among the right people, at the height of the season. A venial folly; after all, are we quite sure that the enlightened Selden is any better for cutting himself off from the life of his country and reading La Bruyère?

Lily Bart has the beauty and vanity which George Eliot thought so wicked in women, but Lily's attractions are energy, an occasional capacity for honesty and innocence. She is not ashamed of her cunning in getting money out of a married man like Gus Trenor for she has used her brains; what really shocks her is the price demanded. Her match is Rosedale, the rich rising Jew who reads her character perfectly, who puts his price up as hers goes down and, in the end, out of sheer admiration for her abilities, is willing to behave disinterestedly. But he is defeated by her gift for last-minute failure: she refuses to silence the women who have ruined her. Pride or a sense of virtue? Neither, I think—and here Mrs. Wharton is very penetrating: those who believe in their star believe also in despair. Lily Bart is a gambler. One enjoys her as one enjoys the electric shocks of roulette, as one enjoys the incorrigible and the plunger. And one enjoys her also because Mrs. Wharton turns her inside out:

> Moral complications existed for her only in the environment that had produced them: she did not mean to slight or ignore them, but they lost their reality when they changed their background.

Or, when it is a matter of getting a financial "tip" out of Trenor:

> She was always scrupulous about keeping up appearances to herself. Her personal fastidiousness had a moral equivalent and when she made a tour of inspection in her own mind there were certain closed doors she did not open.

The only element missing from Lily Bart's character is her obvious sexual coldness to which, when the novel was written, Mrs. Wharton could hardly have referred even if—to suppose the impossible—she had desired to do so.

New York's social scene is expertly set down in *The House of Mirth* with an anthropologist's thoroughness and the novel is remarkable for its skillful visits from one smart set to the smart set on the stair below. These tours are conducted with all Mrs. Wharton's superlative snobbery.

> Mrs. Bry, to Mrs. Fisher's despair, had not progressed beyond the point of weighing her social advantages in public.

There was smart hotel society:

> Through this atmosphere of torrid splendor moved wan beings as richly upholstered as the furniture, beings without definite pursuits or permanent relations, who drifted on a languid tide of curiosity from restaurant to concert hall, from palm garden to music room.

Here reigned Mrs. Hatch, the simple lady who, surrounded by beauty specialists, wished to soar socially; the Bovary of the Gossip columns, who wanted to do what was "nice" and to be taught how to be "lovely."

Mrs. Wharton hated the smart set she had been brought up in and she is good in this novel no doubt because she is anatomizing the monster whose stupidities and provincialities might have crushed her. But the making of her as a novelist is her power to create incident and to conduct great scenes. Strangely enough her ironical power and gift of surprise often recall those of an utterly different novelist—Thomas Hardy. She has—usually under iron control—a persistent sense of fate, a skill in entangling her characters before striking them down. The scene at Gus Trenor's when this magnate turns nasty and looks like going to the point of sexual assault is wonderfully handled and Lily is marvelous in it; every cliché in this well-known situation is avoided, every truth in it discerned and the end is perfect. And Bertha Dorset's revenge on Lily: that is as brilliant a *volte-face* and surprise as one can remember in any plot in social comedy. Mrs. Wharton did not touch these heights afterwards, though even in her weaker novels, there is the same astringency, the same readiness of invention.

Again and again we find that novelists who have attacked the conventions because they stultify the spirit, who attack the group for its cruelty to individuals, will end by pointing out the virtues of submission. Mrs. Wharton may have hated old New York, but she hated the new New York even more. She disliked the prison of silent hypocrisy, but she drew in her skirts when candor came in. Especially after her long life, *en grande luxe* in Europe. What indignation denounces creeps back in the name of sentiment. *The Age of Innocence* shows a man giving in, loyally marrying the conventional girl he does not love, throwing over the Europeanized woman who is his natural equal. It is the surrender to the established bourgeois standard. No great harms come of it; only dullness and disappointment. The sweet young girl he was engaged to was slyer than he thought. She became like her mother-in-law to whose face "a lifelong mastery over trifles had given factitious authority." Perhaps, after all, her husband reflects, that old New York which would not "know" a divorced woman, was rather charming and quite right. Better renunciation than a hole-in-corner affair. Mrs. Wharton always believed in the sterner condition; but her brain resented it. Not even snobbery and respect for "factitious authority" could get her into the Catholic Church at the end of her life. The old Puritan worldling stood out firmly for patching, for facing unpleasantness, making the second best of things, refusing accommodations. Worry, culture and character were the thing. One imagines God wondering if he dared leave a card. The strange thing is that we mistrust her at once when, late in life, she becomes benign.

MISS LONELYHEARTS

Nathanael West is one of the novelists of the breakdown of the American dream in the thirties. His real name was Nathan Weinstein, he moved in fashionable literary society, became a script writer in Hollywood after the success of *Miss Lonelyhearts* and was killed in a motor accident at the age of forty. Two of his novels, *Miss Lonelyhearts*—which is very well known—and *The Day of the Locust* show that a very original talent was cut short. He was preoccupied with hysteria as the price paid for accepting the sentimentalities of the national dream. He feared hysteria in himself, he was morbidly conscious of it in his people; he was attracted and repelled by its false dreams as one might be by a more poisonous way of mixing gin. West did not feel that life was tragic, for the sense of tragedy was lost in the moral collapse of the period he lived in. Like Chekhov—but only in this respect—he was appalled by the banality of city civilization. Instead of being tragic life was terrible, meaningless and without dignity. Mr. Alan Ross, in a warm, if sometimes difficult, introduction to a volume containing all four of West's novels, makes this point and suggests that while the English writers of the thirties reached their conclusions "through a series of well-bred intellectual convictions," Americans like West were thrown helplessly among the brute economic facts. For them the experience was emotional and even theatrically so, because hysterical violence is very near the surface in American life.

West's resources were Art—he learned from the surrealists—and compassion. Except in his satire, *A Cool Million,* which is an American *Candide* done in the manner of a parody too obvious and prolonged, he was not a political writer in the literal sense. He explored the illness behind the political situation. Human beings have always fought misery with dreams, Miss Lonelyhearts observes; the dream and its ignoble deceits, the panic, anger and frustration these deceits expose, gave him his material. In *The Day of the Locust,* his mature novel, it is the boredom exposed by the failure of the Californian dream of an earthly Paradise that puts an expression of hate and destructiveness on the faces of the weary middle-aged population who have retired to Los Angeles. As they pour in to gape at the stars arriving for some world première, they have the look of lynchers. Lynch, in fact, they do and for no reason.

This does not convey that West was a comic writer. He had freakishness, wit and a taste for the absurd from the surrealists, also their sophistication in parody and styles, but moved quickly away from their gratuitous and perverse humor. He became comic and humane. *Miss Lonelyhearts* is a potent and orderly distillation of all the attitudes to human suffering. Miss Lonelyhearts himself is the drunken writer of an Advice Column in a newspaper who begins running it as a joke, a sort of sobbing *Americana,* and ends by becoming overwhelmed by the weight of human misery and by his inability to do anything about it. The office gambits sicken him. Christ, Art, the Karamazov line, the Value of Suffering, back to Nature, on to Hedonism and so on have been taped long ago by Shrike, the editor with the dead-pan face, an expert in "how to play it."

Shrike is one of West's many attacks on the dream-generators of the mass media—an attack in the sense of being one of those unholy recognitions that lie at the center of the comic view of life:

> "I am a great saint," Shrike cried. "I can walk on my own water. Haven't you heard of Shrike's passion in the Luncheonette, or the Agony in the Soda Fountain? Then I compared the wounds in Christ's body to the mouths of a miraculous purse in which we deposit the small change of our sins. It is an excellent conceit. But now let us consider the holes in our own bodies and into what these congenital wounds open. Under the skin of a man is a wondrous jungle where veins like lush tropical growths hang along overripe organs and weed-like entrails writhe in squirming tangles of red and yellow. In this jungle, flitting from rock gray lungs to golden intestines, from liver to lights and back to liver again, lives a bird called the soul."

In the vulgar, exhausted way of the mass media, dead-pan Shrike is an aesthete. His jaunty little face looks like a paralyzed scream of fright. His remarks are pictorial, but without relation to any meaning. Miss Lonelyhearts is muddled by Shrike's cleverness. He would like to be able to believe in the efficacy of Christ, but the name for him has become another word for hysteria, "a snake whose scales are tiny mirrors in which the dead world takes on a semblance of life." He plowters through a series of alcoholic bouts, tries to seduce Shrike's cold and salacious wife, gets into fights in speakeasies, terrorizes and tries to torture an old man in a public lavatory; for Miss Lonelyhearts has strong sadistic fantasies, his pity has a strain of cruelty in it and he has begun to hate the sufferers who had the tempting horror of freaks. He is seduced by the nymphomaniac wife of a cripple, tries illness, love on a farm. These struggles are fuddled but heroic; he feels his "great heart" is a bomb that "will wreck the world without rocking it." In the end he has a vision of the love of Christ and rushes to tell his friend the cripple about it; but the cripple shoots him in a fit of jealousy. Christ may not be hysteria, but he is a tale told by an idiot.

This might have been a slushy book, the derelict lot behind James Barrie's hoardings. It is, instead, a selection of hard, diamond-fine miniatures, a true American fable. West writes very much by the eye and his use of poetic images has a precision which consciously sustains his preoccupation with the human being's infatuation with his dream and inner story. (All his people are spiders living in the webs they spin out of their minds.) Leaves on trees are like thousands of little shields, a woman's breasts are like "pink-tipped thumbs," a thrush sings like a "flute choked with saliva," a cripple limps along "making waste motions, like those of a partially destroyed insect." If we call *Miss Lonelyhearts* a minor star it is because we feel that the Art is stronger than the passion; that, indeed Miss Lonelyhearts himself is capable only of pathos. His advice to the nymphomaniac who is torturing her husband, to "let him win once," is just wise old owlishness; her happiness is to accuse and torture, his to drag his loaded foot. West has not considered that human beings overwhelmingly prefer suffering to happiness and that their sobbing letters are part of the sense of the role or drama that keeps them going. Still, as a performance, *Miss Lonelyhearts* is very nearly faultless.

The Day of the Locust is an advance from fable and from fragments of people, to the courageous full statement of the novel. I say "courageous" because in this kind of transition the writer has to risk showing the weakness of his hand. The artificial lights of the freak show are off in this book and we see human absurdity as something normal. This is a novel about Hollywood. West worked in the hum of the American dream generators and he chose those people who have done more for American culture than their coevals in Europe have done for theirs: the casualties, the wrecks, the failures, the seedy and the fakes. They are the people to whom the leisureless yea-sayers have said "No." The observer is a painter from the East who is dreaming up what sounds like a very bad picture, a sort of Belshazzar's Feast. (He is a vestige of West, the aesthete.) He has fallen for Faye, a daydreaming creature who secretly earns money as a call girl for a "cultured" brothel, and who hopes, like the rest of the people, to get into pictures. She lives among a ramshackle group which includes old stage hangers-on, a ferocious dwarf, a woman who is grooming her son to be a wonder child of the screen, an absurd, fairly genuine cowboy extra and a pathetic hotel clerk from the Middle West. Faye is carefully observed. She is the complete daydreamer, insulated to such an extent by the faculty that it acts as an effective alternative to innocence; she is sexually provoking, cold, little-minded and cruel, but puts gaiety into the roles she takes on and has the survival power of a cork in a storm. If Los Angeles were destroyed by fire she would easily survive, not because she is hard but because she is flimsy. Already, in *Miss Lonelyhearts,* West had been a delicate student of the American bitch.

This Hollywood novel is mature because the compassion has no theatrical pressure; because now West is blocking in a sizeable society, and because his gift for inventing extraordinary scenes has expanded. The novel is dramatized—in Henry James's sense of the word—in every detail, so that each line adds a new glint to the action. His sadistic streak comes out in an astonishing description of an illegal cockfight in a desert lot. His comic powers fill out in the scenes with the angry dwarf and in the pages where the hero gets lost in a film Battle of Waterloo. The psychological entangling is brought to an appalling climax when Faye leaves her exhausted hotel clerk for a Mexican and this leads on to the great final staging of the world première, where riot and lynching are sparked off by the wonder boy of the screen, and the hate behind the Californian myth comes out:

> Once there, they discover that sunshine is not enough. They get tired of oranges, even of avocado pears and passion fruit. Nothing happens. They haven't the mental equipment for leisure, the money nor the physical equipment for pleasure. . . . Their boredom becomes more and more terrible. They realize that they have been tricked and burn with resentment. Every day of their lives they read the newspapers and go to the movies. Both feed them on lynchings, murder, sex crimes, explosions, wrecks, love nests, fires, miracles, revolutions, war. This daily diet makes sophisticates of them. The sun is a joke. Oranges can't titillate their jaded palates. Nothing can be violent enough to make taut their slack minds and bodies.

It was a warning against Fascism; it makes the witch hunt understandable; by extension, it is a statement about the nearness of violence in American life.

The Day of the Locust has the defect of insufficient ambition. It calls for a larger treatment and we have a slight suspicion that the painter-observer is slumming. But West had not the breath for full-length works. Script writing snaps up the clever. His important contribution to the American novel was his polished comedy, which he displayed with the variety of a master and on many levels. If his talent was not sufficiently appreciated in the moral thirties, it was because comedy as a world in itself and as a firm rejection of the respected was not understood. West had something of Europe in him, where it is no crime to know too much.

THE FORSYTES

Galsworthy? A City toff, decent fellow, fond of the Turf. Good shot. A bit damp-eyed. Some trouble with a woman. Gave up shooting birds, took to novel writing and shooting his own class—rich lawyers, company directors—until the Germans unsportingly cleared the covers. In the end, wrote telegraphese like this and forgave all. "The rum thing to me," said Gilbert Murray who admired *The Forsyte Saga*," is that I don't feel that I know in the least what a Forsyte is like and I am not conscious of having seen one." This is not Oxford snobbery: after forty-odd years one feels exactly that. Galsworthy's imagination was lukewarm: thin, partial, thumb-nail sketches of people, poor invention, jog-trot realism, blur when there is a question of feeling, embarrassment or jauntiness when there should be thought.

On the other hand, D. H. Lawrence *did* jump at Forsyteism as a social illness and even respected the satirical force of *The Man of Property*. It opens well and has an idea. Before the family history drifted into genteel soap opera, thousands of readers recognized their relatives; on the Continent and in America, the *Saga* became the standard guide to the English character. Even today, especially on the other side of the Iron Curtain, "the great Galsworthy" is brought out like a trump card when one is playing a hand or two with foreign intellectuals. The world has a hunger for the single, simple explanation and Galsworthy explained where the Victorians had put on a complex, congested, preaching face.

For him property was the English passion; convention disposed of the inconvenient emotions. You bought everything—from houses, pretty country, works of art to women and children. Every human feeling had to pass through a more or less brutalizing shareholders' meeting; it had somehow to pay and, if you had your losses, you put a soothing cream of sentiment over them. The foreigner brought up on Victorian impenetrability was ready for Galsworthy's inside view. It explained that peculiar foreign fantasy: the well-off, buttoned-up, blue-eyed, blank-faced Englishman who was a sort of gun dog to a master called the Right Thing and trained to love life only when it was decently dead. In short, the Forsytes are "rum" because they are a theory. The theory works in *The Man of Property* because Galsworthy's anger is roused; once that dies, the *Saga* becomes a family charade and a hymn to crustiness.

A man of property himself, Galsworthy was a rebel against his own class for reasons of chivalry rather than of deep principle. His private story is very relevant—too relevant. It has long been known and Mr. Dudley Barker has written a mild, tactful and, occasionally, skeptical account of it in a biographical study, *The Man of Principle*. A young man with a handsome allowance and pleasant expectations, Galsworthy amused himself with horse-racing and not much more at Oxford; came down to idle at the Law; was sent round the world to get over a mild, unsuitable love affair; returned to discover religious doubt, guilt about the condition of the poor, and to slip into a liaison with his cousin's wife. In the mercantile euphemism for describing sexual unhappiness, the couple were not "on terms": even worse, she played Chopin and he preferred the Yeomanry. The fear of scandal, ostracism and the danger of hurting his father and, possibly, losing his income made Galsworthy keep the liaison fairly secret for ten years. Then the affair blew up. The central theme of *A Man of Property*—the indecency of property rights in love—was provided. Try to own Beauty and it vanishes.

But once the scandal died down and the divorce was over and the ostracism of Ada Galsworthy came to an end, Galsworthy's rebellion ended too. He continued all his life to be indignant about cruelty and social injustice, but within the system. He became a very likable kind of English crank and this crankiness found an effective outlet in his plays; but as a novelist he sank back into an ironical apologia for the class he represented. Soames, the villain, the only character of any account in *The Forsyte Saga,* becomes Soames the stoic bearing the weight of his own dull, tragic compulsion to possessive love. That development is commendable. Galsworthy has at least seen that possessive men who put a money value to everything are not thereby cut off from tragic or, at any rate, pathetic experience: if Soames is mean, he is also emotional and, in stoicism, he gains a pitiable strength. But gradually Soames becomes Galsworthy's mouthpiece and that is a betrayal of the meaning of the first volume of the *Saga.* Galsworthy has not the talent, the vitality, the conviction, to deepen an idea.

One realizes that Galsworthy is not going to face everything out when one sees his handling of the

Soames-Irene-Bosinney situation. All that is said conveys nothing about Irene and everything of the narcissism of those who admire her: they are caressing their own feelings. She is a sentimental mystery—an erotic dream. If she were not, Galsworthy would have to come out with the plain fact that she is a real female, as ruthless as Soames and indeed a bitch in all the crises of the story. Defending his study of erotic passion in an earlier book, *The Dark Flower,* Galsworthy said too much had been written about the physical realities of erotic passion, too little of its spirit; the truth is that he goes straight into sentimentality by a high-minded evasion of the facts. The famous passivity of Irene is a fantasy: she must be seen as the victim. We must be prevented from seeing that Beauty is making victims of her two husbands and her son. For there is a Galsworthian theory that irresistible Passion comes uncalled for in our lives, transfiguring, destroying, vanishing. So it may, but at least we know what and who hit us. The novelist who does not know will be guilty of one of those moral tergiversations that are fatal to his quality as a writer and even to his craftsmanship. Galsworthy is so bemused by Irene that he cannot even get the woman to speak except in lines that sound like bits of a breathless telegram. And she is, more often than not, sitting by an open window near flowers! Clever woman!

After this central failure, Galsworthy is left to exercise the skill of a gentleman amateur on the surface of social life. Here and there he practices a port-wine irony in his little sketches of testy old men and foolish aunts. There are embarrassing pictures of un-Forsyte-like artists. There are one or two good boardroom scenes, for Galsworthy had observed company meetings when he was idling at the Law. There is some expert comedy: Soames, in Paris, mistaken by a detective for his wife's lover. Or the breakup of horse-racing Montague Dartie's rickety marriage where the maneuvers intended to separate the couple only succeed in reuniting them. Galsworthy's lapses into the raffish are good.

The interesting thing about him is that he was a taught writer: his wife above all, then Edward Garnett, Conrad, a whole committee, worked on his manuscripts in a manner that would have been intolerable to a less determinedly masochistic figure. He slaved away, like a Forsyte at the office, until he attained a nonstop facility which was his personal triumph and, in the end, his downfall. What no one detected was that his weaknesses fitted him for the stage: his simple, sentimental view of the class situation, his feeling for moral melodrama, his eye for the short scene, his topical sense of justice and a reformist temper made acceptable by dialogue done in offhand remarks. He could knock off a play in a few weeks without help from the committee; and actors gave life to what, in his novels, was really lifeless.

It is fashionable to think him crude as a dramatist; and his situations are really head-on collisions in unlikely circumstances. But he got the admiration of Shaw and even Wells, who was no admirer of the novels, was won over. The fact is that Galsworthy was an ingenious craftsman. The sudden entrance of the exquisitely serpentine Jew in gorgeous dressing gown, among a group of the squirarchy struggling into their boiled shirts in the country-house scene of *Loyalties,* "tells" symbolically and theatrically in an instant. Galsworthy also hit the taste of a decade in which—as Mr. Barker says—the Welfare State began to kick in the womb. Plays like *The Silver Spoon, Strife* or *The Skin Game* had much the same effect on its first audiences as *Look Back in Anger* has had in our own time. He had hit upon that mysterious thing—the idiom of a period. The theatre was just the place for those black-and-white notions of Decency and Vice, Property and Poverty, Truth and Pharisaism which were buried in the confusions of his mind. His novels, he once said, were not social criticism, they were "spiritual examinations," conversations between two halves of himself.

As a man Galsworthy was the gentlest of toffs, and a moral toff to the end. Guilty about his inherited wealth, he scrupulously gave away large sums of money to the needy, to hangers-on, to causes and still managed to leave £98,000. He was a soft touch for ex-convicts. He was whimsical about the enormous list of good causes he supported. They ranged from prison and divorce reform, the establishment of a minimum wage in sweated industries, woman's suffrage, slum clearance, down to the protection of prostitutes and animals and the improvement of slaughterhouses. His generosity to servants and tenants infuriated his neighbors. Yet he remained very much the "man at the club window"—a phrase of Edward Garnett's that rankled—in the sense that he found it hard to make real contact with people outside his own class. As Mr. Barker says, he had no notion that the poor had their own life. He was always the district visitor, solemn, formal and modest.

Galsworthy's character appears most clearly in his relations with Ada Galsworthy. She was the daughter of an eccentric doctor who spent many years building an elaborate mausoleum for himself and used to sit in Norwich cemetery gazing at it with pleasure and thinking of little touches to add to it: an apt progenitor for the original of the mysterious, passive, silent Irene. As a muse—a model from whom the novelist was rarely separated—she was, not surprisingly, exigent. She became a hypochondriac and he was her continual nurse. He said that he had found a talent for nursing.

In a sense, he wanted to nurse England. He also said, with a sort of helpless pleasure, that Ada paralyzed him. That Forsyte story was never written.

ROSS AT THE DEPOT

Withheld from the public since the twenties when it was written, T. E. Lawrence's *The Mint* is one of those time bombs of literature which fail to go off when the hour comes. Its mystery, kept alive by a leak here and there, a single copy circulating somewhere or other, and by people "privileged to see," had been artificial; and the habit of building up expectation of "revelations" in his work was brought to a climax by issuing an unexpurgated edition in leather at extra cost. It is an odd comment on our manners that we have contrived to make the short list of four-letter words which are easily turned into the nuggets of a publisher's gold mine. Lawrence was, of course, writing when the revival of the rights of blasphemy and bad language was regarded as an ethical duty; but, for a later generation, military service and war have not been a novelty, linguistically or otherwise, and I doubt whether anyone under forty will want to pay to read exactly what the soldier said so often. No scandal, no sex, no sodomy. *The Mint* is simply an earnest documentary work. It was noted down night after night in the Nissen huts of the R.A.F. Depot, records what went on in the huts and on the square and what it felt like to have one's spirit broken and to be turned into 352087 A/c Ross. This experience has become a commonplace to the majority of living males and dozens of documentaries have described the process. In waiting till 1955 the book had waited too long and disclosed nothing much about Lawrence himself.

All the same, there is a curious period interest in *The Mint.* It is an arty book: Lawrence's own injured romanticism and his self-pity see to that. One sees now a pathos in the stilted originality which was worked into so much of the more ardent prose of the time and which I take to be a hangover from Meredith.

> So the appellant moon easily conjures me outside. . . .
>
> On the western slope swelled the strident activity of red-and-chocolate footballers.

Lawrence's prose attempts to attract attention to its airs and merits; he is a word prig. Occasionally, in a portrait, an eventual touch of fantasy justifies him:

> China . . . is a stocky Camberwell costermonger, with the accent of a stage Cockney. Since childhood he has fought for himself and taken many knocks, but no care about them. He is sure that safety means to be rough among the town's roughs. His deathly white face is smooth as if waxed, the bulging pale eyes seem lidless like a snake's, and out of their fixedness he stares balefully. . . . China has said, "F——" so often, inlaying it monotonously after every second word of his speech with so immense an aspirated "f," that his lips have pouted to it in a curve which sneers across his face like the sound-hole of a fiddle's belly.

It must be said that *The Mint* is more labored in its first painful 165 pages which are based on notes taken certainly too close to the object; the remaining forty pages, based on letters, are both happier in themselves and are more freely written, and this part of the book contains an excellent description of speeding on a motor bike. Lawrence wrote spiritedly about action. Another virtue of *The Mint* lies in its honest effort to get to the bottom of his subject. At first the impression is that what is unique experience for him, in his egocentric way, is commonplace for his fellows, but presently he notices that it will not be commonplace for them either. In 1923, with a million and a half unemployed in England, enlistment meant the open acknowledgment of defeat by life. Having lost their souls, men glumly hesitated as they handed over their last possession: their bodies.

> We include "lads" and their shady equivalent, the hard case. Also the soft and the silly: the vain: the old soldier who is lost without the nails of service: the fallen officer sharply contemptuous of our new company, yet trying to be hail-fellow and not proud. Such a novice dips too willingly at the dirty jobs, while the experienced wage slave stands by, grumbling.
>
> The dressy artisans, alternately allured and repelled by our unlimited profession, dawdle for days over their trade tests, hoping some accident will make up their minds. Our Glasgow blacksmith given only bread and tea one day in dining hall, cried, "Aam gaen whame," muddled his trial job and was instantly turned down. That last afternoon he spent spluttering crazy, non-intelligible confidences at every one of us. A dumpy lad he was, with tear-stained fat cheeks, and so glad to have failed. "Dry bread," he would quiver half-hourly with a sob in his throat.

Simple-minded, like a child, but stiff-minded, too, and dirty; very Scotch.

Lawrence himself joined the R.A.F. under the name of Ross at a time of physical and spiritual exhaustion in his life when (he said) he was capable of only negative decisions. He wanted, he says, to get back to human kind and, halfway through the book, he thinks the plan has failed. It probably did fail: it was loveless and despairing. The malicious and the knowing have described Lawrence's enlistment as an example of his chronic playacting, but human motives are rarely simple; even if he were playacting, this is as serious and complex a compulsion as its opposite, and not less "real" or "sincere." Self-dramatization is common among gifted men and provides its own experience. At the Air Force medical, the doctor noted, Lawrence says (no doubt with some self-infatuation) that he looked as though he had been going short of food for months. If he had, there was no need for him to have done, and he may have half-starved in a sulking desire to show he had not received sufficient attention. That does not alter the fact that a hungry man was abasing himself before the doctor. The theme of abasement already occurs in *The Seven Pillars of Wisdom;* in *The Mint* one is struck by the analogy with religious conversion. The book might indeed be a histrionic footnote to Alfred de Vigny's elaborate comparison of the religious and military vocations. The world is abandoned, and the gates close on the recruit, as private possessions the body and the mind are systematically destroyed, the will is thrown away, the subject is in a condition as abject as that of Saint Ignatius when he stood in rags at Montserrat; only after abasement can obedience become an instinct and the old man give place to the new man, the required automaton, fulfilled in corporate pride and corporate wholeness. That is the ultimate reward; in the interim, he sinks restfully and unresponsibly into the dull, kind, corrupt world of the closed community, where promiscuousness kills the desire for intimacy, where sex is a dirty word, and the last feeble ghosts of private life escape in groans and bablings from the lips in sleep at night. That is purgatory. It is a pity that Lawrence had to leave the R.A.F. and so lost the will to describe the experiences of the technician's heaven.

To his companions, as far as so impersonal a writer can disclose it, Lawrence was an oddity. He could not swear. They were considerate about his age—he was eight years older than most and was physically exhausted more quickly than they. They admired his use of long words, they borrowed a little money. They must have seen him wince at the sight of their bullocky animality. He let them down in one respect: every man has some small advantage he can exploit; why, as a "toff," did he not exploit the fact? There was no masochism in the men, there was no point in being a "mug." This complaint came to a head in the conflict with a sergeant who was one of two or three sadists who made his life hell at the Depot in those days. This sergeant was a killer. One day, when he had reduced his squad to a helpless, gasping collection of sweating and frightened animals, he made a short inspection to finish them off, stopped in front of Lawrence and said: " 'When did you have a bath? Open your collar,' thrust his hand roughly inside against my wet breast. 'Christ, the bloody man's lousy. . . . March the filthy —— out to the wash house and scrub the —— out of him properly.' " Lawrence was marched off by Sailor, who had a great command of picturesque obscenity. The blanks lengthen in Sailor's dialogue: "God if that long —— streak —— pokes his head in here after us, I'll knock seven different sorts of —— out of him. But, mate, you let the flight down, when he takes the mike out of you every time. Give the ignorant —— bag a —— great gob of your toffology."

Pain is the subject of *The Mint* and it is not pain quietly borne. It is relieved by rough kindness. When Lawrence, who slept badly, went for a walk at night he was treated with sympathy, wonder and pity by the sentries. He observed their new character growing up in the men. Once the hell of drill was over and they got to the aircraft, they found the unconscious solace of mass men: the machines belonged to them, not to the silly fools who flew them and messed them up. Lawrence was moved by this, and the puritan in him responded to the dull self-righteousness of unexceptional people. Since he was exceptional himself he must have been divided in mind. It is pretty evident that he knew he had no place there and that the cure—that old, mystical, muddled notion of "going back to the people" —was, stunt or no stunt, a failure. The affair of the motor bicycle suggests the trouble was one that could not be solved by immolation in the corporate life. And there *The Mint* leaves us. It is, in point of writing, one of the first documentaries, tortuous and self-conscious, vivid and affected, powerful and yet weakened by shrillness and mannered introspection. Writing was not his medium. Or, rather, to be his medium it had to have the great, cruel, false, personal, romantic subject, with Carlyle's "dark curtains" coming down on it at the end. The Royal Air Force was precisely not that in 1923 and, in seeing the commonest men only in relation to their failure in civilian life and their military training, he showed his distance from them. Those writers who have succeeded in portraying common men have not made them the acolytes of the writer's own personal rituals. One is left, at the end of *The Mint,* moved by the writer's pain and nagged by the peculiarity of his case. One is not left with very much more.

THE BORED BARBARIANS

In the last decade Mr. Anthony Powell was the first to revive the masculine traditions of English social comedy. He retrieved it on behalf of the upper classes. The joke that he is a Proust Englished by Wodehouse has something in it; in fact, the big influence was Aubrey, but where Aubrey had an almost fretful appetite for scandal and oddity, this was dignified, in Mr. Powell's generation, as the belief in personal relationships. Other values, in the twenties and thirties, were in flux; one could become an anthropologist, a Malinowski of Mayfair, Bloomsbury and country-house life, and try to establish a culture pattern. I confess that I have got more out of Mr. Powell's novels, as each one of them stands, than I have out of his ambition to fill out the social panorama during his period. I am not convinced that any pattern is emerging. It is enough that *A Question of Upbringing, The Acceptance World* and *A Buyer's Market* introduced a new kind of nerve, comic effrontery and invention. They caught and played with that ineradicable core of boredom that has been the resource as well as the blight of upper-class English life, a boredom produced by the inherited genius for ironing out feelings, and doggedly covering the loss with bouts of dottiness, alcohol, adultery and class consciousness. Mr. Powell's English are punishing and punished. Their comedy has no silken threads; the threads are tweed.

What are the characteristics of this masculine tradition in our comedy? It is intelligent rather than sensitive; it is prosaic rather than poetic; it is sane rather than extravagant. It is egocentric and not a little bullying. It has a manner, and that manner is ruthless and unkind. To stand up to the best manners of English society one has to be rude, exclusive and tough. One must be interested in behavior, not in emotions; in the degree to which people hold their forts—and how much money the forts cost—not in what human beings are. The tradition begins with Fielding; it is there, minus the animal spirits, in Jane Austen. Its values are bound to the social class the writer belongs to—in Wells, for example, to the lower middle class. Hardheaded, often gifted, snobbish—for the most part—appreciative of other people's disasters and evasive about their own, self-oppressed and taking it out in horseplay and libertinage, Mr. Powell's characters are a sort of club. They can listen unexhausted to gossip about each other, but their faces become suddenly masked if an outsider comes up. Their privacy is phenomenal. Widmerpool, the go-getter and man of will—a considerable comic creation—is damned because people affect not to remember whether he comes from Northamptonshire, or is it Derby? Mr. Powell's narrator really hounds him. Yet, of course, Widmerpool also hounds himself.

The world Mr. Powell is describing is dull, incurious and barbarous, judged from the outside, but very funny to read about. It certainly defeats foreigners. But the people of high comedy *are* generally dull. (The characters of Henry James's *Portrait of a Lady,* for example, are barely conversible.) The question is, What has Mr. Powell done with them? The early novels like *Afternoon Men* and *Venusberg* and *From a*

View to a Death shared a sharp, electric, almost lyrical, performance. One of the earliest writers to expose people, and even more their way of life, by the follies of their dialogue, Mr. Powell took a number of specimens of the Jazz Age and drily left little commentary. *Afternoon Men* gave one stiff shot of party life; *Venusberg*, romantic yet lapidary, commemorated the love affair abroad; *From a View to a Death*, that social return match: the undesirable artist among the speechless fox hunters. Here Mr. Powell's Stendhalian dryness began to warm and a deadly moralist appeared. For this is the novel of Major Fosdick, a very rare bird indeed in the English Tweedery, and one of ingenious complication. A tendency to overdress, so that even "the skin of his face was covered by small diagonal lines similar in pattern to that of his coat," was not to be attributed to any shortness of genealogy in Major Fosdick; he was far from being a stockbroker. The deep boredom and privacy of English country life had brought out something cross-gartered in his nature. He would lock himself in his dressing room, when the fit was on, and would dress himself in a woman's evening dress and picture hat and then, taking out an exercise book, write poetry. What we so anxiously hope for indeed happens: he is caught by an enemy squire and neighbor in this rig-out and, wits not moving fast in those acres, he might have been able to palm himself off as his own wife. A mustache betrayed him.

A scene of this kind is, of course, a stock one in farce and it is funny enough as it stands. But everything lies in the handling and here we see the first signs of Mr. Powell's coming maturity. He is never satisfied with a mere joke. The encounter has two beauties: first that Fosdick compromises. He takes off the picture hat and swings it absurdly as he talks; second, neither man mentions his astonishment or horror, but treats the whole episode *à l'anglaise,* as a test of character and upbringing. Fosdick knows he will have now to surrender in the long row over his pheasants. He retires, stiff in the upper lip, to a nursing home in the proper way. Mr. Passenger, the squire, will go home and, as is proper, forbid his daughters the house, but he too recognizes moral defeat. He had considered himself a man of independent genius whose luck was always out, a potential superman who had never had his chance. His tragedy is that:

> In this moment of emergency he had been thrown back on the old props of tradition and education and when he might have enjoyed a substantial revenge he had behaved with all the restraint in the world.

The characters in *From a View to a Death* are perennial in the classical English comedy of country life and the national mixture is there, even to the mad cynicism of the cautionary tale. I am thinking of the barrel organ players who appealed for charity on the grounds that they were orphans.

> The postulation rested wholly on the handicap of loss of parents, which because the youngest of the orphans must have been at least forty years of age, was in their case presumed to have persisted into early middle life.

But if the characters are the same, the observation is revised. They are done in new colors. Mr. Powell is, as we know, devoted to Aubrey's *Lives* and his comedy has behind it a stolid native melancholy that is terrifyingly full-blooded. He has wit, but it is not rapier-play; rather it leaves a skillful boxer's marks upon the body of the enemy. The characters retire bruised, not nicked, from the ring. And then an unusual dimension is added to his people: they are reconsidered. They are not only figures of fun and amusement; they have a serious relation to their own experience or to the author's, so that we are shown the comedy of social history's "past." In a world in which standards and values have vanished, to what do we turn? To the attempt to find out a personal pattern—that favorite word of unbelieving anthropologists—to the sober technical question as to where we were accurate and where (through immaturity) off the mark in the consideration of ourselves, our friends and our world. We become the pedants of the cult of personal relationships.

This pedantry is the basis of all Mr. Powell's comedies. *A Buyer's Market* reconsiders the characters of *A Question of Upbringing* and both books fill in at length the social scene that was left out in *Afternoon Men.* So we have a finely painted, detailed picture of the last year at Eton, the London Season, the first ventures in society, the first stages of a career; and in the background the upper classes start on that peculiar course of chasing after artists, drifting into Bohemia, the demi-monde and the business rackets, which has been typical of our age. *A Buyer's Market* contains three absurd figures from this time: Mr. Deacon the aging bad painter, Uncle Giles the shady rebel, and the superb Widmerpool whom we had first seen at Eton—wronged, earnest, narrowed and ambitious. Widmerpool is a wonderful portrait of the go-getting young man—he is Fielding's Blifil, but now in business—whose pursuit of the main chance has given a growing squint to his life. He talks like a Pep book, he calculates absurdly aloud, he is prone to social disasters of the first magnitude. He is not debagged by the young oafs at the debs' ball, but he does get covered with castor sugar; it is he who is made to pay for the Free Love girl's abortion; it is he who drives his car into the ornamental urn at the magnate's castle and who makes a ludicrous appearance behind the bars in the dungeon there. Widmerpool never comes up smiling; muttered indignation attends his injuries. He becomes the victim one cannot love, crouching round the ashes of his private shames, but he has his own private laugh. For his pursuit of private respectability and the windy justifications of the yes-man is always successful.

The farce of Widmerpool gains from the sententious, slow motion manner of Mr. Powell's writing. The deb sprinkles Widmerpool lightly with the sugar pot:

> More from surprise than because she wished additionally to torment him, Barbara did not remove her hand before the whole contents of the vessel—which voided itself in an instant of time—had descended upon his head and shoulders, covering him with sugar more completely than might have been thought possible in so brief a space. Widmerpool's rather sparse hair had been liberally greased with a dressing—the sweetish smell of which I remembered as somewhat disagreeable when applied in France—this lubricant retaining the grains of sugar, which, as they adhered thickly to his skull, gave him the appearance of having turned white with shock at a single stroke, which judging by what could be seen of his expression, he might very well in reality have done underneath the glittering incrustations that enveloped his head and shoulders. He had writhed sideways to avoid the downpour, and a cataract of sugar had entered the space between neck and collar; yet another jet streaming between eyes and spectacles.

Mr. Powell is excellent with the raffish. Some critics have objected to his sententious manner; but even if it is true that this is what happens to Proust if one drains off sensibility and makes him appropriate to clubs, I think the sententious irony succeeds. It is, after all, native and part of the tradition. It adds a very English flavor either of comic tautology or deflation.

> "Shall we leave the gentlemen to their port?" said Mrs. Widmerpool, when finally the subject had been picked bone dry.
>
> She mouthed the words "gentlemen" and "port" as if they might be facetiously disputable as strictly literal descriptions in either case.

That final "in either case" is the devastating torpedo. Mr. Powell may have got overfond of phrases like "in his case" and all those "unquestionably," "alternativelys," "undoubtedlys" and "if anythings," but in their forensic malice, they rub the salt in hard. (The narrator's desire to pass as the impartial norm conceals a fierce melancholy which I suppose to be Mr. Powell's energizing wound as an artist.) The habit of laboring a point may also at last add the macabre to the grotesque:

> A direct hit had excised even the ground floor, so that the basement was revealed as a sunken garden, or site of archaeological excavations long abandoned, where great sprays of willowherb and ragwort flowered through the paving stones; only a few broken milk bottles and a laceless boot recalling contemporary life.

And the deliberate intellectualization of an absurdity may become disturbing:

> The name Casanova's Chinese Restaurant offered one of those unequivocal blendings of disparate elements of the imagination which suggest a whole new state of mind or way of life.

These words come from *Casanova's Chinese Restaurant.* The story has two musicians, three writers, a painter, a biography-writing peeress, a Left Wing peer turning intellectual; we may find ourselves in a country house like Dogdene, a discarded first or second wife may drag us down to Earls Court or Pimlico.

The aim of Mr. Powell's sententiousness is to appall by the judicious: in a sense, his comedy is hysterical. There are several references, in the novel, to a ghost train the narrator and his friends used to go on when they were young; and it is implied that their lives, in the Bohemian period he is describing, have been like this absurd and finally ghastly journey.

But these novels constitute a *roman fleuve*. The same characters reappear, with new wives, husbands, careers, fortunes and fates; they are connected intimately in their social set. They live in a whispering gallery, in a mocking music of echoes from the past. They astonish one another by their unpredictable actions and their new chummings-up. Who would have thought, in *At Lady Molly's*, that Widmerpool would fall for that brassy ex-VAD, Mrs. Haycock? Or, in a later volume, that the grand Mrs. Foxe would take up with a ballet dancer and shower him with presents? Here a difficulty arises. After the deep spate of their early flow, such novels run into shallows. What began as a panorama begins to sound like a gossip column. One noticed this in *At Lady Molly's*; in *Casanova's Chinese Restaurant*, the habit of gossip has really set in and the central interest—the examination of two marriages—is not strong enough to stop it. One has the irritating impression that Jenkins, the narrator, has no other profession but to run about collecting the news; his stability has become fitful. The characters exchange too much hearsay. This is the danger with the *roman fleuve* when it lacks a strongly sustaining idea beyond the convenience of its own existence. I am not sure that the idea of the decadence of a class, anecdotally viewed, is strong enough. I think Mr. Powell has now to guard against the risk that his characters will be so familiar and real to him that he will cease to make them important to us; that they will lose their true strength, *i.e.*, that they are obsessive fictions. The constant difficulty of the novelist is to avoid the engaging demi-monde that lies between art and life. Hearsay enfeebles, if Aubrey's brief emblematic lives become Aubrey's long ones.

Against this natural drift Mr. Powell puts his set comic scenes and uses, of course, his notable organizing powers. But, in *Casanova,* there is only one of these comic set pieces strong enough to stand against the current. It must be said that this particular one is as good as any he has done; it is the scene in which the drunken Stringham mocks the nagging out of the tragic Maclintick's terrible wife, and is himself finally carried off by his old governess. It is marvelously observed and the tragic sequel is all the more forceful for it; one notices here how brilliantly Mr. Powell arranges material that has become immense. He is very accomplished in pulling things up out of the past and planting them massively before us. I put this scene beside the earlier one in *At Lady Molly's* where the General, newly come to psychological studies, makes his absurd, slow motion diagnosis of Widmerpool's sexual misfortune. Mr. Powell is a master of such refracted comedy and that is where the sheer intelligence of the masculine school counts. Such things are far superior to his social commentary.

In praising Mr. Powell for his hard-headed comedy, his mastery of burlesque and farce, I do not undervalue his serious reflections. He does not glow with urbanity. He is melancholy, sane, experienced; there is no cynicism. His epigrams are withering but they do not utterly demolish. Their balance is as formidable as their wit:

> He also lacked that subjective, ruthless love of presiding over other peoples' affairs which often makes basically heartless people adept at offering effective consolation.

He has a sense of proportion, yet he also has edge. It is an uncommon pair of gifts. When one speaks of his melancholy one is not describing a passive condition; one is speaking of a driving force. His almost geological utterances suggest that even Mayfair and Pimlico have their Egdon Heaths:

> Love had received one of those shattering jolts to which it is peculiarly vulnerable from extraneous circumstances.

A sentence like that could go on the title page of *Casanova's Chinese Restaurant*. It contains, down to the very word "peculiarly" the undertones and overtones of this novelist, in whose work the human comedy is grimly engrained.

ALEXANDRIAN HOTHOUSE

In France, Germany and, for a while, in the United States, Lawrence Durrell has been the most admired of British novelists. For ourselves, he is a mixture of traveler, poet and the brilliant raconteur in depth of nonstop loquacity. Our literature grows blooms like this in the expatriate and Imperial hothouses—Mr. Durrell was planted in the Middle East and the Mediterranean—a Ouida as well as a Kipling, a Norman Douglas as well as a D. H. Lawrence; a Byron, but also a Hichens.

Where our exotics excel is in a matchless sense of place which, I believe, is not approached by any literature in the world. Mr. Durrell's evocation of Alexandria, in *Justine, Balthazar, Mountolive,* and *Clea,* is one of the finer mirages in our writing. It is an astonishing collection of fragments, a self-perpetuating generation of vivid pictorial illusions, obsessive, poetic, curious, scholarly, and headily at the mercy of mood and memory. This writing of his is splendid, even when the pedal is down, because the poetic image is the image of precision; and arresting, because contemporary English prose has either—in one of Durrell's phrases—got a hot potato in its mouth or has been nibbled close by the bleak teeth of modern criticism. In either case, it looks like rain. The writer whose subject is illusion, as Durrell's, is entitled to color, image and fantasy and it is no good complaining that, on the subject of cities, he does not write like Smollett who succeeded fearfully in a different way. Fragments stick:

> Streets that run back from the docks with their tattered, rotten supercargo of houses, breathing into each others' mouths, keeling over . . .

> the early spring dawn with its dense dew, sketched upon the silence that engulfs a whole city before the birds awaken it . . . the sweet voice of the blind muezzin hanging like a hair in the palm-cooled upper airs . . .

> in the summer the sea-damp lightly varnished the air. Everything lay under a coat of gum.

And there are the set pieces, like the sight of the desert at the meeting of the Copts, the duck-shoot in the delta. Or those long interiors: the cellar in which the child prostitutes come out by candlelight like a cloud of bats, or the Minister of the Interior's appalling reception room, with the old, sugared and slothful spider pillowing his stomach on the divan.

But as a novelist? A novel can be anything; but, struggle as Mr. Durrell does with his conviction that he is conducting an experiment in "the novel of sliding panels," or creating a mosaic of plot and symbol in layers and depths, he is really a raconteur, a master of the episode. He cannot stop. His novel *Clea* rounds off the Justine series, but he is clearly hankering after new twists and densities. In *Justine* he was all surface; in *Balthazar* he showed us it was a false surface; in *Mountolive,* the political novel which really rooted his characters, he got depth at last. I think this volume is the making of the quartet. But in *Clea,* invention and ingenuity have become a habit. The difficulty is that the war has come, the spell of old Alexandria and the decadent elation that sustained it have gone. There is no artifice to believe in. Pursewarden, who began to shape in *Mountolive,* lectures us for hours about sex, literature and the North in the only too-well-known voice of Norman Douglas. This is not the earlier, difficult Pursewarden of scandalous sexual misbehavior, fighting the Foreign Office, and dumfounding and seducing that honking, hysteric Lesbian, Justine; breaking the lockjaw of her desire for martyrdom by making her laugh at herself for the first time in her life. In *Clea* poor Pursewarden, who has had to bear much from Mr. Durrell, is given a guilty secret; he has committed incest. It is as solemn as the committal to the deep. It is made to sound like one of the seven deadly virtues. The smut is below standard, too.

And then, in *Clea,* those letters, diaries and mimicries which Mr. Durrell has skillfully used to give a change of view to the earlier books, swamp the narrative. There is still good farce which, after place, is one of Mr. Durrell's strong gifts. The saga of Scobie, the Catholic Police Chief with "tendencies" (Eonism) gets broader after his death. This sinning and Cockney prowler, with a bad accent, is canonized as a Moslem saint by accident because of local popularity. His tomb contains his bathtub—no body available—and works miracles. There is Dr. Amaril's romance with a girl for whom he makes an artificial nose, a charming tale; and more dreadful, the tale of Dr. Balthazar's last love affair. In a panic because he is obliged to take to false teeth, and sees in this a sign of declining powers, the philosophical old dabbler in the Cabbala falls in love with a beastly young actor, and is driven to the most extravagant and pitiable humiliations of homosexual jealousy. He ends by attempting to cut off his own hands. (Hand symbols and handcutting occur more than once in Mr. Durrell's quartet, for as he annotates the course of European sexual practice and fantasy from Rabelais to Sade, Sade gets most of the cheers. As a gesture to Home, there are two cheers for D. H. Lawrence.)

Mr. Durrell's ingenious method of sliding the panel and showing us many episodes again with new and unexpected shadows, is dramatic but unoriginal; it cannot disguise the fact that his leading people are not people at all. They are vehicles of events; they are a poet's notes; they are fables, subjects of one another's conversation and, in the case of the women, are seen only in the light of desire. It is Mr. Durrell's point as an artist that they are fervid aspects of the city, created by its moments. They build up, of course, as time passes. Justine, the nymphomaniac, the banker's wife, the narrator's mistress, is shown first as a figure of mystery, then as a raucous hysteric and finally we get a real insight into her nature when we discover that she is diverting her desire to suffer into serious political plotting. Politics calm her sexually. She is the perpetual *intrigante* with a rage for power. When the plot fails she turns upon her husband and becomes not the mysterious holy whore, but the true married scold. So Justine acquires character—but only through the say-so of her lovers who observe her. She is less a woman than gossip. We see the rest of Mr. Durrell's characters as we might see them in Casanova, almost only in their relation to some peculiarities of sexuality, its pleasures, pains, dissimulations, ironies and unpredictable turns.

Mr. Durrell and his people are continually talking. They talk well and wittily, with instructed skepticism and an immense amount of quotation including quite a few old intellectual gags, like Mommsen's about the Celts destroying civilizations and creating none of their own. It indeed often seems that loquacity has been substituted for sex. And *are* they talking about love? Not really; only about narcissism and desire. Sterile, they are talking about its perversity, its sadness, its anecdotage, its variety, its passing. Their sexual love is easy, but after the sexual act there is still unsatisfied desire. Exhausted romantics, they are looking over the sleeping lover's shoulder. Love—and Mr. Durrell as a good Mediterranean prides himself on his knowledge of its variety—rarely grows beyond that first stage in his novels. He speaks in Stendhalian phrase of *amour passion,* but does not give us an example of it. No one is possessed.

Here and there, there is a *glimpse* of love—and we have to grant that he sets out to be a novelist of fragmentation—as when, for example, in a very fine scene, an old man cries for his mistress on his deathbed in hospital. He is an old dealer, she is a cabaret dancer with many customers who has long ago left him. He wants her now, not for comfort, not to expose a broken heart, but to confess to her that he once or twice robbed her and cheated her. He wants to clear his conscience. Surely love is the bloodstream of the moral nature; Mr. Durrell sees human beings as thinned-out spirits off on some kind of erotic hunt who live only in the eyes and the senses, on the nerves, in expert pleasure and in terror. We accept this because he tells us we are in Alexandria, the androgynous, where people are "wounded in their sex"; but it knocks the bottom out of old Pursewarden as a sage. It is noticeable indeed that Mr. Durrell's people acquire character when they are seen outside of love, especially the men. Narouz, the rich Copt and farmer, for example, who murders and is murdered, is far more real than his brother, the mysterious Nessim, the banker who is caught in Justine's affairs. Nessim becomes real only when we see him plotting to run arms into Palestine. Mountolive, the ambassador, becomes real when he is shocked out of his long daydream of desire for Nessim's mother, is caught by political intrigue, and goes through the shocking and terrifying scene in the child's brothel.

If mutability and illusion are the subjects of this novelist who is afloat on fine words and an avidity for art and ideas, his means are shock, boldness and a mastery of intrigue, patterning and storytelling. His experiment in repeated rewritings succeeds to a great extent because the shift has some of the abruptness of the theatre in it. In all things he is an artist; even when he bores he bores us as an artist by striking too many attitudes. When the shift fails it is because he relies excessively on long-winded narrators who are supposed to be new voices but who are in fact as clever in the same way as he is. The influence of Norman Douglas and the desire to out-Juan *Don Juan* have been baneful: it produces Ouida. But one does not forget the absurdities of Scobie, the love life of Pombal, the French diplomat. One admires the caricature, the murder of Narouz, the scene in which Pursewarden fails to make love to Melissa, succeeds when he has confessed a secret to her, and drops her suddenly when she accidentally reveals a trivial yet deadly secret to him; one does not forget Scobie's death, the horror of the brothel—or anything which springs from intrigue. For intrigue buzzes out of Mr. Durrell's tremendous power of observation and invention. His eyes are forever watching; his ears forever hearing. The Decadent palls, the compulsive talker goes on and on, but again and again the romantic inventor breaks through like a hothouse flower.

PAIN AND WILLIAM GOLDING

The essence of the novelist's art—especially the English novelist's—is the quotidian. From the moment Crusoe domesticates and diarizes his desert island, the novel reflects the confidence the individual derives from the society he lives in. The risks of romance are gone; he is safe in the realist's nest: Selkirk was lonely, but Crusoe is the least lonely man in the world. This confidence has lasted in our tradition. But when we look up from our books into the life around us today, we wonder how the prosaic observer in realistic fiction can be so certain of himself. The quotidian art goes on describing and describing and, as far as externals are concerned, we cannot complain that the modern realist fails to describe the features of a changing, violent or collapsing society. But he is the spectator, in some lucky way insured and untouched; rarely does the novelist find the point at which we are involved or committed; rarely does he touch the quick, so that for once the modern alibi—"it is beyond the power of the imagination to grasp, etc., etc."—does not work. The imagination will never grasp until it is awakened; and facts will not awaken it. They merely strengthen opinion; and there is nothing so apt to shut us off from the world as the correct opinion about it. The imagination can be awakened only by the imagination, by the artist who has the power to break us down until the point of secret complicity is reached. It was this point which the writer of romance, undeterred by the day's events, and lost in his world of dramatic wishes, once knew how to reach.

Mr. William Golding is an artist of this kind. His three books, *Lord of the Flies* (1954), *The Inheritors* (1955) and *Pincher Martin* (1956) are romance in the austere sense of the term. They take the leap from the probable to the possible. *Lord of the Flies* has a strong pedigree: island literature from Crusoe to *Coral Island*, *Orphan Island* and *High Wind in Jamaica*. All romance breaks with the realistic novelist's certainties and exposes the characters to transcendent and testing dangers. But Golding does more than break; he bashes, by the power of his overwhelming sense of the detail of the physical world. He is the most original of our contemporaries. Many writers have been concerned, as a matter of argument, with what is rhetorically called "the dilemma of modern man," and have given us, as it were, lantern slide lectures on the anarchy of a poisoned future; they are really essayists sitting in comfort. Golding, on the contrary, scarcely uses an argument or issues a warning. He simply shakes us until we feel in our bones the perennial agony of our species. By their nature, his subjects—prep school boys on a desert island in a world war, the calvary of a sailor who gave the right order but whose half-conscious body is being washed about the gullies of an Atlantic rock, the conflicts of a handful of Neanderthalers—could easily become the pasteboard jigsaw of allegory, pleasing our taste for satire and ingenuity; but the pressure of feeling drives allegory out of the foreground of his stories. He is a writer of intense visual gift, with an overpowering sense of nature and an extraordinary perception of man as a physical being in a physical world, torn between a primitive inheritance and the glimmer of an evolving mind. A dramatic writer and familiar with the strong emotions that go with the instinct of self-preservation—blind love for his kind, hatred, fear and elation—he is without hysteria. He is not cooking up freakish and exotic incident; he is not making large proclamations about man against nature, God, destiny and so on; he is seriously and in precise, individual instances gripped—as if against his will—by the sight of the slow and agonizing accretion of a mind and a civilized will in one or two men, struggling against their tendency to slip back, through passion or folly, and lose their skills in panic. And there is pity for the pain they feel.

Pain is the essence of Mr. Golding's subject. In *The Inheritors* it is the obscure pain of a baffled and dying group of ape men who see themselves supplanted by the more skillful new being called Man. The ape man experiences the pain of the grunt, of trying to communicate from one poor mind to another—"I have a picture. Can you see my picture?"—and also the pain of trying to distinguish, for a moment, what is inside from what is outside himself. From his tree he sees Man who is not afraid of water, as he is, who gets drunk on honey, who has invented love play; he sees with a kind of grieving as an animal might grieve. In *Pincher Martin*, the tale of a modern sailor whose broken body is washed about the Atlantic rock, who eats limpets, is poisoned by his store of food and who eventually goes mad and dies, the pain is in the fight against physical hurt and loss of consciousness, in the struggle to put his educated will against his terrors. It is also in the Job-like protest against a defeat which wrongs everything he has believed in. In *Lord of the Flies*—the first and, I think, the best of these books—a group of schoolboys reenact the *Coral Island* story and the pain is in the struggle between the boys who revert, through fear, to the primitive and turn into savage hunters, and those who are trying vainly to preserve foresight and order. In the end, the boys are rescued, but not before they have lived through the modern political nightmare.

Mr. Golding's sensibility to pain is the spring of his imagination and if, in all three stories, the heroes are smashed up, he is by no means a morbid or sadistic writer. The chest of the creature, running in terror from its enemies, scorches, the calves cramp, the skin tears, the body has to endure what animal panic lets it in for. Pain is simply the whole condition of man; it is the sign that he is awake and struggling with his nature, and especially with the terror which so suddenly scatters the mind. *Lord of the Flies* contains one episode of great horror. The rotting body of a dead parachutist is blown across the island in the night, almost stepping on the trees and the beaches, until it is taken out to sea. The sight is the final and clinching argument to the very young boys that a devouring Beast has really been among them; and one might conclude that this is a decisive symbol of human defeat and the meaninglessness of the struggle. The idea is irrelevant. Mr. Golding's imagination is heroic. Against the flies that buzz round the dangling scarecrow must be put the elation of the adventure, the love of natural life, the curiosity of the eye, that run through the writing. And the compassion.

It is natural to compare *Lord of the Flies* with *Coral Island*—and then with *High Wind in Jamaica.* In *Coral Island* we see the safe community. A century without war and with a settled sense of the human personality has produced it. In Richard Hughes's book, we saw the first sign of disintegration: the psychologists have discovered that children are not small fanciful adults, but are a cut-off, savage race. In *Lord of the Flies* we understand that the children are not cut-off; anthropology, the science of how people live together, not separately, reflects the concern of the modern world which has seen its communities destroyed. The children in *Lord of the Flies* simply reenact the adult, communal drama and by their easy access to the primitive, show how adult communities can break up. Of course, Mr. Golding's improbable romances remain improbable; they are narrow and possible. The modern romancer has the uncluttered chance of going straight to the alienation of the individual and to the personal solitude that is one of the forgotten subjects. In our world, which is so closely organized we are hardly aware of what we are privately up to. We use large words like calamity, disaster, racial suicide, devastation; they are meaningless to us until an artist appears who is gifted enough to identify himself with a precise body being washed up against a precise collection of rocks, a precise being sniffing the night air for his enemy or feeling the full force of a particular blow. Until then, we are muffled in our alibi: "the imagination cannot grasp."

Lord of the Flies is the most accomplished of Mr. Golding's novels. Its portraits of the shipwrecked boys and its understanding of them are touching and delightful and he is master of a rich range of scene and action. In this book his spirit and his serenity are classical. *Pincher Martin* is more chock-a-block, but it has fine descriptions of the roaring, sucking, deafening sea scene on the rock which we know stone by stone. He is a modern writer here in that his eyes are pressed close to the object, so that each thing is enormously magnified. We see how much a man is enclosed by his own eyes. The important quality of all Golding's descriptions is that they are descriptions of movement and continuous change and are marked by brilliant epithets. (One remembers: "three prudish anemones.") There is this picture of the swimming sailor, almost at the rock:

> Ropes held him, slipped and let him go. He saw light, got a mouthful of air and foam. He glimpsed a riven rock face with trees of spray growing up it and the sight of this rock floating in mid-Atlantic was so dreadful that he wasted his air by screaming as if it had been a wild beast. He went under in a green calm, then up and was thrust sideways. The sea no longer played with him. It stayed its wild movement and held him gently, carried him with delicate and careful motion like a retriever with a bird. Hard things touched him about the feet and knees. The sea laid him down gently and retreated. There were hard things touching his face and chest, the side of his forehead. The sea came back and fawned round his face, licked him. He thought movements that did not happen. The sea came back and he thought the movements again and this time they happened because the sea took most of his weight. They moved him forward over the hard things. Each wave and each movement moved him forward. He felt the sea run down to smell at his feet then come back and nuzzle under his arm.

But this book succeeds less when it takes us into the sailor's chaotic recollections of his life. It contains some flashes back to scenes of jealousy and rivalry which are hard to grasp. It may be that Golding's sense of theatre—often strong in writers of romance—has overcome him here. (He is the author of a witty satirical play, *The Brass Butterfly,* which is excellent reading.) But in making us feel in the current of the modern world, instead of being stranded and deadened by it; in providing us with secret parables; in unveiling important parts of the contemporary anguish and making them heroic, knowable and imaginable, he is unique.

AN IRISH OBLOMOV

There is a terrifying sentence in James Stephens's account of his meeting with Joyce in Dublin that unfortunately came to my mind when I was struggling with Samuel Beckett's trilogy, *Molloy, Malone Dies, The Unnamable*—"I looked at him," says Stephens, "without a word in my mouth except vocabulary." Will someone not chart the vivid but interminable ocean of Irish garrulity for us, point out the shallows and the depths, tell us where the words are vocabulary only and where they connote ideas or things, where they are propitiatory magic, where egomania filling in time and place? Where is language used for language's sake, and where is it used as a gabble-gabble ritual to make tolerable the meaninglessness of life? It would be of practical help to know whether a writer was drowning well within his own depth or out of it; and when it would be decent to leave him to it—possibly coming back later, after a smoke, to see how he was getting on.

One does this with *Tristram Shandy.* Pending other guidance, the reader of Beckett's trilogy, *Molloy, Malone Dies* and *The Unnamable,* does the same. They are lawsuits that never end, vexations, litigations joined with the tedium, the grayness, the grief, the fear, the rage, the clownishness, the physical miseries of old age where life is on the ebb, and nature stands by smiling idiotically. Why was I born, get me out of this, let me live on less and less, get me to the grave, the womb, the last door, dragging this ludicrous, feeble, windy broken old bag of pipes with me. Find me a hole. Give me deafness and blindness; chop off the gangrened leg; somewhere on this rubbish dump where I crawl there must be some final dustbin, where I can dribble, laugh, cry and maunder on the this and the that of the general mystery and occasionally give a toothless grin over an obscene word or a farcical sexual memory.

Flight, old age, and the wrangle about personal identity, these are Samuel Beckett's themes. A man is a vestige left to hop around in wearying argy-bargy after his invisible master: punishment, for the old, unremembered sin. Life is the *belle dame* with the mindless smirk and she hardly troubles to look at the victim who has been reduced to the total lethargy of compulsive speech. That is the joke: the mutilated thing can *talk.* In the first volume the man is Molloy, the tramp with crutches, a mixture of simplicity, hurt and lunatic energy. He can still spit with contempt at society:

> One of us at last! Green with anguish. A real little terrestrial! Choking in the chlorophyll. Hugging the slaughterhouse walls! Paltry priests of the irrepressible ephemeral!

He bashes along on his bicycle, through the town, trying to get to his mother. He runs over a dog—

> an ineptness all the more unpardonable as the dog, duly leashed, was not out on the road, but in on the pavement, docile at his mistress's heels. Precautions are like resolutions, to be taken with precaution. The lady must have thought she had left nothing to chance, so far as the safety of her dog was concerned, whereas in reality she was setting the whole system of nature at naught, no less surely than I myself with my insane demands for more light. But instead of groveling in my turn, invoking my great age and infirmities, I made things worse by trying to run away. I was soon overtaken by a bloodthirsty mob of both sexes and all ages, for I caught a glimpse of white beards and little angel faces, and they were preparing to tear me to pieces

—but the lady stopped them, saying she was taking the dog to the vet to be put down, in any case, and he had saved her a painful task.

This volume has all Beckett's headlong comic gift. Molloy is in the clownish state of senility, his disqualified life has the spirit either of a fairy tale or inverted idyll; and in his pestiferous search for "more light" on everything and nothing—mostly the latter—there is a grin half of mockery and half of frenzy on his scabby face. His sexual memories are funny because they are few, take him by surprise, and they are a mixture of the grotesque and touching, the dirty and the modest. He has dragged his body around all his life, and it follows him like some ignorant valet.

There is far more to compare with *Tristram Shandy* in the caprices of this volume and its exploits in self-contradiction in order to hold the floor, than there is with Joyce.

In the second volume, *Malone Dies,* we move from the freedom of rebellion to loneliness. Malone, by the way, may be another aspect of Molloy; he doesn't know who he is. As far as I can make out the scene of the novel is a madhouse or infirmary for the old, and Beckett becomes the grammarian of solitude. The senses are dying. How does Malone know where the veils of air end and the prison walls begin? The body turns in smaller and smaller circles; the mind conjugates trifles. Here Beckett intervenes with some satirical observation of normal people, a trite couple and their favorite son, a piece which might have come out of Sartre's *Nausée,* or Nathalie Sarraute, and we are reminded that Beckett writes his novels first in French.

But we return to endless hair-splitting, metaphysical speculation sliding from association to association, and these convey that as age increases the tedium of life, so the unwearying little talker in the brain with his lawsuit against life bosses every half minute of it. Grief and pity hang between his words; but the book unexpectedly ends in wholesale murder, when the feeble-minded inmates of the infirmary are taken out on a picnic.

In the third volume, Molloy, Malone, Mahood, Murphy—whatever the name now is—is a lump, almost sightless, stone deaf, always weeping, mutilated, immovable, the helpless center of a world that he can be conscious of very rarely. He is about to become Worm, all human identity gone. The archaeological kind of critic who can recover a novel from its ruins may be able to make something of this volume. I find it unreadable, in the sense that I cannot move from paragraph to paragraph, from page to page. It is all significance and no content.

The stream of consciousness, so lively and going dramatically from image to image in Joyce, is here a stream of imageless verbosity occasionally broken by a jab of obscene anger, but gray, gray, and it goes monotonously along in phrases usually about seven words long, like some regularly bumping old tram. This is, of course, not so much the stream of consciousness as the stream of solitude and provides the comedy of overhearing a man talking to himself—Bloom, one recalls, rarely talked; things "came up" in his mind. He was in the midst of drama—a comedy that is genuine enough certainly, but not of boundless interest.

Why is Beckett interesting as a writer? As a contemporary phenomenon, he is one more negative protest against the world going to the slaughterhouse, one more protest on behalf of privacy, a voice for myopia. He is a modern Oblomov, fretful and apathetic, enclosed in private fantasy, dropping off into words instead of sleep. They are eloquent, cunning, unremitting words.

He is far from feeble, for there is a devil-like slyness in the half grin on the faces of his old men who can hit out with their crutches. What tedium! they exclaim—speaking not only of existence and human solitude—but, we suspect, of ourselves. His imagination has the Irish cruelty and self-destructiveness that Yeats once spoke of. Beckett's anti-novels, like all anti-novels, have to deal with small areas of experience because their pretension is to evoke the whole of life, *i.e.*, life unfixed by art; the result is that these verbose books are like long ironical, stinging footnotes in small print to some theme not formulated. But there is a flash of deep insight in the madness he evokes: it is strange that in a generation which has put all its stress on youth and achievement, he alone should have written about old age, loneliness and decrepitude, a subject which arouses perhaps our deepest repressed guilt and fears. He is the product of a civilization which has become suddenly old. He is a considerable, muttering, comic writer, and although he conveys unbearable pain, he also conveys the element of sardonic tenacity and danger that lies at the heart of the comic gift.

CAVALLERIA RUSTICANA

"Growing still, he went off at an ambling pace of his mule, under the burning sun; a sun which split the stones now, and made the stubble crackle as if it was catching fire. At the gully between the two mountains he seemed to enter into a furnace; and the village on top of the height hanging above the precipices, scattered between enormous rocks, mined with caverns which made it seem suspended in the air, blackish, rusted, appeared abandoned, without a shadow, with all the windows open in the heat, like so many black holes, the crosses of the church towers trembling in the sun-dark air."

This is a description of the country north of Catania in the summer. I have taken the paragraph from one of the few descriptive passages in Giovanni Verga's Sicilian novel *Mastro-Don Gesualdo*. Readers who have been in that heat-hammered island will appreciate the exactitude of Verga's eyes and perhaps the jolting of D. H. Lawrence's translation. The critic will observe how the phrases which do not directly describe heat, most intensely convey the sensation of it. "Furnace" is, of course, direct enough, and if you have looked down an industrial furnace, one of those long, ochreous, silent and unsurpassably intent corridors of short flame, the word will not be simply a conventional literary metaphor. Furnace is indeed the only word for a mountain gully under a vertical sun. But the thought of summer in Sicily brings back to my memory those black holes in the stone houses and the darkening, smoked-glass effect of tyrannical light. The sun is an enemy; earth and sun are at war with each other, and the candor of the Mediterranean scene is not disclosed until the evening when the battle has its sudden southern end or in the early morning, before it has begun.

Those are the hours when we can think of Theocritus and the Greeks. But in the middle hours of the day images of violence come into our minds. We think of earthquakes, the *mafia,* the bombs and shots of the factions and all those tales of boiling jealousy, the Judas kiss of the duelist and the long knife lying in the flat of the hand. It was, after all, upon Verga's story, *Cavalleria Rusticana,* that Mascagni built his opera. The story was not romantic, southern hyperbole. We saw Sicilian violence transplanted in Chicago a few years after Verga's death, a violence still naïve, spontaneous and quite outside the range of our usual judgments. It belonged to an earlier culture than ours, and strangely enough to that pastoral world of the delightful Theocritus. The sweet notes of the reed were drawn from the lips of men enjoined to kill in certain psychological situations. But what went on behind the violence? What was life like in the broken streets of the mountain towns and villages? Verga, who had been born near Catania in the seventies, came back from Naples when he was about forty to find out. His journey was one of those returns to the source which are commonly fruitful in the lives of artists. He was tired of writing novels about leisured people who make love to one another's wives and who go on chewing over the really not very astonishing sensations which they have detached from the meat of living. He had nothing new and certainly nothing brilliant to say about the subject. He came to Sicily to get back to something more important, which was going to be stark in the manner of Zola. And, first of all, Verga was very stark. *Cavalleria Rusticana* is an admirable, naked story, ruthlessly economical and as plain a piece of surgery on the passions as you could ask for. It is more than surgery; the more terrible Sicilian knife is at work. *La Lupa,* the story of a man-devouring peasant woman who has to be killed by her son-in-law, is another of the same kind. There is something superb, an excess which amounts to the poetry of pride, about these acts of transcendent psychological justice among people who are blinded by the rage of honor, amid starvation, crippling toil and rags.

Unlike Mérimée who looked at the violent and idyllic remnant of pastoral culture in the Mediterranean with the eyes of a connoisseur, Verga was committed. The Sicilians were his own people. He got back inside them. There was not much inside them, in our sense anyway, for they were southerners without introspection, black and white in their souls, like their light; but as a society they had a great deal. Verga planned to write five novels, each one to deal with a class in Sicilian society. The first dealt with the poor. (An American translation exists.) The second dealt with the people who are just above the masses; and this one, *Mastro-Don Gesualdo,* was translated by D. H. Lawrence, who was just the man to feel an idiom. In this book we find what it is that lies behind the Sicilian violence. The answer, according to Verga, is more violence. Violence of tongue, violence of will, greed, push, scramble, gossip, the awful ruthless, comic, bitter, incorrigible barnyard belligerence of family life; fights for money, fights for food, fights for possession. Misery is the basis of it, the misery of poor land, the misery of the isolated towns where the nail scratches of scandal and contempt are scrawled over everyone's life. The beautiful are the humble and submissive who refuse to join the fight; worse luck for them, they are kicked out and trodden on and their poor-spiritedness is a byword. So we should describe the people in Verga's novel and yet they do not distress us. Only the suburban townsman idealizes the countryman and is shocked by the malignance of country life and its poisoned solitudes. Only the suburban townsman conveniently forgets that the countryman must fight for money and property like the rest of the world. Far from distressing us, Verga's people gradually take possession of our minds, seize us with their grasping hands, harangue us about their case until we are forced to see the point of it, and to see that here, in this ludicrous family screeching about pride, money, marriages, and ownership, something elemental is taking place. His people are able to convince us of this not merely because it is true but because Verga is a very considerable novelist. He has a rich range of mood, a pungency of metaphor; something in him is equal to the clamor of the heart; he has a comprehensive grasp of scene; and without being naturalistic he seems to be able to pull up people by the roots straight out of nature and put them, rife as they are, upon the page. They come out with such vocal, physical emphasis that at first one is stunned and deafened. Verga depends on the crackle of his dialogue and on an allusive atmosphere which each sentence creates. You have to watch that and keep your senses keen or you will miss his transitions. And then these Sicilians think and feel at the tops of their voices. Their bellies are "full of poison," their mouths "spit bile"—a vast amount of bile is spat in this book; Lawrence must have loved the anger of it—and in a few pages you will see people compared to vipers, wolves, hounds, tigers, wasps, pigs, cows, donkeys, scorpions and vampires, a whole menagerie. All this makes the early chapters trying until you acquire a kind of sardonic animal grin yourself; then things go splendidly.

You notice that Verga is not a regional novelist in the provincial sense of the word. *Mastro-Don Gesualdo* is no more regional in this rather derogatory meaning, than Turgenev was in *Lear of the Steppes.* No, Verga is European and modern. His visual power, which is heightened by his constant use of peasant metaphor and his identification with the peasant mind, is very modern. This visual quality is one which literature has developed to fill the place previously taken by traditional, moral and religious generalizations; the traditional Catholic novel, for example, about Sicily had no need of this physical vividness. Verga, no doubt like Cézanne, supposed he was being scientific. Now the visual, oral style becomes monotonous, unless the human heat of the book grows until it becomes convulsive and momentous. And Verga's story does grow. We see Mastro-Don Gesualdo, a common worker on the roads, in his first rise in the world. First his fight against his own family over their petty trade; then his marriage and the fight against his wife's aristocratic relations—they are a scarecrow lot of decayed aristocrats but not too grand to smell the main chance a long way off —then his fight against the town's jealousy of his wealth. And finally his fight against his daughter and her husband who is a duke. In that last fight Don Gesualdo attains the rigor of spiritual agony. The struggle begins when the cholera has driven his patriarchal family to the mountains. It develops when revolutionaries from Palermo incite the peasants to get back the common lands which he has taken. It gets the better of him when he has to fight for command not merely of his property but of his wife and daughter. He defeats his daughter but loses the wife who has never loved him. The whole world rises against him. They see his weakness. He is not a monster but, searching for power, he has forgotten he is capable of sorrow; and meaner people spring upon the shoulders of this man whose will has been exorbitant. There is the Sicilian subject as one sees it in Verga; exorbitance. A man must carry his passions to the extreme, and fate, like a counter-logic, will come down the road to meet and defeat him, not with one clean blow but a long, slow bludgeoning, beating him to his knees and then down into the dust of the greedy generations from which he sprang.

The intensity of Verga is achieved by dense detail. He is totally without rhetoric. Of a suspicious man he writes: "Don Ferdinando, always after them, sewed to their heels, silent. . . ." Of the Duke's servants in Palermo in the wonderful final scene when Gesualdo lies dying among the idle footmen in his daughter's grand house: "An army of lazy rascals, lackeys and chambermen, yawning with their mouths shut, walking on tiptoe and serving you without saying a word. . . ." Those phrases take one back to Browning's *Ring and the Book.* But thinking about this intensity has led me to forget Verga's comic gift. Verga saw the fantastic comedy of the family struggle. He saw the sardonic farce of Sicilian politics, and how much they depended upon local personality. The intruding priest, for example, who gets the men of property on to the revolutionary side so that they can save their property, is a real, slippery beauty. Who has not met that busy little ferret? Then there is the young baron seducing the awful touring actress by sending her food to guzzle from his mean mother's larder; and there is the christening scene where all the relations get in their digs at the right point. They all hate Don Gesualdo, and very likely, they point out, the child is not his. An important point to notice in Verga's dialogue is that people do not always talk to one another. They declaim out of themselves.

> Don Gesualdo kept on chatting with Cousin Zacco, each of them with his heart in his hand, oh so friendly! Then the baroness spat out the question that was boiling inside her:
>
> "Is it true that your husband lends him money —on the quiet?—Have you seen him come here to him? Tell me, what do you know?"
>
> "Certainly, certainly," replied Don Gesualdo at that moment. "You must take children as they come."
>
> To confirm this Zacco pointed to his own girls ranged in a row like so many organ pipes, modest and pleasing.
>
> "Look you. I have five girls, and I'm fond of them all alike."
>
> "Why, of course," replied Limoli. "That's why you don't want to marry any of them off."
>
> Donna Lavinia, the eldest, threw an ugly look behind her. "Ah, are you there?" said the baron. "You are always ready, like the devil, in the litany, you are!"
>
> All at once down in the square below there exploded the deuce of a noise of crackers. . . . It was Santo, Don Gesualdo's brother, celebrating the baptism of his niece in that fashion, in his short sleeves, on all fours down there below, with a lighted fuse. Don Gesualdo opened the window to pour out a sackful of abuse.
>
> "Fool! You'd have to be doing something! Fool!" The friends calmed him.

"Poor chap! Let him alone! It's one way of showing his pleasure."

A novelist is tested by his power of sustaining long scenes and large groups of people and by his power of continual dramatization. It is his duty to break a marriage, a birth, a death, or some enterprise into living fragments. This gift of fragmentation is given only to the greatest novelist; lacking it, the glib, second-rate ones are perhaps more quickly read. They are certainly quickly forgotten. But Verga is one of the great in this novel, a Balzacian. He sees a society and that society working in men and women. Perhaps, like the Sicilian sun, he hammers his words too pitilessly on our heads and batters us with the theme of self-interest; but he has the space of the masters. I would say to any young novelist who wanted to shake himself into a fresh consideration of the art of the novel, to get hold of Verga quickly. When Italians boasted about him in Paris before the war they were not far wrong.

POOR RELATIONS

The small house on the cliff of Passy hanging like a cage between an upper and lower street, so that by a trick of relativity, the top floor of the Rue Berton is the ground floor of the Rue Raynouard, has often been taken as a symbol of the life of Balzac. The custodian of the house—now a Balzac museum with the novelist's eternal coffeepot, his dictionary of universal knowledge and with his appalling proof sheets framed on the wall—shows one the trap door by which Balzac escaped to the lower floor in the Rue Berton. Down it the fat breathless novelist of forty-one went stumbling and blurting, like his own prose, to the Seine. Two houses in one, a life with two front doors, dream and reality; the novelist, naïve and yet shrewd, not troubling to distinguish between one and the other. Symbol of Balzac's life, the house is a symbol of the frontier life, the trap-door life of the great artists, who have always lived between two worlds. There Balzac wrote his letters to Madame Hanska in Poland, the almost too comprehensive, explanatory and eloquent letters of a famous and experienced writer who has the art, indeed the habit, of self-projection at his fingertips; there, when the letters were posted, he went to bed with the docile housekeeper who was finally to turn round and blackmail him, and so provide him with the horrifying last chapters of *Le Cousin Pons.* At this house in the worst year of his life, the least blessed with that calm which is—quite erroneously—supposed to be essential to the novelist, Balzac wrote this book and *La Cousine Bette,* respectively the best constructed and the most fluent and subtle of his novels.

A new life of Balzac was published in Paris in 1944. It is called simply *Vie de Balzac* and is by André Billy. This biography contains nothing new, but it gathers all the immense biographical material in a couple of volumes. Its detail is as lively and exhaustive as a Balzac novel; the manner is warm but skeptical, thorough but not dry. Very rightly, M. Billy looks twice and three times at everything Balzac said about his life, for he is dealing with the hallucinations of the most extraordinary egotist in the history of literature. One can imagine a less diffuse biography; one in which the picture of his time played a greater part and where every detail of a chaotic Bohemian career was not played up to the same pitch. But given the gluttony of Balzac's egotism and the fertility of his comedy, one is not inclined to complain.

Like the tons of bronze and antiques—Balzac estimated the weight and value of himself with the care of an auctioneer's valuer—with which he darkened the house he finally took for Madame Hanska when he had got his hands on some of her fortune, the novels of Balzac weigh upon the memory. The reader is as exhausted as the novelist by the sheer weight of collection. One is tempted to see him as the stolid bulldozer of documentation, the quarrying and expatiating realist, sharpening his tools on some hard view of his own time. He seems to be stuck in his task. Yet this impression is a false one, as we find whenever we open a novel of his again. Balzac is certainly the novelist who most completely exemplifies the "our time" novelist, but not by his judgments on his society. He simply *is* his time. He is identified with it, by all the greedy innocence of genius. The society of rich peasants brought to power by revolution and dictatorship, pushing into business and speculation, buying up houses and antiques, founding families, grabbing at money and pleasure, haunted by their tradition of parsimony and hard work, and with the peasant's black and white ideas about everything, and above all their weakness for fixed ideas, is Balzac himself. He shares their illusions. Like them he was humble when he was poor, arrogant when he was rich. As with them, his extravagance was one side of the coin; on the other was the face of the peasant miser. The cynic lived in a world of romantic optimism. We see the dramatic phase of a century's illusions, before they have been assimilated and trodden down into the familiar hypocrisies. To us Balzac's preoccupation with money appears first to be the searching, scientific and prosaic interest of the documentary artist. On the contrary, for him money was romantic; it was hope and ideal. It was despair and evil. It was not the dreary background, but the animating and theatrical spirit.

Balzac learned about money, as M. Billy says, at his printing works in the Rue du Marais. He expected to find that fallen aristocrat, the goddess Fortune of the eighteenth century; instead he found that in the nineteenth century the goddess had become a bourgeois bookkeeper. His laundry bills, his tailor's bill, his jeweler's bills were mixed with the printing accounts. The imagination of the businessman is always governable; Balzac's was not. Financially speaking, Balzac was out of date. Like his father, who also was willing to work hard enough, he sought for Fortune, not for Profit; far from being an example of Balzac's realism, his attitude to money is really the earliest example of his Romantic spirit. Balzac's attitude to money was that of a man who did not understand money, who could not keep it in his hands, the plagued spendthrift and natural bankrupt. His promissory notes were a kind of poetry in his early years; later on they became articles of moral indignation; in the end—to quote M. Billy's delightful euphemism, he lost all "pudeur morale." The creation of debts began as exuberance; it became an appetite, one of those dominant passions which he thought occurred in all natures, but which really occur only among the most monstrous egotists. Madame Hanska's fortune did not calm him. He went on buying here and there, incurring more debts, scheming without check. And the last people he thought of paying were his wretched relations and especially his mother. To her, he behaved with the hypocrisy and meanness of a miser and the worse he treated her the more he attacked her.

At this point it is interesting to compare Balzac with Scott whom he admired and consciously imitated. Madame Hanska's estate in Poland was for many years his visionary Abbotsford; the passion for antiques, the debts, and the crushing labor, the days and nights of writing without sleep, were Abbotsford too. Balzac saw himself as an aristocrat; Scott saw himself as a laird: they are by no means the first or last writers to provide themselves with distinguished ancestors. He went to the length of traveling to Vienna as a Marquis, with coronets on his luggage; it was ruinous, he discovered, in tips. But the honorable Scott was broken by debts; they drove him to work as a duty; they wore out his imagination. Balzac, on the contrary, was certainly not ruined as a writer by his debts. His debts were a natural expression of a voracious imagination. One may doubt whether any of his mistresses moved his inspiration—though clearly their maternal sympathy was necessary—but one can be certain that Balzac's imagination was ignited by the romance of purchase, by the mere sensual possession of things. The moving impulse in his life was, as he said, the discovery of the "material of civilization," the literal materials; and although he considered this a scientific discovery, it was really a mysticism of things. Every object he bought, from the famous walking stick to the museum pieces, represented an act of self-intoxication that released the capacity—so vital to the creative artist—to become unreal.

It is easy, as M. Billy says, a hundred years after, to blame Madame Hanska for delaying her marriage with Balzac and for adding the afflictions of reluctance and jealousy to his life of appalling labor, but obviously he was possessed by a kind of madness, and he would have stripped her of all her property. One understands her hesitation after reading his later and maniacal letters about money and things.

"Je suis sûr qu'au poids il y aura, dans notre maison, trois mille kilogrammes de cuivres et bronzes dorés. C'est effrayant, le bronze! Cette maison est, comme je te le disais, une mine de cuivre doré, car mon ébéniste me disait qu'il y en a mille kilogrammes. Á huit frances le kilo, à vendre aux chaudronniers, c'est trente-deux mille francs de valeur réelle. Juge de la valeur, en y ajoutant le valeur d'art."

Ruinous. There was no "valeur d'art." His brain gave way under the strain of his schemes and combinations. Yet, *Le Cousin Pons* and *La Cousine Bette* were written in that year; and when Pons makes the fortune of his persecutors with his collection of antiques which they had despised, one sees Balzac avenging himself for the complaints of his mistress. No; he was not weighed down by debts, in the sense of having his talent ruined by them. His extravagances floated him on the vital stream of unreality. He was the Micawber for whom things were only too continuously "turning up," a Micawber who worked. Balzac and Micawber are, it is interesting to note, contemporary financiers of the period.

The ox-like groans, the animal straining and lamentation of Balzac, his boasting, his bosom-beating letters to women like Madame Carraud before whom he parades in the role of the indomitable martyr of circumstance, have created an imaginary Balzac. One sees—his own phrase—"the galley slave of fame." A rather different impression was formed by his contemporaries. Once he had put his pen down he was childishly gay:

Naïveté, puérilité, bonté, ces trois mots reviennent sous la plume de tous les contemporains. Le portrait de Balzac que nous a laissé le poète des *Meditations* se trouve confirmé en tous points par celui qu'a tracé George Sand: puéril et puis-

> sant, toujours envieux d'un bibelot et jamais jaloux d'une gloire, sincère jusqu'à la modestie, vantard jusqu'à la hâblerie, confiant en lui-même et dans des autres, très expansif, très bon et très fou, avec un sanctuaire de raison intérieure où il rentrait pour tout dominer dans son oeuvre, cynique dans la chasteté, ivre en buvant de l'eau, intempérant de travail et sobre d'autres passions, positif et romanesque avec un égal excès, crédule et sceptique, plein de contrastes et de mystères. . . .

Some indeed found him grubby, ill-kempt and uncouth. Hans Andersen hardly recognized the dandy of the evening party in the tousled Bohemian of the following day. There was a Rue Raynouard and a Rue Berton in his appearance and in his nature.

Instant in his admirations and schemes, Balzac was like a child for whom everything happens *now* and in a *now* that is connected with no future. Certainly with no future of incurred obligations. The burden of Balzac's life is not apparent until one sees him at work; and then we see that not debt but his method of writing was the fatal aggravation.

In a sense Balzac is a made, or rather re-made writer. There were times when he rushed down to the printers at eleven o'clock at night and they took the chapter of his novel page by page as he wrote it. But such moments of inspired exhibitionism were rare. In general Balzac strikes one as being the gifted talker whose mind congests when he sits down to write what he has just spoken. No doubt he could have turned out the cheap thrillers of his early period as easily as he spoke; but with his other books the process was agonizing. There would be several versions of the text, each one smothered with erasures and additions; chapters were put into different places, more chapters were sandwiched in between. Pages and pages scrapped, more pages added. The historian of the contemporary scene had only to go out of his door to see a new thing to squeeze somewhere into the text. And this was not the end of the confusion and the struggle. Once the printers had sorted out the manuscript and had produced their galleys, the ungovernable author began a hardly less drastic process of destruction and reconstruction. Night after night, from midnight until seven—and these were merely regular hours. There were days and nights of almost continuous labor without sleep. "Il ne savait pas sa langue," said Gautier. The time spent and the printers' costs would have eaten seriously into earnings not already mortgaged by extravagance.

Let us return to the double house in the Rue Raynouard and look once more at the two great novels Balzac wrote in that small room above the trap door, when his brain was already breaking under the appetites he imposed upon it. Open *Le Cousin Pons.* There is the expected chapter, that roughly and in a domineering way generalizes and clears a space for the characters in the Parisian scene. And then, like a blow in the face, comes the brutal sentence: "On n'a jamais peint les exigences de la gueule." One stops dead. What on earth has poor Pons done that his fastidious habit of dining at the expense of his better-off relations should become a treatise on the trough? Comically treated, of course; Balzac examined the dossier of human nature with the quizzical detachment of some nail-biting, cigar-stained Chief of Police who is going rapidly up in the world; who has seen so many cases; who thanks heaven that he does not make the moral law and that a worldly Church stands between himself and the Almighty. Passion, even when it is a passion for the best food, always becomes—in the experience of the Chief of Police—a transaction; Pons trades the little errands he runs on behalf of the family for the indispensable surprises of the gourmet. In the pursuit of that appetite he is prepared to ruin himself where other men, more voluptuously equipped by nature, will wreck themselves in the capture and establishment of courtesans. Sex or food, money or penury, envy or ambition—Balzac knows all the roads to ruin. If only men and women were content with their habits instead of craving the sublimity of their appetites.

But *Pons* is a type. He is a poor relation. In that isolation of a type, one detects the main difference between the French and English novels. The English novel has never lived down its early association with the theatre, and has always had to wrestle with a picaresque or artificial plot. But even if this had not been so, we could never have been a nation of moralists. Our instinct is to act; our interest in morals is a practical interest in results. The French novel—and how obvious this is in Balzac—is dominated on the contrary by a sense of law. Behind the individual lies the type, behind the act lies a law governing the act. The French novelists are the lawyers of the passions; they proceed from the prototype to the particular and then carry it back for comparison. Subtle and litigious in tactic, they conclude that human experience, however bizarre, however affecting, can never escape the deep inscription of its category or evade the ordinance of some general idea.

To an English taste there must always be something arbitrary in such a structure. Natural Protestants, we resist a determinism so Roman and so Catholic. But we must be abashed by the double reference in which French fiction is so rich. Look at the delightful Pons. His character has so many departments. He is an old man, an ugly man, an outmoded but respected musician, a dandy survived from an earlier period, a collector of antiques, a poor man, a careful man, a simple man who is not quite so simple—see his valuable collection of pictures and bric-à-brac cunningly picked up for next to nothing—a sexless man, a gourmet, a hanger-on, shrewd in his own world, lost in the society into which he has grown up. Pons is the kind of character who, inevitably, becomes fantastic in the English novel simply because no general laws pin him down. He would become a static "character." Instead Balzac takes all these aspects of Pons and mounts each one, so that Pons is constructed before our eyes. We have a double interest: the story or plot, which is excellent in suspense, drama and form—this is one of Balzac's well-constructed novels, as it is also one of the most moving—and the exact completion, brick by brick, of Pons and his circle. There are the historical Pons—he is an *incroyable* left-over from the Directoire—the artistic Pons, the financial Pons, the sociable Pons, the moral Pons, and in the end Pons dying, plundered, defiant, a man awakened from his simplicity and fighting back, the exquisitely humble artist turned proud, sovereign and dangerous in his debacle. Pons is a faceted stone, and part of the drama is the relation of each facet with the others. Thus his fantastic dress is related, via dandyism, to his small, esteemed, but out-of-date position in the world of art. That adjoins his love of good living—picked up in smarter days—which links up with the solitariness and social spryness of the bachelor, his timidity and his sexual innocence. We have the portrait of a man who in every trait suggests some aspect of the society in which he lives. The history of his time is explicit in him. Yet he is not a period piece. A period piece is incapable of moral development and the development of a moral theme is everything in the novels of Balzac, who facilitates it by giving every character not merely a time and place, but also an obsession. Among English novelists only Henry James, George Eliot and, on occasions, Meredith, advance their drama not from incident to incident, but from one moral situation or statement to the next. (In Meredith's *The Egoist* one recalls the tension, tightening page by page, that precedes the accusation: "You are an egoist.") So it is with the story of Pons. He is snubbed by his ignorant relations who do not realize even the financial value of his collection of antiques and pictures. In consequence, rather than be dropped or ridiculed, he gives up his beautiful dinners and retires to taste the blessings of the concierge's motherly cooking and pure friendship with the delightful Schmucke, a man even more simple than himself. At that point an English novelist might have given up. The lesson was clear. But Balzac, like Henry James, saw that drama lies in the fact that there is no end to moral issues. For him—recomplication, further research. And so, just as Pons is getting a little tired of his landlady's cooking, society tempts him again. His relations apologize, and Pons is one of those good men who cannot bear other people to say they are in the wrong. He conceives a grandiose scheme for returning good for evil. He will find a husband for the unmarriageable daughter. He will announce the enormous value of his collection and leave it to her in his will. Result, gratitude? Not a bit of it. The family is longing to wipe out the memory of their humiliating apology by vengeance, and when the marriage scheme collapses, they finish with Pons. Once more we have come to a natural end of the novel. But once more Balzac recomplicates. Pons falls into the grip of his concierge, who has suddenly become covetous now that she has two harmless, childless, womanless old men in her power; and his downfall is insured by the very innocence of Schmucke, who cannot believe evil of anyone.

Balzac is the novelist of our appetites, obsessions and our *idées fixes,* but his great gift is his sense of the complexity of the human situation. He had both perceptions, one supposes, from his peasant origins, for among peasants, as he was fond of saying, the *idée fixe* is easily started; and their sense of circumstance overpowers all other consideration in their lives. A character in Balzac is thus variously situated in history, in money, in family, class and in his type to begin with; but on top of this, Balzac's genius was richly inventive in the field least exploited by the mass of novelists: the field of probability. It is very hard to invent probabilities. This simply means that Balzac knew his people as few novelists ever know their characters. The marriage scene in *Le Cousin Pons* for example: there we have the rich German all set to marry the daughter of the family. The awful facts of the "régime dotal"—a phrase repeated in pious chorus by the family with the unction usually reserved for statements like "God is Love"—have been accepted by him. He has merely to say the word. At this tense moment the German electrifies everyone by asking the unexpected question: Is the girl an only child? Yes, she is. Then he must withdraw. A man of forty is an idiot who marries a girl who has been spoiled in her childhood. She will use the fact that he is so much older than herself to prove she is always right. That way lies hell. The respectability of the institution of marriage is in itself no satisfaction.

But *Le Cousin Pons* moves from one surprising probability to the next, backed by the massed ranks of human circumstance. The change in the character of the charming, motherly landlady of Pons who suddenly takes on the general professional character of the concierges of her district creates another powerful situation—powerful because so isolated are we, so obsessed with possibility and hope, that the probable is unperceived by us. The last thing we care to believe is that we are governed by type and environment. Balzac believed nothing else.

I do not know that I would put anything in *Le Cousin Pons* above the first part of *La Cousine Bette,* though I like Pons better as a whole. Pons is the old bachelor. Bette is the old maid. The growth of her malevolence is less subtly presented than the course of Pons's disillusion, because Balzac had the genius to show Pons living with a man even simpler than himself. One sees two degrees of simplicity, one lighting the other, whereas Bette stands alone; indeed it may be complained that she is gradually swamped by the other characters. She is best in her obscurity, the despised poor relation, the sullen peasant, masculine, counting her humiliations and her economies like a miser, startling people with her bizarre reflections. They laugh at her and do not conceive the monstrous fantasies of her painful virginity. And we are moved by her in these early pages when she is hiding her Polish artist, shutting him in his room like a son, driving him to work; or, later, when Madame Marneffe gives Bette the shabby furniture. Bette is a wronged soul; and when her passion does break, it is, as Balzac says, sublime and terrifying. Her advance to sheer wickedness and vengeance is less convincing, or, rather, less engrossing. It is a good point that she is the eager handmaid and not the igniting cause of ruin; but one draws back, incredulously, before some of her plots and lies. Acceptable when they are naïve, they are unacceptable when they fit too efficiently the melodramatic intrigue of the second part of the book. But the genius for character and situation is here again. La Marneffe, rooted in love's new middle-class hypocrisy and turning into a sanctimonious courtesan, is nicely contrasted with the besotted baron who had grown up in an earlier period—"between the wars" in fact—when the fashion of love was brisker and more candid. That situation alone is a comic one. The diplomatic farce of La Marneffe's supposed pregnancy is brilliant.

The lies and short repentances of the sexagenarian baron are perfect. Only Adeline does not, to my mind, come off in this novel; and here we come upon Balzac's rather dubious advocacy of marital fidelity. He sounds as little convinced as a public speaker haranguing his way to conviction. Adeline's pathetic attempt to sell herself, in order to save her husband's fortunes, is embarrassing to read; are we to admire virtue because it is stupid? Balzac protests too much.

No one has surpassed Balzac in revealing the great part played by money in middle-class life; nor has anyone excelled him in the portraits of the parvenu. Henry James alone, coming at the zenith of middle-class power, perceived the moral corruption caused by money; but money had ripened. It glowed like a peach that is just about to fall. Balzac arrived when the new money, the new finance of the post-Napoleonic world was starting on its violent course; when money was an obsession and was putting down a foundation for middle-class morals. In these two novels about the poor relation, he made his most palatable, his least acrid and most human statements about this grotesque period of middle-class history.

THE BOHEMIAN

The English visitor to the Continent is always surprised by the part played by students in society and in politics. They have even become the subjects of music and literature by a sort of natural right which has not existed in England except possibly at the time of Chaucer. The drinking songs and the tales of Heidelberg, a book like Murger's *Scènes de la Vie de Bohème,* have no parallel in England; and the explanation seems to be that the English universities preserved the monasticism of the Middle Ages but cut themselves off from the medieval spirit. A student tradition, one that goes back to Abélard and Villon, is not nurtured in seclusion; it depends upon poverty and mingling with the ferment of the town. This has not been in the character of any of our older universities; for us the student does not exist. We have never idolized youth. Our idol, until *Lucky Jim* appeared has been the Schoolboy when a Frenchman asks us for the parallel to Murger's book, we are forced to hush up the fact that *Charley's Aunt* is the only play about an undergraduate, and to divert his attention to the enormous importance of *Tom Brown's Schooldays.* Among the Anglo-Saxons it was the unsecluded Americans, rather than ourselves, who took to the Quartier Latin as ducks to Pernod.

Like most English readers, when I was young I owed my first notions of the Quartier Latin to the sentimental and watered-down works of Thackeray, Du Maurier and W. J. Locke. These fanciful last two imitators of Murger were said to be harmless; while the sentiment, the tears and the picaresque farce of Murger were condemned as misleading. A Bohemia like his had never existed. Or, if it had, it certainly existed no more. Only lately I have read his *Scènes de la Vie de Bohème,* and I regret, as usual, that I did not go to the fountainhead before. Some of it is tedious, but the sketches have very amusing moments. Murger had that acute Parisian sense of comic pose, a kind of wit of situation as well as a wit of words and ideas, that crisply feathers the surface of life as he skims along. But the interesting thing about *La Vie de Bohème* is less the story than its success. Not entirely does Murger owe that to the accident of Puccini's opera. Murger had already made a very successful play of the book before Puccini took it up. A suggestive light is thrown by a remark of the Goncourts which they put down in their *Journal* in 1856:

> When Murger wrote La Vie de Bohème, he had no notion that he was writing the history of a social world which was to become a power within five or six years, yet that is the fact today.

The Bohemians, they say, bar the way to the well-born who are damned as amateurs. "The advent of Bohemia means the domination of socialism in literature." They should have written "the domination of that new uprooted class 'the intelligentsia.' "

If socialism does owe something to Bohemia, what Bohemia really did to artists and writers in the long run was, of course, to isolate them from society. Not socialism, but art for art's sake came out of the Bohemian myth and produced in figures like Gauguin, Verlaine and Modigliani an isolation more haggard and stark than anything the frittering Murger and his little circle ever knew. Murger went to seed among the obliging tears of a small Parisian clique. The Goncourts maliciously note his first tailcoat, and his official break with the hungry past when he set up at the Café Riche. He became a journalistic slave, and in the words of his own Rudolphe honestly said, as we all have:

> "Je veux bien consenter à regarder le passé, mais ce sera au travers d'une bouteille de vrai vin, et assis dans un bon fauteuil. Qu'est-ce-que tu veux?—je suis un corrompu. Je n'aime plus que ce qui est bon."

He had, the Goncourts remarked, one of the largest funeral processions of his time, and among the mourners of the poet of hunger was Théophile Gautier, who talked, not very suitably, of the influence of cattle cake on the flavor of steak, all the way to the cemetery.

Where the Goncourts' sharp nose for tendency was right was in detecting the enormous potential of publicity in the early idea of Bohemia. Murger, who was half-German, had given a halo to romantic disorder and, by the end of the century, Puccini and English bestsellers like Du Maurier and W. J. Locke, had carried the idea triumphantly into every vicarage and suburban villa. If you sat on the floor or boiled an egg unassisted you became a Bohemian. The romance of the fifties had become the myth of the century. The English Bohemians of Du Maurier and Locke are no longer poor students. They are the sons of rich parents. The famous Trilby is a model, but she comes from a distinguished Irish family! Du Maurier's Laird—the only agreeable character in a dreadfully coy book—has his Broadwood and his furniture sent over from England to the Quartier Latin; and Locke's heroes always belong to the best county families and are tired of their clubs. The strange thing is that we are shown the lives of poor artists no more, but the lives of people whose ambition is to throw up everything and become poor in order to be artists or to live near them. Middle-class society is kicking over the traces. It is in conflict with itself. Yet the conflict is, so far, not very profound. The illusion of the new Bohemia was that it could preserve the middle-class amenities while throwing over the irksome conventions that protected them. And by the twenties we had arrived at a paradoxical situation which would have soured the faces of Murger's circle at the Café Riche: the bourgeois had been converted to art. All the world was bent upon becoming artistic. The Quartier Latin and Montparnasse had become the quarters of the rich. I remember my own early bewilderment in Paris. Brought up to believe that my intellectual emancipation depended on my finding a cheap room to live in on the Left bank of the Seine, and that damnation awaited those who dwelt on the Right, I gloomily remember I could not afford to be a Bohemian. Life was cheaper in Passy; one went to Montparnasse or the Rue de Seine to borrow money and to wonder what spirit of perversity and masochism had possessed the sons of rentiers that they must put on fancy dress and live among the worst drains of Europe. The Goncourts were right—Bohemia had become a racket, a greater racket than they could have guessed.

No doubt I exaggerate. My nose, insufficiently Bohemian, has led me out of the malodorous pensions of the Mont St. Geneviève and so closed a world to me except as a spectator. I recognize my own facial expressions in Murger's picture of the bourgeois who used to go night after night to the café to watch with a craving he dreaded to reveal. There is, and will always be, the temporary Bohemianism like that of Murger's Rudolphe; and always, no doubt, what Murger called the Bohemianism of the *impasse*. That gaunt man with the Christ-like face and the invalid's straggling beard, who sat all day over his cup of coffee and who looked as if he were starving, was a one-time silk salesman despite his "artistic" appearance. But he was in fact starving, God knows why, and they picked him up half dead in the street. The Bohemians of the *impasse* were, as Murger said, chronically unproductive and garrulous. If I wish to visualize a Bohemian of this kind I always think of a middle-aged man who, as an alleged fashion journalist, spent his days with the mannequins of the Rue de la Paix and played the harmonium on Sundays at a Methodist chapel. Murger knew his subject. It was his only subject. He knew and illustrated in his own life and work the drift into finicking which the life of the clique encourages. The frenzied hunt for the *pièce de cent sous,* the strangling estimate of whether the next meal lies north, south, east or west as you leave the door, are not the only enemies of the Bohemian; nor the hospital its final dread. The dreaded enemy is self-discovery. The inner terror which Murger described in another of his books is the fear not that the talent for which one suffers is insufficient, but that it simply is not there at all.

Socialists—the most respectable of men—have come to attack Bohemia for its disorder and its philosophy of isolation; but I wonder whether those who do so really attack it from a rival Bohemia of their own, the equally ancient Bohemia of the exile and refugee. Political Bohemia from the time of Herzen and through the life of Marx, offers a story no less wretched and picaresque than the lives of students and artists. If the Bohemia of the artist had been taken over wholesale by middle-class society in 1931, and had gone, its place was taken by this revived Bohemia of the refugee. Colorless and despondent, watchful and suspicious, whispering in groups over the backs of chairs at the Coupole or the Dôme, the exiles sat waiting for news from home, where the gaudy and gregarious figures of the earlier decade hoped they'd heard the last of it. And perhaps that is a portent. Mr. E. M. Forster has lately recommended a return to Bohemia for writers; but tomorrow independent political thought, not art, may be one of the seven deadly and unremunerative sins. Du Maurier's Little Billee turned "deathly pale" when he saw Trilby, a lady of one of the best Irish families, posing for "the altogether"; his grandson may crumple up if he catches her indecently exposing the charms of a minority mind to oblige a few friends.

I have said very little about Murger's sketches themselves. They have a boulevard wit and when, later on in life, Murger decided to give up the fastidiousness of art and to go after money in the theatre he made the right decision. He was not a natural highbrow. His melancholy temperament was that of the clown, not of the poet; he was a born writer of farce, and his young men have that too eternal youth of the theatre. His student wit is exact. And his sense of *blague* never fails him. The youth who paints a luxurious room on screens in lieu of furniture, the expert borrower who has noted down where he can get a free meal for every day of the month and, going out for it, discovers his host has left and is on his way to see the borrower on the same mission—these are the brainwaves of the theatre. The light sentiment, the conventional Parisian irony, punctuated by an occasional real phrase taken from life, are agreeable enough in short snatches. And the Mimi of the book, whose life with Rudolphe is frankly, if rather cozily, described as a hell of jealousy and injudicious expense—hats and boots were Mimi's weakness—is a good deal livelier than the Mimi of the play or the opera. The ornately facetious style is not the journalese of the comic writers, though I don't know that makes it any better. Really, there is no serious reproach which can be fairly made against Murger. He is simply a little writer, a brilliant dabbler in unreality, high spirits and sadness, whose very melancholy, as it ripples along, reveals a fundamental lack of seriousness. His letters with their outcry against hunger and their hard tale of work, describe with bitter dignity a Vie de Bohème which he glossed over with a phrase or two in the sketches. His own horrible death—his flesh was decaying; shortly before he died his lip fell off when he was shaving—and the death of the real Mimi, were the end of a story very different from his light elegy of lost youth.

THE ENGLISH FRENCHMAN

"He counted on a certain repugnance in those who most admired him, as men of his disposition count on the help of a certain instinctive dislike in those of whom they are most anxious to make themselves masters."

So wrote Arthur Symons in an acute preface to a collection of Prosper Mérimée's stories. Repugnance certainly disturbs our admiration of them; indeed, between Mérimée and the reader one might say that repugnances are exchanged like the names of seconds in a duel. We open *Colomba* or *Mateo Falcone* with the feeling that it is sunrise, that presently our infinitely accomplished adversary will come coolly through the woods and in a couple of minutes put a bullet through our lungs. We shall have died for God knows what, though Mérimée himself will suggest that our fate was no more than the icy flash of a diamond on the dark finger of death. For Mérimée a life is a campaign.

For us who have two wars in our blood such a writer has a peculiar interest. He can count on our repugnance and our attraction still. As a writer of *nouvelles* he is, without question, a master; and in the construction of stories of action or, perhaps one should say, in stories of the consciously active man, he is inhumanly exact. "I have spent my nights lately writing for posterity," he wrote in the *Lettres à une Inconnue.* It is true. As bodies are preserved endlessly in ice, or the fly forever printed flawlessly in amber, so his stories appear new to the minds of every generation, and we cannot imagine a time when *Carmen* is forgotten or *Colomba* unreadable. It is an effort to approach and read many of the overwhelming figures of literature. But Mérimée remains crystalline, exact, apparent; he can be approached at once. The interesting thing is his refusal to be great; I mean his refusal to be a great man in the histrionic manner of the nineteenth century. Where his contemporaries in France and England seem to have gone to the wigmakers to dress for the character part of prophet, thinker and visionary, and to prepare the long oration of their careers, Mérimée steps back. Where they are positive and aggressive, he is negative and critical. They, in the manner of the century, are going to be great men. Their role and their audience will be everything to them. But when we look at Mérimée it appears to us that the sight of so many vibrant egotisms, warming up their engines and preparing to take off with a roar, must have produced in him a perverse decision, a decision without modesty, to stay isolated on the ground. And we know that it was his aim—a singular one for a writer—not to be a great man, but to obtain regard as a scholar and a gentleman; an English gentleman, of all things, as romantic Frenchmen conceive that character to be. In this, Mérimée was just as much an actor, just as much an heir of the Romantics and just as much a prophet as the rest of his contemporaries. He was simply the reverse of the medal. Like Stendhal, he discloses that the other side of Romanticism is the quest for personal power and for a primitive justification of it. He is not an aristocrat who inherits power in some sense as a trust; he is the intellectual, the clerk or servant of aristocrats, who becomes the libertine of the will to power, pursuing it, inciting it, probing it, and in the story of *Colomba,* exalting it. The themes of *Carmen,* of *Tamango,* of his superb historical novel, the *Chronicle of Charles IX,* of *Mateo Falcone,* and even of that ironical little comedy of manners, *L'Abbé Aubain,* are all alike in this respect: they describe ruthless private wars; his people are goaded by pride or vanity to seek dominion. And when one side or the other has won, or when both have destroyed each other—what is left? Mérimée is too honest an artist and too clear-minded to suggest that anything can be left for people like this but the emptiness of conquest. War in the heart and mind destroys as infallibly as war on a continent. It is an absolute evil. A shocking laugh there may be, like Colomba's derision when she sits back well-fed by revenge; but in general Mérimée leaves us abruptly and we see an empty stage where pity cannot tread. For pity has not been born.

In this attitude of mind Mérimée was prophetic. He foreshadowed one kind of writer who would succeed the prophets. His critical intelligence, the hard rapier-like sound of an intellect without heart, evokes an echo in ourselves. He is the scholar, the artist, the poet of insensibility. He is—one hardly likes to breathe the suggestion—tough. We have often thought that the visions, the sentiment, the complacencies of the nineteenth century deluded us; we turn for respite to Mérimée who encases his heart, prepares to repel by a skilled display of strategy and marksmanship, and declares that the aim of man must be a self-control so established, a mistrust so masked, that he can never be duped. That decision of his, "not to be duped," is famous. The word recalls a word fashionable in our forties: disabused.

And yet how refreshing Mérimée is! What brilliant uses may be made of an arrested development! The shock does not come, after all, until the ends of his stories: when Tamango's broken glory fades into a Governor's anecdote, or when Carmen's death is merely a gloss on the customs of the gypsies. And that final shock is wiped out by the memory of the first shock we get when we begin a new story; the shock of pleasure and exhilaration in something new and strange. Mérimée is never boring. He writes like a gifted raconteur who is nonchalant, entirely at ease, but always alert in the presence of his circle. A bore has been defined as a man who tells us everything, and Mérimée never falls into the trap. He rewrote *Colomba* sixteen times to be sure of avoiding it. His economy of narrative is native to his guarded and scholarly mind. One may resent a curtness which was the fruit of mistrust, and one may add that the man who is not duped does not live to the full—"life is time's fool"—but if Mérimée is curt, he also has the rare gift of order, which I take to be the first essential of good narrative. Mérimée's gift of order enables him to place his scenes, as Turgenev and Pushkin placed theirs, briefly but infallibly before our eyes; to know, in *Colomba*, for example, how much of Corsica to describe, how far to dilate on local custom, how far to build up his anecdotes about the vendetta until the main vendetta of the story looms over us like an iron cloud, impassable and momentous on a mountain road. A great part of the pleasure of reading his stories comes from our awareness of their construction. At each phase we are conscious of being set free from the irrelevancies by which other writers mystify the reader, and of being directed by a mind that knows how to eliminate. One of the many difficulties the novelist has is to discern his situation clearly and many greater writers than Mérimée fail to do this; whatever Mérimée may lose by his gift of isolating certain elements of character, he gains by the clarification of issues. So that we are able in *Colomba* simultaneously to hold in the mind many contrary things. We watch Colomba's will to revenge working on her brother's mind, but we do not lose sight of the civilization he has, or the difficult nervous English girl he has left in Ajaccio. Even at the crisis of the book, when Colomba's conspiracy breaks and murder, somehow and somewhere, is inevitable, we never lose sight of the sunlight and the fog on the maquis and of the chattering Colonel and his daughter ambling cheerfully toward the awful hour when—as the bandit says—there will be fresh meat for sale in the town. Mérimée, of course, gets his effect by a lucid prose style which deliberately lowers the emotional temperature in order to heighten the intellectual excitement. He excels in his skill at rendering the depths by keeping to the surface, by attending to the beguiling and untrustworthy smile of life. His own emotions abstain from the narrative and, as I said before, we are free—that sense of freedom is the great gift of the Romantic tradition. With him we are free, also, of the Romantic burden. And even at the end, when the shock comes, as it always does in Mérimée, when we see him going too far and Colomba jeering at the broken father whose sons have been murdred, we are left reluctantly admiring the wicked perfection of the scene, the injurious irony. In the same way the end of *Tamango* is perfect.

In their dissociation of power and energy and pride from the rest of life, Stendhal and Mérimée are prophetic of an aspect of fascism. And Mérimée added a predilection for primitive types. He is saved from the complete accusation by his scholarship and by his detachment. Mérimée does not desire to return to the primitive or to a world without mercy. He declined to have an organic conception of history. He was an anthropologist, not a mystic. Even his Byronism was moderated to the temper of what became a gentleman with the spleen. He has a little in common with Pushkin, whom he translated, a harder, frozen Pushkin always on guard. His mind was skeptical. There is a clear statement of his skepticism in his historical novel, *The Chronicle of Charles IX*, where he extracts the utmost irony out of the religious wars and the massacres of St. Bartholomew and detaches himself from the tale halfway through in order to explain his method of writing history to the reader. "This is not the last time brothers will kill each other in France," says the dying convert to his Huguenot brother; and Mérimée excels in describing the ambiguities of conscience in an age when professions of faith do violence to the soul. This novel set out to undermine the laden and stolid histories of Sir Walter Scott, and it reads as if it were written, not in the first half of the nineteenth century, but in the last twenty years. There is a succession of incomparable scenes, and there is no dead wood. Again, our pleasure is a double one; we are watching the building of the characters and the story while we are borne along by it. And again we are struck by another aspect of Mérimée which brings him close to us: what he passes off as his belief in anecdote is really his perfunctory name for documentation. Unfeeling he may be, but he can reconstruct an environment, a period, the corner of a battlefield, a gaming table, a Corsican hut or a house of rendezvous in Seville, with a fidelity to their normal condition which many a more profuse writer, and more humane, has failed to achieve. He has the patience, the grace, the exactitude if he has also the perfunctoriness of the amateur. A writer might learn his art from him and dread the perfection he had learned.

HUGO'S IMPERSONATIONS

"Hugo began life as a mature man and is only now entering on adolescence." The words of Vigny's referred to Hugo's life when he was twenty-seven, not to his work, but they come back when we read *Notre Dame de Paris* and *Les Misérables*. There are the dreams we dream no longer, powerful frescoes without intimacy. They belong to the volcanic periods of life—so apt to return—when the unconscious erupts, when the superego pronounces, when the monstrous and the ideal hog or transfigure our natures, when the self is still molten and has not been hardened into unproductive habit. In Hugo, it never became hardened. He spread into journalism and epic. Content to impersonate medieval history in *Notre Dame de Paris,* Hugo became universal history, man, justice, natural and spiritual law, the Infinite by the time he came to the 2900 pages of *Les Misérables.* It has been said that, like Balzac, he had too much confidence in his own genius. So had all the Romantics. The criticism is useless: take away excess from Hugo and the genius vanishes. One has to agree with M. André Maurois's comment that Hugo had by nature the gift of portraying the gigantic, the excessive, the theatrical and the panoramic, and is justified by the truth and nobility of his feelings. Our difficulty is that we can nowadays recognize, by general psychological aid and the torture chambers of contemporary history, the monstrous side of a book like *Notre Dame de Paris,* but have disconnected it from the ideal. We can recognize horror and grotesque, and even respond to the rhetoric of darkness; we are unable to credit the rhetoric of light. We are too absorbed in the rediscovery of evil. For Hugo, the black and white artist, one could not exist without the other. He was a primitive in that respect—or a commercial.

In *Notre Dame de Paris* Hugo's dreams are magnified in outline, microscopic in detail. They are true but are made magical by the enlargement of pictorial close-up, not by grandiloquent fading. Compare the treatment of the theme of the love that survives death in this book with the not dissimilar theme in *Wuthering Heights.* Catherine and Heathcliffe are eternal as the wretched wind that whines at the northern casement. They are impalpable and bound in their eternal pursuit. A more terrible and more precise fate is given by Hugo to Quasimodo after death. The hunchback's skeleton is found clasping the skeleton of the gypsy girl in the charnel house. We see it with our eyes. And his skeleton falls into dust when it is touched, in that marvelous last line of the novel. Where love is lost, it is lost even beyond the grave. The reader is made to see this finality with his own eyes. If we object that Hugo's world is rhetorical, his skepticism, irony and wit give the rhetoric earth to stand on. Quasimodo is put to the torture in a ferocious scene, but it follows a trial which is based on the stock stagy comedy of deaf prisoner at odds with deaf judge. The novel is a romance, but its parts exist in equilibrium. Interwoven with the tragedians—Quasimodo, the girl, the lusting priest—is the pedestrian Gringoire who has been quick to make his peace with the world, like some Shakespearean clown. He grows before our eyes, as all the characters grow. Beginning as a bore, he becomes the nervous smile on the face of that practical pusillanimity which we call the common experience and the instinct to survive. (We live by our genius for hope; we survive by our talent for dispensing with it. Turning to M. Maurois's *Life* and recognizing that part of Hugo's greatness lay in his efficiency in using every item of his life, we wonder if Gringoire was some malicious version of a Sainte-Beuve, for he has married the Muse platonically. He will be a critic.) "What makes you so attached to your life?" the haunted archdeacon asks him. Gringoire makes the gracious Pyrrhonian reply about the sun, flowers, birds and books and adds the sublime sentence: "And then I have the happiness of spending every day, from morning to night, in the company of a man of genius, myself. It is very pleasant."

Hugo was the impresario of a split personality. Out of the depths came the monsters created by chastity: lust, cruelty, jealousy, violence, maiming, murder, in pursuit of the innocent, the loving and the merciful. The black and white view is relieved by the courage of the priest's feckless brother and the skepticism of Gringoire, the whole is made workable by poetic and pictorial instinct. It has often been pointed out that Hugo had the eye that sees for itself. Where Balzac described things out of descriptive gluttony, so that parts of his novels are an undiscriminating buyer's catalogue; where Scott describes out of antiquarian zeal, Hugo brings things to life by implicating them with persons in the action in rapid "takes." In this sense, *Notre Dame de Paris* was the perfect film script. Every stone plays its part. We can be sure the bells of Notre Dame are not there merely to ring; they will act upon a life; and, in fact, they deafen Quasimodo and that deafness ruins him in the courts, saves him and ruins him in love. In *Les Misérables* we can be sure Hugo does not describe, say, the inn sign at the Thénaudiers' out of sheer love of describing inn signs; a volume later Thénaudier turns up with it, in another setting, trying to palm it off as a picture by David. Once we have caught on to this clinching habit of Hugo's, every scene springs to action. We are waiting for the magic to work. Sometimes the trick is too obvious: we know the dancing girl will find her mother, by matching her shoe. "The reader will have guessed"—a ham phrase often repeated, but therein lies half the pleasure. We *have* guessed, as we guess in magic.

More important than this, for the critic, is the fact that Hugo's simplifications of the inner life are required by a superb sense of the theatre. He works entirely within its terms. One can see where he was trained. He works by stage scenes. The scene before Notre Dame is a stage set. He has the art of placing a situation, opposing an obstacle, creating a new situation, reversing it, doubling and redoubling. Rushing in the dark to save the gypsy in the tower of the cathedral from her attacker, Quasimodo triumphs in his strength, but when he discovers the attacker is his master, the priest, all his will and strength collapse. Yet if the priest wins that round he loses it because of the new situation; it is he, the master, who has the bitterness of being enslaved. Not merely by lust for the girl, but by the new thing—jealousy of his hunchback servant. Hugo was popular but not necessarily false because he put the obsessive and strong situations in simple theatrical terms. He is rich in dramatic irony. There is a purely stage scene where Louis IX inspects at length the construction of a wooden cage in which a prisoner is wailing for mercy. The king does not notice the prisoner because, in his avarice, he is too interested in the cost of the wood. Yet when another prisoner appeals for mercy the king lets him off out of whim. Fate rules us all, the Wheel of Fortune is a trickster. Hugo's whole method as a novelist is contained in these dramatic ironies and reversals, but he applies it in such a variety of ways and at so many levels that we do not notice the mechanics of it. In storytelling the method has the immense advantage of a delaying tactic: see the manner in which the dreadful Thénaudier in *Les Misérables* is made to reveal his adroitness, chance by chance. And if we ask ourselves whether Hugo's characters live outside the theatre, Thénaudier provides one answer. Hugo has to see them in that spotlight in order to see them truthfully at all. A typical passage of Ciceronian oratory on Thénaudier's wickedness ends with the typical epigram which contains a truth: in this wicked man there was "*quelque chose qui était hidieux comme le mal et poignant comme le vrai.*" The ideal world is a world of opposites; in the rhetorical evocation of it, it is the last short sentence of the harangue that makes the dramatic point and clinches the scene. Hugo never fails with that sentence. The old dying Jacobin denounces the Church like an orator for pages on end and, for reply, the saintly Abbé simply kneels and says: "Give me your blessing." That is good theatre for it does not make the priest theatrical; it convinces us that he is alive. One has to admit that Hugo can overdo it. In the very next line, the old Jacobin falls back dead. That is too much. The critics who warned Hugo of his excess of originality and of his weakness for doubling his metaphors and his points, were right; at a deeper level there is the objection that a love of paradox is likely to turn into the high-flown belief that everything equals everything in the end. (Which one is pursuer, which pursued: Javert or Valjean?) But the highest moment of an art so ingeniously staged in its particulars is not metaphysics but spectacle. The attack on Notre Dame by the army of beggars; the preparations for the execution of the gypsy girl and her escape; the scenario of Waterloo—these are all crises on the grand scale and classical operatic instances of the mass scene.

The fact that Hugo's characters are larger than life as individuals and are only life-size when they are part of a crowd—judges, soldiers, beggars, populace—does not mean, of course, that they are not individual and recognizable, or even that they are either allegorical or caricature. There are no unconvincing or sentimentalized characters in *Notre Dame* or *Les Misérables,* as there are in Scott. (The two novelists are not really comparable; it would be more sensible to call Hugo "incurious Dostoevsky" rather than "inferior Scott." Hugo was simply too extroverted to know how morbid the sources of some of his ideas were; he merely knew that they drove his brother mad, not himself.) If *Les Misérables* is a lesser and more ambitious work than *Notre Dame,* this is partly because it is humorless and has little comedy. But Hugo's genius was for the creation of simple and recognizable myth. The huge success of *Les Misérables* as a didactic work on behalf of the poor and oppressed is due to its poetic and myth-enlarged view of human nature—intermingled with that fundamental regard for human cunning which a popular culture seems to call for. Hugo himself called this novel "a religious work"; and it has indeed the necessary air of having been written by God in one of

His more accessible and salable moods. Myth and theatre, rather than fact and dogma, are what have made Quasimodo, Valjean, Javert universal in popular esteem. It is remarkable that the eight hundred superfluous pages of digression did not wreck the book.

THE CENTENARY OF ANATOLE FRANCE *

Anatole France was born on April 16, 1844. He ripened with the century and died (overripe, the critics said) in 1924. His centenary comes too soon, for it has caught his reputation floating indeterminately in the trough that always follows a wave of fame. We find it hard to face the elders whom we admired when we were young and who dominated our scene, for they contain too much of our discarded life. Reading them again we find them mocking us with our own image, like a parent or a brother who is ourselves yet not ourselves. And yet it is not hard to disentangle oneself from Anatole France. Despite his artifice, his epicureanism, his air of ripeness and skepticism, he is at heart an adolescent writer. His world—as he says toward the end of his last autobiographical book, *The Bloom of Life*—is the world of desire and illusion. His way

* This essay was written in 1944.

is the primrose path of nostalgia, sensual pessimism and self-love. The famous irony is the artful weapon of the bookish man who never grows up, who tastes life and history. They are a gourmet's dish, sweetened by the senses, salted by horror. He observes, but does not experience; and, beginning as a dreamer, a writer of historical pastiche, a faun-like comedian of the museums and the libraries, he ends in moral nihilism. One is reminded of his own phrase about Van Dongen's portrait in his old age: "It makes me look like a Camembert that is running."

The notes of tenderness and the naïve which appear in both the sentimental and the savage writings of Anatole France led many critics to feel that, if he was appalled by human nature, he also pitied it. But now one begins to doubt. One does not pity men until one understands their dignity. As one reads his life and rereads his books one builds a picture of Anatole France shut up in a daydream world, protected by all the authority of a superb culture, tortured by self-pity and not by pity for mankind. His reminiscences of childhood and youth, his essays in the archaic improprieties of history, and his two or three realistic novels reveal a man who chooses to exploit the pleasure, the terrors and the final anarchy of a personal solitude. He became a kind of Gibbon who has lost the love of liberty in the love and hatred of himself and who, tactfully withdrawing from the battle of history, contents himself with the footnotes. It is the course of the bookish man, the man who has tippled the illusions of the library and whose irony scarcely conceals the complacency of the noncombatant. One might suppose, after reading his novel about the Terror, *The Gods are Athirst,* that the French Revolution was an idle piece of human sadism caused by boredom or some northern incursion of the sirocco, and that the forces of history are really nothing but the agglomerated aberrations of human character. The complacency of this view is as shocking as the Terror. It is not a cold complacency; it is the complacency of the daydream and self-love.

To this passive and cunning view of life, Anatole France brought the genial resources of his unorganized reading, the power to crystallize it in anecdote and to link the anecdotes together, with the subtlety and wit of the French tradition. One is rummaging in a second-hand bookshop—and, of course, he was the son of a famous bookseller—and each volume has its human habit and voice. As a novelist Anatole France was less a creator of characters than a compressor of them. He squeezed them out of books, as wine drips out of the press. His naïve priests and his fanatics, his trenchermen and his sluts, his always bedable girls, his politicians gulled by their own corruption are the fantasies of the library, jocosely or morbidly removed from the treadmill of life. There is scathing diagnosis—see his handling of the Dreyfus case in *Penguin Island*—there is art. But a heavy price is paid for this intellectual high-coloring of France's characters: we cannot take them seriously. They have wine instead of blood; sex but not vitality. The Terror in *The Gods are Athirst* does not terrorize except as a theory about the Terror. We are engaged by the sensational notion that hundreds offered themselves voluntarily to the guillotine, that the Moscow confessions were anticipated, that a woman would cling to her lover with a wilder ardor and attain an even more powerful satisfaction, when she knew he had that morning condemned innocent men peremptorily to death. For we know that some women do offer themselves to murderers with special zeal. And yet, in the end, we put down this novel which was to blast the puritan out of us and to replace him by the mellow and stoical reader of Lucretius—we put it down with the feeling that we have been tricked. Surely, we say, huge scenes have been left out. Surely it is perverse to personify the Revolution in a narrow prig like Gamelin and to treat the Terror as an outburst of self-righteousness or to isolate it as a clinical instance of insanity. Is it enough to regard the Terror merely as one of the frenzies of human nature? Was it not inevitable and therefore tragic? Is it not an insult to those cartloads of human beings jolting toward the guillotine, to give them the pathos of marionettes, to treat them as a cat treats a mouse, to use them as a psychiatrist's anecdote? The sadism and pity of Anatole France are certainly powerful and unrelenting in this book; but, in the end, one comes to regard it as a piece of erotica, while its judgment—that after revolutions have done their worst, life eventually goes on exactly as before—relies on an obvious confusion of ideas.

I see nothing humane in this book. On the contrary, it seems to me a plea for human isolation, and it has paid the price of such pleas; it has missed the sight of human dignity. Irony has made horror trivial. One sees it through a keyhole. Anatole France professed to recover something of the eighteenth century, but the humanity of the eighteenth century was not the fruit of a philosophy of contemplation. Gibbon recorded the crimes and follies of mankind, but his History was imbued with a hatred of tyranny; and Voltaire, that "chaos of clear ideas"—was driven by the same passion. The humanity of the eighteenth century was an active faith, enlarged by the variety, not desiccated by the absurdity of human nature; and men like Gibbon and Voltaire did not suppose themselves to be standing on some magically stationary point in history. A mystic like Blake did not think of the Terror as chiefly an example of the savor of human cruelty.

The purely literary critic would say that the talent of Anatole France was the talent of annotation. He was, like so many of his characters, a collector of bric-à-brac, a *bouquiniste* of the quays, a conversationalist. He arranges his material. He does not build with it. The pleasure we get from a book like *At the Sign of the Reine Pedauque* springs from grotesque contrasts. The salacious is followed by the lyrical, the philosophical by the picaresque. The patchwork manuscripts of Anatole France, posted into ledger-like notebooks from diverse rewritings, show the care with which he placed each sentence and each episode. No one could have arranged *bibelots* on a table more maliciously. But the failure to rise to the fullness of a great theme is curious in a brain and taste so greatly gifted. One is tempted to turn away from literary criticism and to explain the failure, as Mr. Edmund Wilson has done, as the result of the lack of some comprehensive and energizing philosophy of life. Bourgeois culture had become static and self-contained. Anatole France has written enough about himself—and very honestly, too—to show that he was essentially a timid and egotistical writer; and one can understand how the first World War must have scattered his learned dreams by showing him History out on the hunt and with a purpose in its eye. But a writer cannot have a comprehensive philosophy of life just for the asking. And if there is no comprehensive view about mankind in Anatole France beyond the notion that we are going round in circles, there is a pretty constant view about one subject in his books—that is, the Church. There his skepticism could bite because it had something for his teeth to bite on. The fame and influence of Anatole France with the large public were due, one suspects, to his response to the religious crisis of the late nineteenth century. After all the sneers, the comedies and the satire at the expense of the Church, there remains a nostalgia, like his own nostalgia for his childhood, which was typical of the minds of those caught in this religious conflict. And, especially in England, his sophisticated and Rabelaisian manner, alternating with the pretty manner of the folktale, soothed the struggles of our overstrenuous consciences. For at least a generation no English writer offered the same irreverent consolations.

My own taste is divided between the autobiographical books about childhood and the one or two realistic novels. *Le Petit Pierre* and *Pierre Nozière* are studied, but they are graceful and convey the dogged smallness and anxiety of childhood. They evoke, as *The Crime of Sylvestre Bonnard* does also, the life of the narrow streets of the Quartier Latin and of the Quais, so that one seems to be treading again the shadows of the plane trees and seeing the severe ripples of the Seine. The quality of meditation is filled with Latin sentiment; the fairy tale charm is of the period. (That it may be a little fake is part of the charm.) The Bohemianism is harsh and native. It belongs to an entirely French society, unpolluted by the raucous Bohemia of Montparnasse. The tragedy of Anatole France was that he drifted from this fanciful world into the more violent world of religious, political and historical fable. The realism of books like *The Elm Tree on the Mall* or *The Red Lily* has a smaller scope, but its note is truer. One cannot call a book like *The Red Lily* a great novel about jealousy, but in its severe frame it reflects a few things perfectly and with supreme economy. Formal and quite unspeculative, it makes its comment on "moeurs" with a clarity that is worth all the juicy Abbés, the tavern sluts and tedious scholars of the epicurean novels. These are good for a page, or good for a chapter, but they have the tedium of marginalia. They are a connoisseur's collection, a professor's conundrum, a bookseller's whisper. The great foot of Rabelais comes down upon the pretty pickle and leaves it looking flat.

HENRY DE MONTHERLANT

Henry de Montherlant was born in 1896. He belongs to the brilliant generation of rebels on whom the label Recalcitrant and Unseizable can be fixed. "There have been three passions in my life: independence, indifference and physical delight," he has written; the words were sharpened in the trenches of the first World War to which we can trace his anti-romanticism and the determination to strip away the disguises of experience and to present only the "authentic." In *La Rose de Sable* (*Desert Love*) he wrote: "For we should all be most suspicious of any venture of spirit or conscience which we knew had begun by being merely one of the heart." His hostile studies of women, more particularly bourgeois women, in the pre-war novels, sprang from this mistrust of the duplicity of the heart: their speciality. Desire revitalizes; love corrupts because it is corrupt in itself. In an interesting introduction Mr. Quennell reminds us that the ruthless Montherlant hero used to be compared with Renaissance man. Well! Well! Nowadays he looks simply like one more writer; tough indeed, but evasively bent on self-preservation. In a long account of how he set out to make his life in his *Selected Essays*, he describes how he broke his ties with France after the first World War and went off to live anonymously and alone, in complete freedom in Algeria. He had ceased to be a Catholic; he was attracted to Spanish mysticism. Spanish critics found in him that intellectual excess which they always dislike in French culture when it seeks an exotic, foreign trellis. The essays are the work of a man of changeable and restless temper and the ones he wrote during the thirties when Hitler was rising, are egotistical and, on the whole, silly. Where he impressed, as Mr. Quennell says, is as a descriptive writer. In this volume, Montherlant's account of his irritable, defensive acquaintanceship with a Jewish soldier during the first World War is worth the rest of the book. It is at once a portrait and an exact, cold estimate of his own prejudices as a stupid young man.

Since the second World War, Montherlant has emerged as a fine playwright. His novels seem less important. His attitude to life is interesting now only as it contributes to his descriptive power. Montherlant's descriptions are drained of personal excess and present a scene as if it were the residue left when dozens of conflicting eyes and minds have moved away from it. There is one novel which, because it lies outside his usual belligerence, begins to look like lasting. This is *The Bachelors* (*Les Célibataires*) published in 1934. It is translated by Terence Kilmartin. It is one of those carefully framed, precise and acid studies on a small canvas in which French writers again and again excel. The small becomes vast. Coziness vanishes from cozy corners. Eccentricity is seen to be tragic. Two absurd old men cease to be only absurd; their comedy is dreadful. Their tale contains one of the repressed subjects of our time, one of the subjects that has in fact been secreted while our society has been devoting itself to "independence, indifference and physical delight," for Montherlant's three passions were not peculiar to him; they are principles that, by now, have taken possession of two generations. The subject is old age.

The two bachelors are an elderly uncle and his nephew, the survivors of a family of the Breton nobility who share a little house in filth and poverty in the Boulevard Arago. We meet the older one standing outside a lighted shop window reading a newspaper with the help of a stamp collector's magnifying glass. He looks like a tramp. His clothes date back to the fashions of 1885; his overcoat and all his clothes are fastened by safety pins, his boots are tied with string. His pockets contain an old crust of bread, two lumps of sugar, bits of tobacco, solid bread pellets and a beautiful gold watch with his coat of arms on it. He is Elie de Coëtquidan, a baron. At home, he sleeps in a filthy bed. He is hysterically devoted to cats. He is a keen remover of stamps from envelopes. He has fits of writing scandalous anonymous letters for he delights in causing trouble. He is avaricious and dishonest. The only secret in his life is that he is a virgin; but since his principle is to frighten his other surviving relation, a rich banker, he pretends that a Jewish lady, to whom he takes a few sausages or cakes every Saturday, has been his mistress for thirty years or more and may make claims on the family. He is maliciously trading on the family's latent anti-Semitism.

The nephew, Léon de Coantrés, goes about in workman's clothes. After a promising beginning—he excelled at Latin verse, played the piano, invented a photographic enlarger—he sank into neurotic sloth. His natural direction was downhill. He loathes Society and his ideal is to be an odd-job man or laborer, fetching coal, sweeping up, polishing floors—anything that requires no thought and no worry. He has by now cut himself off from women of his own class; in any case, his love affairs had been with servants and prostitutes; the sudden disappearance of one of these for whom he had a tenderness had given him a powerful shock. For twenty-five years he has dreamed of her and never spoken to a woman. He washes once a fortnight. His whole life is based on a resentment of his aristocratic birth; and he suffers from the public scorn given to the French aristocracy. A clue to his neurotic condition is that his father had ruined the family and that he, the son, is being stripped, little by little, by a swarm of newly discovered creditors. With bewilderment he sees his tiny income vanishing. When the novel opens we see him trying to make his uncle face up to the terrible fact that they will have to sell up and separate. The loneliness of old age is about to set in.

And here the familiar French drama of avarice and hypocrisy begins. Uncle and nephew visit lawyers and their rich relative Octave, a banker—a beautifully drawn study in the evasions of a man who covers up his dishonesties by convincing himself of his own charitableness. He insures himself by openly deceiving himself. For example, when he realizes that he is about to be touched by the old gentlemen, he at once gives a largish sum to an orphanage so that he will be able to say "in all honesty" that he has "so many claims." His other motive is that he is being sued by a tenant for charging an illegal rent, and the charity is a sop to his conscience. The gift is secret, yet in his idiotic way, he feels it will help his lawsuit morally!

Of the two supplicants, the malign elder is more successful. In a splendid scene he bluntly blackmails the banker with the totally unreal threat that he will go and live with his Jewish "mistress." He gets an allowance at once and then sits in the banker's splendid office and refuses to go, getting the utmost out of Octave's humiliation.

Being fundamentally innocent, Léon does worse. He is down to his last few francs and still the banker shuffles and evades. The household is broken up and then, suddenly, the baron reluctantly lets him live in the lodge of his summer château. The last evening of the two old men together is nearly wrecked by a small incident. The old one is rolling up a filthy bread pellet as he chatters and suddenly he stops and a wild look comes into his eyes.

> "What is it Uncle?" asked Léon anxiously.
>
> "I've lost my pellet," said the old man with a look of desperation. Léon got down on his hands and knees and searched with him. When he saw it, he hesitated; then he remembered that it was his last evening with his uncle and, in the name of the past, the family and his mother's memory, he picked up the ignoble object and gave it to him.

We come to the final scene where Léon goes enthusiastically to the little place of his own in the country. He will be "away from Society," in the "bosom of nature," "living the life of the common people." (Montherlant is mordant about class masochism.) He eats with the laborers at the inn who call him Monsieur le Comte for a day or two, but stop at once in terrible silence when he tells them he is poor. The minuteness of Montherlant's descriptions of a sick old man's empty days is terrible. One can count the hours. He can't think of anything to do, so he lies in bed; but once he is in bed, a log rolls off the fire or the chimney smokes and he has to get out. He begins to feel dizzy and ill.

> Like a drowning man searching desperately for something to cling on to, he wanted to concentrate on some action or other, so he snatched up a pair of nail clippers and cut his nails . . . He went to look at himself in the mirror, convinced that it must show in his face that he was a sick man. But he could see nothing abnormal in his face. He simply found it ludicrous.

Outside he can see the formations of wild geese flying away over the dunes in their autumn migration. The lines might come out of a Russian novel.

Montherlant's picture of old age is searing in its intimacy and the effect is all the more keen because he has a searching comic gift. The snobbish, negligent and dirty country doctor to whom Léon goes is a comic figure; and, back in the Paris pages, there is a brilliant short sketch of an aristocratic lady who finds Léon and pretends not to notice he is looking like a tramp, and shouts with ecstasy about his "simple life" and how "ravishing" it is. She would (Montherlant observes) have called *The Critique of Pure Reason* ravishing. Montherlant never skims the surface; he knows the habits of life, mind and speech of the different social classes, and especially of the aristocracy; and without laboring his points, can exactly place any word or act in its context. His sense of *milieu* is exact. His epigrams do not wear so well—it was clever in the thirties for a novelist to make a mocking intervention; it was a dig at literature. But his irony devastates. After Léon's death, the innkeeper sends to Octave the banker a heavy bill for drinks the wretched Léon has never had; and Octave pays up willingly. He can now quieten his own conscience with the happy delusion that Léon's total failure as a human being was due to alcohol. The key to Montherlant's outlook on life is contained in an armed sentence: "People do not do us all the harm they are capable of." One lives in danger, on the edge of things. Montherlant's distinction is that he writes a prose that catches perfectly this sense that the course of life is perilous and unexpected.

Algeria, the romantic and patriotic cult of the Sahara: Henry de Montherlant's *Desert Love* (*La Rose de Sable*) is a novelist's response to "the colonial situation" and the private dilemma of the conqueror. The introduction is not clear about this book. It has been drastically cut. The translation is from the French edition of 1955 and this is an extract from a much longer manuscript written in 1932. I am not sure whether this has ever been published; the suppressed portion is political. Why suppressed? Out of date, perhaps; or the author has changed his mind. We ought to be told and we are not. The book is evidently an attack on the conventional, upper-class European, nature's Second-in-command. His class has dulled him. The present story contains the love story only of the original manuscript, and this is complete in itself. Love is M. de Montherlant's speciality: women are pitiable or contemptible instruments, men are exasperated executants. The curse upon man is the worship of maturity. Love is regarded as a delusive transaction between technicians who have engaged in it out of *amour propre* and are surprised by emptiness, hypocrisy, suffering and loneliness. Passivity predominates in his characters; from this they go on to cruelty and pity. They are hurt and hurting. Aiming at exactitude (which is not possible without heart) Montherlant's view is fundamentally perverse, but it has edge and clarity. He lacks the faculty and humility of human blindness.

Desert Love is one more of his examinations of the insulted and the injured. By the influence of his patriotic and socially influential mother, Lieutenant Auligny is posted to a remote station in the Sahara. She wants the glamor of a son "out there." He, too, is willing to believe in it. Lacking intellect, he is a passive passenger of contemporary rhetoric. He is ready to believe in the Sahara myth and when this illusion is quickly killed he falls back on the grumpy chauvinism of small things. This is good: upper-class chauvinism has become petty. Auligny is good, upright, kind, without military ambition and stupid. He is also morbidly sensitive. If we compare him with his English opposite number, the nice or decent fellow, Auligny probably lacks the group or social instinct which is second nature to the English and is their conventional hideout when in personal difficulties. Auligny tries to think consistently; his opposite number would grope his way through an undergrowth of sentiment and worry. Auligny finds that the Sahara post is hell on earth. Heat, squalor, boredom, have driven the older hands to near-madness, drink and squalid nights with the one local prostitute. Auligny decides that he can keep his sanity if he finds an Arab girl companion. There must be some human tenderness which will give him security of spirit. A girl is quite easily contracted for; she is hardly more than an inarticulate, illiterate and obedient child. It upsets Auligny that he has had to rent her; it fusses him that the contract requires that she shall remain virgin—a conflict here between honor and personal vanity.

Auligny is a man without self-confidence. He invites a friend (the familiar artist-Casanova of French fiction whom one never really believes in) to share the girl. Guiscart-Casanova foresees the worst; a connoisseur of bizarre sexual situations, he refuses at the last minute. The effect on Auligny is excessive. The girl yields to him suddenly and he is in love with her. He is not only mentally entangled now; he becomes pro-Arab.

> Nobody even suspects the business of carnal love at the root of this or that action of ours which today seems so distinterested. And presumably this is all to the good. For we should all be most suspicious of any venture of spirit or conscience which we knew had begun by being merely one of the heart.

The last sentence there is more interesting than the first: as a minor La Rochefoucauld, Montherlant is apt to fire only on one cylinder.

A parallel sympathy for the French is not, as we can see, aroused in the sandy, illiterate and passive girl.

Goodness knows—Montherlant doesn't—what sex does for her. She is well drawn and is certainly not sentimentalized. Once awakened she quickly tires; in any case, Auligny is a man who watches. He does not give. Neither she nor her father sees in him anything but the conqueror who commands and pays. Their desperate hunger is not sexual. The soft-hearted Auligny wishes to get more out of sex alone than can be bought, or is even there to buy. He is rejected. She and the one or two Arabs are silent when he makes pro-Arab remarks—a characteristic situation of the thirties.

They do not hate him. They find him laughable. The reason seems to be that they are secure through living with their race; he is insecure, like a child whose pride is to pretend to be alone. There is the passing gaiety of the flesh. What else is there? (Auligny asks.) He calls the girl "the sand rose" because "she resembled those little petrifications in being as charming as their petals on the surface, but underneath as cold and inert as the stone of which they are formed."

Montherlant is a tender and exact analyst of the pagan processes of lust and his descriptions of carnal love are intimate without coarseness. He is not one of those erotic novelists who describe in order to excite themselves. Even in a brutal or squalid scene he keeps his head. His success here springs from the fact that he is more interested in the mind as the body affects it. His chief curiosity is for the character of Auligny, in pulling to pieces a character who combines stupidity and sensibility. Above all Montherlant is interested in the worry and pathos of human inconsistency. In "the colonial situation," indeed in any human situation, there is no such thing as a fixed type. Montherlant's other novels have left an impression of emotional immaturity, but this works to his advantage in describing the abortive love of transaction. And if there is something intrinsically mean in the scale and people of the episode, his strong physical feeling for the desert gives a larger impression of loneliness, desuetude and the grinding-down of life:

> For he was now wide awake, in the center of the bivouac, drowned in the pungency of the troop's leather, and staring into starless sky. With strident whinnies, just like so many women laughing, some of the horses struggled and stamped their hooves, trying to get free from their hobbles. A man went across to tighten the knots. At last there was quiet. Auligny rolled over on the other side. Under the ash, the fire seemed to be out, but every now and then a little flame leapt up to illuminate the *shesh*-enwrapped head of one of the men, a shadowy bundle on the ground. . . . All around him his men lay asleep, their faces completely covered or with the *shesh* concealing their mouths. They sprawled like children, some so covered and bundled up that one would not have suspected they were human beings at all, others the opposite stretched out in the naïvest postures. Some forearms were stretched up stiff in the air. There were lovely rings on the fingers of some of the uncouth soldiers. Their knuckles gleamed.

Were they human, was the Berber girl human? The conqueror's mind was tortured. He had the vanity of his principles, the burden of his backslidings. The sandstorm reduced one to frantic animal restlessness. It blew up the stench of smoke, turned the air to glue and rustled maddeningly on the dunes. In the heat one could have been lying under the furnace of a locomotive. A knife could have been stuck fast in the dense air. They told Auligny to keep cool by singing: "Lah, lah, lah, lah."

The portrait of Auligny is dispassionate and exhaustive. He is the well-brought-up young man, uprooted and lost. His difficulty is his inadequacy for the role of conqueror; very few can naturally fill it—those who know and those who do not ask. Auligny even lacks the desire for military distinction. His sensibility is really self-regarding and, when out of his depth, he is either brutal or wounded. His "case"—if he has one—is that he has never really moved out of Paris and in any very serious novel about the colonial situation, he is really not strong enough to be fully in it. He never really finds out about the Arabs, indeed in his humiliation, he cries out against the High Command for sending inexperienced men who do not know the language to the country. He is taken aback when he observes a "human" reaction in the Arabs—if he sees tears or some "unreasonable" behavior. He is crushed when the girl he has bought does not love him and tells lies.

What has all this to do with Algeria? Isn't it a good deal just the dear old French theme of the bought little mistress, something neat about the disappointments of too-neat an idea? It is not Montherlant's fault that the Auligny situation is now out of date. He has done what he set out to do—to reduce the exotic Sahara myth to the experience of one of its nonentities. Implicit in this is also the exposure of nonentity love: the love that fears to meet an equal. In its erotic pages French literature has colonized wildly since the Romantic movement. That is now put right. Auligny rides off with his dream in his head, like any other sad officer in French fiction, but "trampled underfoot." It is "a closed dream." The road back is barred by ridicule. He has not even the consolation of remorse. It is as if the young ladies in Chekhov had had no intention ever of going to Moscow. There is not even good-bye. End of the European myth of the departing garrison.

THE MILITARY NECESSITY

It has taken nearly one hundred and twenty years for Alfred de Vigny's apologia for the military life to come once more into its own. It has had to wait for the tide of peace to turn and for the birth of two war generations. Like some writers of our own twenties, Vigny had imagined that negotiation was bound to succeed war in the diplomacy of nations and that science would eventually bring in the world state and make war impossible. He did not see that it would make war more alluring and interesting. Yet his accent is persuasive when he expresses this feeling, for he had the art of keeping rational hope faint but alive and of surrounding it with compassion for its insignificance. A lesson to propagandists: the pessimism which addresses itself to the last feeble spark of reason in our minds has a longer life than the bullying good will which slaps and pushes us along. From our point of view Vigny's personal aloofness and melancholy hit the mark. Humphrey Hare, who has made the present excellent translation, says that Vigny was never temperamentally at home in the circumstances of his life which were, indeed, generally dejecting, and that the crisis of the Revolution seemed to be "perpetually alive in him." He was not born until 1797 but his mind was formed by the eighteenth century, his parents were aristocrats whose property was sequestered, and although he was brought up to the idea of military glory, he was also taught that Bonaparte was an impostor. His coldness and remoteness were the formal mask of the man who finds himself between two worlds, but they were not the Byronic mask of a "doomed" or "lost" generation, for Vigny was a natural stoic who understood abnegation and pity. He had little egoism. He astonished and amused people like Dumas and Hugo by his fastidiousness—his mistress said she had only once seen him eat, and then only a carrot; as a soldier, he treated the army stiffly, as a "nomad monastery," a place for order, solitude, contemplation and self-effacement. Sainte-Beuve mocked him for being a Trappist and Vigny himself put down his failure in the army to having brought a passive and reflective mind to an active avocation. Vocation it certainly was not.

Vigny had the aristocratic dignity, the sense that Duty is Fate. This gave him a backbone which is lacking in the other disillusioned Romantics. When he occasionally falls into their inflated manner he writes poorly. "In the universal foundering of creeds," which was felt in his time, as it has been in ours, he believed in the aristocratic and "earthly religion" of honor, "the virtue of the life of this world." The argument and the stories that make up *The Military Necessity* are based on this sense, and it enabled him to define the moral essence of a soldier's life and the tragic mutilation of the individual, humane soul by the corporate spirit. The key to his thought lies in his account of the explosion at Vincennes when the kindly overzealous quartermaster is blown to pieces.

> Like a stone from a sling his head and torso had been hurled sixty feet up against the chapel wall, and the powder, impregnating this appalling bust, had cut its outline deeply on the wall at whose foot he had fallen back. Although we gazed at it

for a long time, no one uttered a word of pity. Possibly because to have pitied him would have been to have pitied ourselves for having run the self-same danger.

Any society requires the inhibition of feeling in its members and Vigny's point is that this is inevitable, and perhaps desirable. But he also indicates the price that has to be paid: a loss of heart and above all a loss of compassion. We should feel most compassionate of all to the soldier who sacrifices himself to society's requirement that he shall have no compassion:

> The army is blind and dumb, strikes down unquestioningly those to whom it is opposed, desires nothing for itself and acts under compulsion. It is a great machine wound up to kill; but it is, too, a machine capable of suffering.

For Vigny the modern army is a "body divorced from the great body of the nation." It is the scapegoat. In his long time of service he was painfully sensitive to these definitions, because he himself saw no active service against a foreign enemy: the most he had to do was to help quell a riot of liberal citizens in the town of Pau. It was bad enough to be the licensed murderer abroad; but to have that role in one's own country was pathetic and false. (This is the situation Stendhal angrily described in *Lucien Leuwen*). What Vigny is commemorating is the frustration of the old Napoleonic sense of glory—Napoleon appears unsympathetically in one of the stories in this book—the loss of romance.

Does the modern soldier still feel himself to be in a false position, in Vigny's sense? By 1914-8 he certainly did, but has the feeling continued in the conscripted, peacetime armies? Some have felt military service to be a happy return to their schooldays; but for most men the experience is that of the guinea pig who is made to suffer the effects of a major psychological operation. Like the novice, he submits to mutilation in order to obtain a special kind of soul. Like the soldier of Vigny's time he is a man "thrown, changed, recast, shaped forever to a common pattern. The man is lost in the soldier"—as he is lost in the monk. Routine, the check on the intelligence, reserve, obedience to artificial authority, bring out the melancholy and coarseness of boredom in military life; the gain, Vigny says, is abnegation and sacrifice:

> This utter abnegation of which I have been speaking, together with the constant and careless expectation of death, the complete renunciation of all liberty of thought and action, the delays suffered by a limited ambition and the impossibility of acquiring riches, all produce virtues which are much rarer among those classes of men who remain free and independent.

A monastery, a prison, the chains gladly accepted—such are Vigny's metaphors. A stoical doctrine, yet if it is wisdom and even freedom to submit to Fate and to obey, this submission is as corrupting as the pride of the man who believes he is free. Vigny wrote as a soldier of the peacetime bodyguard and garrison; he did not know the passion of action except by hearsay and he was austerely, humorlessly unaware of the corruption of the bored camp. He himself wasted a large part of his life in a profession to which he was unsuited—except that it gave him this book.

As a personal document, in which the self is disciplined to the point of anonymity, *The Military Necessity* is a classically clear and direct piece of writing. It is originally conceived. Vigny is an artist-philosopher. He sets out his theme a little at a time and then breaks off to tell at leisure a story that illustrates it. The military argument is a frame (as Turgenev's after-dinner conversations were or Mérimée's reflections on travel and custom) for three dramatic stories of character and action. This method of writing a short story will always attract the aspirant because it seems to be the easiest, for it gives the writer points of rest and provides him with the easy opportunity of stating an argument or a moral. The reader is deceived: for the requirement of this art is that one shall state a case without appearing to do so. Mr. Humphrey Hare quotes Sainte-Beuve's praise of Vigny's poetry:

> He never . . . produces his tears as tears; he transforms them . . . If he wishes to give vent to the anguish of genius or to the loneliness of a poet's heart, he does not do so directly as would M. de Lamartine, with a lyrical effusion, instead he takes the indirect method.

Vigny is always concrete. He is various and resilient in feeling and in portraiture. The poor quartermaster is blown up at Vincennes but the tragic irony of this perfunctory death is effective because we had seen the old man in his youth, in his fairy tale love affair, his love of homely music, in his fussing care and his fantastic life-long luck. Vigny has taken care to move us; his very arguments about the military life are feelings purged of personal rancor. His second virtue is that of surprise. When we meet the broken officer who is trailing through the mud of Flanders, with a mad girl in the cart behind him, we expect some tale of the misery of war, but it turns out to be far worse, an affair of political execution and the sea. The soldier has been ordered to shoot the girl's lover and he has saddled himself with his guilt. The officer with the malacca cane in the next story is similarly engaged in expiation. By doing their duty all his soldiers isolate themselves from humanity and accept a guilt which they cannot forget, and which is not "their fault." They are the martyrs of society. The event which causes this, in every case, is always astonishing, sudden and fearful.

Vigny has an exquisite sensibility to atmosphere and place. One will not easily forget the Flanders road, the attack on the Château at Reims, the simple barrack scenes at Vincennes or the long, dull, noiseless night in Paris deserted on the eve of the Revolution; such scenes have the supreme deceptive and allaying effect found only in the great storytellers. What are those fires? The shopkeepers are merely burning down the trees that have darkened their shops; so does a revolution begin. It is on the day when nothing happens that everything happens. Then, at the critical moment of action, this quiet and reflective writer breaks into unforgettable physical detail. It is detail, uniquely of the occasion, which a writer of stories must always seek—the muddle of the execution at sea when the girl is put by mistake in full view of her lover's death; the terrible moment in *The Malacca Cane,* when Captain Renaud, afraid of being afraid, runs his sword into a body during the night scrimmage at the Chateau:

> an elderly officer, a big strong man, though his hair was gray, rose like a ghost, uttered a fearful cry at the sight of what I had done, and thrusting violently at my face with a sword, fell instantly beneath the bayonets. I, too, fell to a sitting position beside him, stunned by a blow between the eyes, and I heard near me the dying voice of a child saying, "Papa."

Thus we know that Captain Renaud has killed a child, not a man, before its father's eyes. Or there is the dramatic eavesdropping on the meeting of Napoleon and the Pope. These crises are burned in all their special detail upon the reader's mind, as the outline of the quartermaster's body was printed by blast on the wall. One never forgets the physical scene which has been exactly caught from the chaos of feeling by a cool artist.

The admirable thing in *The Military Necessity* is the

novel and unobtrusive interweaving of story and argument. Again and again, when we think we are about to be fobbed off with an anecdote or a memory, we find Vigny going much further. Though the story of the malacca cane culminates in the episode at the Château, it has taken us through the life of Admiral Collingwood, through a consideration of the character of Bonaparte and the seductions and errors of the idea of glory. It has discussed whether we shall serve men or principles; it has discussed the dehumanization of man; the acceptance of retribution; the fact that ultimately life will deny us justice. We are always in deeper than we expect; we retrieve the idea of "the military necessity," just at the moment when it seemed forgotten and when false freedom seemed to be breaking in. The book does set up against the amorphous literature of our day, the dramatic blessings of an original and ingenious sense of form, the value of a decisive sense not merely of material but of fundamental subject. The latter is what we lack today. Vigny's life suggests that subjects are best found by writers who submit themselves to an intolerable spiritual pressure.

THE RUSSIAN DAY

What is it that attracts us to the Russian novelists of the nineteenth century? The aristocratic culture made more vivid by its twilight? The feeling, so readily understood by English readers, for ennui? No. The real attraction of that censored literature is its freedom —the freedom from our kind of didacticism and our plots. The characters of our novels, from Fielding to Forster, get up in the morning, wash, dress and are then drilled for their roles. They are propelled to some practical issue in morality, psychology or Fortune before the book is done. In nineteenth-century Russia, under the simpler feudal division of society, there is more room to breathe, to let the will drift, and the disparate impulses have their ancient solitary reign. In all those Russian novels we seem to hear a voice saying: "The meaning of life? One day that will be revealed to us—probably on a Thursday." And the day, not the insistence of the plot or purpose, is the melodic bar. We see life again, as we indeed know it, as something written in days; its dramas not directed by the superior foreknowledge of the writer, but seeming to ebb and flow among the climaxes, the anti-climaxes, the yawnings of the hours. Turgenev, who knew English literature well, used to say that he envied the English novelists their power to make plots; but, of course, he really disdained it. The surprises of life, the sudden shudders of its skin, are fresher and more astonishing than the imposed surprises of literary convention or the teacher's lesson. And in seeing people in terms of their anonymous days, the Russians achieved, by a paradox, a sense of timelessness in their books. Gogol, for example, seems to date far less than Dickens. In the Russians there is a humility before the important fact of human inertia, the half-heartedness of its wish to move and grow, its habit of returning into itself. This is true of Turgenev; obviously true of Chekhov, and I think also of Dostoevsky. His dynamism and complex narratives are the threshings and confusions of a writer who—if we consult his notebooks and letters—could never bind his mind to a settled subject or a fixed plot.

Yet the use of the eventless day could not alone give the Russian novel its curious power; indeed, it can be its weakness. No novelists are easier to parody than the Russians. These people picking their noses at the windows or trying on their boots while they go through passion and remorse! The day is a convention like any other. What gives those novels their power, and these persons their gift of moving us, is something which comes from a profound sense of a presence haunting the day. There lies on those persons, even on the most trivial, the shadow of a fate more richly definitive than the fate of any individual human being. Their feet stand in time and in history. Their fate is corporate. It is the fate of Russia itself, a fate so often adjured with eloquence and nostalgia, oftener still with that medieval humility which has been unknown to us since the Renaissance, and which the Russians sometimes mystically identify with the fate of humanity itself.

I have been reading Turgenev again and dipping occasionally into Avrahm Yarmolinsky's thorough and discerning evaluation of him. It was a great advantage to the Russian novelists that they were obliged to react to the Russian question; a great advantage, too, that the Russian question was to become a universal one: the question of the rise of the masses. The consequence is that Turgenev's political novels—especially *Rudin* and even *Fathers and Sons*—are less dated outside of Russia than they are inside it, for we can afford to ignore the detail of their historical context. I first read *Rudin* during the Spanish Civil War and, when he died on his foreign barricade, Rudin seemed to me (and still does seem) one of "the heroes of our own time." At the end of all Turgenev's political stories one may detect the invisible words "And yet . . ." left there by his hesitant and tentative genius. He is so close to the ripple of life's process of becoming, that at the very moments of decision, departure, farewell, he seems to revise and rejuvenate. The leaf falls, but the new bud is disclosed beneath the broken stalk.

Turgenev solved the Russian problem for himself, as he solved his personal question by an ingenious psychological trick. It is rather irritating, it is a little comic when we see it in the light of his personal character, but it was serious and successful. It was the trick of assuming a premature old age. Now this device was a legacy of Byronism. One can see how it must have infuriated his younger contemporaries to hear him declare that at thirty-five his life was finished; and then to have him live another thirty years in full possession of his gracious and pertinent faculties. The trick was a kind of alibi. For behind the mist of regret, that autumnal resignation, the tenderness and the wave of the scented handkerchief in a good-bye that was never quite good-bye, there was a markman's eye. Yarmolinsky speaks of him stalking his characters as he stalked his grouse on the steppe of Orel or Kaluga. Every time he picks off his man and notes, as he does so, his place in the Russian fauna. Look at this from *A Nest of Gentlefolk:*

> I want above all to know what you are like, what are your views and convictions, what you have become, what life has taught. (Mihailovitch still preserved the phraseology of 1830.)

The comic side of this adroit sense of time—so precise, so poetic and moving in his writing—comes out in Turgenev's private life. His autumnal disguise enabled him to give his large number of love affairs a protective fragility. The autumn is the hunting season. *A Sportsman's Sketches, A Nest of Gentlefolk, Fathers and Sons*—those are the perfect books. Turgenev is the poet of spring who eludes the exhausting decisions and fulfillments of summer and finds in the autumn a second and safer spring. He is the novelist of the moments after meetings and of the moments before partings. He watches the young heart rise the first time. He watches it fall, winged, to the common distorted lot. The young and the old are his fullest characters: the homecoming and death of Bazarov and the mourning of his parents are among the truest and most moving things in literature. To this tenderness, this capacity to observe the growth of characters and the changes of the heart, as the slow days of the steppe change into the years that rattle by in Petersburg or Baden, there is, as I have said, a shrewd, hard-headed counterpart, the experienced shot:

> In the general the good nature innate in all Russians was intensified by that special kind of geniality which is peculiar to all people who have done something disgraceful.

Or:

> Of his wife there is scarcely anything to be said. Her name was Kalliopa Karlovna. There was always a tear in her left eye, on the strength of which Kalliopa Karlovna (she was, one must add,

> of German extraction) considered herself a woman of great sensibility.

Or:

> Panshin's father, a retired cavalry officer and a notorious gambler, was a man of insinuating eyes, a battered countenance, and a nervous twitch about the mouth.

Looking back over the novels, one cannot remember any falsified character. One is taken from the dusty carriage to the great house, one meets the landowners and the servants, and then one watches life produce its surprises as the day goes by. Turgenev has the perfect discretion. He refrains from knowing in advance. In *Rudin* we are impressed by the bellows of the local Dr. Johnson; enter Rudin, and the brilliant young man demolishes the doctor, like a young Shelley; only himself to suffer exposure as the next day shows us more of his character. His people expose themselves, as in life people expose themselves, fitfully and with contradiction. The art is directed by a sense which the English novel has never had—unless Jane Austen had something of it—the sense of a man's character and life being divisible into subjects. Career, love, religion, money, politics, illness and the phases of the years are in turn isolated in a spirit which is both poetic and scientific. There is no muddle in Turgenev. Romantic as he may be, there is always clarity, order and economy. He writes novels as if he were not a storyteller, but a biographer.

It was Edward Garnett who, in defending the disputed portrait of Bazarov, pointed out that Bazarov ought to have been judged as the portrait not of a political type, but of the scientific temperament. (There is nothing wrong with Bazarov really, except that Turgenev placed him in the country, where he was a fish out of water, instead of in the city.) This temperament was Turgenev's, and because of it one easily discounts the inevitable sad diminuendo of his tales, the languid dying away which is the shadow of his own wish in his work. The rest stands clearly and without date. But the method has one serious weakness. It almost certainly involved drawing directly from life, and especially it meant that Turgenev was (or thought he was) stimulated to write by an interest in living persons for their own sakes. Turgenev knew his own lack of invention, his reliance on personal experience, and he studied character with the zeal of a botanist watching a flower; but, in fact, the study of character, for a novelist, means the selection or abstraction of character. What is selected is inevitably less than what is there, and since Turgenev was (as he said) governed by the actual life story which he saw, he does not add to or transform his people. They have the clarity of something a little less than life. What is missing from them is that from which he personally recoiled—fulfillment. There are spring and autumn—there is no summer. If success is described, it is by hearsay. Marriage, for Turgenev, is either scandal or rather embarrassing domesticity, something for a fond, indulgent smile, but a quick getaway. Strangely enough, it is his objectivity which leads to his limpness.

There are two qualifications to add to this criticism. One is suggested by A *Sportsman's Sketches*. His people derive a certain fullness from their part in the scene of the steppe, which none described better than he. In this book, his scrupulous habit or necessity of stopping short at what he saw and heard gave his portraits a laconic power and a terrible beauty. There the Russian day brings people to life in their random moments. The shapelessness of these pieces is the powerful shapelessness of time itself. The other qualification is the one I have indicated at the beginning of this essay.

If his people lack the power to realize themselves because Turgenev himself lacked it in his own life, they have their roots in the fate of Russia. You localize them in a destiny which is beyond their own—tragic, comic, whatever they are—in the destiny of their society. They may fail, Russia goes on. One remembers that startling chapter at the end of *A Nest of Gentlefolk,* where, after the bitter end of Liza's love, the novelist returns to the house. One expects the last obligatory chords of romantic sorrow, but instead, there is the cruel perennial shock of spring:

> Marfa Dmitrievna's house seemed to have grown younger; its freshly painted walls gave a bright welcome; and the panes of its open windows were crimson, shining in the setting sun; from these windows the light merry sound of ringing young voices and continual laughter floated into the street.

The new generation had grown up. It is the most tragic moment of his writing, the one most burdened with the mystery of time as it flows through the empty light of our daily life.

THE HYPOCRITE

We walk down a street in the dead hours of the afternoon, looking at the windows of the villas as we pass by. They are glass cases; they are the domestic aquarium, and what our idle eye is seeking, is a sight of the human fish within. And presently we are taken by surprise. We see a face in one of those rooms. Agape, bemused, suspended like some torpid trout, a man or woman is standing alone there, doing nothing, and sunk in the formidable pathos of human inertia, isolation and ennui. It is always a surprising sight and, to a novelist, always a disturbing one. We are used to the actions of human beings, not to their stillness. We are taken aback suddenly to our childhood, when time went by so slowly, and when we, too, were shut in a room with some grownup who was occupied entirely by the mysterious, enormous process of sitting. How they could sit! And sit alone! And how their figures grew larger and larger in our eyes, until their solitude and silence seemed to burst the room. It was, I think, one of the first intimations of mortality in early childhood.

The Russian novelists of the nineteenth century owe everything to their response to the man or woman sitting alone in a room, to the isolation, inertia, the missed-beat in human character. They are naturally aware of what André Malraux has called, in a recent book, "the crevasse that separates us from universal life." The chief subject of the Russian novelists—the monotonous life of the country house which is scores of miles from its neighbors—draws this response from them. And as they stand alone in the room, drumming their fingers on the window and looking out at the slow, cumbrous changes of cloud in the Russian sky over the steppe, the characters of the Russian novel fill out with the unoccupied hours of life. Loneliness intensifies character. The great personages of literature have so often been the solitary natures who overflow into the void that surrounds them, who transcend their personal lives and expand until they become prototypes. The Russian novel abounds in such figures. Oblomov is an example. Stefan Trofimovitch in *The Possessed* is another. Iudushka of *The Golovlyov Family* belongs to this category. One is tempted to say novels are important only when they create these abnormal, comprehensive people. But in saying this it is important to note one difference between the Russian figures and those of the West. Those strong-minded, bossy, tyrannical Varvara Petrovnas and Arina Petrovnas who honk their way through Russian life like so many vehement geese; those quietly mad, stagnant, frittering men who spend their time dodging these masterful women, are different from the English eccentrics. Our eccentricity or excess is a protest against the pressure of society; the Russian excessives of the nineteenth century were the normal product of a world which was so lax that it exercised no pressure at all. "We Russians," Shchedrin wrote, "are not drilled, we are not trained to be champions and propagandists of this or that set of moral principles, but are simply allowed to grow as nettles grow by a fence." Iudushka and Oblomov are natural weeds of a neglected soil. They grow by running rife and they derive their force not from private fantasy alone, as Pecksniff or Micawber do, but from the Russian situation. They are puffed out by the sluggish, forgotten hours and days of the steppe. For in the empty hours and the blank distance which separate them from their neighbors, all the fate, the history, the significance of Russia itself, is gazing back at their gaping eyes.

After reading Shchedrin's *The Golovlyov Family* one sees why a character like Iudushka, the liar and humbug, is greater than Pecksniff who is, I suppose, the nearest English parallel. Iudushka is greater, firstly, because he has Russia inside him, and, secondly, because he is encumbered with the dead weight of human dullness and vulgarity. He is greater because he is a bore. I do not mean that Iudushka is boring to read about. I mean that Dickens did not mind that Pecksniff was a boring and vulgar man; Dickens's genius was attracted only to the dramatic and absurd exterior of the whited sepulcher. Shchedrin did not stop at the farce of human hypocrisy, for the tricks of hypocrisy are really too crude and blatant. Shchedrin went on collecting the evidence with the patience of one of those static realists like Richardson; and he presently came upon the really terrible thing in Iudushka's character. We can laugh (Shchedrin seems to say) at the obvious hypocrisies of Iudushka and, like his neighbors, we can grin at his eye rolling, his genuflections and his slimy whimsicalities; but there is something more serious. The real evil is the moral stagnation in Iudushka's character. The real evil is the muddle, the tangle of evasions, words, intrigues by which he instinctively seeks to dodge reality. We forgive his sins; what eludes forgiveness is the fact that his nature has gone bad; so that he himself does not know the difference between good and evil. He is a ghastly example of self-preservation at any price. In middle age he is befuddled by daydreams. He will pass a morning working out fantastic conundrums such as, how much money he would make out of milk if all the cows in the neighborhood died except his own. He works out the most detailed but essentially ridiculous systems of bookkeeping, and imagines that he is working. Less and less is he able to face any decision, however small. He is a hive buzzing with activity—but it is the act of procrastination. I do not ever remember seeing such a picture of our character in any English novel; yet the humbug's art of evading an issue by confusing it is a universal one. There is one remarkable picture of Iudushka's evasion in the account of his behavior to the servant girl whom he has got with child. Iudushka manages never to admit that the child is his, but allows everyone around to say it is. His own reaction is to groan and to say "This is unbearable"—subtly conveying that his sufferings, not his act, are the unbearable thing. Iudushka reaches the sublimity of self-deception here. He has achieved detachment and isolation from his own actions. And the strange thing is that we begin to pity him at this point. He feels an agony and we wince with him. We share with him the agony of being driven back step by step against the wall and being brought face to face with an intolerable fact.

There is nothing notably remote from our experience in *The Golovlyov Family*. Neither the emancipation of the serfs which stupefies Arina Petrovna, nor the fact that one is reading about a remote, semi-feudal estate, makes the book seem exotic or alien to us. Our own Arina Petrovnas do not starve their sons to death, but they have driven some to alchoholism; our own Iudushkas do not publicly drive their sons to suicide. But, in the main, we must be struck by the essential closeness of Shchedrin's novel to the life of the successful middle class in England. Iudushka's prayers for guidance have a sinister echo. Walter Bagehot, I believe, said that the mind of the businessman lived in a kind of twilight, and the character of Iudushka is a remarkable example of a man whose cunning requires an atmosphere of vagueness and meaningless moral maxims. He has the stupidity of the slippery. In the end, it is not so much his wickedness that shocks his nieces, as the fact that he has become such a talker, such a vulgar babbler and bore. Cucumbers, pickles and the mercy of God indiscriminately mix in his mind. He bores one of the girls out of the house; and one of the most terrible chapters in the book is that one toward the end when the girl comes back to his house to die and wonders whether she can bear to spend her last weeks in the house of a man who never stops driveling on and on about trivialities. She can tolerate him only by persecuting him. This picture of the triviality of Iudushka's mind is Shchedrin's master stroke.

The Golovlyov Family has been described as the gloomiest of the Russian novels. Certainly the characters are all wretched or unpleasant, and the reader of novels who professes that strange but common English attitude to literature: "Would I like to meet these people?" must leave the book alone. Yet Shchedrin's book is not gloomy; it is powerful. It communicates power. It places an enormous experience in our hands. How many of the realists simply indulge in an orgy of determinism and seek only the evidence that indicates damnation. Shchedrin does this up to a point, but he is not looking for quick moral returns. His method is exhaustive and not summary. Old Arina Petrovna is a tyrant; but her lonely old age has its peculiar rewards. She enjoys guzzling with Iudushka, she adores his boring conversation; she is delighted to queer his pitch when he seduces the servant girl. The compensations of life are not moral; they are simply more life of a different kind. Here are the last years of her life:

> She spent the greater part of the day dozing. She would sit down in her armchair in front of a table on which smelly cards were spread out, and doze. Then she would wake up with a start, glance at the window, and without any conscious thought in her mind gaze for hours at the wide expanse of fields, stretching into the distance as far as the eye could see. Pogorelka was a sad-looking place. . . . But as Arina Petrovna had lived all her life in the country, hardly ever leaving it, this poor scenery did not seem dismal to her, it touched her heart, stirring the remains of feeling that still smoldered in it. The best part of her being lived in those bare, boundless fields, and her eyes instinctively turned to them at every moment. She looked intently into the distance, gazing at the villages soaked with rain that showed like black

> specks on the horizon, at the white churches of the countryside, at the patches of shadow cast by the wandering clouds on the sunlit plain, at the peasant walking between the furrows, and it seemed to her that he never moved at all. But she did not think of anything or, rather, her thoughts were so disconnected that they could dwell on nothing for any length of time. She merely gazed and gazed until the drowsiness of old age began to ring in her ears, covering with a mist the fields, the churches, the villages, and the peasant walking far away.

No, Shchedrin is not gloomy because he does not soften. He undertakes to scald us with the evidence; he does not pretend that it will make vulgarity romantic or ignorance pretty. He is powerful because he remains severe. And so, at the end, when Iudushka and his niece, after their awful drunken quarrels, suddenly admit their despair to each other, and Iudushka makes the one truly heartrending cry of his life, we are moved beyond description. "Where are they all?" he cries, thinking of the mother, the brothers, the sons he has tricked and bedeviled into the very grave. He has felt the clammy coldness of a hand touching him —and the hand is his own. His cry is like Lear's. And it is all the more appalling that he utters this cry when his broken niece is still with him; if he had cried out when he was alone we would not believe. One had indeed not grasped it until then—the total disappearance of a family, the total disappearance of all that suffering and hatred. And the force of the book is all the greater because we do not look back upon a number of dramatic intrigues capped by their scenes, but we see Russia in our mind's eye, the steppe, the little-changing sky, the distance of people from each other, and the empty hours of all those lives. The English novel of family life inevitably turns from such a pessimism, but not, I think, because the English family is or was any nicer than the Golovlyovs were. The middle class, up to now, have lived in an expanding economy, which has enabled people to be independent where they could not be indulgent. If that economy becomes static or if it is put on the defensive, then a different tale will appear. The story of our money and of our religion has yet to be written.

THE GREAT ABSENTEE

If literature were to follow the excellent custom of the Catholic Church which adds a new saint to the calendar in every generation, and with more than half an eye on the needs of the time, it is easy to see which character in fiction is now ripe for canonization. Not the propagandizing figure of Don Quixote; not the innocent Pickwick; certainly not Robinson Crusoe, that too industrious town planner running-up a new society. The function of the saints is to assuage the wishes of the unconscious, to appeal to that part of a man which is least apparent to himself, and today we must turn away from the heroic, the energetic, expansive and productive characters. Falstaff the coward, Oblomov the sublime sluggard and absentee, seem to me our natural candidates. Oblomov above all. In a world of planners he plans himself to sleep. In a world of action he discovers the poetry of procrastination. In a world of passion he discovers the delicacies of reluctance. And when we reject his passivity he bears our secret desire for it like a martyr. For us he sleeps, for us he lies in bed daydreaming, for us his mind goes back to the Arcadia of childhood, drinking the opiate of memory. For our sakes who live in clean rooms and who jump out of bed when the alarm clock goes, Oblomov lies among his cobwebs and his fleas, his books unread, his ink dry in the bottle, his letters unanswered. While we prosper, he is cheated. And at the end of our racketing day we see his face—the moonlike face of the obese and the slack, and with that wry kink of fret and faint madness which the moon sometimes has on it—we see his face looking upon us with the penetrating, disturbing criticism of the incurable, the mysterious reproach of the man who is in the wrong. Slowly, guiltily, his foot comes out of the bedclothes and dangles furtively above the slipper on the floor and then, with a tremor of modesty before the implication of an act so obscenely decisive, the foot is withdrawn. Who knows what valuable grains of sensibility are lost to the soul when man is persuaded to stand upright?

In all the great mad literature of nineteenth-century Russia, Goncharov's novel is, to my mind, the gentlest and most sympathetic in its feeling. Like so many great books, *Oblomov* grew beyond its author's intention. Goncharov was one of the new realists and reformers. He wrote to satirize the sluggishness of the old-fashioned landowner. The industrialization of Russia was beginning, and he wrote to praise the virtues of the new businessman. *Oblomov* is an excellent example of the ambiguous value of propagandist purpose to a novelist: in a great novelist this will stimulate the talent until it swallows the purpose. Without genius Goncharov might have written a tract. Having genius, he has created one of the sublime comedies of all literature. After we have read this book we do not hate idleness, escapism, daydreaming: we love Oblomov. We have discovered a man, a new man whose existence we had never suspected; a ludicrous Russian nobleman who, we realize, has dwelt for a long time not in Russia but in ourselves. And, so deceptive is the relation of moral purpose and literature, we are not in the least impressed by Stolz, the busy, cheerful man of affairs, who is held up for our admiration. It is easy and natural to admire *him;* we take *him* in our stride; our sense of justice, our humanity and our sense of adventure, demand more delicate and difficult tasks. Oblomov loses Olga, Stolz marries her; but, like Olga, after her years of happy and successful marriage, we have an intuition that something was lost when Oblomov was cast away. As Goncharov wrote—and he spent many years on this book—he began to see beyond the comedy of Oblomov's condition and discern the value of it. Propaganda does not become art until it has the grace and the courage to welcome the transposition of its purpose.

There is reason to regret—though such regrets are really irrelevant to criticism—that Goncharov did have a purpose, and that he took it seriously enough to create the character of the virtuous Stolz. I do not mean that Stolz is a failure as a character. Goncharov had the gift of original observation; he was incapable of palming off on us a wooden or sentimental idealization as some of our Victorian novelists have done. He has the kind of closeness to fact which Trollope had. One's criticism of Stolz is simply that he exists at all. The book could get on quite as well, indeed it might have taken a more startling and imaginative turn, without him. And this is not pure conjecture. We now know enough about Goncharov to see that he was not merely a pedestrian realist; Russian critics have pointed out that *Oblomov* is a much more subjective book than it appears to be at first sight. There is more than one hint in the drawing of Oblomov's character. That he should pay for his torpor by being filthy and getting swindled we easily see. What other price is there? Ill health, of course. But there is something more. A faint furrow comes sometimes between those bland and mooning brows; a perceptible dryness gives, once in a while, an unguarded edge to his voice. Oblomov has the horrors. Under that passivity lies a possible madness, a frantic, abysmal, screaming despair. Now, that element is neglected by the book. Goncharov's preoccupation with Stolz took his mind from it. And so, once Oblomov has retreated from his affair with Olga with all the faultless strategic skill of the neurotic, he slumps to a comfortable, though pilfered, life in the arms of his landlady. He is ill. She mothers him. She recognizes in him an innocent. This is a shock to a moral man like Stolz, who believes in self-mastery, self-knowledge, the muscular development of human character; to Stolz, Oblomov is like a man who has gone native. But benign to the end, ineffectual, happy and blessed by Fate, Oblomov dies in his sleep, protected from his enemies and wept by the few who loved him.

Nothing could be more assuring. There is a transcendent gentleness, an ineffable prosaic delicacy, in the book. But we can't get away from it; the second part, although benign and moral, is dull. Suppose, for one moment, that Goncharov had not kept up his guard. Suppose that, undirected by Stolz and moral purpose, he had told much more of the truth. For Goncharov was, of course, a potential Oblomov—the fat man with the phlegmatic and malicious tongue, they called him. And Goncharov did have the horrors; he knew what they were. His life is one of those tales of mania that shadow literature, as we are said to be shadowed all our lives by the agonies of birth. Goncharov's minutely observant disposition concealed a nature eaten up by malice and jealousy. A slow, vegetating writer who wrote little, he could never forgive Turgenev for his adroitness, his skill and his success. He conceived the notion that Turgenev had stolen one of his plots and some of his characters, and even a humiliating public arbitration on the matter did not cure him. As the years went by and Turgenev's fame grew, Goncharov built up a fantastic dossier of Turgenev's supposed plagiarisms. Jealousy grew, as it will, into persecution mania. That is the drama which is missing: Oblomov's hatred of Stolz. Alternatively Oblomov's hatred of himself. Dostoevsky would have seen that; but, thank heaven, Dostoevsky did not seize the character of Oblomov. He would have made him one more Russian Christ.

Looking back on that paragraph, I begin to wonder if I have not strayed into a too strenuous conception of Oblomov's character and have forgotten his humility and its complement, his immense and passive conceit. No one can say that Oblomov is a divided man, he is as perfectly integrated as a blancmange. Oblomov's relation with the swindling Zahar, his servant, is like that of wife and husband; and the master rises to feminine heights in the wonderful quarrel which takes place in the early pages. Like some inured husband Zahar watches with resignation the familiar sight of Ilya Ilyitch Oblomov building up an emotional scene:

> "Then why did you talk of moving?" said Oblomov. "Why, no man can stand it!"
>
> "I merely thought other people are no worse than us, and if they move we can," Zahar said.
>
> "What? What?" Ilya Ilyitch asked in surprise. "What did you say?"
>
> Zahar was confused, not knowing what he could have said to cause his master's dramatic gesture and question. He was silent.

"Other people are no worse!" Ilya Ilyitch repeated with horror.

"That is what you have come to! I shall know now that I am the same as 'other people' to you!"

Oblomov bowed to Zahar ironically, looking deeply insulted.

"But Ilya Ilyitch, I've never said you were the same as anyone else . . ."

"Out of my sight!" Oblomov commanded, pointing to the door. "I can't bear to look at you. Ah, 'other people'! Very well!"

The scene goes on. Oblomov calls for kvass, and begins again on an ominously quiet note:

"Well, how do you feel?" Ilya Ilyitch asked gently. "You aren't happy, are you? Do you repent your transgression?"

"Whatever is this?" Zahar wondered bitterly. "Something heartrending, I expect; one is bound to cry if he goes for one like this. How have I grieved you, Ilya Ilyitch?"

"How?" Oblomov repeated. "Why have you considered what *other people* are? Comparing me to 'other people,' " Oblomov said. "Why, do I rush about or work? Don't I eat enough? Do I look thin and wretched? Do I go short of things? I should hope I have someone to wait on me and do things for me. Thank heaven I've never in my life put on my stockings myself. As though I would trouble! Why should I?"

And so he goes, pulling out all the stops, to the final words of this sublime quarrel, until Zahar is sobbing with contrition which—experience has taught him—is a necessary part of the play:

"And you," Oblomov went on, not listening to him, "you should be ashamed to say such things! That's the snake I've warmed in my bosom."

"Snake!" Zahar cried, clasping his hands and setting up such a howl that it sounded exactly as though two dozen bumblebees had flown into the room and started buzzing. "When have I mentioned a snake?" he said amidst his sobs. "I never even dream of the cursed thing."

Both had ceased to understand each other and now no longer understood themselves.

Goncharov had all the comic gifts. He had the art of capping one absurdity with another yet more absurd. He is fantastic in this scene; but in the beautiful chapter which describes Oblomov's childhood and youth, he is also the master of the quieter humor of real record. The talk about the evenings drawing in, in the Oblomov drawing room, is a perfect fragment of satirical observation. Again his purely descriptive drollery is superb. There is the hour of the siesta when, the family and servants, having guzzled in their plump and sunny Arcadia, all are asleep. It is a folk picture, a scene from the *Sleeping Beauty*, a fairy tale—to those scenes Russian humor owes a profound debt:

> The gardener stretched himself out under a bush in the garden beside his mattock, and the coachman was asleep in the stables. Ilya Ilyitch peeped into the servants' hall; everyone was lying down on the benches, on the floor, and in the entry; the children, left to their devices, were crawling about the yard and rummaging in the sand. The dogs retreated into the depths of their kennels, since there was no one to bark at. One could walk straight through the house and not meet anyone; one could steal everything that was about and cart it away unhindered—but there were no thieves in these parts. It was an overwhelming irresistible sleep, a true semblance of death. There was no life anywhere: only sounds of snoring of various pitch and quality came from every corner. Occasionally some sleeper would raise his head, look in senseless surprise about him and turn over or spit without opening his eyes, and munch-

> ing with his lips or muttering under his breath, drop asleep once more. Another would suddenly, without any preliminaries, jump off his couch as though afraid of losing precious moments, seize the jug of kvass, blow the flies that floated in it, causing them to move violently in the hope of improving their position, take a drink, and again fall on the bed as though shot dead.

The undertone of dream and fairy tale runs through the book like the murmur of a stream, so that to call Goncharov a realist is misleading. Oblomov himself becomes one of those transfigured characters which have grown over a long period of writing, which exist on several planes, and which go on growing in the mind after the book is put down. Now he seems to symbolize the soul, now he is the folly of idleness, now he is the accuser of success. He is an enormous character.

One other character ought to be mentioned: Olga. She is a direct descendant of Pushkin's Tatiana. In drawing her Goncharov achieved something unusual. Ever observant, he set about describing the birth and growth of a girl's personality; and especially he set out to describe what most novelists—always too much in love with their heroines—omit: the growth of their will. Goncharov showed that the apparently incalculable Olga was really quite calculable. He was aware of how much she would change from week to week. It is an oddly cool psychological analysis of "the young person" and something I do not remember seeing as clearly done anywhere outside of Henry James. Much might be written about her, and much more still about a comic masterpiece which does not agitate the mind as some comedies do, but which seems to become grafted into it.

All the Russian critics have pointed out—as Janko Lavrin says in a useful little book—that Goncharov was a divided man. As a child of the rising merchant class who were introducing modern capitalism into Russia, he observed the feudalism of the land-owning class with both disapproval and nostalgia; and Professor Lavrin even suggests that one reason why he did not engage in the reformist enthusiasms of the Herzen circle at the University may have been that these were the speciality of the sons of the land-owning class. How can we know the buried jealousies of early childhood? At any rate Goncharov's heart had been formed by the sight and experience of the old patriarchal life, if his calculating head was formed by progressive ideas. There is an accident of personal life to be taken into account also; his father died when he was four and, like Oblomov himself, he longed for the rest and passive pleasure of lying in a mother's arms. There, in one form or other, the life of his heart and imagination was vested.

The theme appears in simplified and didactic fashion in Goncharov's first novel, *A Common Story,* translated in the nineties by Constance Garnett. It is a Trollopian novel, simple but effective in mechanism, equable in manner and movement, smiling, ironical and pleasantly conventional. A young man leaves the provincial Arcady to make a career for himself in St. Petersburg. He arrives full of romantic idealism at the house of a discreetly worldly uncle who amuses himself by puncturing everything the boy believes in. The boy's romanticism (the uncle explains) is silly, his poems are idiotic, his education useless as a preparation for the world of affairs. As for love, it does not last; friendship is precarious and is best confined to one's business friends; marriage cannot be based on love and, when successful, is a matter of congenial habits and to be managed by guile. There is no happiness without prudence. The uncle is one of those skillful small hedonists of the golden mean. First, an absurd, pretty love affair with a young coquette and then a groaning and glutting passion for a clinging, possessive and yearning widow, cure the young man of his illusions. Uncle is right. But uncle had not noticed that the cure of illusions means the death of the heart and the ossifying of the soul. We leave the nephew becoming exactly like uncle just at the moment when uncle, at the age of fifty, has suddenly realized that his own cautious philosophy has destroyed not only himself but the heart of his wife. Uncle has a chronic pain in the back—the respectable price for a life of prudence—and the nephew knows he too must be on the right course because he has had the twinges of the same malady. By their illnesses ye shall know them.

A Common Story is an amusing novel. Self-mutilated, no doubt divided, a wry-faced spectator, Goncharov found himself with a neat and tender comic gift. The opening character describing the boy's departure is exquisite and touching; the next, which describes the uncle reading the boy's letters and throwing his sweetheart's present out of the window, is very funny. There is an excellent scene when the uncle reads the disobliging things his indignant nephew has written about him and calmly forces the boy to take down, at dictation speed, the other side of the story. Goncharov understood the tricks of comedy and especially that of repeating the same situation in different circumstances. The love scenes are aware of caprice and mood, pique, over-dramatic folly, small lies and satiety. But this is more than a novel about sense and sensibility, head and heart, city and Arcadia. It is a novel about loss. And here Goncharov is moving to Oblomov. Two years later he was to write the famous *Oblomov's Dream* as a separate story, which was eventually the core of the great book. The young man in *A Common Story* settles for the death of the heart and makes a marriage of convenience. Oblomov absents himself from such dilemmas: the key to happiness is daydreaming, sleep, sloth, complete passivity. The great outsize characters in fiction, like Oblomov, are the revenges of the unconscious.

THE MINOR DOSTOEVSKY

I have been reading the shorter novels of Dostoevsky. It is natural to pause before doing so for one last glance at the exalted glaciers of the major works. We stand in the sun on the modest contours of the foothills, looking up at the haggard and fog-hung precipices of Mounts Karamazov, Myshkin, Stavrogin and Raskolnikov, rather awed to think we have been up there, shuddering at the memory of it, impelled to go again, but glad of an excuse not to try it this time. We have been so lost on those heights; laughter at the wrong moments was so apt to cap the ecstasy of our expeditions. We would have periods of asking, with Tolstoy and Turgenev, whether our leader need be so shameless; and our Western natures rebelled at the notion of returning with the hangdog air of petty criminals. We conceived society to be our neighbors and their works; not a spawn of souls, half-born and without even an hour's civilization. And then, in the twenties, too heady a tradition of salvation was hung around those peaks, and it was the wrong kind of salvation. The world is not saved by novelists; and the unreason of the psychological mystics of the twenties seems to us now, I think, a rather shady attempt to get to God by the stage door. One thing scientific culture has done for us is to give us a desire for order and for intellectual propriety, and I hope we are beginning to see again that egging readers on to personal conversion is not one of the functions of the novel. In any case, the kind of salvation which Dostoevsky appeared to urge was not as private as it seemed to his adorers of twenty years ago; he did not offer a personal salvation in the form of a semi-religious psychoanalysis. The people of Dostoevsky's novels are notable not for their isolation but for their gregariousness. The infection is common. They run in crowds. If they plan to suicide or murder they tell everyone. They are missionaries in mass morbidity, mass guilt, and mass confusion. Even when alone they are not absolutely alone; they have at least two selves. One hears not the private groan but the public lamentation. I can well imagine that the next time I read the great works of Dostoevsky—and we are growing nearer and nearer to his temper—I shall find he has everything to say to a Europe which is becoming a morass of broken pride, vengeance, humiliation and remorse. As a political journalist he will have a great deal to say about Christianity and Socialism, about Germany and Russia, about the criminality of Europe; as a novelist he will seem to show a profound instinct for the character of groups of people, their ideas and the common hungers that bind them.

The irrational is no longer the novelty it was, and we are consequently less struck by the madness of Dostoevsky than we used to be. A sensationalist he was; but now, whenever I open a novel of his, my first impression is one of realism and sanity. He knows the world from behind the scenes. The accent is decisive.

The voice bristles with satire and expands with a capacious humor. Dostoevsky at his best writes like a hunted man who, for the moment, has fooled the bloodhounds and has time to confess and to laugh before the baying drives him on again. He is laughing hotly from the midst of experience. He is not laughing in order to forget it. The shorter novels of Dostoevsky —and in shorter works like *The Eternal Husband, An Unpleasant Predicament* and *Uncle's Dream,* we see the ground plan of all his greater works—are festive with experience of human society. Dostoevsky could see the terrors of our double natures, the fever in which our inner ghosts encounter each other, but he saw the raw comedy of this conjunction. It is frightful that we have so many selves and that the unconscious may wreck us; on the other hand there is something bizarre, something comic, something pitiable, in this squabbling assembly that has somehow got into one unpleasant pair of trousers. Look at *Uncle's Dream* for a moment. It is a farce; a masterful provincial lady in a scandal-mongering clique, attempts to marry off her beautiful daughter to a decrepit prince. One can picture the whole story as a very funny and quite unreal piece of theatre. But even this mechanical piece of fooling lives on several planes. One moment the Prince, with his wig, his false beard and his derelict body, is a horror; the next moment he is ridiculous. Then, suddenly, he appears delightful. We long for him to appear again as we long for Stefan Trofimovitch in *The Possessed.* The Prince even attains a rickety dignity, and from dignity, he dwindles to a thing of pity. After all, we say, he did not really lie when he said his proposal of marriage was a dream. The conventional comic writer draws his characters to a single pattern of wit or makes the world a convenience for his joke. Dostoevsky does not do this. He is one of the great comic writers because, however satirically he may begin, he always grows into humor, and the humor is not imposed on life but arises out of it. He is aware of the collisions that take place in our natures. Somewhere—I forget where—Dostoevsky said he merely pushed things to extremes where other people went only halfway. And yet when we compare Dickens's *A Christmas Carol* with Dostoevsky's *An Unpleasant Predicament,* it is Dickens who seems to be the unreal and exaggerating artist. For Dickens exaggerated in seeing only one side of his characters. (Tony Weller's life is reduced to a reaction to widders, Barkis is merely "willin'," and so on.) Dostoevsky explored the whole, and the thing that is comic on one page may become tragic on the next. The profoundly humorous writers are humorous because they are responsive to the hopeless, uncouth concatenations of life.

In *An Unpleasant Predicament* we have the simple story of a pompous official who, in an access of philanthropical conceit, goes uninvited to his clerk's wedding celebrations, just to show that all men are brothers and that he is above social prejudice. Far from having a good effect, the visit ends in his total disgrace and almost succeeds in wrecking the marriage. The stages of Ivan Ilyitch's downfall, until he is carried dead drunk to the bridal bed and breaks up the wedding, are brilliantly described, and Dostoevsky, who, like all the nineteenth-century romantics, excelled in describing the moods of crowds, keeps us in uncertainty until the end. Exploring all the possibilities, that is to say raising all the mystifying issues which can be raised, as if he were writing a long novel and not a short story, he ends with justice to all. Ivan Ilyitch is not alone to blame. The poor clerk, with his pride and his private quarrels with his wife, is in a muddle as well. We cannot be made responsible for the unnerving manners of our friends. No one is malignant, but everyone is to blame. It is all very well to talk about humanity and brotherhood, but be careful that in doing so you are not forgetting your own pride when you contemplate the pride of other people. Each man and woman, I warn you (says Dostoevsky, the incurable novelist), is capable of becoming a novel in himself, a novel by Dostoevsky, moreover. I warn you it is impossible to do anything whatever with any human being, unless you are fully willing to take the tumultuous consequences of his being human.

As I said before, it is odd that Dostoevsky should ever have been regarded as the novelist of the isolated soul. I can only suppose that very few readers read these comedies and do not know *The House of the Dead*, that wonderful documentary mine in which Dostoevsky describes his Siberian experiences, without hysteria or ideological puffing. In the great novels he is so blatantly the writer of spiritual headlines; in *The House of the Dead* he was content with the laconic news. No one who has read it can say that he ignored the problems of society. Like Balzac, on the contrary, he plunders society. He is acutely aware of class differences. So gregarious and populated is the unconscious, that in the typical dreams of his characters crowds of people will appear. There are, for example, the dramatic dreams in *The Eternal Husband*, Dostoevsky's most purely intellectual and accomplished comic novel. The sinister gangs of dream figures stamp up Veltchaninov's stairs and point at him with horror as he lies asleep in his guilt. In this novel it has been said that Dostoevsky parodied himself—it was written after *The Idiot* and *Crime and Punishment*—and certainly all his ideas are here: the double, the unconscious, the fantasies, dreams, persecutions, suspicions, shames and exchanges of personality. Even a child is tortured. But surely this comic masterpiece, a comedy which (as always in Dostoevsky) carries its own underworld along with it, stands completely on its own feet. In the first place the growth of Veltchaninov's sense of guilt from a vague irritation to mind and health into definite consciousness is described with wonderful objectivity and suspense. The value of psychological analysis to the novel lay, for Dostoevsky, in its latent dramatic quality. Psychology was dramatic; for us it becomes more and more a metaphor or explanation. The farcical duel between Veltchaninov and "the eternal husband" whom he has cuckolded, has an undertone of imaginative gravity which makes the farce more dangerous. Dostoevsky, once more, is pushing things to extremes because at the end of the extreme is the pity of human nature. Halfway—where other writers leave this kind of story—lie the conventions of melodrama and intellectual comedy; and, mad though the story is, it is full of the madness we all know about in the lives of people. The madness is the madness of life, not the madness of the mind. No one will ever accuse Dostoevsky of failing to complicate a situation, and this book is a succession of superb complications. The very last one, in which "the eternal husband" is being bullied by his new wife, and has silently to beg Veltchaninov not to cuckold him again, is one of the funniest and most moving in comic literature. The unconscious, Dostoevsky discovered, gave probability to the most bizarre situations and turned coincidence into fate. And, it is interesting to note, in the middle of this comic novel there occurs one of the very few pictures of normal, happy, family life to be found in his work.

The Eternal Husband is no doubt so refreshingly precise in its psychology, so well composed and economically written, so brilliant in its commentary because—for the time being—Dostoevsky had exhausted his anxiety for salvation. This is his one Western novel. It came from that part of him that liked to cut a social figure and was written during a rare period of equipoise and untroubled self-satisfaction. It has the genial air of a successful presumption, and it might easily have been written in our century, not his. And yet it could not have been. For the effect of psychological intuitions and discoveries upon our novel is to make it reminiscent, autobiographical, plotless; whereas in Dostoevsky's hands the novel became inventive, dramatic and far richer in plot than the rest of Russian fiction. How rich *The Eternal Husband* is in episodes; the absurd house-watching scene, the dramatic interviews, the discovery that the husband is torturing his child, the scandal at the brothel, the visit to the country, the nights which husband and lover spend together, where the husband first poses as his wife's ghost and later attempts murder! When one compares the realism of Chekhov with the romantic realism of Dostoevsky one sees how much was thrown away when novelists threw out plot. When plot went, the isolation of characters began; and though, by Dostoevsky's time, plots were stale, he showed that even the most hackneyed and novelette-like plot became rich and new when it was replenished by a new view of human nature.

A RUSSIAN CINDERELLA

And what happened after the glass slipper fitted and Cinderella married the beautiful Prince? Marriage changes the character of women; what kind of woman did Cinderella become? Going back through the story and looking for those experiences which must have marked Cinderella's life, we cannot but be alarmed by the probabilities. How humiliation must have intensified her emotional and imaginative life! What a crowd of impulses will fly up, fierce and disparate in their flight, like birds suddenly set free, when the years and years of repression come to an end! What an appetite for life, for pre-eminence, for power, for perpetuating the glittering success, will come to the downtrodden and humiliated one. Heaven protect us (we say aloud, as we glance at the history of society) from the tongue, the will, the parading ego, the unstable moods of the slave set free! And how did Cinderella escape—if she did escape it—the worst evil that can puddle the eyes and slur the lips of a beautiful woman: the vice of touchiness?

I know of no book that presents this case with more imagination and percipience than Aksakov's *A Russian Gentleman.* Sofya Nicolayevna, in that most limpid of the Russian autobiographies, is a portrait of Aksakov's mother. For years she had been outrageously treated by a stepmother. Then had followed a time of extravagant social success. At the time of her marriage, when she came as a guarded and resolute stranger into the patriarchal family of pioneers who had settled in the swollen and luscious region of Ufa, the old Abrahamic grandfather of the family judged her character:

> "Well, now, friend Ivan, what can say you of the daughter-in-law? As a man you are a better judge of the point than women are." Karatayeff, disregarding a signal from his wife, burst out with enthusiasm: "I do assure you, batyushka, that such another dazzler"—he always used this phrase of a beautiful woman—"as brother Alexyei has bagged is not to be found in the whole world. A look from her is as good as a shilling. And her cleverness! It's past all telling. But there's one thing, batyushka: she's proud: she can't stand a joke. When you try to have a little fun with her, she gives you a look that makes you bite off the end of your tongue."

And Aksakov himself says of the mother he adored and who adored him with all the violence of her heart, "Reluctantly," he says, "I must confess that love of power was one of her ruling passions; and the germs of this passion, now that she had been released from the cruel oppression of her stepmother, were sprouting actively at this time." Much, evidently, would depend upon the Prince. But power-loving women who are the belles of local society have a surprising tendency to fall for nonentities. They do not marry Princes. They look for slaves.

In Aksakov's father, Sofya Nicolayevna found a man whose deference, obedience and humility made him the perfect, the passionate slave. She would rule him, raise him up, mold him to the shape of her brilliant, town-bred ideas. She would scare him into wakefulness, blow him up in scene after scene till she had made him into another being. It was a bad beginning. But strong characters are often convinced that there is virtue not for themselves alone but for everyone else in violent purges of self-expression; and Sofya Nicolayevna was too young and too blindly herself to discern that violent outbursts appalled her husband, paralyzed him and drove him into the consuming daydreams of disillusion and resentment. She won her victory—but what a victory! It was empty. For she had begun by destroying his power of candor. Like many weak people, Alexyei had learned under the despotism of his father to develop a capacity for strategic retreat and adjustment. The weak—and how it maddens the strong! —have their own resources. The strong—and how it surprises the weak!—are so subject to sudden collapse, hysterical dependence, remorse and despair. Aksakov's father had his moments of pre-eminence. And in any case there are always compensations in life. He would leave the tumultuous bedroom to sit by the deep river which tumbled past the house, watching the sight which—Aksakov says—no Russian can resist: the sight of moving water. There was superb, Homeric fishing at Ufa; and the end of a scene (Sofya Nicolayevna would observe in despair) was often a fishing expedition, when the perch came out of the river by the dozen and—engrossed now by an unhuman antagonist—her husband would be seen in his boat, playing an heroic bream. Flustered by human nature, he could slip away from the incomprehensible campaigns of love into a passion no less solacing or primitive, the passion of the chase. In the crystalline air of the steppe and among the evening fogs of the water meadows and birch woods he would wait for the rising quail which had been decoyed by the peasant's flute, and shoot, undeterred, at the hare bolting for cover.

The real Prince was Sofya Nicolayevna's father-in-law, the stupendous grandfather whose portrait dominates the book and whose wise, patriarchal mind and arbitrary nature seem to reign over every page. In this old despot, with his terrifying rages, his implacable regard for truth, god-like in the solemnity of his habits, so that every eccentricity—chopping his shirts up on the doorstep, dragging his wife about by the hair, or standing more or less naked in the farmyard every morning to watch the sun rise—had the weight of something like the whole Mosaic Law behind it—in this tribal hero Sofya Nicolayevna recognized a force more powerful than her own and an indispensable ally among the jealousies of the family. Here she came upon her match in love and found her quality justly estimated and admired. The love of this old man for his daughter-in-law, in a family rat-ridden with that fear and that jealousy which natures too strong always create around them, is incomparably moving. In this first volume of his recollections, when Aksakov was describing the early life of his grandfather and his parents, he was an imaginative artist of the highest order.

In the second volume of his recollections, called *A Russian Schoolboy,* Aksakov reveals the second great passion of Sofya Nicolayevna. It was for himself. Intense in all her passions, she directed her whole life upon the ailing boy and he depended utterly on her. Their separations brought them both to fevers, fits and the brink of suicide. One must suppose that the fixity and joy of this overpowering and constant emotion must have been the cause of Aksakov's minute and exalted memory of his childhood, a memory that is hardly surpassed by Proust's. To Aksakov, childhood was the Golden Age. Not a bird song, not the flight of a butterfly or flash of a fish was forgotten. They were embalmed in the stillness of an unhesitating recollection. Like Goncharov's recollections of his childhood in *Oblomov,* Aksakov's have the warmth of some tale of the folk, where the sun always shines and where even the wickedness of man or the savagery of nature charms us as legends do, illuminating our lives without overpowering them. Aksakov's recollections are a retrospect without remorse. We are endeared by the permanence of human types and the profit and loss of living. The turbulent emotion of Aksakov's adoration of his mother has calmed into one of those deep and now untroubled feelings so beneficent to works of art. No other Russian writer, not even Tolstoy, has achieved the extraordinary stillness and ecstasy of Aksakov's picture of family life. No other Russian writer has held the mirror up to life so steadily, so that we see how the hours pass at Ufa in all their enchanting detail, without a tremor of the glass. In Proust, the act of remembering, the search for the past, the sensibility of the seeker, are important, perhaps the most important elements, in the task of memory; in Aksakov's mirror the agitation and flaws of such a brilliant egoism are not there to distract. Aksakov is not speculative. He is simple, tender, comic, delicate and factual.

> The dinner passed off in the usual fashion. The young pair sat side by side between the old couple; there were a great many courses, one richer and more indigestible than another; the cook, Stepan, had been lavish with his spice, cloves and pepper, and especially with his butter. The bride ate the dainties pressed upon her by Stepan Mihailovitch, and prayed that she might not die in the night. There was little talking, partly because every mouth was occupied and also because the party were not good at conversation. Indeed, they were all uncomfortable in their own ways. Yerlykin in his sober intervals drank nothing but water, and hardly spoke at all at such times, which gained him a reputation for exceptional intelligence; and Karatayeff dared not open his mouth in the presence of Stepan Mihailovitch except to answer a question, and went no farther than repeating the last words of other people's remarks.

> If they said "The hay crop will be good if we get no rain" or "The rye made a good start till the sudden frost came"—Karatayeff came in like an echo "if we get no rain," "till the frost came"; and his repetitions were sometimes ill-timed . . . Mazan with long boots smelling of tar on his feet, and wearing a long coat which made him look like a bear dressed up in sacking, handed round the loving cup. . . .

How is it that so still, so conservative a memory nevertheless conveys to us an impression of animation, excitement and suspense? For nothing like the airless gleam of a Dutch interior halts the descriptions of the scene. The answer must be that Aksakov's memory conceals the act of remembering, that his imagination works in hiding; he holds the mirror so still that we see not the writer but the movement of life itself, as the hunter or watcher of birds does when he sits in the fields unmoving for hours until life has the courage to resume its business. We watch with Aksakov and observe the huge suspense that hangs upon every detail of life from minute to minute.

Aksakov was a slavophile and a conservative. No hint of the political problems that were to disturb Turgenev and his successors comes into his work. To him the life of the country house in Russia—at least as he knew it—was as sound as an apple. It is true there may be sadistic and drunken landowners who beat and even murder their serfs. It is true that his grandfather was a violent man who expected to be obeyed on the spot and gave summary punishment. But such things are in the order of nature. His grandfather prospered. His people or tribe prospered. To be relieved of evil we must all pray to God. One cannot say that Aksakov was indifferent or complacent. He was simply under a spell.

It was the spell of private life; that life which goes

on whether there is justice or injustice, war or peace, struggle or inertia, the web we spin. One reads Aksakov now with a natural nostalgia, not indeed for the past, not for the delectable life of landed prosperity; not even for the abundance of food and drink for what is the story of family life but the story of the hours spent between one meal and the next?—but for the fixed state of living, some settled condition of judgment. Aksakov's grandfather sat watching the happy young couple, Sofya Nicolayevna and her husband:

> His happiness had a shade of fear and of disbelief in the solidity and permanence of a state of things in itself so charming. He would have liked to speak his mind on the subject, to give them some hints or some useful advice; but whenever he began, he could not find the right words for thoughts and feelings which he could not make clear even to himself; and he went no farther than those trivial commonplaces, which, for all their triviality, have been bequeathed to us by the practical wisdom of past generations and are verified by our own experience.

What is it we admire about these words? We admire their closeness to a simple mind. But above all we admire the spaciousness of the experience from which they come. To that sense of space, in the Russian novels of the nineteenth century, we return eagerly again and again.

A RUSSIAN OUTSIDER

The great Russian novels of the nineteenth century so dominate their scene that we forget they stand on the shoulders of minor figures who would impress the reader in any less fertile literature. One of these minor figures is Nicolai Leskov. I am not sure whether, considered as a writer of short stories, Leskov can justly be called minor. In England, translation of Aksakov came very late in the day, when his contemporaries like Turgenev and Dostoevsky were already established with us. There has been a greater delay in translating Leskov. A small collection of his tales called *The Sentry* was translated by A. E. Charnot and given to us by Edward Garnett in 1922; then in 1926 Gorky introduced us to *The Enchanted Wanderer;* and since then there has been one more volume: *The Musk Ox,* translated by Mr. L. Norman. Those who read *The Sentry* will remember Leskov's quality in that powerful story of squalid murder called *The Lady Macbeth of the Mzinsk District* and in the bishop's dramatic tale of his mission to Siberia, called *On the Edge of the World.*

Nicolai Leskov was born in 1831 and died in 1895. He was born of mixed class—clergy, merchants and the gentry were his forbears—and this puts his range of observation closer to Dostoevsky's than to the landowner writers. His origins are not very different from

Dostoevsky's. For a long period of his life Leskov worked for an Englishman who was managing one of the great estates—the Englishman is amusingly drawn in the tale called *The Stinger* in Mr. Norman's translation—and he traveled all over Russia. When Leskov came to write he had a wide, traveling experience of Russian life and custom to draw on, an experience which had been formed without literary intent. He "went to the people" not as a self-conscious intellectual, but as a practical man of affairs. One can see how this worked both advantageously and disadvantageously on Leskov's talent. He is, we are told, one of the "unplaced" writers of the nineteenth century, very popular with the public but regarded with caution by the critics; and this caution comes from the suspicion that many of Leskov's stories are ready made. They come too unevenly, too amateurishly and only partly digested out of life. They smack sometimes of the reminiscences of a District Commissioner. It seems to be a fact that a writer of the highest class must be driven by the instinct of the artist to strike a balance between life and literature very early; then only will he have time and place in his mind for the hourly discipline of imagination and sensibility which is essential to the well-being of a talent. The sight of the self-conscious artist "going to the people" or doing the opposite and shrinking from external experience, is a subject for satire and, nowadays, for sociological attack; but the artist is in the right of it. The greatest artists have always rationed themselves. In the life of Leskov one can see that he paid for the rich experience which enabled him, among other things, to form an astonishing ear for the real speaking habits of people by beginning to write too late in life. One has only to compare his manner of narration with Turgenev's. Both Leskov and Turgenev used what is now considered the old-fashioned device of setting a story within a story. The

Baron puts down his glass after dinner and is reminded of an extraordinary man or woman he met years before. Or he retells something he heard when he was a student, or when he was out shooting. Now in Turgenev the convention is graceful, because we feel that he has invented the setting. There never was such a Baron with his glass of wine, nor such a student. The device convinces because it is an artifice. In Leskov one has no similar illusion. We feel that his beginnings, his containing stories are muddled up with real life and, by the great paradox of art, they are distracting and unconvincing just because they are probably true.

Another reason for the uncertainty about Leskov's talent and the neglect of it in Russia is said to be political. A practical and experienced man, Leskov attacked the Left, especially the Nihilists, and was boycotted by the Liberal papers and critics for the rest of his life. He was also especially interested in the religious subject, and was accused of being a debased clerical writer fond of mixing lewdness and religion. He deserted the impressive ranks of Russian pessimism for a gentler, more tolerant and warmer view of life. I can only say that I do not believe Leskov's position was seriously affected by these sins. Dostoevsky did far worse in *The Possessed*, and Turgenev went almost as far in *Fathers and Sons* and *Virgin Soil*, and both survived the anger of the political fanatics. Aksakov was a Conservative of the Conservatives. If Leskov's position was unsatisfactory to the critics the reason is plain. He brought the independence, the originality of the man who has put his own life and experience before his political and religious views. Revolutionaries, Liberals and Conservatives all disliked him; and perhaps they had some right on their side, perhaps there is no special merit in refusing to be labeled. That kind of independence is frequently egotistical and unstable.

There are eight stories in *The Musk Ox,* and many of them stop at the point where Dostoevsky would have begun to inflate them. Leskov is in many respects a Dostoevsky without the epileptic fits. The tale called *The Musk Ox* is about an uncouth and vagabondish fellow who is deeply religious and is in training to be a priest. But he cannot get on with people. He is dirty, he is difficult, he has no pliancy. He becomes a tutor and finds the family he is with are corrupt, and goes scowling away at a moment's notice to tramp the roads. Everyone, according to him, is tainted. There are fewer and fewer people worth seeing or talking to, and so, tramp-like and morose, refusing to work, demanding his bread at any door, he loses himself in the depths of society, looking for signs of the resurrection of the human spirit among the outcasts and disinherited. In the end, he finds a reformed estate run by a hard and thriving businessman who recognizes his originality and lets him hang around. The businessman knows that "the musk ox" will try and upset his workers by preaching his peculiar Gospel Hall revolution to them; but the businessman also knows that the workers will regard the tramp not as a messiah but as a comedian. And so it turns out. They love "the musk ox" and humor him. Everyone loves and humors him, and this is too much. "The musk ox" has depended on getting on badly with people; humored, he goes and hangs himself.

Like many of Leskov's stories, this one is slow in starting. He is best in describing the unexpected reactions of peasant people and in recording their devious or stone-walling conversation. And he is especially attractive because of his sympathy. Leskov had a particular gift for leading one, step by step, into the quiet obstinacies of sainthood, and for creating the awkward, the almost humdrum saint, the very ordinary man who has become isolated from the beliefs of his fellows by the force of experience. Where other writers interest us in ordinary people by giving them some bizarre habit of life or mind, or by turning them into eccentrics, Leskov sticks closer to his observation. The King Charles's head is not an amusing decoration in these people's lives; it is very often the main, clumsy, immovable piece of furniture. In one of his tales, the mournful chair mender who is made to change his name by an erratic nobleman, lives with the new name all his life, as if it were a sofa or a sideboard he was keeping for someone. He lives with it religiously, without comprehension; there is nothing eccentric in this. For the new name is his luck. Too perturbing to be thought ludicrous, too useful to be inquired into. Again and again in Leskov's stories, something comes into the lives of the people and settles there immovably like an animal. There is the sensation of a thing or a presence mysteriously "in occupation," a sensation one has also in stories of Kafka's. When the Lady Macbeth of the Mzinsk district commits adultery, we detect at once a change in the character of her husband's house. She herself walks about like an empress giving orders, quieting the whispers about her adultery, with gifts, until the servants say, "That's all. It's her affair—she will have to answer for it." When she goes from adultery to murder, we see guilt living in the house. In a remarkable passage Leskov actually gives a form to this presence—there is a symbol in all his stories—without deviating into fantasy, but indeed by adding to psychological truth. After her first murder when she is lying down on her husband's bed dreaming of her lover, Katerina Lvovna sees a cat come on to the bed and she strokes it. She is puzzled because there is no cat belonging to the house. She does not realize that she is dreaming the cat.

In this dreadful story, in all of Leskov's best work, every sentence adds and tells, and Katerina moves toward her doom trammeled by her crimes, and only death can set her free of them. Circumstance, we feel, has moved into her life like the hostile figures of a dream, and has ousted her will. Her drama is impelled. And because of the laconic simplicity of the writing and the awkward garnishment of plain but real dialogue, her lot seems to us unanswerable and cuts speculation short.

Leskov's powers as a writer were brought out most strongly in his religious stories; but unlike most religious writers he was capable of many moods. He comes closest, I suppose, to the one or two Irish writers who are sometimes pious, sometimes skeptical, sometimes even ribald; and while he satirized the clergy or described religious failure, he also described the search for pure religion. And he did this, as a novelist should, without being didactic. His mind was saturated with the religious folklore of the peasants. Leskov seems to have a more genuinely religious nature than "the great sinner," as we can see in the story called *On the Edge of the World.* Here the mystery of faith and the question of the nature of Christ are described as a search, and indeed, paradoxically, as a gradual shedding of what is formally thought to be Christian. A young bishop is obliged to put his life in the hands of a pagan tribesman during a Siberian blizzard; they exist together on an animal level, and at every turn the dull, ignorant peasant who refuses to be baptized and whose simple mind argues in a maddening and small circle, obliges the bishop to shed one certainty of dogma after another. The setting is unforgettable. In some way the religious mystery has moved into the bishop's life in the shape of the stinking, stoical, immovable tribesman. And the bishop is not presented as an obtuse or conventional figure of satire; he is sensitive, educated, courageous and altogether a delightful human being. There is a wonderful scene at the height of the blizzard when the peasant covers the bishop with a reeking reindeer skin and then crawls underneath with him, puts his nose against him and snorts his bad warm breath into the bishop's nose in order to keep him alive.

The Musk Ox is not as good a selection of Leskov's stories as *The Sentry* is, nor is it as well translated. The translator of Leskov has a cardinal difficulty. Leskov excelled as a writer of common speech and wrote many of his stories as they would be spoken in a kind of vernacular, which he sometimes stylized. This must have given his work a quality which escapes translation.

THE YOUNG GORKY

The lasting work of Gorky is to be found in the three volumes of autobiography which he wrote between 1913 and 1924 and in the famous portraits of Tolstoy and Andreyev. Most foreign readers have been appalled by the scenes of squalor and gloom which Gorky set down from his life. The opening pages of *Childhood* are characteristic: Gorky's young and merry father lies dead in the room, the grandmother and the pregnant wife are lamenting, the police are at the door to hurry the funeral, and grief suddenly brings on the wretched mother's labor pains. The child has a terrifying vision of death and birth and there is the inevitable Russian touch of farce: frogs jump on top of the father's coffin as it is lowered into the muddy grave and are buried there. We foresee that Gorky's mother is one of those austere, sensitive, fine women doomed to be destroyed by the brutality and hopelessness of life; and so it turns out, when she takes the child to her father's house. Grandpa has a small dyeworks and is a man of substance. But he has an uncontrollable temper; in his sadistic bouts and partly on pious principle, he beats up the women and children of his family and also his employees. He is surrounded by drunken, quarreling, vindictive and covetous relatives all whining for his money. Uncle Mike crowns everything by setting the family dyeworks on fire and, in general, one can only say that the cruelty of Nature and the viciousness of the social system are outmatched by the natural animal malice of one human being to another in this book. There *are* scattered moments of goodness and quiet, but the general gloom is relieved by one figure alone: Gorky's grandmother. This captivating old lady is the soul of love and pagan sweetness and a storyteller of genius; there is a strange mixture of mysticism, poetry and stoicism in her nature, and she seems to be a throwback to some earlier, Arcadian phase of the Russian folk. It is because of her influence, as we read on, that our disgust declines. We find we are being seduced by the expressiveness of all Gorky's people, by their self-abandon and by what, later on, Gorky is to call their capacity for turning their sorrows into carnival. Fatalism does not always degrade: it often enlarges.

Gorky does not snarl; he neither maunders nor does he coarsely glut a secret appetite. He is totally free of that hysterical connivance which we get from Zola; he is never prolonging a private orgy. He is not a sensationalist wallowing in the sins of society; nor is he here a social realist congratulating himself, like some Victorian reformer, that he at any rate has the right social and political views. We are elated because in these books Gorky has the heroic eye, a sort of giant-creating eye; because he has the strongest compassion, and practices an almost saintly exclusion of himself from his own story. What matters to him is the broad spectacle of humanity. The boy grows, but the world grows too; everything is in physical movement. Gorky has a memory, we say, that allows the world to have existed to the full, without first having to ask a tacit moral or intellectual permission from himself. He has his standards, of course, he has his fastidiousness and there *is* a judgment, but none of these distorts his emotions or robs his "extraordinary" eye of its pity and its liberty.

Some critics have pointed out that Gorky's realism is a revolt against the puritanism of earlier Russian writers; if this is so, we notice that it takes a puritan to revolt, though many puritans relapse instead and go to seed. Gorky retains the puritan core, and the puritan energy and tenacity; he is moved by what he mixes in with—the orgy at Petrovsky's in *My Universities*, for example—he is marked by it, yet he retains his integrity and he is not corrupted. An interesting reflection on his pessimism is made by Mirsky in his *History of Russian Literature.*

> Gorky (he says) is not a pessimist and if he is, his pessimism has nothing to do with his representation of Russian life, but rather with the chaotic state of his philosophical views, which he has never succeeded in making serve his optimism, in spite of all his efforts in that direction. As it is Gorky's autobiographical series represents the world as ugly but not unrelieved—the redeem-

ing points which may and must save humanity, are enlightenment, beauty and sympathy.

This is the optimism native to all artists which is always more important than what they *think* they believe and is frequently at complete variance with it. In the course of his sometimes portentous self-education, Gorky was never able to tame his "extraordinary eye." It remained autonomous and unweakened, a kind of person in itself like one of those boys who lead the blind. Indeed that is how Gorky often seems to us: a powerful, blind man being led by a voracious, all-seeing child.

To an astonishing extent all Russian literature is led blindly on by the inconsequence of the eye. Russian fantasy, the effect of the naïve and childish, the sudden dislocations which make the Russian novel so loose and life-like, above all the sense of the grotesque, owe everything to it. To some extent this use of the eye—and also the habit of describing violently contradictory feelings almost in the same breath—have stereotyped Russian literature for the foreign reader who is, perforce, unable to see differences of style. But one has only to compare Tolstoy's superb use of the eye with Gorky's to see there *are* differences and that this is not a national manner alone. Tolstoy watches life unblinkingly, like some subtle, impartial animal whose many-faceted lenses reflect all without effort. He lies still and natural life is imprinted on him line by line. Gorky, on the other hand, is like a hundred-eyed man who goes aggressively into life catching detail at every blink and who amazes us by forgetting nothing. Where he looks something is always happening. If a foolish soldier has turned to face his tormentors, Gorky sees him tuck his shirt in; if half a dozen chickens are being chased on a boat, he will see three fly overboard;

he will remember how many times his grandmother told him to get from under her feet, when the dye-works caught fire, and afterwards see her blow on her scorched fingers as she talks; he will remember thousands of faces and gestures, every change of mood, every word spoken in his grandpa's tormented family, in the shops, ships and sheds where he worked, or on the roads where he tramped. The seeing and hearing are consuming. If the whole is invented memory, it is invented down to the most casual acts and finest shades and in a manner seemingly effortless. As far as I can define it the art seems to lie in combining contrasting things; in his accounts of people he first describes their appearance or their life from the outside and then catches something unexpected which reveals a part of the inner life that is bubbling away inside them. This is what human beings look like (he seems to say)—violent, vindictive, malicious, foolish, innocent, unfortunate, rascally or good—but what is on their minds all day, how do they get through the hours? So much fighting, scheming, quarreling, hoping, suffering—but what is deposited by it all for their empty moments, what is their particular form of the human bewilderment? So, for example, when the boy is left with the temper of his uncontrollable grandfather:

> I lost all interest in grandpa's talk which grew duller, more nagging, more self-pitying, day by day. It had practically become a habit with him to quarrel with grandma and forbid her the house, and then she stayed at Uncle Mike's or Uncle Jake's. Once she was away for a number of days and grandpa cooked for us. He burned his fingers, yelled, cursed, smashed dishes; and he became noticeably gluttonous. Coming to my little hut, now and then, he would take his ease on my turf bench and, after watching me for a time would suddenly ask: "Why so quiet?"

"Because I prefer it. Why?"

And that would precipitate a lecture. "We're not upper crust. No one bothers about our education. We have to learn by ourselves. For them books are written and schools are built; but no time is thrown away on us. We have to get along by ourselves." And he lapsed into a preoccupied silence; he made me feel uncomfortable and tense, as he sat there inert and oblivious.

The next moment the pious, diddling old savage is turning his old wife out of the house, saying that he has fed her long enough. But whereas a pitiless satirist like Shchedrin portrayed such a man in the storming and whining hypocrite Iudushka, Gorky sees people as victims of forces they do not understand and not as souls wicked in themselves. Grandpa is horrible, but he is also absurd, touching and not without a queer, half-frightened dignity.

Gorky's judgments are instinctive, not intellectual. He is torn between compassion and an aggressive resentment, himself as contradictory as the characters he draws. As he reflects upon the murderous quarrels in the home where he was brought up, he says:

> In time I came to understand that out of the misery and murk of their lives the Russian people had learned to make sorrow a diversion, to play with it like a child's toy; seldom are they diffident about showing their unhappiness. And so through the tedious weekdays, they make a carnival of grief; a fire is entertainment, and on a vacant face a bruise becomes an adornment.

A carnival, these three volumes of autobiography are, a carnival that wanders all over the Russia that existed before the beginning of this century, steadied here and there by one or two serious people of goodwill and illuminated by the gracious old figure of the grandmother, the pagan saint and storyteller. This old woman is beaten from time to time, like everyone else in the book, but she takes that with a guileless and humble laugh, goes on with her stories and her simple pantheism. She has the civilization and humanity of a poet. What Gorky understood as an artist he must have learned from her. She chanted her tales:

> When she had finished I begged for another, and this is an example of what I got. "Now an old goblin lives in the stove. Once he ran a splinter into his paw. As he rocked back and forth with the pain, he whined 'I can't bear it, little mice, it hurts so much.' "
>
> And she lifted her own foot in her hands and rocked it comically, screwing up her face as if she actually felt the pain.
>
> The bearded, good natured sailors would listen, too, and applauding the stories would urge: "Give us another, grandma." And in reward they would invite us to supper with them. There they plied her with vodka and me with watermelon. This was done in secret, for there was a man patrolling the boat, dressed like an official, who forbade the eating of fruit, confiscating whatever he found and throwing it overboard. Everybody kept out of the way of this man who, besides, was perpetually drunk.

The story and Gorky's epilogue have the same turn of inconsequence, the same immediate candor and acceptance of life.

Gorky is a writer strong as cheese and raw as onion. It is strange to think of him reading Fielding and praising the trim English as the originators and masters of realism, for his vision is heroic. He had a primitive directness of apprehension, a sensibilty unspoiled by civilization. That he was idolized by the people was just; like them he was growing; like them he drew his imaginative forces from the past. He was really a life rather than a novelist, a learned and circumspect vagrant who became, for one period, as Mirsky says, the only alternative government in Russia. What he lived and saw, not what he constructed, contained his importance. Often intellectually indigestible as a writer he is always a blind, moving force.

THE CID

Until fifty years ago our interest in the great epic heroes was literary and nothing else. Figures like Arthur, Roland, the Cid and many others, had been revived by the Romantic movement and were charged by its taste for hero-worship and history. So slight was their relationship with anything going on in the world in the nineteenth century, that the interest in them looks like an attempt to escape from a grey mercantile present into a glamorous past. It was not entirely that; there were the psychological sympathies of the power lovers, the hankerings after the superman in the Victorian age, the desire to reduce the hero to the outstanding bourgeois. And there were occasional emotional rebounds as well. Southey's superb translation of *The Chronicles of the Cid* may have owed something to emotions stirred by the citizens of the Revolution or the figure of Napoleon, as well as to the dramatic personal contact with Spain. Yet all these responses remain literary and even antiquarian, and some readers must have felt, as I very often have, that the epic heroes were epic bores of featureless and exhausting simplicity.

Times have changed. The conditions out of which a living epic literature might arise have appeared in many parts of the world. Not in the West, perhaps, but certainly in continents where there has been continuous war, and where new orders are forming themselves. We have seen popular movements give a legendary character to their leaders. We have seen leaders looking about them for useful myths. Myth-like figures bob up continually in popular culture. They do not last, for one eclipses another. But the myth-making faculty has generally revived, is no longer derided, is eagerly studied and is made to serve the ends of government—political, religious and psychological. We are back at a moment when a magic, like the discovery of the bones of St. James at Compostela, is firmly exploited. In this climate the epic heroes come closer to us and we can see their roots in life. A book like Mr. W. S. Merwin's translation of the *Poem of the Cid,* has now an extra dimension, and since Southey wrote, the Cid has been liberated by that great Spanish scholar Ramón Menéndez Pidal. The Champion now stands clearly and firmly on the dusty soil of Castile and we can know for what solid reasons he became the legendary national hero, and why one of the impulses behind the writing of the poem was what we would now call propaganda. We can see a myth being used, and why it was used.

Rodrigo Diaz, the Cid or Lord, as the Moors called him, the Champion as he was called by the Castilians, was born in 1045 in the village of Vivar in the cornlands near Burgos. He died fifty-six years later in Valencia and the *Poem* of his real or fantastic feats was written forty years after his death by a Mozarábe (*i.e.,* a Christian born under Moorish rule) who may have known him. Many who knew him must have still been alive. Vivar was a frontier town. As a boy the Cid fought in the frontier wars of Navarre, and he was brought up at court. He could write. He came of noble stock, though not of the highest nobility, a matter of great importance and strong resentment in his life. The effect of the endless wars had been to increase the number of lesser nobility, the men who had horsemen and vassals, and the Cid belonged to this group. In Navarre whole populations became armigerous. They had their property in land and mills. (The Cid was mocked for his mills.) Their road to great wealth was to obtain the spoils of war and here the Cid enormously succeeded. His "ill-shod outcasts" told the Count of Barcelona: "We keep alive by taking from you and others." The prodigious loot obtained by him from his enemies turned him into a type of self-made millionaire whose daughters are sought for their money by the high nobility, but who, like their father, are socially despised. The *Poem* brings out strongly the private pride in something like a democratic attitude to life which was the great strength of the spirit of Castile, or which made that kingdom, and not feudal Leon, the leader in the wars of Reconquest and the most powerful of the Spanish states. The *Poem* is, in this sense, the voice of an unconscious wartime revolution.

The Cid has often been described as a freebooter, a soldier of fortune who sold himself to Moors and Christians, according to where the profit lay. This is not at all what he would have seemed to his contemporaries. At his birth, Christian Spain lay in the north, Moslem Spain in the south and east; but the majority of Spanish Moslems were, after three hundred years, of Ibero-Roman or Gothic stock. There was a mingling of races which had been made possible by Islamic rationalism.

The people were bilingual. The Cid appears at the moment when a Moorish dynasty was weakening and becoming more penetrable by guerillas who could capture castles if they could not gain territory, and when many Moors had become vassals of the Christian north. In the eleventh century it was not astonishing that a Moorish king should entrust the government of his land to the Cid, nor that the Cid should fight for the Moorish Emir of Saragossa against the Count of Barcelona, nor that he should at other times extend Moorish lands at the expense of Aragon and Castile. The strange thing is that his loyalty to his own King, who had banished him and wronged him out of personal envy and perhaps because of the intrigue of the great landowners and high nobility of Burgos, was constant.

Slaughter and booty are the trades of the Cid. One of the famous moments of the poem occurs after the siege of Valencia where he takes his frightened wife up to the top of a tower so that she can watch the battle and "see how they earn their bread." In its terse, plain, homely, always concrete fashion, the poem sets out the labors of an astute fighting man's life, in the sense that he is earning his living and doing what he wishes with his own. Religion is there, but hardly more than formally recognized. There is little of the ideological crusader in him. He is a generous conqueror. There is frequent stress on his legal rights. He insists at the court on every tittle of them but always bows to the law himself. The amusing and well-known episode of borrowing money from the Jews on a false security—the boxes of sand said to be boxes of gold—indicates that the writer of the poem was aware of the economics of guerilla warfare and knew all about calling on bankers and arranging for commission. This plainness about the ordinary things of a country dealer's life, and the charming small touches—the little girl of nine who explains to the Cid that her family cannot allow a banished man into the house—set the hero in a recognizable world that he loves, and as a man to be esteemed. His pain at parting from his wife is not written up, but is thought of as an excruciating physical pain, in the traditional manner of Spanish realism:

> "now we part; God knows
>   when we shall come together"
> Weeping from his eyes
>   you have never seen such grief
> Thus parted the one from the others
>   as the nail from the flesh.

He is a real man among real things even when his exploits are fantastic:

> There the rout began
>   as it pleased God.
> My Cid and his Knights
>   rode in pursuit;
> You would have seen so many ten cords
>   snapped, and the poles down,
> And so many embroidered tents lying on the
>   ground.

And in the court brawl where the Cid storms at the rich nobles who have married his daughters and then left them stripped and beaten in a wood because they are not good enough socially, the scene has the roughness of nature. Here, above all, one sees the Cid stiffly affirming the law. He is not a lawless man.

This plain, bare, directness of the *Poem,* its lack of hyperbole and of elaborate message, is in itself delightful; but there is another aspect in which we see the myth-making faculty at work. Brenan discusses this in his *Literature of the Spanish People* and it can be followed in more detail in Pidal. The *Poem of the Cid* was written directly under the influence of the *Chanson de Roland* which commemorated the greatness of

Charlemagne three hundred years after his death, whereas the *Poem of the Cid* was almost contemporary. The *Chanson* has a quality, Brenan says, peculiar to French art but never found in Spanish. It does not stop at telling a story, "it sets up a universal pattern or example. Already in this period we can see the French mind at work, consciously and deliberately creating ideas and values." It is a work animated by the crusading spirit and fortified by national and religious propaganda; for it was the French, and especially the Benedictines of Cluny, the intellectual commissars of Europe, who had established the figure of St. James of Compostela as a symbol of the Christian drive against Islam, and who had established the pilgrimage route across the Pyrenees to the shrine as a sort of political duty. The famous battle at Roncesvalles occurs on the pilgrims' road over the Pyrenees and is an incident in ideological warfare.

But as the Spaniards fought back against a real occupation of their country, they began to resist the centralizing sophisticated ambitions of a remote French Europe. The Spanish peasant disliked the new feudal tenures the Cluniac monks sought to impose. There was strong opposition to the introduction of the Roman rite. The Cid's handwriting itself is in the old script, not the new standard script being introduced by the planners of the new Europe. The *Poem of the Cid* is, in short, the assertion of the Spanishness of the struggle. The Cid is more than a great fighter, he represents the appearance of a Spanish view, opposed to the spirit of the French propagandists. Brenan says there is nothing in French literature of the twelfth century to compare with the assured and responsible political feeling of the *Poem of the Cid* and that one of the reasons for this was that the Spaniards were not taken up with the international question of the relations of the Church to the civil authorities. There was no ideological right and wrong for the Spaniards; on the contrary, from the simple view of the ordinary free man, the tone is set by that famous line: "God, what a good vassal, if only he had a good lord." If we are to look for a contemporary parallel—admittedly a dangerous amusement—we see the Spanish relation to the new monolithic system of France and Rome as something like, say, the relation of Yugoslavs to Russians. The situation is as primitive. The other point is that heroes may rise spontaneously, but they are not heroes unless they arise out of fundamental situations in their age —they are not merely courageous, fortunate men or splendidly tragic men—and that no myth crystallizes about these popular figures except through the means of an acceptable propaganda. The French genius had to suggest an idea; the Spanish genius, to be effective politically, had to turn to a man and to convey that Islam was conquered and Europe saved, not by a complex organization and an ideology, but by a banished man of just instincts, well set in his own land.

QUIXOTE'S TRANSLATORS

Don Quixote has been called the novel that killed a country by knocking the heart out of it and extinguishing its belief in itself for ever. The argument might really be the other way on. *Don Quixote* was written by the poor soldier and broken tax collector with the hand maimed in his country's battles because the Spanish dream of Christian chivalry and total power had passed the crisis of success. The price of an illusion was already being paid and Cervantes marked it down. When Don Quixote recovered his sanity, his soul lost its forces, and he died. What must strike the foreign reader is the difference between the book as it appears to Spaniards and as it appears to the world outside of Spain. The difference is that in Spain *Don Quixote* had a basis in contemporary fact; outside of Spain it is morality, metaphysics, fable. The romances of chivalry were read during the Counter-Reformation and specifically moved two of the Spanish saints to action—Santa Teresa and St. Ignatius de Loyola. Longing for the freedom of a man as her brothers went off to the New World, Santa Teresa read these books with excitement, and Loyola's famous vigil at Manresa was made consciously in imitation of Amadis, and might be a chapter of *Don Quixote.*

Outside of Spain, the novel began a new life in countries where the idea of chivalry had no tradition of national awakening and power, where the tragic core was missing. To the English and French translators who got to work a few years after the book was published, *Don Quixote* was simply the greatest of the picaresque novels, indeed the only great one in a *genre* which elsewhere kept strictly to exaggeration, meaninglessness and popular anarchy. The book became farce—though the contemporary Shelton sins far less than Motteux who translated the book at the beginning of the eighteenth century—a string of adventures and scenes of horseplay tied up with ironical conversations about the noble disadvantages of idealism and its conflict with proverbial self-interest. If we turn to the English novelists who, in the early eighteenth century, were deeply influenced by the tale, we can see how they altered the characters of Don Quixote and Sancho to suit the new middle-class morality. Don Quixote, especially, the violent and subtle madman with his visions of the lost Golden Age, becomes in England a mere eccentric, an unaccountable squire, an hilarious Scot in Smollett, an unworldly but rough-and-tumble clergyman in Fielding. Figures like Parson Adams are misfits, cranks, clowns, often enlightened but always simple and without authority; whereas Don Quixote's mind is darkened and dignified by the counsels of his madness. He has the endless resource of the neurotic; he has pride and the habits of pride and command. In England, the ingenious gentleman is opposed by the worthy forces of self-interest, so much admired in Cheapside. The question is practical: idealism or realism? The answer always sentimental: failure is lovable and what is lovable is commercial. These imitators in the sensible eighteenth-century delight in freaks because they love individuality; but they do not enter, as Cervantes in his great mercy did, into that universal region of the human spirit where the imagination reigns like an ungovernable and fretful exile in a court of shadows.

I have lately read a newish translation of *Don Quixote* and of three of the *Exemplary Novels* by the late Samuel Putnam. These are handsome volumes printed on a fine large page—a great advantage—and contain a critical account of many earlier translations and a very large collection of valuable notes; altogether a scholarly piece of work by an American amateur. He had translated a good deal of Brazilian literature. Mr. Putnam believed *Don Quixote* to be one of the dying classics and thought an accurate and contemporary translation might revive it. Compared with Shelton, the abominated Motteux—the one guessed and the other added color—with Ormsby, Jervas and even the Penguin done efficaciously (especially in the dialogue) by J. M. Cohen, Putnam's translation is toned down. This means that the fine shading of the irony of Cervantes becomes clear and Mr. Putnam has taken great trouble with the difficult proverbs. A few contemporary colloquialisms, mainly American, surprise but do not seem out of place; there is often a mildness in Mr. Putnam which leads him to choose a weak word or phrase where the Castilian is strong, terse and concrete; and in straining after accuracy he has missed sometimes the note of repartee or satirical echo in the conversations of Don Quixote and Sancho. In the scene at the inn with Maritornes and the muleteer, and in the chapter following, Motteux, Jervas and Cohen—to take only three—are superior in vigor to Mr. Putnam whose colloquial phrases have a citified smoothness from easy overuse. To give an example: Don Quixote is about to reveal that the daughter of the supposed Castilian had come to him in the night, but stops to make Sancho swear that he will tell no one about this until after the Knight is dead for he will not allow anyone's honor to be damaged. Sancho replies, without tact, that he swears, but hopes that he will be free to reveal the secret tomorrow, on the grounds that: "It's just that I am opposed to keeping things too long—I don't like them to spoil on my hands."

Both Motteux and Cohen stick closer to the more vigorous original image. The Spanish word is "go mouldy" or even "rot," and not "spoil." Literally "go mouldy on me." In the earlier chapter one can catch Motteux adding direct, eighteenth-century animal coarseness where Cervantes is not coarse at all; in fact, *Don Quixote* is unique in picaresque literature in its virtual freedom from obscenity, except in some of the oaths. When Maritornes rushes to Sancho's bed to hide there from her angry master, Motteux writes:

> The wench . . . fled for shelter to Sancho's sty, where he lay snoring to some tune; there she pigged in and lay snug as an egg.

This is picturesque, but it has arisen from the mistranslation of two words in the text. Possibly it is an improvement on Cervantes who wrote merely that "she went to Sancho's bed and curled up in a ball." Mr. Putnam's pedantry spoils his accuracy here for, instead of "ball," he writes "ball of yarn." The objection to Motteux is that in making Cervantes picturesque and giving him Saxon robustness, he endangers the elegance and the finely drawn out subtleties of the original. Motteux was halfway to Smollett, which is a long way from Cervantes. The picturesque and pungent in Cervantes lie wholly in Sancho's proverbs where Mr. Putnam excels. When Doña Rodriguez says that she can see "the advantage which a maiden duenna has over a widow, but he who clipped us kept the scissors," Sancho comes out strong and to the life:

> "For all of that," Sancho said, "when it comes to duennas there's so much to be clipped, according to what my barber tells me, that it would be better not to stir the rice even though it sticks."

Don Quixote begins as the description of a shy, timid, simple, eccentric provincial gentleman who, after the first clash with reality, develops an always growing complexity of mind that is the satisfying and diverting substance of the book. For as he goes deeper into delusion, so he is dogged by a dreadful doubt and self-knowledge. At the end, when Sancho returns home leading his master, with their roles reversed—for it is he, the realist, who has triumphed, having governed an island and having even rescued maidens in distress —Don Quixote is said to have failed in all but to have known glory and to have won the supreme victory: victory over himself. The novel is a powerful example of the process of the growth of a work of art in a writer's mind, and of the luck of writing. For at the end of the first part which Cervantes at one time regarded as the end of the book, one can see the idea in crisis and at the point of breaking down. Some critics have thought that the irrelevant stories stuffed into the end of the First Part show a fear that the reader will be bored by the colloquies of two characters only: and that he also wished to show that he was not a mere popular writer, but could write a polished, psychological short story in the best manner of the time. (He, indeed, succeeded in the story of Don Fernando and Dorothea and, in the latter, drew a delightful analytical portrait of cleverness in women.) But in the long interval between the two parts, the idea matured and became richer in fantasy, invention and intellectual body; the range of character became wider and success—so bitterly delayed in Cervantes's life—released confident powers that delight us because they delight in themselves. Not only does Don Quixote's own case branch out into full intricacy; not only are we now taken into all the casuistries of the imaginative life; by a master stroke, Sancho is infected. The peasant gets his dream of material power, like some homely Trade Unionist, to put against the gentleman's dream of glory. Realism turns out to be as infectible by fantasy as idealism is. *Don Quixote* begins as a province, turns into Spain and ends as a universe, and far from becoming vaguer as it becomes more suggestive, it becomes earthier more concrete, more certain in real speech and physical action. *Don Quixote* does not collapse as the Second Part of Gogol's *Dead Souls* does, because Cervantes is not mad. He remains pragmatic, skeptical and merciful; whereas Gogol got the Russian Messianic bit between his teeth and went off his head. Spanish fantasy goes step by step with Spanish sanity. Nor, if we read *Don Quixote* truly, can it be described as a work of disillusion, if we mean by that the spiritual exhaustion which follows a great expense of spirit. The Spanish crackup had begun, but it had only just begun. The force of that national passion was still felt. Though Cervantes was the broken soldier, though he was imprisoned, hauled before the Inquisition, and knew all the misery and confusion that the Spanish expansion abroad had left behind at home, he was not the enemy of the Spanish idea. He valued arms more than literature, as he explicitly said—incidentally in the character of Cardenio he drew an excellent portrait of a coward. What *Don Quixote* does is to enact the tragedy of experience as something still passionate though commingled with reflection; experience now more deeply felt. The comic spirit of the book is not satirical or tired, but is vital, fully engaged and positive. The wisdom runs with the events, not after them. It is stoical, not epicurean; sunlit, not eupeptic; civilized, not merely robust. *Don Quixote* bridges the gulf between two cultures, not by an inhuman cult of the people, but by excellence of intellect, by the passion a writer has for his means, by irony and love.

A VIENNESE

A start has been made in the translation of Robert Musil's immense unfinished novel, *The Man Without Qualities*, which this Czech-Austrian began writing in the twenties and was still working on when he died an exile in Geneva in 1942. It is a wonderful and prolonged firework display, a well-peopled comedy of ideas, on the one hand; on the other, an infiltration into the base areas of what we call "the contemporary predicament." There is the pleasure of a cleverness which is not stupid about life: "Even mistrust of oneself and one's destiny here assumed the character of profound self-certainty," Musil wrote—not altogether ironically—of the Austrian character and these words suggest the conflict which keeps the book going at its cracking speed. Of course, Musil's kind of egoism had a long run in the first twenty years of the century and he has been—the translators tell us—written off by the standard German literary histories. Musil's tongue does indeed run away with him, but it is stupid to denigrate him. Proust and Joyce, with whom he has been exaggeratedly compared, approached the self by way of the aesthetic imagination; Musil reconstructs egos intellectually. What ideas do our sensations suggest? What processes are we involved in? If Musil has come to us regrettably late, if he sticks for his subject matter to the old pre-1914 Vienna and has some of that period flavor, he is not stranded there. The revival of Henry James has taught us that writers who live passively within history may be more deeply aware of what is really going on than those who turn up in every spot where the news is breaking.

The nearest parallel to Musil is not Proust but Italo Svevo in *The Confessions of Zeno*. Musil is very much an intellectual of that strain. The two writers represent opposite sides of the same Viennese school. They are restless, headlong psychologists and skeptical talkers, to some extent café writers. Like Zeno, the Ulrich of *The Man Without Qualities* is a gifted and self-consuming man. He burns up his experience. But whereas Zeno is a hypochondriac, a man of endless self-doubt, the clown of the imagination and the heart, whose great comic effect is obtained by the pursuit of folly with passionate seriousness, Ulrich is a healthy, athletic, extraverted and worldly character whose inquiring brain captivates and disturbs men of action. He is a mind before he is a sensibility. He has only to appear for others to behave absurdly; his irony muddles them; his perception alarms. Musil's achievement is to make this formidable character tolerable and engaging. Ulrich is endlessly, perhaps pitilessly patient; he has learned that humility of the intellect which comes of continuous use and which is necessary to those who look into other people for what may be useful to their own imaginative and intellectual search. Like Zeno he can never resist a theory; but whereas Zeno's love for other people is really a kind of remorse for having had so many ideas about himself, the love of Ulrich is a feeling of gratitude to others for suggesting so many ideas that he has been free of them personally. His attraction and power come from an imagination which transposes. Here is a comment on one of his comic characters, a cabaret singer, a Juno of refinement who has a passion for eating. After a good meal she would feel obliged to repay her lover:

> She would stand up and tranquilly, but full throatedly lift up her voice in song. For her protector such evenings were like pages torn out of an album, animated by all sorts of inspirations and ideas, but mummified, as everything becomes when it is torn out of its context, loaded with the tyrannical spell of all that will now remain eternally the way it is, the thing that is the uncanny fascination of *tableaux vivants* when it is as though life had suddenly been given a sleeping draught; and now there it stands, rigid, perfectly correlated within it itself, clearly outlined in its

immense futility against the background of the world.

One can see, after this, why Musil has been compared with Proust—though, if the translation is to be relied upon, he does not write as well—yet, where Proust seeks to crystallize a past, Musil is always pushing through that strange undergrowth to find out, if possible, where he is, where life is tending, and what is the explanation. His book is a crab-wise search for a future, for what has not yet been given the sleeping draught.

In the opening volume, the people, the time and scene are the Vienna of the Austrian Empire. The main episodes are Ulrich's love affairs with the guzzling singer and with a rueful nymphomaniac; his friendship with a gifted but unstable girl and with a superb bourgeois lady, notorious for mind, whom he calls Diotima, and who goes in for the True, the Good, the Beautiful on the grand scale. Diotima is a monument, an outsize schoolgirl. But the larger themes are political and social. Before long we have, by brilliant implication, an amusing but moving picture of a complete society whose intentions become nobler the nearer it is to destruction. Nobler and more absurd. For Musil has invented a wonderful farce called the Collateral Campaign. This vague political movement is meant somehow and simultaneously to celebrate the Emperor's birthday, boost Austrian culture—with a meaning glance at the Germans—preserve the stagnant existing order and yet arise spontaneously from the hearts of the common people and bring new spiritual life to the greatest minds dessicated by skepticism, intellectualism, etc. In short it is an all-purpose piece of uplift which is touchingly sincere and hopelessly muddled. It is very fond of the word "true"—not patriotism but "true" patriotism, not values but "true" values. The comic beauty of the Collateral Campaign is that it can never settle on its precise form; it swells into committees, exhausts all the clichés, and turns into its opposite: a movement for chauvinism and rearmament. Really it is a midwife of Fascism. Nothing is more certain of comic reward than Musil's sympathy. It is tender and deadly.

The people of the Collateral Campaign are "good." They are responsible. They represent "the best elements." They can choose. They choose ridiculously. But what of the bad, the irresponsible who cannot choose—a man like the homicidal maniac Moosbrugger who may or may not be executed? (He wants to be executed because he has an almost pettifogging regard for the law.) The Moosbrugger case puts its shadow on all the characters in the book and one of Musil's feats as a novelist is to show us exactly how Moosbrugger seeps into every mind in some way or other. If society is tending towards progress what is it going to do about this Caliban? Ulrich reflects; "If mankind could dream collectively it would dream Moosbrugger." If we do not know by what absolute standards to settle the Moosbrugger case, then a great social catastrophe is inevitable. Writing in the twenties Musil could hardly have been more prophetic.

There is an interesting account of Musil's life in the very good introduction to this edition of his novel. He came, we are told, of a gifted family. He was educated for the Army, fought in the 1914 war, became a civil engineer, a distinguished inventor, a mathematician, a psychologist, and was about to teach philosophy at Munich before he turned to writing. Musil brought to his writing not only the capacity for setting but also the habit of hypothesis. Ulrich is, in many ways, Musil translated. In his several attempts to define what he means by "the man without qualities," he notes,

> He will perform actions that mean something different to him from what they mean to others, but is reassured about everything as soon as it can be summed up in an extraordinary idea.

Or again, the translators give us these lines from the page he was adding to the last volume of his novel on the day he died:

> Of course it was clear to him that the two kinds of human being . . . could mean nothing else than a man without qualities and, in contrast, the man with all the qualities that anyone could manage to display. And the one might be called a nihilist, dreaming of God's dreams—in contrast to the activist who is, however, with his impatient way of acting, a kind of God's dreamer too, and anything but a realist, who goes about being worldly clear and worldly active.

Consciousness was Musil's real subject, not the "stream" but the architecture, the process of building, stylizing and demolishing that goes on in the mind. How does an idea like the Collateral Campaign grow in various minds? How, sensuously, does it breed? At what point does sensation become idea? How does reality look after that intoxication? These things bring out Musil's alacrity and focusing power as a novelist; for though he never stops talking he always enacts what he sees. He has a poetic yet practical ability for showing an idea coming to someone—a slow-minded and simple aristocrat, a blackamoor servant, a woman beginning to feel indignation and remorse in love, any transition in fact from one state of consciousness to another. He has the merit of loving people for their essence. There is, to take one example, a striking study of that special bourgeois protégé, the failed artist who takes to blaming his failure on the collapse of culture. From a hero he has turned into a petty domestic tyrant and rules his wife, who has ceased to love him, by making her play duets on the piano. Their marriage is sustained by a neurotic frenzy of piano playing:

> The next moment Clarisse and Walter shot away like two railway engines racing side by side. The music that they were playing came flying towards their eyes like the glittering rails, then vanished under the thundering engine and spread out behind them, as a chiming, resonant, miraculously permanent landscape. . . . Precise to a fraction of a second, gaiety, sadness, anger, fear, love and hatred, longing and weariness went flying through Walter and Clarisse. It was a union like in a great panic. But it was not the same mindless, overwhelming force that life has. . . .

The more music sublimely unites them, the more they are separated in life, each thinking his way away from the other. Walter, the rejected husband, fearing failure and impotence, begins to slip into thoughts comfortably too large for him, and ends by playing Wagner for erotic reassurance. Here he begins to strike wrong notes. Clarisse's mind jumps from image to image and to questions becoming more and more savage: does civilized life yearn for brutality? Does peacefulness call for cruelty? For there is an empty room in Clarisse where "something tore at the chains." At the end of this volume we get a glimpse of that empty room.

In making raids like this into Musil's novel one risks making it sound thin or melodramatic in the heavy Central European way; a pound of realism to a ton of essay writing. He is, on the contrary, subtle, light, liquid, serious. He is, no doubt, a bit over-fond of himself, perhaps a bit too tolerant to the "I" who is never brought up against anything stronger than itself; a bit too much on the spot, especially in the love affairs. What the novel does show is that the habit of intellectual analysis is not stultifying to drama, movement or invention, but enhances them. It is a delightful insight that a movement like the Collateral Campaign, which has no distinctive idea, will inevitably attract all those people in the Austrian Empire who have only one idea; it is perfect that Ulrich shall be put in charge of sorting out these cranks. His theories, the whole apparatus of the book, are the forgiveness of the artist, not the examination papers of the master. Consciousness is, for him, a pardonable folly. Some critics have discerned what they believe to be a mythological foundation to this novel, in the manner of *Ulysses;* the density, suggestiveness and range could support the view. For it is cunningly engineered.

The second volume of *The Man Without Qualities* sustains the impression of a major writer of comedy in the Viennese manner, and of an original imagination. A French friend of Musil's, M. Bernard Guillemin, has been good enough to add something to the comments I made on the mysterious English title of this novel. What Musil meant by "a man without Qualities" (*Mann ohne Eigenschaften*), he says, was "a man completely disengaged and uncommitted or of a man in quest of nonaccidental attributes and responsibilities self-chosen—the German counterpart of Gide's "*homme disponible*" though there is nothing of Gide in Musil's work. In the later volumes, it is said to have worried Musil himself, that a character as disengaged as Ulrich is, will eventually become isolated and bypassed by life. The sense of adventure which exhilarates the early volumes becomes paralyzed in the later ones, where the intellectually liberated man is not able to take the next step into "right action." It is significant that Musil's novel was never finished. He had spun a brilliant web of perceptions round himself and was imprisoned by them.

In this second volume, the absurd Collateral Campaign is still going on in Austria. Diotima, the lofty-minded Egeria, who runs the social side, who discovers the "soul," is getting tired of her husband, a high government official. She has risen out of the middle classes into aristocratic society, and she plants this idea of the soul in an international financier and arms manufacturer, a German called Arnheim. There are Generals who come in because "the Army must keep an eye on things"; Diotima's social rivals appear to keep an eye on her, and so on. There is a wonderful complete picture of a society at the edge of the precipice of 1914. The novelist's comic sense of character is speculative, and is strengthened by his penetration into the kinds of consciousness current at the time, into how private ideas become public, and public ideas affect the emotions of private life.

In the meantime, the Moosbrugger case, which underlies the social picture and which has been deceptively dormant, revives and adds a disturbing footnote. What about the law's attitude to insanity in murder; what about violence in the State, in personal life? At the most unexpected moments, Moosbrugger —who is merely a name in the papers to most of the characters—raises his idiot head and poses his devastating questions. "Ordinary life," Ulrich concludes, "is an intermediate state made up of all our possible crimes." So Musil dresses a platitude in epigramatic form; he has become rather free with epigrams; but his gift is to enact epigrams imaginatively.

In this volume the analysis of character is done at much greater length than in the introductory volume and so there is more discussion and less action. Of the portraits, Arnheim's and the absurd yet subtle General's are the most impressive, but we must not omit the girl Gerda and her lover who are moving towards an early form of Fascism. Musil's Arnheim is by far the most cogent and exhaustive study of a millionaire magnate's mind that I have ever read. The irony is exact and continuous. Arnheim, for example, had "the gift of being a paragon":

> Through his understanding of this delicate interlocking of all forms of life, which only the blind arrogance of the ideologist can forget, Arnheim came to see the prince of commerce as the synthesis of revolution and permanence, of armed power and bourgeois civilization, of reasoned audacity and honest to goodness knowledge, but essentially as a symbolic prefiguration of the kind of democracy that was about to come into existence . . . he hoped to meet the new age halfway.

Under the influence of his love for Diotima, Arnheim seeks to bring about the "fusion of interests between Business and the Soul." His craving for power leads him to writing books: "with positively spectral prolixity" his pen began to pour out reflections on "the need of this fusion" and "it is equally certain that his ambition to master all there was to be known . . . found in the soul a means of devaluing everything that his intellect could not master." Arnheim is morally devastated by his love for Diotima for she is monumentally high-minded; and Musil has the pleasure of showing us a sumptuous, high-minded *femme du monde* reduced to the frantic condition of a woman forced to the bed of a testy, cynical husband, and a magnate paradoxically reverting to his native instincts the more his "soul" is elevated. All roads leave from the soul, Musil reflects, but none lead back to it: Arnheim is no more than a magnate after all and, once Diotima can be his, he falls back on the old maxim that in love, as in business, one had better spend only the interest, not the capital. Arnheim's character again reminds us of Walter Bagehot's dictum: a kind of intellectual twilight, with all its vagueness, is necessary to the man of business; and, towards the end of this volume, Musil reveals what Arnheim is really after in the ideological mists of the Collateral Campaign and the higher life of Diotima: he is after control of the Galician oilfields.

Ulrich, the man without qualities, is the natural enemy of Arnheim; his natural foil is the comic General. An air of unworldliness in civilian life is an obligatory mask of the military profession; all "a poor soldier man" may permit himself to point out is that, if the military have a virtue, it is their sense of order. There is a farcical scene of discussion when this soldier describes his visit to the National Library where he approaches the whole task of improving his mind in the spirit of the strategist. The General is a wit in his way. Even after a carefully worked out campaign of reading, in which he allows for substantial casualties, he discovers it will still take him ten thousand years to read what is necessary. "There must be something wrong about that," he says, raising his glass of brandy.

Musil writes with the heightened sensibility of a man in love; that is to say, under the influence of the unrest of seeking a harmony and completion in things. The Collateral Campaign itself is a kind of communal love affair. In the description of love affairs and especially in the portraits of women in love, Musil is truly original; in managing scenes of physical love, he has not been approached by any writer of the last fifty years. What has been missing, in those accounts, has been Musil's transcendent subject: the sense of the changing architecture of consciousness. He brings the effect of the imagination into the fears and desires of these women, their sense of living out an idea which may indeed well be a love fantasy about quite a different lover from the one in whose bed they lie. He is sensitive to the power of "erotic distraction"; of Rachel, the maid who goes to bed with a fellow servant because she has been stirred by the touch of a guest's hand, he writes:

> The object of this yearning was actually Ulrich, and Solimon was cast in the role of the man whom one does not love and to whom one will nevertheless abandon oneself—a point on which Rachel was in no sort of doubt whatsoever. For the fact that she was not allowed to be with him, that for some time past they had hardly ever spoken to each other except in a whisper, and that the displeasure of those in authority over them had descended upon them both, had much the effect on her as a night full of uncertainty, uncanny happenings, and sighs has on anyone in love; it all concentrated her smouldering fancies like a burning glass, the beam of which is felt less as an agreeable warmth than as something one will not be able to stand much longer.

The high-minded love affair, the violently neurotic, the absurd one, the desperate affair carried on against the will, the one crossed by other lives; from all these Musil extracts the essence with dignity and gaiety, the comi-tragedy of human loss and incompleteness. The history of love is the history of absence, of arrival and departure. He is able to do what no contemporary ever does: to move from the imaginative and emotional to the physical without change of voice; even the naked fight on the bed or the brazen or terrified undressings are not marred by the worst fault of our erotic realism: its unconscious grotesque. The tenderness, subtlety and disinterestedness of Musil's intelligence enable him to do this; and the almost conversational style. Critics tell us that, whatever the awkwardness of translation may be, he has in German a style that is as lucid as that of Anatole France and less florid than Proust's. One cannot judge this, though the translation of this second volume seems to me an improvement on the first. (The whole difficulty has been to avoid translating German abstractions into the kind of technical or administrative super-jargon which these become in English.) Musil is an addiction. The most irrelevant criticism made of him by some Germans and Austrians is that his kind of café sensibility is out of date. It may certainly be familiar in Schnitzler and Svevo, but Musil's whole scheme prophetically describes the bureaucratic condition of our world, and what can only be called the awful, deadly serious and self-deceptive love affair of one committee for another. And he detects the violence underneath it all. In only one sense is he out of date: he can conceive of a future; of civilized consciousness flowing on and not turning back, sick and doomed, upon itself.

Index

About the Author

V. S. PRITCHETT was born in England in 1900. He is a short-story writer, novelist, critic, and traveler. His collected stories have appeared in America under the title *The Sailor and the Saint.* Among his novels are *When My Girl Comes Home, Mr. Beluncle,* and *The Key to My Heart* (which will be published by Random House in the fall of 1964). Most of his critical essays appeared originally in *The New Statesman* under "The Living Novel" and "Books in General" columns. He is now a director of this paper and a lifelong contributor. He also contributes to *The New Yorker, Encounter,* and *Holiday.*

Mr. Pritchett has traveled extensively in Europe, the Middle East, and South America. He considers *Marching Spain* and *The Spanish Temper* his two most important books of travel. He has also visited the United States, where he gave the Christian Gauss lectures at Princeton, and was recently Beckman Professor at Berkeley, California.

His book on London, entitled *London Perceived,* with photographs by Evelyn Hofer, has been published in the United States, and he is now working on a companion volume about New York as well as on new short stories.

Mr. Pritchett is married and lives in London.

About the Author